W9-AYV-022

KETCHIKAN PUBLIC LIBRARY
KETCHIKAN, ALASKA 99901

ON MONSTERS

NSTERS

AN UNNATURAL HISTORY
OF OUR WORST FEARS

Stephen T. Asma

KETCHIKAN PUBLIC LIBRARY
KETCHIKAN, ALASKA 99901

OXFORD
UNIVERSITY PRESS

2009

OXFORD
UNIVERSITY PRESS

Oxford University Press, Inc., publishes works that further
Oxford University's objective of excellence
in research, scholarship, and education.

Oxford   New York
Auckland   Cape Town   Dar es Salaam   Hong Kong   Karachi
Kuala Lumpur   Madrid   Melbourne   Mexico City   Nairobi
New Delhi   Shanghai   Taipei   Toronto

With offices in
Argentina   Austria   Brazil   Chile   Czech Republic   France   Greece
Guatemala   Hungary   Italy   Japan   Poland   Portugal   Singapore
South Korea   Switzerland   Thailand   Turkey   Ukraine   Vietnam

Copyright © 2009 by Stephen T. Asma

Published by Oxford University Press, Inc.
198 Madison Avenue, New York, NY 10016

www.oup.com

Oxford is a registered trademark of Oxford University Press

All rights reserved. No part of this publication may be reproduced,
stored in a retrieval system, or transmitted, in any form or by any means,
electronic, mechanical, photocopying, recording, or otherwise,
without the prior permission of Oxford University Press.

Library of Congress Cataloging-in-Publication Data
Asma, Stephen T.
On monsters : an unnatural history of our worst fears / Stephen T. Asma.
p.   cm.
Includes bibliographical references and index.
ISBN 978-0-19-533616-0
1. Monsters.   I. Title.
GR825.A86 2009
398.24'54—dc22
2009007219

2 4 6 8 9 7 5 3 1

Printed in the United States of America
on acid-free paper

For my favorite little monster, Julien—
cast from no mold, spinning out of control, and beautiful.

CONTENTS

ACKNOWLEDGMENTS

WINSTON CHURCHILL ONCE said that "writing a book is an adventure. To begin with, it is a toy and an amusement; then it becomes a mistress, and then it becomes a master, and then a tyrant. The last phase is that just as you are about to be reconciled to your servitude, you kill the monster, and fling him out to the public."

I have written half a dozen books now, and I think Churchill has captured the process perfectly. I am happy to fling this monster out to the public. But I'm proud of it, and I'll probably miss my long servitude to it. Of course no monster gets built alone; even Dr. Frankenstein had Igor's help (at least in the movies). At the risk of offending my friends and family by associating them with a hunchbacked imbecile, I wish to thank my many collaborators.

My family is a team of tireless supporters. Heartfelt thanks go to my parents, Ed and Carol, and brothers, Dave and Dan, plus the entire Asma tribe. My dearest Wen and Julien waited patiently for Baba to climb out of the laboratory; I am grateful for their patience and their help with the voltage generators, test tubes, and that one time when we had to beat back the torch-wielding villagers.

Anatomy was frowned upon in the eighteenth century, and the body snatchers who dug up cadavers for secret scientific study were known as "resurrection men." My resurrection men were Bob Long and Roland Hansen, both of whom exhumed obscure texts and sources. A writer could not ask for better research assistants. Lauren Dubeau and Loni Diep helped me find many wonderful images of monsters. Joanna Ebenstein, David Driesbach, and Peter Olson very generously contributed their own excellent artwork to the book.

I am grateful to Steve Kapelke, provost of Columbia College, for having the vision to create a "distinguished scholar" rank and for having the lapse of good judgment to name me as one. Complicit in this happy gaffe were my chair, Lisa Brock, and Deans Cheryl Johnson-Odim and Deborah Holdstein. I'm thankful to many other friends at Columbia College, including Sara Livingston, Garnet Kilberg Cohen, Kate Hamerton, Teresa Prados-Torreira, Micki Leventhal, Keith Cleveland, Oscar Valdez, Krista Macewko, Jeff Abel, and drinking partner Baheej Khleif.

This book and my intellectual life would be much poorer if it wasn't for my small and voracious reading group, Tom Greif and Rami Gabriel. Many thanks to them for reading large chunks of this book, but also for weekly torture sessions with obscure philosophers, evolutionary psychologists, cognitive scientists, revolutionaries, and more.

Many others need to be thanked: Alex Kafka, Kendrick Frazier, Raja Halwani, Gianofer Fields, Pei Lun, Michael Shermer, Donna Seaman, Robyn Von Swank, Adrienne Mayor, Leigh Novak, Jim Graham, Greg Brandenburgh, Jim Krantz, Harold Henderson, Doctor Swing, Michael Harvey, the honorable David Brodsky, wingman Brian Wingert, Tomo and Dave Eddington, and all my friends at Lake Shore Unitarian Society in Winnetka, Illinois. Special thanks to my excellent editor at Oxford, Cybele Tom, who believed in this monstrous project and also helped amputate its unnecessary tentacles, and to Christine Dahlin and Judith Hoover. As always, I alone am responsible for the flaws of my creature.

ON MONSTERS

What a chimera, then, is man! What a novelty, what a monster, what a chaos, what a subject of contradiction, what a prodigy! A judge of all things, feeble worm of the earth, depositary of the truth, cloaca of uncertainty and error, the glory and the shame.

BLAISE PASCAL

I consider it useless and tedious to represent what exists, because nothing that exists satisfies me. Nature is ugly, and I prefer the monsters of my fancy to what is positively trivial.

CHARLES BAUDELAIRE

I have never seen a greater monster or miracle than myself.

MICHEL DE MONTAIGNE

Introduction

Extraordinary Beings

PHOBIAS

EVER SINCE I WAS A SMALL BOY I've had a phobia about deep
murky water, or more accurately, a fear of what might be living in
such waters. A seemingly harmless swim in a weedy lake sends my
imagination into overdrive and I can almost see the behemoths and levia-
thans rising up to gnaw off my extremities. I'm a grown man, for God's
sake, and a skeptic as well. But no amount of reasoning with myself can
begin to dispel the apprehension. I've never ruined a beach picnic by refusing to get in the water, nor have I needed to be talked down from an anxiety attack. Like most other "lite" phobics I just cringe a little bit and get on
with the swimming. I'm annoyed by my irrational fear of sea monsters, but
I've resigned myself to coping with it.

When I was living in Cambodia I occasionally went swimming in the
muddy Mekong, but I winced at the idea that more species of giant fish
live in the Mekong than in any other river in the world. Mekong catfish
can grow to be eight or nine feet long and weigh between six hundred and
seven hundred pounds, and goliath freshwater stingrays can be over twelve
hundred pounds. Moving geographically to the deep seas of the Atlantic
and the Mediterranean, one finds an enormously long silvery snake-like
beast called an oarfish. This nightmarish fish lives at depths of three thousand feet and has been seen and captured only after rare surfacing episodes
due to illness. This ribbon-like giant, with striking red-headed "plumage,"
can grow up to fifty feet in length and probably inspired many early sailor

The Kraken is a mythical sea monster that has troubled sailors' dreams for centuries. The legend may be based on glimpses of giant squids or abnormally large octopi. Drawing of the Kraken, complete with faux scientific nomenclature, by artist Peter Olson © 2008. Reprinted by kind permission of the artist. www.peterolsonbirds.com.

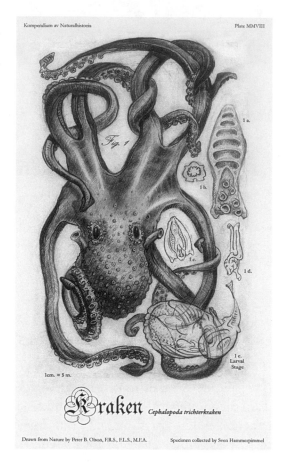

tales of sea monsters. Add to this sort of oddity the fact that every once in a while science dredges up some hitherto unknown specimen from the deep, such as the ancient coelacanth or rare evidence of the giant squid.[1] I can almost hear my reptilian brain telling my neocortex, "See, I told you! Don't go in the water." But these real monsters are nothing compared to the nefarious beasts that swim in my head. These are modified versions of the real creatures, but always with sharper and more copious dentition, more poisonous dorsal spikes, and more razor-like claws for effortless laceration. And of course they're bigger too.

When the first two crazy people, I mean *scientists*, descended a quarter of a mile into the ocean in a crude bathysphere, they found unimaginable creatures. Off a Bermudan island in 1930 William Beebe and Otis Barton witnessed swarms of bioluminescent creatures—transparent eels, shrimp, and nightmarish fish—and giant shadowy figures looming just outside the range of their spotlight. They could descend only a fraction of the actual sea depth, but when asked to describe the receding waters below them, Beebe said that the abyss "looked like the black pit-mouth of hell itself."[2]

A survey of popular culture indicates that I am not alone in my fear of sea monsters. Television, movies, and video games are rife with neck-tensing narratives about underwater peril. The literature and imagery of high culture, too, have long been fascinated with the idea of watery fiends.[3] But there may be deeper reasons, below the stratum of culture, for the ubiquitous sea monster phobia. Evolution may have built this into our species over the span of many prehistoric millennia. Fear of murky water may have been a good survival strategy for ancestors who regularly fell victim to real predators; trepidation at water's edge may have been just the thing that helped some hominids to leave progeny. This is speculative, but it is consistent with basic Darwinian assumptions about the evolution of instincts.

In a telling passage from *The Descent of Man*, Darwin scandalously compares the intellects and emotions of humans and animals.[4] He tells several stories of his experiments at the Zoological Gardens, in particular his research at the monkey house. Darwin knew that monkeys had an "instinctive dread" of snakes, so he took a dead, stuffed, and coiled-up snake down to the monkey house. "The excitement thus caused was one of the most curious spectacles which I ever beheld," he wrote. A stuffed snake was too horrifying and the monkeys stayed far away from it, but a dead fish, a mouse, and even a live turtle eventually drew the monkeys in and they displayed no fear in handling them. Pushing the experiment further, Darwin placed a live snake in a bag and put this inside the cage. "One of the monkeys immediately approached, cautiously opened the bag a little, peeped in, and instantly dashed away." But then, in a human-like act of curiosity, "monkey after monkey, with head raised high and turned on one side, could not resist taking a momentary peep into the upright bag, at the dreadful object lying quietly at the bottom."[5]

To monkeys, snakes are monstrously threatening and so their instincts err on the side of caution. In a state of nature many snakes are real threats; from an evolutionary point of view, any monkeys that happened to be extra timid around them probably lived to procreate another day. One might say that monkeys have an *emotional caricature* of snakes in their instinctual vocabulary. The monsters of our human imagination may be similar caricatures, originally built on legitimate threats but eventually spiraling into the autonomous elaborations that only big brains can produce. In my brain, the piranha becomes the Loch Ness Monster.

Arachnophobia, or fear of spiders, seems to be a universal human dread, especially in children. The biologist Tim Flannery asks, "Why do so many

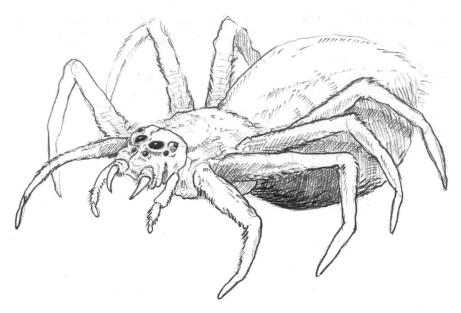

Many monster archetypes seem to tap into widespread arachnophobia. Some evolutionary psychologists believe that spider and snake phobias are the result of natural selection. Pencil drawing by Stephen T. Asma © 2008.

of us react so strongly, and with such primal fear, to spiders? The world is full of far more dangerous creatures such as stinging jellyfish, stonefish, and blue ringed octopi that—by comparison—appear to barely worry most people."[6] Flannery speculates that a Darwinian story connects human arachnophobia to our African prehistory. Because *Homo sapiens* emerged in Africa, he wonders whether a species or genus of spider could have been present as an environmental pressure. Africa is the place where the human mind acquired many of its useful instincts. If humans evolved in an environment with venomous spiders, a phobia could have been advantageous for human survival and could be expected to gain greater frequency in the larger human population. The six-eyed sand spider of western and southern Africa actually fits that speculation very well. It is a crab-like spider that hides in the sand and leaps out to capture prey; its venom is extremely harmful to children. One can see how a fear of spiders would have been highly advantageous in this context. Our contemporary arachnophobia may be a leftover from our prehistory on the savanna.[7]

In recent cognitive science debates, fears of snakes, spiders, and other creatures have been held up as examples of preset mental circuits in the human brain.[8] Though it is a controversial idea, a growing number of theorists argue that our brains come hard-wired with some belief content, such as "snakes = bad." The fact that phobias seem so resistant to revision in light of new experiences suggests that they are closed information systems. Even after a phobic person is told that a snake is not poisonous or witnesses the removal of the venom ducts, he or she still dreads handling the reptile. The phobia stays like a stubborn piece of antiquated furniture in the architecture of the mind.[9] Perhaps monsters are also part of our furnished mind. As cultural and psychological realities, monsters certainly seem unwilling to go away, no matter how much light we shine in their direction.

More important for my thesis, however, is the wonderfully ambivalent tension in Darwin's zoo monkeys. The monkey cannot fully confront the snake, but he cannot leave it alone either. He is repelled *and* attracted. Of course, we are just like him; we cannot "resist taking a momentary peep...at the dreadful object lying quietly at the bottom."

REPULSION AND ATTRACTION

While perusing the disturbing deformed specimens at the Hunterian Museum in London,[10] I found myself standing beside a young boy and his mother. We were all staring at a display case that contained a series of tragically malformed babies floating in large jars of alcohol.

"Oh my God!" the boy cried out. He repeatedly shrieked as he moved around the frightening display cases. The Hunterian Museum is a treasure trove of macabre specimens, some dating back to the mid-1700s. The collection, like the one in the American Mutter Museum in Philadelphia, is an unsettling compendium of the ways Nature can go wrong.

"Oh Lord, I can't believe it!" the boy gasped in his thick north England accent. He was moving into the pathology section of the museum now, and he was being drawn into the morose magic of Hunter's collection. As he stared intensely at a fetus with two fused heads, his mother suddenly turned to him and asked, "Is this disturbing to you, William?" He didn't look away from the cases, but responded, "God, yes. Very."

"Shall we go, then, dear?"

"No," he shot back, "absolutely not."

WHEN MY SON AND I LIVED IN CHINA he demonstrated the same ambivalent human impulse. In China today, as in other parts of the developing world, it is still possible to see adults who suffer from birth defects that would have been routinely remedied in the West by early surgeries or procedures. Lack of decent health care has doomed many poor people to lifelong struggles with otherwise easily curable maladies.

Similar to those of the Hunterian and Mutter Museums, here is a vitrine of teratological birth defects from the Vrolik Museum. Many of us find them difficult to look at, and yet it is difficult to look away. Photo by Joanna Ebenstein © 2008. Reprinted by kind permission of the artist and the Vrolik Museum, University of Amsterdam.

In our neighborhood, an undeveloped suburb of Shanghai, my three-year-old son and I walked to school every day and stopped to drop a few coins in the begging cup of a hydrocephalic woman. Her head was swollen to the size of a large beach ball, perhaps three times normal size, and she rested it sideways on her shoulder as she sat on the sidewalk. My son was frightened of her, but he staunchly resisted my attempts to avoid her and insisted every day that we stop to say "Ni hao" to the "big head lady," as he referred to her.

These are examples of what we've all experienced at some time or other: the simultaneous lure and repulsion of the abnormal or extraordinary being. This duality is an important aspect of our notion of monsters too.

Monster is a flexible, multiuse concept. Until quite recently it applied to unfortunate souls like the hydrocephalic woman. During the nineteenth century "freak shows" and "monster spectacles" were common; such exploitation of genetically and developmentally disabled people must be one of the lowest points on the ethical meter of our civilization.[11] We have moved away from this particular pejorative use of *monster*, yet we still employ the term and concept to apply to *inhuman* creatures of every stripe, even if they come from our own species. The concept of the monster has evolved to become a moral term in addition to a biological and theological term. We live in an age, for example, in which recent memory can recall many sadistic political monsters.

INHUMAN

In 2003 I lived within walking distance of the infamous Security Prison S21, a torture compound in Cambodia. It took months for me to get up the nerve to visit. Pierrot, the Swiss owner of my guesthouse, told me that he still refused to go after ten years in Phnom Penh. "You will not get me in that place, mon ami." He explained, "It is the maker of bad dreams, and I wish to sleep well." Like Pierrot, I didn't want to go to S21 either. But S21 was a place of monsters, real monsters and real victims, and I could not altogether leave it alone.

Over and over again one hears the same story of torturers—whether Nazis, Pinochet lackeys, American soldiers at Abu Ghraib, or Khmer Rouge teenagers at S21—the story that they were just "following orders." But before we dismiss these people as demons that bear no resemblance to us, we should remember Stanley Milgram's famous experiment on the psychology of obedience to authority, in which average Americans were made to believe they were shocking other average Americans with lethal doses of electricity simply because a man in a white lab coat insisted that they do so.[12]

Most people who hear about Milgram's study ask themselves what they would do as a test subject. Or we wonder how we would respond if we were told that prisoner *X* is an enemy of freedom and that we must pressure him to give up information about an imminent terrorist plan. Or worse yet, we wonder what we would do if someone held a gun to our head and told us to cut someone else's throat. That's what happened at S21, over and over again. If we were in that situation, would we become monsters? Or does such heinous action require freewill agency in order to qualify the perpetrator as monstrous?

A torture bed in the Khmer Rouge prison S21. Seventeen thousand Cambodians lost their lives in this monstrous place. The building is now a memorial museum in Phnom Penh, Cambodia. Photo by Stephen T. Asma © 2008.

The term *monster* is often applied to human beings who have, by their own horrific actions, abdicated their humanity. In *The Fragility of Goodness* Martha Nussbaum makes the Aristotelian argument that our humanity is indeed a fragile mantle, one that can be corrupted by forces internal and external to us.[13] Like Hecuba in the Greek tragedy, who finds her child dead, a human being can lose so much that is precious to her, through war or persecution or chance, that she sinks to the level of an animal, or worse. Everyone has the potential to become monstrous.[14]

In Cambodia I walked the dusty dirt roads to the uneventful-looking compound S21. It looked uneventful because before 1975 it was simply known as the Tuol Svay Prey High School. It was converted into Security Prison 21 by Pol Pot's security forces, and it became the central detention center for suspected enemies of Angkar, the mysterious and authoritative higher organization or party of the Khmer Rouge.[15] By 1976 approximately twenty-five hundred prisoners had passed through the bloody corridors of S21, and each year that followed saw increased numbers of tortured prisoners, until they totaled around seventeen thousand by 1979, when the Vietnamese Army liberated Phnom Penh. When Vietnamese soldiers stormed S21 they were horrified by the carnage they discovered there. Only seven survivors were found alive in the compound; no one else who entered S21—not one of the seventeen thousand people—made it out alive.

My guide for the tour was Ladin, a small woman in her thirties with a broad and somewhat sad face. She smiled and gestured for me to walk with her across a small field of dust and burned grass. We were the only people moving through the compound. All the classrooms of this former high school had been converted into prison cells and torture chambers. Iron bars were installed over the windows and doors and barbed wire snaked everywhere. On the ground floor little brick cells had been fabricated to hold one prisoner each, with not even enough space to lie down. Larger rooms held hundreds of prisoners chained together, unable to move—starving, dehydrated, injured from their interrogations, dying.

Ladin led me to one of the torture chambers. The floor was checkered with tile, and the walls were mottled and dirty. A battered bed frame sat in the center of the room; shackles and chains lay on the bed. Underneath the bed was a huge dried stain of blood that had pooled there from countless victims. The room was left just as it was found when S21 finally fell in 1979. The last victim, tortured to death as the Vietnamese were entering Phnom Penh, was discovered here and photographed. The gruesome photo now hangs over the bed. It shows a mangled man lying in this bed before me, his head caved in, his throat slit, blood everywhere, a rooster standing on the body picking at the corpse. I left the room quickly.

The phenomenon of this torture prison is a testament to human depravity, because the vast majority of the men, women, and children who were brought here had done absolutely nothing wrong and were as mystified by their imprisonment as you or I would be if someone dragged us out of bed tonight and charged us with bogus crimes. Hearsay, suspicion, and paranoia led the Khmer Rouge's Security Office, Central Committee, and Ministry of Defense to descend violently upon innocent farmers, teachers, engineers, students, workers, and whole families, accusing them of being enemies of the revolution.[16]

My guide, Ladin, explained to me that she was ten years old when the Khmer Rouge came to her home, forcibly removed her father and brother, and sent her to work in the fields from sunrise to sunset until she almost starved to death. She never saw her father and brother again and still has no knowledge of their fate. I wondered how she could come to this wretched place day after day and offer tours of events that had shred her own life. Perhaps walking these terrible hallways had some paradoxical therapeutic effect on her. I didn't understand it. I didn't understand any of it.

One aspect of the monster concept seems to be the breakdown of intelligibility. An action or a person or a thing is monstrous when it can't be processed by our rationality, and also when we cannot readily relate to the emotional range involved. We know what it's like to hate, for example, but when we designate a monstrous hate, we are acknowledging that it is off our chart. We don't have to go all the way to Pol Pot's Cambodia to find modern monsters. Many more are very close to home.

On May 11, 2005, thirty-four-year-old Jerry Hobbs was charged in Lake County, Illinois, with the brutal murder of his eight-year-old daughter, Laura, and her best friend, Krystal Tobias. In a videotaped confession, Hobbs described killing the girls after he argued with his daughter in Beulah Park in Zion, Illinois. Hobbs, who had only recently been released from a Texas jail for an unrelated 2001 aggravated assault (chasing a guy with a chainsaw), believed that his daughter had stolen money from her mother. According to him, Laura was supposed to be grounded, but she had gone to the park to play and Hobbs followed her there. When his daughter argued with him and refused to come home, he said, he attacked her. According to his confession, Laura's friend produced a small "potato knife" to defend herself, but Hobbs wrestled it away from her and used it to stab the children repeatedly until they were dead.

This story achieved national attention in the spring of 2005, and Hobbs is currently awaiting trial in Lake County. He now claims that his confession was coerced by police and that he is innocent. In addition, many of the facts of his story don't add up. There doesn't appear to be physical evidence linking him to the crime, and the defense claims there is some physical evidence linking a different, unnamed person to the crime scene.

The principal investigator for Hobbs's defense team is my brother, David Asma, one of the investigators for the Lake County Public Defender's Office. Like dozens of previous grisly crimes, this one ended up on his desk within hours of the formal charge. My first reaction to hearing about the case was to recoil at the very sight of "monster Hobbs," so dubbed by the strident CNN legal commentator Nancy Grace, but my second reaction was "How can anyone defend this monster?"

The Public Defender's Office, and in particular my brother's job, is a gruesome world of mutilated bodies, rape, insanity, arson, guns, drugs, mendacity, and sadism. It is a place where the most monstrous of human behaviors are on display. But my brother's position is that "monsters" are matters of perception. A person is demonized, according to him, by people who stand to benefit from the derogatory labeling. Monsters are "constructed" and serve as scapegoats for expedient political agendas. He, and most other public defenders, make a heuristic commitment to the innocence of their clients. My brother assumes that everybody he defends is (at least from 9 to 5) misunderstood. Hobbs's defense team argued, for example, that his confession was coerced by police who kept him awake and under questioning for an unhealthy stretch of time. The recent spate of death row pardons based on DNA evidence (even when there were confessions) makes this a more reasonable position than it first appears. Whether or not Hobbs committed the murder is something for a jury to decide. But his defenders cannot think of him as a monster if they are to do their jobs effectively. In addition, Dave must emotionally distance himself, for professional reasons, from the murders themselves. "I have looked at photos," he explains, "of the most grisly murders—sometimes for a whole year straight, everyday—but I cannot look at the victims as little girls or whatever the case may be. I must look at them, study them forensically, as *evidence*." When I press my brother, he admits that, yes, whoever did kill these little girls is a monster, but *on the job* he must adopt the working hypothesis that the killer is not his client (or in other cases, that his client may have done the deed but has mitigating issues).

It's worth noting, too, that the nature of most client-council relations would tend to bring the humanity of the accused to the forefront, would tend to de-monster them. The defender always sees another side of the accused than the wider public does. This is not, I suspect, the result of some deep moral mission or heart-of-gold goodwill on the part of the defender, but rather the result of mundane daily interactions and conversations. Over the course of many interviews and meetings, accused criminals and their counsel often end up sharing cigarettes and chatting about everything from recent sports scores to their similar musical tastes. The person you are defending may or may not actually be a monster, but it must be harder and harder to see him as such if you get to know him.[17]

UNMANAGEABLE

Of course not all monsters are evil. Dragons in China, for example, are so loved that the Chinese consider themselves to be the "children of the dragon."[18] Some monsters start out harmless, but their own nature forces a turn toward malevolence. Mary Shelley's creature in *Frankenstein* is perhaps the most famous of the gentle-hearted giants gone bad. It is the failure of Victor Frankenstein and society generally to provide a space for him in the human family that turns the creature into a monster. "Shall

The Golem is a bumbling monster of Jewish folklore. The clay creature was animated by Rabbi Judah Loew to protect the Jewish ghetto but could not be controlled and wreaked havoc in Prague. Pen and ink drawing by Stephen T. Asma © 2008.

each man," the creature bitterly asks, "find a wife for his bosom, and each beast have his mate, and I be alone?"[19] The creature is so alienated that he cannot even find solidarity with the nonhuman animals. This novel gives us a glimpse into the subjective interior of the monster's life and gives us a tragic archetype of the misunderstood outcast.

Long before *Frankenstein* we had the Jewish version: the bumbling, innocent, but also dangerous Golem of Prague.[20] Versions of the legend differ somewhat, but one iteration tells of a giant creature fashioned out of clay by a sixteenth-century rabbi, Judah Loew. At a time when the Jewish ghetto of Prague was regularly under anti-Semitic attacks, Rabbi Loew brought the giant clay sculpture to life by writing the word *emet* (Hebrew for "truth") on his forehead. The animated monster was to protect the Jewish people from outside aggression. It was strong and powerful, but it was also stupid and followed directions too literally or incorrectly. The Golem began by protecting the Jews, but its clumsy nature eventually led to its accidentally harming them, sending the community into greater chaos. In the original Golem story the rabbi is able to shut down the bumbling giant and prevent further disaster by erasing the *e* from *emet* to create the Hebrew word for *death*. According to legend, the Golem's body still lies dormant in the attic of the Altneuschul temple in Prague, awaiting reanimation should the need arise.

In the stories of the Frankenstein creature and the Golem we see another important version of the monster concept: a creature or person who is dangerous to us, but not intentionally so. We might call them "accidental monsters." They've had a significant rebirth in recent science fiction that considers our possible encounter with alien life forms.[21]

THE LITERAL AND THE SYMBOLIC

Monster derives from the Latin word *monstrum*, which in turn derives from the root *monere* (to warn). To be a monster is to be an omen. Sometimes the monster is a display of God's wrath, a portent of the future, a symbol of moral virtue or vice, or an accident of nature. The monster is more than an odious creature of the imagination; it is a kind of *cultural category*, employed in domains as diverse as religion, biology, literature, and politics.

As a *literal* creature, the monster is still a vital actor on the stage of indigenous folk cultures,[22] and it's safe to say that even in our developed and otherwise secular world, the idea of a literal demon or devil still haunts the minds of many evangelical and mainstream Christians. In this book I am concerned with literal monsters, but the monster as metaphor is probably more relevant for us now. In some cases, the literal and the metaphorical merge in a dance of causation, as in the case that Teresa Goddu tells of a vampire clan in Murray, Kentucky, in the late 1990s.[23] Here the legends of vampire activity, such as drinking blood and killing, actually inspired some teenagers to role-play, acting to such a degree that they murdered a parent.

Thankfully, most people don't have to worry about actual blood drinking and instead employ the monster concept metaphorically rather than literally. But even so, we have begun to realize the important role that metaphors play in shaping our thoughts and our experiences. According to the theorists Mark Johnson and George Lakoff, we have many conceptual metaphors that act like lenses for filtering and organizing our experiences: "Our ordinary conceptual system, in terms of which we both think and act, is fundamentally metaphorical in nature. The concepts that govern our thought are not just matters of the intellect. They also govern our everyday functioning, down to the most mundane details. Our concepts structure what we perceive, how we get around in the world, and how we relate to other people."[24] When we say "He was a monster," our listeners have a general sense of what we mean because they conceptually map some inhuman qualities onto the person we're talking about. We perform a metaphorical operation that helps us to understand one domain of action by seeing it through another, more concrete domain of action. When trying to convey the way your colleague at work "uses people" and seems to "feed" on their weaknesses, you refer to him as a "vampire." It's a classic case of using an obvious activity (drinking someone's blood for nourishment) to clarify a more subtle and intangible activity of instigated workplace drama. Johnson and Lakoff claim that these metaphors are often prelinguistic aspects of our thinking, shaped by cultural conventions and native psychophysical tendencies.[25] I suspect that monsters are metaphorical archetypes of this nature, and I want to trace the anatomy and evolution of some of these metaphors.

Hand in hand with this idea that metaphors shape our thinking, communicating, and even feeling is the idea that *imagination* is more active in our picture of reality than we previously acknowledged. The monster, of course, is a product of and a regular inhabitant of the imagination, but the imagination is a driving force behind our entire perception of the world. If we find monsters in our world, it is sometimes because they are really there and sometimes because we have brought them with us.

BOTH THE EAST AND THE WEST are rife with monsters of every stripe. Demons, dragons, ghosts, wrathful Buddhas, and supernatural animals occupy the theology, folklore, and daily rituals of religious cultures around the globe. The "hungry ghost" is a common creature in Asia. It usually represents a monstrous afterlife for a person who was gluttonous or greedy in this life; in the afterlife, the person is tortured by his insatiable hunger. These creatures, sometimes imagined with a giant stomach and a pinhole mouth or no mouth at all, continue to play an important role in Eastern cultures; Southeast Asia and China still have annual hungry ghost festivals. They are imaginative symbols of the frustrations of hedonism and the doomed pursuit of pleasure. A comparative study of similar Christian, Hindu, and Buddhist monsters could give us important insight into our common search for the ecstatic experience, our ascetic bifurcation of spirit and flesh, our quest for ideals and perfections, and our retreat from evil. Indeed, any comparative cross-cultural study of monsters in Eastern and Western cultures could provide an interesting picture of what is common and what is unique in our hopes and fears. But, anxious that such an East-West project might be too big for an in-depth analysis, I have chosen an only slightly less daunting endeavor: a cultural and conceptual history of Western monsters. Here, too, the terrain is immense, but I believe that a coherent thread can be followed from the ancient to the contemporary. The concept of monster has evolved over time, and I hope to track some of the main branches of that Western genealogy. And I hold out the hope that some future book will take the East as its primary focus.

IT SEEMS IMPORTANT TO SAY A WORD about the *word* "monster." Obviously it's not a complimentary term. Like the words *imbecile* and *moron*, which psychologists once used as technical descriptors for IQ levels, the word *monster* once had a slightly less pejorative set of connotations but has now slipped wholly into the derogatory. The term was never entirely friendly, but in certain eras it was used to, among other things, designate those persons whom we now refer to as developmentally or genetically disabled. Perhaps the word is so charged with prejudicial values that it can never again be used in an objective or purely descriptive manner. No one who finds himself at the receiving end of the monster epithet can be confused about its negative connotations, and it is probably fair to say that, in reference to humans, there is no longer any truly *literal* sense of the term. To be completely accurate I should, throughout this book, place every instance of *monster* in scare quotes to indicate my ironic use of the term. This would be stylistically tedious, even irritating. So we'll have to be satisfied with a disclaimer: no disrespect is intended by the author to any particular monsters, living or dead.

PART

I

Ancient Monsters

I

Alexander Fights Monsters in India

The whole earth echoed with their hissing.
ALEXANDER'S LETTER TO ARISTOTLE

FTER DEFEATING KING PORUS IN THE PUNJAB REGION, Alexander the Great chased the tyrant farther into India. "However," Alexander reported, "it commonly happens that when a man achieves some success, this is pretty soon followed by adversity."[1] Lost in the deserts of the Indus Valley, Alexander and his army found themselves dehydrated and demoralized by a fierce and hostile environment. Alexander relates the frightening events of that campaign in a letter to his old teacher, Aristotle.[2] Marching through the desert, Alexander's forces were so thirsty that some of the soldiers began to lick iron, drink oil, and even drink their own urine. A devoted soldier named Zefirus found a tiny puddle of water in the hollow of a rock, poured it into his helmet, and brought it to Alexander to drink. Alexander was moved by the soldier's generosity, but he poured the water out on the ground in front of the whole army to demonstrate that he, as their leader, would suffer with them. This show of strength and solidarity gave inspiration to the troops and they marched on until they finally reached a river. But frustration rose further when they discovered that the river was poisonous and undrinkable.

In the middle of this large river sat a strange island castle. Alexander tried to communicate with the naked Indians therein, asking them where he might find good water, but they were unresponsive and took to hiding. Two hundred lightly armed soldiers were sent wading through the water to try to pressure the castle's inhabitants for help. When the soldiers were a quarter of the way through the river, a terrible turbulence began to churn and the men began screaming and disappearing underwater. "We saw emerging from the deep," Alexander explains, "a number of hippopotamuses, bigger than elephants. We could only watch and wail as they devoured the Macedonians whom we had sent to swim the river." Alexander was so enraged by this calamity that he gathered together the guides, local men who had betrayed them by leading them into this hostile land, and marched them into the deadly water. "Then the hippopotamuses began to swarm like ants and devoured them all."

After another day of marching, the exhausted and dehydrated soldiers finally came to a "lake of sweet water" and a surrounding thick forest. All the men drank their fill and regained some of their strength. They pitched camp there at the sweet water lake, cutting down huge swaths of forest to build fifteen hundred fires. They organized their legions into defense formations in case something should attack in the night, and settled down to rest. "When the moon began to rise," Alexander reports, "scorpions suddenly arrived to drink at the lake; then there came huge beasts and serpents, of various colors, some red, some black or white, some gold; the whole earth echoed with their hissing and filled us with considerable fear."

It's not hard to imagine the terror. Soldiers don't lack fear, after all; they just override it with stoic resolve. Anyone who has ever been in a strange forest after dark knows the pulse-quickening fears that can take hold. If you've ever tent-camped in grizzly country you'll have an inkling of the dread that must have filled these soldiers. The fears of the Macedonians, however, were not just imagined but actually realized over the course of that long night.

After killing some of the serpents the soldiers were relieved to see the creatures retreat. But their hopes of finally getting some sleep were dashed when dragons began to slither out of the woods toward them. They were larger than the serpents, thicker than columns, with a crest on their head, breasts upright, and mouths wide open to spew poisonous breath. "They came down from the nearby mountains and likewise made for the water." After an hour of fighting, the monsters had killed thirty servants and twenty soldiers. Alexander could see that his men were overwhelmed by the strangeness and resilience of the dragons, so he leaped into the fray and told them to follow his monster-slaying technique. Covering himself with his shield, he used nets to tangle the enemy and then struck at them viciously with his sword. Seeing his success, the soldiers rallied and finally drove back the dragons. But then came the giant crabs and crocodiles. Spears and swords were ineffective

Alexander and his army fight a parade of monsters in India. Scene from the *Romance of Alexander*, France (Rouen), c. 1445. Royal MS 15 EVI. From Alixe Bovey, *Monsters and Grotesques in Medieval Manuscripts* (University of Toronto Press, 2002). Reprinted by permission of the British Library.

against the impenetrable shells of these enormous crabs, so the soldiers used fire to kill many of them and drive the rest back to the forest. Alexander lists the subsequent parade of foes:

> It was now the fifth watch of the night and we wanted to rest; but now white lions arrived, bigger than bulls; they shook their heads and roared loudly, and charged at us; but we met them with the points of our hunting spears and killed them. There was great consternation in the camp at all these alarms. The next creatures to arrive were enormous pigs of various colors; we fought with them too in the same way. Then came bats as big as doves with teeth like those of men; they flew right in our face and some of the soldiers were wounded.

As if this onslaught were not enough, the men were astonished next to see an enormous beast, larger than an elephant, emerge from the forest. The behemoth, first appearing in the distance, headed for the lake to drink but then saw Alexander's encampment. It turned quickly, revealing three ominous horns on its forehead, and began charging toward the men. Alexander ordered a squadron of soldiers to meet the earth-shaking juggernaut head-on, but they were overrun. After engaging the monster in difficult battle for some time, the soldiers managed finally to kill it, but only after the creature had taken seventy-six Macedonian warriors to a bloody end.

Still shocked and shaken, the tattered army watched with horror as oversized shrews skulked out of the darkness and fed upon the dead bodies strewn around the beach. Dawn mercifully broke and vultures began to line the bank of the lake. The ordeal was over.

"Then I was angry," Alexander says, "at the guides who had brought us to this dreadful place. I had their legs broken and left them to be eaten alive by serpents. I also had their hands cut off, so that their punishment was proportionate to their crime."

EMBELLISHING

Alexander's letter is almost certainly apocryphal, but it has formed an important part of the legend and mythology of Alexander.[3] Most of the letter's descriptions of frightening creatures come from a book about India written by Ctesias in the fifth century BCE, so, although the events of the letter are fabulous, the monsters were a commonplace in the ancient belief system. An ancient Greek or Roman citizen would have had no trouble believing this story of Alexander's difficulties in exotic India. In fact, the Roman natural philosopher Pliny the Elder (23–79 CE) reinforces the point a few centuries later, when he writes, "India and regions of Ethiopia are especially full of wonders.…There are men with their feet reversed and with eight toes on each foot. On many mountains there are men with dog's heads who are covered with wild beasts' skins; they bark instead of speaking and live by hunting and fowling, for which they use their nails."[4]

The story of Alexander's monster battle at the sweet water lake may be wholly invented by ancient writers, or it may be partially true with significant embellishments. Psychologists have identified a common human tendency to unconsciously exaggerate perceptions. These misperceptions are heavily influenced by our subjective emotional and cognitive states. People who are startled to discover a burglar in their home, for example, usually report the size of the intruder as much larger than he actually is. The cognitive scientist Dennis R. Proffitt has amassed significant empirical data that demonstrate the tendency of those afraid of heights to actually see a greater distance between themselves and the ground. We don't need science to deliver up commonly understood truths, but scientific validation is helpful. Proffitt speculates that perceptual exaggeration of spatial distances probably evolved as a safeguard to promote caution and prevent recklessness when our ancestors engaged in climbing activities. "With respect to fear of falling," he explains, "…the perceptual exaggeration of steep hills and high places increases their apparent threat, and thereby promotes caution and its adaptive advantage."[5] Applying this Darwinian notion to our perception of monsters, it seems useful for humans to see a creature as more dangerous than it truly is.

The creatures described in Alexander's letter may have been real exotic animals, such as cobras and rhinoceroses, which were then multiplied and enlarged by fear-filled misperceptions. Add to this misperception the embellishments of self-report (e.g., the fisherman's syndrome of magnifying the dimensions of the one that got away) and you have a recipe for a fantastic monster story.[6]

Regardless of the veracity of Alexander's description, the symbolic nature of the story is provocative. Among other things, the narrative is a testament to masculine stereotypes of courage and resilience. Wherever we find monsters, there, too, we also find heroes. The Macedonians were intensely afraid to be in such uncharted territory, then wave after relentless wave of dangerous attack came at them from out of the jungle. Yet though they took losses and even occasionally waned in commitment, they ultimately stood their ground against inhuman enemies. It's a manly story of virile strength and valor. When dawn finally broke at the sweet water lake, Alexander reminded his worn-out soldiers "to be brave and not to give up in adversity like women."

The travelers' stories of encounters with exotica are certainly filled with wonder, but they are equal parts fight stories, demonstrations and justifications of martial masculinity. According to this view, the exotic world is not benign, and we must make our way defensively and aggressively. Monsters live with the barbarians, and indeed are the most extreme form of barbarian. One cannot meet them with rational persuasion because they lack the proper faculties, nor can the arts of diplomacy pave a road to compromise.

MANLINESS

There is a lesson in such monster stories as Alexander's victory at the sweet water lake. Each of us will eventually encounter some awful obstacles in life, obstacles that will make us want to lie down, give up, or go away. The lesson is: don't.

As we will see in the discussion of *Beowulf* in part II, in our more liberal intellectual culture macho monster fights have become a quaint genre of outmoded heroics. After all, why must *men*, who cause these aggression problems in the first place, go around slaying dragons? The monster-killing man has become a bit of a joke, trivialized by the ivory tower as too obvious. Hollywood, however, continues to understand this feature of the monster story very well. In 2007 Will Smith starred in a film version of Richard Matheson's 1954 sci-fi classic *I Am Legend*, playing the vampire-slaying last man in New York City. In 2005 Steven Spielberg's remake of H. G. Wells's *War of the Worlds* pitched Tom Cruise against the blood-sucking aliens from a distant planet. Or consider M. Night Shyamalan's 2002 blockbuster *Signs*, with Mel Gibson and Joaquin Phoenix fighting off the invading aliens. All these films portrayed the monster killers as fathers, family men forced to extremes to protect their children. As Robert Neville (Will Smith) in *I Am Legend* tells his daughter, "Don't worry, Daddy's going to take away the monsters." This may seem trivial, obvious, and even naïve to the cynical cognoscenti, but what father hasn't felt this same impulse deep in his bones?

Contrary to the narrative of early twentieth-century anthropology, early humans were probably not bold, assertive predators, marching confidently through the savanna to spear their threatening competitors. Male aggression, we were told, was put to good use in the realm of the hunt and of course in primitive warfare. This kind of domination and mastery of the field was helped along by some burgeoning brain power, but such domination of the other animals led to much further cognitive and cultural progress. Barbara Ehrenreich, in her book *Blood Rites*, surveys more recent anthropology and corrects the old story. We should not think about "man the hunter" in Paleolithic times, she writes, but "man the hunted." She reminds us that humans are fragile creatures: "Our biology is alone enough to suggest an alarming level of vulnerability to the exceptionally hungry or casual prowler."[7] If we are to infer some aspects of human psychology from the evolutionary environment in which they developed, than we had better get an accurate picture of that environment and our status in it. Early humans were not uber predators but scavengers, waiting in the bushes to sneak in and pilfer morsels. It doesn't occur to us anymore to factor in the huge role that big cats, for example, must have played in the cognitive, emotional, and imaginative lives of our progenitors, but we were constantly harassed and victimized by them. Moreover, even in recent history, when the numbers of such predators are way down, a staggering number of deaths from lions, tigers, crocodiles, and wolves have been chronicled. "The British," Ehrenreich reports, "started recording the numbers of humans lost to tigers [on the Indian subcontinent] in 1800, and found that by the end of the century, approximately three hundred thousand people had been killed, along with 6 to 10 million farm animals." Though it may seem a remote possibility to us now, during the formation of the human brain the fear of being grabbed by sharp claws, dragged into a dark hole, and eaten alive was not an abstraction.

Men tend to respond to fear and vulnerability with aggression. The philosopher Harvey Mansfield writes, "Men have aggression to spare; they keep it in stock so as to have it ready when it is needed and even, or especially, when it is unneeded and unwanted."[8] Before men ever fought for honor or economic gain or even turf they must have fought for their own children and mates. Monsters, both real and imagined, are bound up with our feelings of insecurity and our responses to those anxieties. Masculine audacity and bravado is the reflex response to vulnerability.

This universal paternal impulse to protect and use whatever aggression is necessary is rehearsed again in Cormac McCarthy's Pulitzer Prize–winning 2006 novel *The Road*. McCarthy gives us a powerful story about a father trying to protect his son in a postapocalyptic world of roaming cannibals. The father must safeguard his son, lest he become a captive catamite slave whose limbs are harvested by cannibal monsters. Among other things, it is an allegorical story about the need to shelter the good, which is fragile, from the monstrous world.

To a young boy, monsters are exciting and alluring. They are invoked daily as the imaginary foes of the playground. Anyone, I think, who has raised a boy gets this point. When that boy becomes a man, however, he feels keenly, rightly or wrongly, that monsters have become his responsibility, part of his job.[9]

2

Monsters Are Nature's Playthings

Creations at which to marvel.

PLINY THE ELDER

IN ALEXANDER'S ADMITTEDLY SEXIST PEP TALK to his troops, we have an expression of a perennial attitude toward exotic creatures, peoples, and lands. Imperialist campaigns like Alexander's are not for traipsing through strange lands to collect aesthetic oddities and make friends with strangers. They are for coming to subdue, exploit, and civilize the savage world.

Monsters seem to represent the most extreme personified point of unfamiliarity; they push our sense of abnormality beyond the usual anthropological xenophobia. People with customs different from ours are weird, but perhaps different skin colors are weirder still, and people with a dog's head and headless people with a mouth in their chest, well…Animals are similarly conceptualized on a continuum of strangeness: first, nonnative species, then familiar beasts with unfamiliar sizes or modified body parts, then hybrids of surprising combination, and finally, at the furthest margins, shape-shifters and indescribable creatures.

In Homer's *Odyssey*, Odysseus and twelve of his men became trapped in a cave with a giant Cyclops named Polyphemus. "He was a horrid creature," Odysseus informs us, "not like a human being at all, but resembling rather some crag that stands out boldly against the sky on the top of a high mountain."[1] Odysseus at first tries to do some fast talking, but the Cyclops is not moved to mercy and breaks off discussion abruptly. Odysseus reports, "With a sudden clutch he gripped up two of my men at once and dashed them down upon the ground as though they had been puppies. Their brains were splashed upon the ground, and the earth was wet with their blood. Then he tore them limb from limb and dined upon them. He gobbled them up like a lion in the wilderness, flesh, bones, marrow, and entrails, without leaving anything uneaten. As for us, we wept and lifted up our hands to heaven on seeing such a horrid sight, for we did not know what else to do."[2]

Monsters and fabulous beasts like the Cyclopes generally originate in the myths and legends of poetry and allegory.[3] Homer and Hesiod are probably the earliest fountains of Western monster archetypes (e.g., chimeras, Cerberus, Hydra, Minotaur). But these literary creatures evolve and new species are added to the list in the popular tales of travelers. As explorers, soldiers, and traders penetrated strange lands, they absorbed local legends and encountered unfamiliar creatures, bringing all this back to urban Greece and Rome. Additionally, around the time of Herodotus, travel stories and myths were taken up by emerging writers of *natural history*, a budding science of description. These three literatures of monsters and beasts—poetry, travel tales, and natural history—continued to feed each other all the way down to the seventeenth century.

GRIFFINS

The griffins are an interesting case study. They are common characters in Greek literature; Aeschylus refers to them in his tragedy *Prometheus Bound* (460 BCE) as "sharp beaked." In later texts, such as Pliny's *Natural History* (77 CE), the gryps or griffins are bigger and winged. In the fourteenth century, in *Travels of Sir John Mandeville*, Mandeville expands the legend further by claiming that "one griffin hath the body more great and is more strong than eight lions, of such lions as be on this half, and more great and stronger than a hundred eagles such as we have amongst us."[4] This monstrous griffin helps us understand how an unexplainable observation can snowball into an elaborate cultural narrative, a narrative that grows so huge as to conceal its original source altogether.

Most scholars since the seventeenth century have uniformly considered the ancient griffins to be purely fanciful combinations of lion and eagle bodies, a product of the overactive Greek imagination. But one researcher, Adrienne Mayor, has argued that these mythical griffins are literary descriptions of real, albeit extinct, monsters.[5] These creatures are not pure fantasy, but actually appear to have zoological origins.

The first known use of the Greek word *gryph*, meaning "hooked" like a claw, occurs in the writings of Aristeas in the seventh century BCE. Aristeas's book *Arimaspea* is now lost but it was popular in the ancient world and chronicled his travels into Central Asia, where he encountered the Scythian people, a Greek term referring to all the nomadic people who lived between the Black Sea and Mongolia. Over two hundred years later we find Aeschylus relying on the *Arimaspea* for scene-setting details in his *Prometheus Bound* tragedy, set in Asia. Aeschylus describes a frightening land where live the Phorcides, old mumbling maids, swan-shaped, having only one eye and tooth to share between them; the Gorgons, three sisters with snakes for hair who kill you if you gaze at them; fierce griffins; and a race of one-eyed nomadic men called Arimaspeans, who mine the region for its rich gold deposits. Herodotus (484–425 BCE), who traveled through western Scythia himself, also cited Aristeas and tried to corroborate the additional claim that these one-eyed nomadic men were in constant combat with the griffins, who apparently nested in the gold-saturated sands of the region.

For the next six hundred years or so the legend of the griffins expanded and received further nuances from the ancient writers Ctesias, Pliny, and Appolonius. The basic anatomy of this Greek version of the monster, a giant quadruped with a sharp beak, echoes peculiar representations from Scythian art dating back to the eighth century BCE. Scythian tombs, originally created during the time of Herodotus and Aeschylus, were excavated in the twentieth century by Russian archaeologists, revealing scores of gold figurines of beaked quadrupeds.

These cultural convergences regarding the morphology and environment of the griffins suggest that more than fable held this monster together. The regions between the Altai and Tien Shan mountains are extremely rich in fossil deposits, and in the 1920s the paleontologist Roy Chapman Andrews began searching this region after hearing Chinese folklore about dragons' teeth and bones. He discovered massive fields of windblown strata with the skeletons of late Cretaceous dinosaurs strewn over the landscape. Perhaps the most eerie sight was a giant nesting ground of Protoceratops, with juvenile skeletons and even fossilized egg clutches.[6] Andrews was the first to dig out over one hundred Protoceratops from this land, but if Adrienne Mayor is correct, Andrews was not the first to discover these bones; they were regularly picked up and examined by ancient Scythian nomads between 800 BCE and 300 CE. A skeleton of a Protoceratops, and especially the psittacosaurus or "parrot-beaked" dinosaur (also found in the Dzungarian basin), looks exactly as you might imagine a gryph skeleton to look. Mayor summarizes the matter:

> The most common remains, including eggs and young, are of the Protoceratops (ceratops means "horned head"). This creature appears to combine

A skeleton of a Protoceratops, especially the psittacosaurus or "parrot-beaked" dinosaur found in the Dzungarian basin, looks exactly as you might imagine a griffin skeleton. Attempts to make sense of dinosaur fossils certainly stimulated monster speculations in the ancient world. Pen and ink drawing by Stephen T. Asma © 2008, based on a sketch by Albrecht Dürer.

the features of a mammal and bird of prey in a striking way. The body is about seven or eight feet long, and resembles that of a carnivore, but the skull has a powerful beak. The large nostrils and eye sockets and the knobs and frills of protoceratopsids (and distinct skulls, beaks, and giant claws of other dinosaur species) may explain the features of the archaic images of the gryps (and might account for some other unidentified animals in Scythian art).

Russian archaeologists excavating throughout the first half of the twentieth century discovered more than one hundred ancient gold mines in this area of Central Asia, some dating back to 1500 BCE. Mayor and Michael

Heaney speculate that nomads and traders sifted these areas for gold for centuries, regularly stumbling on the skeletons of frightening creatures that seemed to have perished in a series of large-scale battles with their neighbor enemies, the mythical one-eyed Arimaspeans. For the nomads, this would constitute a very plausible story for how these animals became extinct, or how they came to be absent in current times.

MONSTROUS BONES

This raises an interesting point about extinction in general. Today, living on the other side of Darwin, we dig monsters out of the ground all the time and have theoretical concepts such as evolution and extinction to make perfect sense out of why we don't see monsters walking among us anymore. But the intellectual landscape of ancient Greece was quite different from our own, and ideas such as evolution were marginal. So how, generally, did the ancients understand the monstrous bones they discovered? Were the creatures really extinct? Were the bones representative of species or just isolated giant individuals? Did these creatures continue to live on elsewhere, in distant lands?

Pliny the Elder gives us an idea of how the ancients viewed fossils in his account of a giant skeleton found near Joppa (present-day Tel Aviv), interpreted to be the skeleton of a huge Triton, a kind of merman.[7] He seems quite confident that Tritons exist and reports that Emperor Tiberius was assured of their existence by ambassadors from Olisipo (Lisbon). He adds credibility to his belief in Tritons by invoking "two illustrious knights" who witnessed, near Gades (Cadiz, Spain), the giant mermen climbing onto the sides of ships to sit, occasionally capsizing boats in the process. These bones caused quite a stir when brought to the imperial capital. "The bones of this monster, to which Andromeda was said to have been exposed, were brought by Marcus Scaurus from Joppa in Judaea during his aedileship and shown at Rome among the rest of the amazing items displayed. The monster was over 40 feet long, and the height of its ribs was greater than that of Indian elephants, while its spine was 1 and 1/2 feet thick."[8]

We have additional evidence that the ancients were aware of and intrigued by giant fossils (Miocene and Pleistocene mammals), but of course they didn't have a modern concept of such vanished species or a concept of geological time. Suetonius (69–130 CE) tells us in *Lives of the Caesars* that Caesar Augustus liked to display fossils in his home: "His own villas, which were modest enough, he decorated not so much with handsome statues and pictures as with terraces, groves, and objects noteworthy

The Cyclops legend was fueled by ancient Greek misinterpretations of mastodon skulls found in Mediterranean caves. Pencil drawing and collage by Stephen T. Asma © 2008.

for their antiquity and rarity; for example, at Capreae the monstrous bones of huge sea monsters and wild beasts, called the 'bones of the giants,' and the 'weapons of the heroes.'"[9]

It's not entirely clear whether the ancients conceived of their monsters as extinct species.[10] The examples above suggest that the creatures were believed to be rare but not entirely gone. One wonders, for example, if the exaggerated three-horned monster that Alexander faced at the sweet water lake (called an Odontotyrannus or "tooth-tyrant") was a fantasy based on the author's encounter with a fossil skull. The Austrian paleontologist Othenio Abel (1875–1945) argued in 1914 that the Greek myths of the Cyclopes were grounded in people's encounters with fossil elephant skulls, which are plentiful in Mediterranean coastal caves. The large nasal cavity in the center of the skull looks very much like the eye socket of a giant creature.

In a world relatively unexplored and so much larger than it is now, it would be quite reasonable to conclude that dinosaur-like creatures were living in India and other far-off, mysterious places. In fact, naturalists as late as the eighteenth century assumed that the giants whose remains we regularly unearth were still alive in the unexplored regions of the world. Thomas Jefferson, for example, introduced a strange fossil to the scientific community at a meeting of the American Philosophical Society in Philadelphia in the 1790s;[11] he called it Megalonyx, or "Great Claw." Jefferson believed that the enormous claw, discovered in a cave in Virginia, must have belonged to a monstrous cat-like creature; modern researchers have identified it as the giant ground sloth. The interesting point for our purpose is that Jefferson did not think the creature was extinct, but rather living somewhere in the uncharted frontier. "In the present interior of our continent," he suggests, "there is surely space and range enough for elephants and lions, if in that climate they could subsist; and the mammoths [mastodons] and megalonyxes who may subsist there. Our entire ignorance of the immense country to the West and North-West, and of its contents, does not authorise us to say what it does not contain." When he sent Lewis and Clark westward, Jefferson encouraged them to keep a lookout for giant living creatures. Suffice it to say that the ancients were no clearer on this issue than was Jefferson.

NATURAL HISTORY AND CREDULITY

The issue is not whether the ancients were more credulous than we are today, but what theories are available and reasonable in a given age. Even today cryptozoology, the study or search for legendary creatures (e.g., the Loch Ness Monster, yeti, chupacabra), is a reasonable venture, albeit marginal and easily lampooned. How much more reasonable and widespread would belief in cryptids be in the ancient world? Wouldn't monsters qualify as an odious subgroup inside this larger taxon of marvelous beings? Unlike much of today's science, ancient natural history, together with travelers' tales, often increased the credibility of monsters. More accurately, natural history, both ancient and modern, tends to live on the boundary line between the credible and the incredible.

Aristotle, a notable skeptic, was *not* particularly skeptical about the existence of a large hairy quadruped called a Bolinthus that fought its enemies by spraying acid-like excrement great distances.[12] He describes a beast that is bigger and stronger than an ox, with a long shaggy mane, that "defends itself by kicking and voiding excrement over a distance of about twenty-four feet." The excretion is so pungent that it burns the hair off dogs.[13] The animal appears to be an embellished version of the European bison. Even a beacon of rationality like Aristotle can seriously entertain marvelous stories from faraway lands.

One of the most important characters in the history of monsterology, Pliny the Elder, also waffled between reflective skepticism and gullibility. As the historian Margaret Robinson puts it, "It was Pliny's *Natural History* that persisted as the ultimate authority on the subject [of marvelous beasts] for fifteen hundred years."[14] His natural history transmitted the ancient beliefs about exotica into the medieval world; St. Augustine referred to him as "a man of great learning."[15] But today Pliny is considered more of a scrivener, an unreliable inventory taker, rather than a systematic synthesizer like Aristotle. With a little effort, however, reading his passages reveals some important cultural undercurrents.

As a general rule, Pliny accepted almost everything that was reported to him. He informs us, for example, that eels living in the Ganges River in India grow to be three hundred feet long, and that "King Pyrrhus' big toe on his right foot cured an inflamed spleen by touch. The story goes that when he was cremated his big toe would not burn along with the rest of his body; it was put in a chest in a temple."[16] To the long list of amazing descriptions Pliny adds a monster called the manticore, from the Greek for "man-eater." This beast is first described by Ctesias, and Aristotle cites the same description in his *History of Animals*; they all believe the creature to live in India. Pliny says it has "a triple row of teeth like a comb, the face and ears of a man, grey eyes, a blood-red color, a lion's body, and inflicts stings with its tail like a scorpion. The manticore has a voice that sounds like a pan-pipe combined with a trumpet, achieves great speed and is especially keen on human flesh."[17]

It's hard to imagine something that Pliny would *not* assent to in his considerations of nature, but then, rather surprisingly, he suddenly draws a line. "I am obliged to consider," he informs us "and with confidence—that the assertion that men are turned into wolves and back to themselves again is false, otherwise we must also believe in all the other things that over so many generations we have discovered to be fabulous." Apparently werewolves cross the line of credibility for Pliny.

In his explanation of the werewolf story, which comes from Arcadia, Pliny unwittingly reveals an interesting criterion for accepting or rejecting a fabulous narrative. Arcadian legend has it that someone chosen by lottery

The manticore monster was thought to favor human flesh. Descriptions of the beast appear in the natural history texts of Ctesias, Aristotle, and Pliny. Pencil drawing by Stephen T. Asma © 2008, based on a sketch from Edward Topsell's seventeenth-century bestiary.

is led to a marsh. He hangs his clothes on an oak tree and swims naked through the swamp to a deserted territory. "There he is turned into a wolf and associates with other wolves for nine years. If he has avoided contact with a human during that period, he returns to the same marsh, swims across it and regains his shape with nine years' age added to his former appearance."[18] The story so far is dubious, but not more so than the griffin or the three-hundred-foot eel or the Triton, all of which Pliny reports without editorializing. The giveaway for Pliny is that the werewolf, now returned to human form, actually gets back into the nine-year-old clothes hanging on the oak tree. That really tears it for Pliny, and he sighs, "It is astonishing how far Greek gullibility will go."

It may seem the height of hypocrisy to accept all manner of monster but then bar the entrance for the poor werewolf. And yet a deeper logic may be at work. The tipping point appears to be the story itself. Something about the narrative of this man—leaving his clothes on a tree, turning into a wolf and back, and dressing again in the same clothes—feels like a joke, both for us and for Pliny apparently. He can't rule out the werewolf on its own terms; after all, weirder creatures are acceptable to him. It's the literary conventions of the story itself that seem too much like a comedy to accept. Mimesis, or the imitation of life in the techniques of art and literature, was very well understood by the ancients; Aristotle devotes much of his *Poetics* to the philosophy of mimesis. It is not the monster itself that gives Pliny pause, but the "bad play" quality of the story.

Why is a werewolf itself *not* a cause for skepticism? For the same reason that a manticore or a race of one-eyed men are not intrinsically doubtful: nature is stranger than fiction. This is a time when strange monsters in the form of exotic animals are really being discovered in far-off lands. During the reign of Claudius Caesar, Pliny claims to have actually seen the corpse of a hippocentaur (half-man, half-horse) preserved in a vat of honey and brought from Egypt.[19] One suspects that the animal was some other exotic species honestly misidentified or perhaps an early form of Barnum-style hucksterism. In any case, we have to put ourselves in ancient shoes to remember that the Greeks had only recently, relatively speaking, come into contact with elephants and rhinoceroses. With these discoveries still somewhat fresh, it was hard to rule out fantastic creatures. The safest bet was credulity.

Credulity and incredulity are highly relative frames of mind and indigenous to *all* eras. Pliny tells a story about a monstrous octopus weighing more than seven hundred pounds and with thirty-foot tentacles that used to swim into the uncovered tanks of a fish farm in Cartiea. When the farmers realized that the creature was foraging for food in the fish farm, they sealed off the inlet with fences. At night the beast returned and finding no way to swim to the food, actually scaled a large tree and thereby crossed over the fence barrier. Pliny explains that the octopus could be caught only by employing hunting dogs.

> These surrounded the octopus as it was returning at night and roused the overseers, who were terrified by its strange appearance. Its size was unheard of, and likewise its color; it was smeared with brine and had a dreadful smell. Who would have expected to find an octopus there, or to recognize it against such a background? They seemed to be locked in a struggle with something out of this world, for it nauseated the dogs with its terrible breath, lashed them with its tentacles, round which one could scarcely put both arms, which it used in the manner of clubs. After great trouble it was dispatched with the aid of many tridents.[20]

When I read Pliny's description of a tree-climbing octopus, I laughed smugly for half an hour. Gosh, I thought, Pliny cracks me up. Then a nagging thought occurred to me, and after some research into cephalopod biology, I discovered to my embarrassment that octopi do indeed occasionally crawl on land, especially in pursuit of turtles or to get from one tide pool to another. The size of the creature may have been exaggerated by Pliny, but probably not the incredible behavior. I, like Pliny, cannot be sure what creatures are capable of, because they keep surprising me.

Skepticism gives one a certain sense of pleasure, perhaps the pleasure of feeling superior, of not being had. But *belief*, especially in the fantastic, is also very pleasurable. Indeed, with its emotional abandonment of improbability, it seems to trump the cool satisfactions of doubt. The Scottish philosopher David Hume (1711–1776) reminds us that the passions of "surprise and wonder" are very "agreeable emotions," and when they are triggered by anecdotes or reports these passions actually lend a sheen of credibility to those reports. "With what greediness are the miraculous accounts of travelers received, their descriptions of sea and land monsters, their relations of wonderful adventures, strange men and uncouth manners?"[21]

MONSTROUS RACES

"Strange men and uncouth manners" were important topics for ancient writers who wished to explore the "monstrous races" of the human species. The interest in monstrous animals such as the griffin was outdone only by these early anthropological impulses. And again India, which was shorthand for the entire East, was the assumed habitat of these exotic beings.

Most ancient Greeks and Romans considered all human ethnic groups other than their own to be barbarians, but another group of humanoid creatures fell outside the usual bounds of cultural and ethnic difference. The literature of the ancients reveals a continuum of degrees, whereby races of men decline further and further away from their ethnocentric starting place. Some of these humans are monstrous because their culture is considered odious, like Pliny's Scythian tribes who feed on human bodies. But some of these humans strain the category itself and exist somewhere between man and animal, as shown in a report by Megasthenes (350–290 BCE) of Indian men who have reversed feet with eight toes on each foot, or men with a dog's head who bark instead of speak. Or consider the umbrella-footed race of creatures reported by Ctesias (and repeated by Pliny), who have only one leg and hop at astonishing speed and who also lie on their back and raise their large foot to act as an umbrella against inclement weather. In his chapter "Man" Pliny tells us of satyrs living in the eastern mountains of India who "are very fast moving animals, sometimes running on all fours, sometimes upright like humans."[22] The satyrs may have been monkeys in reality, but many ancients knew little about nonhuman primates and tended to interpret reports of them as exotic pseudo-human races.[23] The dog-headed men, for example, may have been an embellishment based on travelers' reports of Old World yellow baboons (*Papio cynocephalus*) from eastern Africa.

These humanoid oddities are bordering on human because of some morphological and cultural similarities with "normal" humans, but properly speaking they are *lusus naturae*, "freaks of nature." More than the occasional individual monster (such as Medusa), whole classes of unclassifiable creatures were admitted by the ancients into the category *human*. These monstrous races will become increasingly important in the medieval imagination, as Christians begin to contemplate their spiritual status: Can these races be redeemed by the gospel?

For the most part, in the ancient world the bigotries about other peoples were not theological in nature. It is true that the Bible carves up races into the descendants of Noah's children, but Greek and Roman ideas about species and race were somewhat more naturalistic. Homer and Hesiod describe a variety of human origins; in addition to the predictable "created by gods" story, we are also born of water, and sometimes born of earth (in the case of autochthones). There was no single orthodox belief on the question of origins. More important, the philosophers all pushed a variety of pseudo-scientific explanations, favoring a kind of spontaneous generation of human beings. Xenophanes, Parmenides, Democritus, and Epicurus all believed that mankind was born of slime.[24] Slime is, indeed, a humble and somewhat egalitarian beginning. For the most part, then, the ancients were ethnocentric for cultural rather than metaphysical reasons.[25]

The Far East was a land of romantic and fearful projections for ancient Westerners. Foreign people, such as Persians, Indians, and Chinese, were often linked with the strange and alien creatures of bogus natural history and mythology. Sometimes the stereotyping was mild or innocuous, as when Pliny says, "The Chinese are mild in character, but resemble wild animals in that they shun the company of the rest of their fellow men and wait for traders to come to them."[26] But sometimes the stereotyping was more pernicious. Herodotus, Plutarch, and Diodorus all demonized the Persians as autocratic and alien, in contrast to Greeks, who apparently loved freedom and rationality.[27] Dehumanizing one's enemy is nothing new, nor is it a purely Western hobby of mind. The Indian epics *Mahabharata* and *Ramayana* describe foreign tribes (presumably Westerners) as *karnapravarana*, giant-eared races, with ears so large that one could wrap up in them to sleep.[28]

Imagining a group of people as monstrous can serve political agendas quite well. The literary theorist Edward Said has famously called this form of political stereotyping "orientalism," a term that refers to the way Occidental writers, artists, and politicians invent a negative category of cultural qualities for Asian and African people in order to better justify Western imperial interests.[29] Scholars like Said, who believe that all knowledge is a kind of power, would certainly see the early anthropology of the ancients as a thinly veiled attempt to create an "us versus them" political dynamic. Maybe this is true; we will have many more opportunities to reflect on it later in this book. But for now it is important to articulate what these fantastical races and creatures meant to the ancients themselves. Before importing too much theory about the *latent* meaning of extraordinary creatures, we need to give great weight to their *manifest* meaning.[30]

Pliny himself shows us the way when he asks the natural question, Why do these monsters and wonders exist at all? He concludes that amazing creatures exist as Nature's "playthings." If they have any purpose at all, it is to create the experiences of wonder, marvel, and astonishment in us. Referring to disappearing "ghost-men" in Africa, Pliny grows philosophical and says, "These and similar kinds of human beings ingenious Nature has made to be playthings for herself and for us, creations at which to marvel. Indeed, who could list the things she does day by day and almost every hour? Let it be sufficient for the revelation of her power to have included races of men among her marvels."[31]

3

Hermaphrodites and Man-headed Oxen

The glutted earth swarms even now with savage beasts.

LUCRETIUS

PRODIGIES AND PORTENTS were perceived to be everywhere in the ancient world. All of nature was sending signals foretelling the future. If one could read the signs properly, which was the job of augurs in Rome and oracles in Greece, then one could predict the fate of military campaigns, the health of marriages, or the prosperity of business ventures. The Romans practiced an art of prophesy that came down from the Etruscans and involved reading the liver of a sacrificed animal. The liver, thought to be the source of blood and life itself, was charted into subdivisions that corresponded to deities. Cults of fortune-tellers evolved an elaborate and secret science of viscera interpretation.

The Roman historian Livy (59 BCE–17 CE) tells a typical story about the bad omen of a sacrifice in 90 BCE. The Roman consul Rutilius Lupus sacrificed an animal and "failed to find the lobe of the liver among the organs; ignoring the omen he lost his army and was killed in battle."[1] In contrast, in 43 BCE Caesar Augustus sacrificed an animal on the eve of his military campaign against Marc Antony. Livy reports that "the animal he sacrificed had twin sets of internal organs. Success followed him."

IN-BETWEEN BEINGS

Like a missing liver lobe, the discovery of a hermaphrodite human was considered by most Romans to be very bad for the health of the state.[2]

Apparently the founder of Rome himself, Romulus, felt threatened by hermaphrodites and ordered them to be drowned upon discovery. The logic of this custom, as with many customs, is unclear. The classicist Carlin Barton suggests that hermaphrodites, with their ambiguous, unclassifiable sexuality, may have been simultaneously threatening to the increasingly rigid official Roman culture but also alluring and exciting to those Romans who felt repressed by the bureaucratic, authoritarian, and hierarchic mores of an expanding empire.[3] The ambiguously gendered person did not conform to traditional male or female parameters.[4] Hermaphrodites, on this account, represented a dangerous freedom, in the same way that "noble savages" must have done for Enlightenment-era urbanites. A more prosaic, and probably accurate, explanation is that monstrous offspring represented a terrible economic and energy burden on the family, and if they should make it to adulthood they would be a burden on the state as well. It's reasonable to expect laws and taboos to emerge in a society that reinforces the specific ecological survival needs of its families. This practice of drowning hermaphrodites was extended to all seriously disabled children in the Roman Laws of the Twelve Tables: "A father shall immediately put to death a son recently born, who is a monster, or has a form different from that of members of the human race."[5]

The hermaphrodite is a liminal being. *Liminal* comes from the Latin word *limen*, meaning "threshold." When you are on a threshold, you are neither inside nor outside but in between. Hermaphrodites, with their ambiguous genitalia, are in between the traditional categories of male and female. One sees, immediately I think, that the idea of a liminal being, something between categories, is a very useful way to think about many of the subjects of this book, not just hermaphrodites. Griffins, with their ambiguous avian-quadruped shape, would qualify as liminal, as would centaurs, the chimera, the Gorgons, the Minotaur, and the Hydra. Mosaic beings, grafted together or hybridized by nature or artifice, reappear throughout the history of Western monsters as the Golem, Frankenstein's creature, and transgenic animals. Even zombies, though not hybridized, are liminal monsters because they exist between the living and the dead. In short, liminality is a significant category for the uncategorizable. Of course, the extraordinary and the ordinary are often just different by degree rather than kind. So the extent to which *everyone* is a little hard to categorize is the extent to which we are all liminal.

Theory aside, Livy chronicled many murders of hermaphrodites in the last two centuries before the Common Era. A short sampling of his very long list will suffice to demonstrate the common perception of hermaphrodites

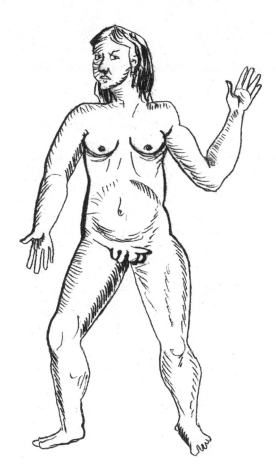

The practice of drowning hermaphrodites was extended to all seriously disabled children in the Roman Laws of the Twelve Tables. "A father shall immediately put to death a son recently born, who is a monster, or has a form different from that of members of the human race." Pen and ink drawing by Stephen T. Asma © 2008, based on a hermaphrodite sketch in Ambroise Paré's sixteenth-century *On Monsters*.

as monsters. In 133, "in the region of Ferentium, a hermaphrodite was born and thrown into the river"; in 119 "a hermaphrodite eight years old was discovered in the region of Rome and consigned to the sea"; in 117 "a hermaphrodite ten years old was discovered and was drowned in the sea"; in 98 "a hermaphrodite was thrown into the sea."

Many other types of monsters are cited in Livy's encyclopedic history, including many unfortunate developmentally disabled children. A sad litany of abnormalities is offered as examples of bad omens, including conjoined twins and babies born with no hands and feet or too many hands and feet. Livy himself seems completely unmoved by any of these stories and recites them as though he's reading sports scores. His entry for 108 BCE reads, "At Nursia twins were born to a freeborn woman, the girl with all members intact the boy with the following deformities; in front his abdomen was open, so that the uncovered intestine could be seen, and behind he had no anal opening; at birth he cried out once and died. The war against Jugurtha was carried on successfully." But things seemed to be looking up for hermaphrodites, at least, by the time Pliny writes his *Natural History*. We find a refreshing tolerance developing toward hermaphrodites when he states, "There are people who have the characteristics of both sexes. We call them hermaphrodites, the Greeks *androgyny*. Once considered portents, now they are sources of entertainment."[6]

Some scholars see a teleological arc here. That is to say, the transition from superstitious murder of hermaphrodites to benign neglect and even amusement looks like progress. It looks like progress because it *is* progress, ethically speaking. But history and ethics don't always converge on the righteous path. The classicist Luc Brisson and the gender theorist Anne Fausto-Sterling both suggest that hermaphrodites suffered terribly in the early days of Roman law, but then rational progress ultimately created a more hospitable Rome for first-century hermaphrodites.[7]

But even while Pliny was assuring the reader that hermaphrodites were in the clear, so to speak, drownings continued.[8] Monsters did not simply evaporate as rational humanism came on the scene. The fear of monsters hung on in the vast stretches of darkness, while the thin flare of rationality, possessed by a few elite philosophers, swept around the terrain, without much illumination or impact.[9]

REASON AND SUPERSTITION

The ancient story about monsters does not progress from crazy paranoia to cool-headed tolerance. Instead, superstition and rationalism shared territory, just as they do today. But it is still important to notice, even without the triumphal narrative, that cool-headed tolerance *did* evolve in the ancient world. The failure of the masses to adopt a scientific attitude toward abnormal beings does not diminish the impressive achievements of the rational minority who did. Anaxagoras's examination of a deformed ram's head is a good example to illustrate the uneasy simultaneity of ancient mysticism and empiricism.

The Greek historian Plutarch (46–127 CE) chronicled the moral characters of esteemed Greek and Roman leaders. One of his subjects was the ruler of Athens in the Golden Age, Pericles (495–429 BCE), who happened to be a good friend of the Ionian philosopher Anaxagoras (500–428). Anaxagoras, who had an unflappable character, was a great inspiration to Pericles. According to Plutarch, Anaxagoras was once accosted in the marketplace by an abusive citizen who hurled several hours of insult and even followed him to continue the diatribe outside Anaxagoras's home.

Completely unfazed by the verbal abuse, Anaxagoras saw that it was growing dark and "ordered one of his servants to take a light and to go along with the man and see him safe home."[10]

But it was Anaxagoras's scientific acumen that not only won Pericles' respect but also ushered in a new phase of natural philosophy. Anaxagoras developed a mechanical theory to explain the origin and motions of the heavenly bodies, suggesting that a powerful sifting force he called *Nous*, or Mind, slowly differentiated the material soup of the early cosmos. Presaging the materialism of later atomist philosophers, he argued that every physical thing had small bits of other substances hidden within it. So the transformations in nature that we see, such as growth and decay, are really the result of these invisible mechanical processes. He looked for predictable causes, rather than superstitious divinations, and his ideas demystified the natural world.

One day Pericles heard that a monstrous ram had been born on one of his farms and he sent for the animal. When it arrived at his court, a crowd gathered around and studied the strange anomaly. The animal had only one horn growing from the center of its head. A revered fortune-teller named Lampon announced that the current political struggle between Pericles and his rival Thucydides would finally be resolved in Pericles' favor. The monstrous ram, found on Pericles' estate, was the auspicious sign indicating political victory. Lampon read the monster as a good omen.

Anaxagoras, who was present for the spectacle, made a careful examination of the one-horned ram and then chopped its head in half. Plutarch reports, "Anaxagoras, cleaving the skull in sunder, showed to the bystanders that the brain had not filled up its natural place, but being oblong, like an egg, had collected from all parts of the vessel which contained it, in a point to that place from whence the root of the horn took its rise." In other words, he offered a scientific, causal explanation of the monster. A developmental glitch had produced a wonder.

Apparently this bit of demonstrable empiricism won Anaxagoras a moment of respect and admiration from the many bystanders at the court. People could actually see with their own eyes the mechanical causes of the monstrosity. But this was a very short-lived triumph of reason over superstition, because a brief time later Pericles did indeed prevail over his political rival and then Lampon the seer was the court darling all over again. This suggests, for one thing, that rational science was not exactly a juggernaut of truth, crushing the culture of superstition in its path. It also suggests that neither science nor superstition ever definitively rules out the other one. Explaining *how* a monster came to be monstrous, as Anaxagoras did, still failed to explain the monster's *purpose*. The purpose or teleology of monsters remained a vital concern for the ancients, and then the medievals, long after the mechanical explanations emerged.

This widespread cultural anxiety about the purpose of portentous monsters was partly a reflection of scientific naïveté in the uneducated classes, but more essentially it was a reflection of human nature. The Roman philosopher Lucretius, writing some three centuries after Anaxagoras, still laments the human tendency to fall into destructive emotions such as fear. Praising his philosophical mentor Epicurus (341–270 BCE), Lucretius tells his readers that Hercules himself, and most of the other gods, were not as impressive as his rationalist hero, who banished the mental monsters of superstition. But he acknowledges the inevitable tendency for undisciplined minds to fall back into fright and trepidation. Even if monsters exist, he exclaims, they cannot really hurt you if your mind is well trained. We should fear more the internal irrational emotions.

> And the rest of all those monsters slain, even if alive,
> Unconquered still, what injury could they do?
> None, as I guess. For so the glutted earth
> Swarms even now with savage beasts, even now
> Is filled with anxious terrors through the woods
> And mighty mountains and the forest deeps—
> Quarters 'tis ours in general to avoid.
> But lest the mind be purged, what conflicts then,
> What perils, must bosom, in our own despite!
> O then how great and keen the cares of lust
> That split the man distraught! How great the fears!
> And lo, the pride, grim greed, and wantonness—
> How great the slaughters in their train! and lo,
> Debaucheries and every breed of sloth!
> Therefore that man who subjugated these,
> And from the mind expelled, by words indeed,
> Not arms, O shall it not be seemly him
> To dignify by ranking with the gods?[11]

Controlling the mind and controlling nature are ways for men to become god-like on this earth. Knowledge, according to the philosophers, is a great weapon against internal and external monsters. When the philosopher Thales (624–546 BCE) was shown a centaur, he actually laughed and offered a very mundane, albeit disturbing, explanation for it.[12] A young shepherd who tended the flocks of Periander, the ruler of Corinth, brought a newborn foal to show the ruler. Jorge Luis Borges retells the humorous story in his *Book of Imaginary Beings*: "The newborn's face, neck, and arms were human, while the rest of its body was that of a horse. It cried like a baby, and everyone thought this a terrifying omen. The wise Thales looked at it, however, laughed, and told Periander that he should either not employ such young men as keepers of his horses or provide wives for them."[13]

ARISTOTLE'S MONSTERS

Aristotle (384–322 BCE) followed the rationalist lead of Thales and Anaxagoras, developing the most impressive and ambitious scientific research program to be found anywhere in the ancient world. He had a knack for getting his hands dirty in areas of study that would have repelled his more refined and academic teacher Plato. When Aristotle was motivating his hesitant students to roll up their sleeves and actually do the animal dissections necessary for the understanding of physiology and anatomy, he told them of Heraclitus's kitchen. A group of dignitaries came to visit Heraclitus and found him warming himself at the stove of his kitchen. They hesitated to enter because kitchens were considered undignified places, especially for serious discussions. Heraclitus said, "Come in, don't be afraid. There are gods here too."[14]

This willingness to investigate the undignified and indecorous aspects of nature led Aristotle to study monsters directly. Being the son of a physician, he had little interest in mythical creatures or phantasms, but focused instead on teratology, the study of developmental malformations that emerge during gestation. Actually, to introduce them as "developmental" is misleading, since it was part of Aristotle's great accomplishment to *notice* (through dissections) that embryogenesis and growth are epigenetic; that is, embryos grow from simple blobs to highly articulated forms. This seems obvious to us, raised as we are on amazing PBS-style microscopy images and documentary films of time-lapse fetal development. *Of course* the egg develops from simple to complex. But the ancients were not privy to this kind of technology-wrested information, and we should also remember that no one even knew that mammals produced eggs until the 1820s, when Karl Ernst von Baer made the discovery. A competing theory, called preformationism, suggested that the fully formed animal was already *complete* at the beginning of gestation, a kind of miniature seed animal; growth was simply a process of getting bigger, not progressive development. This actually seemed more reasonable than epigenesis because the ancients could not understand how molding forces could get inside the womb to sculpt the changing fetal material. By analogy, a piece of leather takes on complex form only when a cobbler works on it, and proponents of preformation could not see any such transformative assembly in utero, so, they concluded, the zygote must be a micro person already.

Aristotle could not agree. He noticed that embryos developed from homogeneous-looking material to heterogeneous structures or forms, but he believed that an underlying *logical* and *metaphysical* reality existed beneath that *physical* process. In describing biological development, he says, "In order of time...the material and the generative process must necessarily be anterior to the being that is generated; but in logical order the definitive character and form of each being precedes the material."[15] In order for a biological process to be regular, predictable, coherent, and successful, it has to know where it's going. An embryo doesn't literally *know* where it's going (as tissues form organs, etc.); it's not a conscious process. But the very fact that animals develop so predictably over and over again, and do not slosh chaotically into a biotic mess, is a kind of proof that organisms have blueprints of some kind. Organisms have internal formal instructions that tell them to make a leg here and a tongue there and when to *stop* making arms, mouths, and so on.[16] This blueprint Aristotle called the essential form, and this essential form is what guarantees that acorns always grow into oak trees, dogs always give birth to dogs, and humans always give birth to humans.[17]

Aristotle was more than familiar with his intellectual predecessors; he had studied them carefully and always took time to consider their teachings. One of his more illustrious forerunners was Empedocles (490–430 BCE), who seriously considered monsters a generation before Aristotle.[18] Empedocles offered a theory of animal origins that looks very similar to Darwinian natural selection, whereby organisms form randomly and the environment selects the more successful experiments. He claimed that in the distant past, before contemporary species, single parts of animals arose separate from each other. Heads without necks rolled pathetically around the environment, trying to survive. Arms, legs, spleens, and eyes presumably crawled the earth in a grotesque parade. Occasionally these organs and limbs accidentally clumped together and managed to survive for a short time, whereas others perished quickly. Among these monstrous creatures, Empedocles mentions the "man-headed oxen" as just one example of random hybrid weirdness. Only your imagination need limit the permutations of viscera. While these beasts were being winnowed by the harsh environment, Empedocles imagines, humanoid creatures without sexual differentiation evolved out of mud. The final stage was the evolution of male and female genders.

Aristotle did not like the idea that we were all monsters once and that "chance fitness" sorted us into our current zoological forms. But unlike today's creationists he did not object on religious grounds. Instead, he thought Empedocles was doing bad science.[19] According to Aristotle, Empedocles had the *causal* story exactly backward. "The process of development," Aristotle explains, "is for the sake of the thing finally developed, and not this for the sake of the process. Empedocles, then, was in error when he said that many of the characters presented by animals were merely the results of incidental occurrences during their development."[20] For Aristotle, the "essential form of a man" is what directs the developmental changes, bringing about a coherent biological process; the "essential form of an ox" similarly guides the process of oxen reproduction. Without the fixed essence, we would see reproductive chaos on a regular basis: monsters would be the norm rather than the exception. Since we don't see that chaos, we can conclude that all development (embryological or evolutionary) must be working toward some fixed goal. If Aristotle had lived to see the birth of modern genetics, with its theory of stored hereditary information in the form of DNA, he would have celebrated it as a kind of formal recipe that guides growth and development. As it is, he had no such knowledge and made the best science he could with what he had.

So we did not have a monstrous past, where parts of creatures accidentally clumped into organisms, because "parts" exist only as components of "wholes." "That this is true," Aristotle says, "is manifest by induction; for a house does not exist for the sake of bricks and stones, but these materials for the sake of the house; and the same is the case with the materials of other bodies."[21] In contrast to this rather philosophical argument, Lucretius offers more mundane proof against monstrous ancestors: monsters would have needed the exact matching sexual organs in order to procreate, and that fit seems even harder to believe if chance is the only cause.[22] In the same passage, he offers an interesting argument for why centaurs could not exist. Lucretius points out that humans mature at a much slower rate than horses do; young foals are independent very quickly after birth, whereas humans are dependent on their mother for years. Consequently, the half-man half-horse would be ridiculous; when the back half of the monster was well grown, independent, and capable of running and jumping, the front half would not even be able to hold up its head. Lucretius uses this logic to eliminate the possibility of any hybrid monsters that are similarly discordant in terms of their developmental trajectories.

Aristotle further reasoned that monsters are simply *mistakes* that occur when normal reproductive processes are interrupted or otherwise corrupted. Nature inadvertently creates monsters when the "essence" of the animal (its final or formal cause) is corrupted by wayward matter. In the same way that grammatical mistakes can creep into an author's writings,

Aristotle suggests, so, too, can biological mistakes creep into the purposeful direction of nature.

Feminist historians have rightfully highlighted the gender implications of Aristotle's biology. Aristotle argues that an essential form is uniform, the same for everyone in a given species. The form, being a kind of biological recipe, has a degree of specificity that differentiates one species of animal from another. Because *matter* is the same in every physical thing (earth, air, fire, and water, and their mixed "tissues"), it must be *form* that separates one kind of thing from another. Form is the cookie cutter, so to speak, and matter is the dough. When a man and a woman have sex, Aristotle says, the form of the offspring is passed along via the man's semen. The woman's uterine blood provides the raw matter upon which the semen information goes to work, concocting and shaping the eventual fetus. The recipe provided from the male would, if it could, create an exact replica of itself, but the clumsy interference of unpredictable matter (too much of this, too little of that) actually corrupts the replication process. So *heredity* is explained by the male contribution to procreation, and *variation* and *diversity* are explained by the female contribution.[23]

In an illuminating passage in *Generation of Animals*, Aristotle gives the ancient world a new view of monsters: "Even he who does not resemble his parents is already in a certain sense a monstrosity."[24] In other words, where there is deviation from the type (and there always is), one sees the minor errors inherent in reproduction. Everyone is just a little bit monster, in this trivial sense, but a more dramatic deviation (again caused by matter) creates the true "grotesques" of teratology: conjoined twins, craniofacial anomalies, missing limbs, polydactyls, hermaphrodites, and so on. He even offers a mundane scientific suggestion for why we don't see more human monsters. "Why is it," he asks, "that quadrupeds of a small size most often give birth to monstrosities; whereas man and the larger quadrupeds such as horses and asses do so less often? Is it because small quadrupeds such as dogs, pigs, goats, and sheep, have more abundant progeny than the larger animals, which either always or usually produce only one offspring at a time?"[25]

Unlike many ancients who loved to speculate on the meaning or purpose of a particular monstrous birth, Aristotle concluded that monsters have no purpose or special meaning. To ascribe such meanings to natural accidents would be as wrongheaded as saying that a crack in the sidewalk is *for the purpose* of letting grass grow through. Monsters are just cases of biological bad luck and therefore don't require special explanations. Aristotle joins the other scientists in claiming that there is no additional purpose or portent in bizarre ram's horns (Anaxagoras) or seeming centaurs (Thales).

All of Nature, according to Aristotle, should be understood in terms of purpose (teleology), such as when he says that an eye must be explained by its purpose of seeing and an acorn's purpose is the oak tree. But despite this framework, or rather because of it, there are no special purposes for monsters beyond the usual species-specific goals. A monster born of humans, no matter what it looks like, is a failed attempt to actualize a human essence. It is not a new species or a hybrid species or an alien creature or even a message from the gods. It is just an anomalous or abnormal human being.[26] But Aristotle's demystification of monsters turned out to be a minority report, largely ignored by the ancient populace. Anomalous births continued to augur important revelations for superstitious Greeks and Romans.

PHANTOM IMAGES

If the ancient scientists were right in their general skepticism about monsters, was everyone else just stupid and naïve? Lucretius offers a charitable clarification of why people continued to believe in monsters. The reason, which seems paradoxical at first, is that people continued to *see* monsters. But now Lucretius, following the general atomistic theory, redefined this "seeing" of monsters within an overall paradigm of perception.

According to atomists, all physical objects are constantly shedding gossamer-thin films of themselves, phantom images that emanate off the object. A horse, for example, is always emitting a transparent copy of itself, fluid-like, through the medium of air until it reaches my eye. I take in this representation through the eyes and it travels on to the mind. This process transmits to the *inside* of a person a little image or replica (material in nature, but very subtle matter) of an *outside* material thing. This theory of perception is quite far from our notion of light bouncing off objects and entering the retina, to be reorganized in the back of the brain by the visual cortex. But it's still an impressive way to solve the riddle of how we get representational information.

These gossamer webs, which are constantly radiating off objects, do not stop impinging on us when we go to sleep. In fact, their infiltration into our senses and then our minds while we're sleeping is the atomistic explanation for dreaming. But while we sleep, Lucretius claims, we cannot separate the true images from the false because our intelligence is dormant. When we dream of our dead father, it is because some leftover image film, floating free of its deceased source object, has drifted into our senses. On this account, monstrous hybrids and fantastical creatures are common "perceptions" because separate gossamers, from separate animals, have mingled and conjoined while floating through the air. A horse gossamer and a man gossamer have mingled their atoms accidentally, and when they are received by the perceiver they are confused as one. As Lucretius explains:

> The Cerberus-visages of dogs we see,
> And images of people gone before—
> Dead men whose bones earth bosomed long ago;
> Because the images of every kind
> Are everywhere about us borne—in part
> Those which are gendered in the very air
> Of own accord, in part those others which
> From divers things do part away, and those
> Which are compounded, made from out their shapes.
> For truly from no living Centaur is
> That phantom gendered, since no breed of beast
> Like him was ever; but, when images
> Of horse and man by chance have come together,
> They easily cohere, as aforesaid,
> At once, through subtle nature and fabric thin.
> In the same fashion others of this ilk
> Are created. And when they're quickly borne
> In their exceeding lightness, easily
> (As earlier I showed) one subtle image,
> Compounded, moves by its one stroke the mind,
> Itself so subtle and so strangely quick.[27]

In one deft move Lucretius and the atomists were able to eliminate the superstitions of belief in monsters and portentous dreams, but also acknowledge their real experiential basis. Confused phantom images (hybridized creatures, dead people, etc.) were actually entering our senses (because the air is thick with a metaphysical mist of images), but people were misinterpreting these as objectively real. Like Aristotle, however, Lucretius failed to have much impact (despite turning atomism into a *poem*) on the everyday culture of the ancient world. Shortly after Lucretius, Livy was still giving great weight to omens, dreams, and monsters, and this trend continued right through to the fourth century CE in the form of popular books of omens.[28]

4

Monstrous Desire

A multitudinous, many-headed monster.
PLATO

WHILE HIKING THE BANKS OF THE ILISSUS RIVER,
Socrates discussed the monstrous side of human desire with his
friend Phaedrus.[1] It was a regular topic for Plato and for many
Greek artists and intellectuals. Classicism is usually characterized by cool-
headed reason, symmetry, and order, but just beneath this calm surface is a
writhing mess of Dionysian reality.

In the dialogue named for him, Phaedrus asks Socrates if he believes
in mythical tales of Gorgons, hippocentaurs, and so on, and the sage holds
forth on the various debates and disputations surrounding the credibility
of myths. Ultimately he says, "I have no leisure for such enquiries; shall
I tell you why? I must first know myself, as the Delphian inscription says;
to be curious about that which is not my concern, while I am still in ignorance of my own self, would be ridiculous."

Unlike the scientifically minded ancients discussed earlier, Socrates had
no interest in debunking myths, monsters, dreams, or gods. He was not even
concerned enough with these things to qualify as a skeptic. He was simply
fascinated by other things, particularly the human psyche. Redirecting the
monster question inward, Socrates says, "I bid farewell to all this [mythol-
ogy]; the common opinion is enough for me. For, as I was saying, I want to
know not about this, but about myself: am I a monster more complicated
and swollen with passion than the serpent Typho, or a creature of a gentler
and simpler sort, to whom Nature has given a diviner and lowlier destiny?"

The answer to this last question turns out to be *both*—and then some. Plato is a careful observer of the conflicted inner agencies at work inside each human being. While he is famous for giving us an allegory of rational enlightenment, the well-known myth of the cave, he is also willing to dig below the surface to plumb the subterranean gutters of human craving. In a less well-known passage of the *Republic*, for example, he builds a monster.[2]

PLATO'S MONSTER

"Let us make an image of the psyche," Socrates explains. "An ideal image of the psyche, like the composite creations of ancient mythology, such as the Chimera, or Scylla, or Cerberus, and there are many others in which two or more different natures are said to grow into one." He asks his friends to compose in their mind's eye a writhing mass of arms, legs, heads, teeth, and claws, all capable of shape-shifting and mutating into new hideous forms: in short, a "multitudinous, many-headed monster," as he calls it. Next he asks his friends to imagine a lion, and finally a rather small man. These are the three ingredients of his mongrel composition, and Socrates says, "Now join them, and let the three grow into one." "Next," he says, "fashion the outside of them into a single image, as of a man, so that he who is not able to look within, and sees only the outer hull, may believe the beast to be a single human creature." At this point we have arrived at a hybrid monster, one part multiheaded fiend, one part lion, and one part man, but they are all hidden within a normal-looking human figure. This creature is actually a symbolic culmination of Plato's entire argument in the *Republic*. It is necessary to analyze the meaning of this symbol in order to grasp ancient ideas about frightening internal monsters (alien parts of the human psyche), the damage they can do, and the proposed cures or solutions for such miasmas.

The human psyche, according to Socrates and many of his Greek contemporaries, is made up of three basic functions: reasoning power (*logistikon*), emotional conviction (*thumos*), and appetite or desire (*epithymia*). We can refer to these as "faculties" or aspects of the soul—simply stated: reason, emotion, and appetite.

The multiheaded monster represents the appetites, the lion signifies the emotions, and the small homunculus is reason, all melded together into one creature. To have a healthy psychology (soul), we must organize this creature in just the right way. We must, according to Socrates, cultivate an inner life where our goals are set by the "smart" part of our psyche (reason), while our convictions ("emotions" that are guided by our rationality) drive us to overcome hardships and challenges and our instinctual drives (the appetites) get pressed into moderate forms by the "higher" parts of the soul. This harmonic relation—reason ruling over emotion (thumos) and both reason and emotion ruling over the fiery appetites (epithymia)—is the condition of the healthy psyche. It turns out that this natural division of labor is precisely the harmonious relationship that we refer to as *justice* in the state, whereby the wise rule over the courageous warrior class, and together they rule over the temperate craftsmen class. Thus, reaching the culmination of the *Republic*, Socrates is finally able to say *what* justice is: the harmony of reason over emotion over appetite. But now, *why* be just?

A gangster, criminal, or unjust person, while appearing successful with his lavish stuff and beautiful sycophants, is ultimately the most miserable of people. He seems to be the free-wheeling big shot everybody respects but is really a slave to his appetites whom everybody fears. Socrates explains that the psyche of the gangster personality (the tyrant) becomes "either by nature or by habits or both" like a drunkard's (or a junkie's) psyche. The harmony of reason over emotion over appetite has become unbalanced, and the lowest part of the soul (the appetites) has become the ruling part of the soul.[3] Here then is the response that Socrates can finally offer to the pessimists. Justice is not a set of actions or behaviors that pay off in some future consequences. Justice is the psychological peace of mind that comes from a fully integrated rational psyche. According to Socrates, nothing can be more *intrinsically* worthwhile than this harmony.[4]

The overriding metaphor of the *Republic* is the equation of justice with the healthy condition of an organism and injustice with the diseased condition. But more than merely asserting the analogy, Plato sets out to show the diseased nature of an immoral person by showing the tyrant mind as a state of inner slavery. The fascinating thing about the ethical theory of the *Republic* is its developmental approach. People aren't born saints or born criminals, they are made that way through bad nurturing and personal habits of indulging the wrong appetites. Plato is telling us how normal people can become monstrous over time.

When he and his friends have assembled their tripartite symbolic monster, Socrates uses it to demonstrate the unfortunate consequences of the pessimist's pursuit of unjust hedonism:

> And now, to him who maintains that it is profitable for the human creature to be unjust, and unprofitable to be just, let us reply that, if he be right, it is profitable for this creature to feast the multitudinous monster and strengthen the lion and the lion-like qualities, but to starve and weaken the man, who is consequently liable to be dragged about at the mercy of either

of the other two; and he is not to attempt to familiarize or harmonize them with one another—he ought rather to suffer them to fight, and bite and devour one another.

Instead of this chaos, in which the internal parts are warring with and even devouring each other, we should ally the more human parts (rationality in particular) against the more monstrous (desires): "He should watch over the many-headed monster like a good husbandman, fostering and cultivating the gentle qualities, and preventing the wild ones from growing; he should be making the lion-heart his ally, and in common care of them all should be uniting the several parts with one another and with himself." If the lion (thumos) rises to the ruling position without the guidance of reason, then hot-headed, overly aggressive, and passionate "animals" result.

A recent headline in a Chicago newspaper reported that a man who became angry with his cab driver dragged the cabbie from the taxi, got behind the wheel, and then repeatedly drove over the cabbie, killing him. This is a frightening case of immoderate thumos, unguided by reason and self-control. If the multiheaded desires (epithymia) rise to the dominant position (above reason and thumos), addictive hedonism tortures the individual with terminal unfulfillment and also tortures his or her immediate social circle with crime, betrayal, and treachery.

Plato gives us a theory about how human monsters, of the psychological variety, actually emerge and evolve, and how they can be prevented. At the beginning of book IX of the *Republic* he says that all human beings have lawless desires within them. The evidence is provided by our own dream life: when we go to sleep our reason slumbers with us, and the beastly and savage parts of us awake in search of gratification. "You know that there is nothing it [epithymia] won't dare to do at such a time, free of all control by shame or reason. It doesn't shrink from trying to have sex with a mother, as it supposes, or with anyone else at all, whether man, god, or beast." The Freudian aspects of Plato's theory give it a very modern-sounding ring, but it is only evidence that the Greeks were more subtle psychologists than sometimes granted.

With Plato's dreams of bestiality and incest we have certainly arrived at the gutter of human desires. But even normal erotic love has the potential (perhaps the inevitability) to go seriously sour. In the remainder of Socrates' discussion with Phaedrus he details how erotic attraction to another is very much like "being possessed": it is a kind of madness that comes over you and forces you to do incredibly stupid things. Of course, anyone who has ever been infatuated with another person knows exactly what he's talking about. But this small-scale common neurosis can grow, if unchecked, into monstrous proportions.[5] Which leads us to look briefly at a famous monster of ancient culture, Medea.

MONSTROUS MOTHER

Medea, a mother who kills her own children, may be one of the most chilling characters of all time.[6] The most famous version of Medea comes from Greek tragedian Euripides (480–406 BCE), but Seneca also contemplated the ancient infanticide and versions of the tragedy have echoed down to become contemporary narratives as well.[7]

Medea is the daughter of Aeetes, king of Colchis. Aeetes possesses the famous Golden Fleece that Jason and the Argonauts are trying to acquire, and Medea falls in love with Jason, aiding him in his capture of the precious fleece. She uses her exceptional arts as an herbalist to drug Jason's foes and flees the island with him, her father in hot pursuit. She unambiguously demonstrates her willingness to sink low by chopping up her brother, who is unlucky enough to have joined her on Jason's boat, and dumping him overboard piecemeal so that her grieving father will have to collect the bits for a proper burial. All this is backstory to Euripides' *Medea*, which begins sometime later in Corinth, after Jason and Medea have produced two boys.

Jason betrays Medea, setting out to climb the political ladder by proposing marriage to the daughter of Creon, the king of Corinth. Medea is devastated and vows revenge. Euripides' play is a surprising tour of the interior emotional, psychological torment of a scorned lover. Medea herself understands that she has become a new kind of person. "In other things," she says, "a woman may be timid—in watching battles or seeing steel, but when she's hurt in love, her marriage violated, there's no heart more desperate for blood than hers."[8] Before she sinks to this monstrous echelon of infanticide Medea wrestles with the virtual devil and angel on her shoulders, briefly contemplating an exile for her sons rather than death. But finally she succumbs to the lust for vengeance by saying, "The evil done to me has won the day. I understand too well the dreadful act I'm going to commit, but my judgment can't check my anger, and that incites the greatest evils human beings do."[9]

The philosophical Chorus of the play articulates the crux of the trouble when they chant, "Love with too much passion brings with it no fine reputation, brings nothing virtuous to men. But if Aphrodite comes in smaller doses, no other god is so desirable." Overwhelmed by a seemingly toxic dose of Aphrodite, Medea designs a reprisal that is both shocking in its brutality and amazing in its comprehensiveness. She creates a poison-soaked

Medea, pictured here in Lars von Trier's film version of the play, getting ready to hang her own son. From Lars von Trier's 1988 television film *Medea* (Danmarks Radio, Denmark). Courtesy of Photofest.

cloak for Jason's new bride, which manages to melt first the bride and then her father, Creon, who embraces her in desperation over his loss. Then she murders her own two boys in a scene that has them crying out in pain and surprise, begging for mercy from the woman who bore them.

When Jason learns that his children have been murdered, he explicitly demotes Medea from the normal human status of woman. In a passage that tellingly synthesizes her foreign, non-Greek ethnicity with her abominable actions, he says, "When you married me and bore my children, in your lust for sex and our marriage bed, you killed them. No woman from Greece would dare to do this, but I chose you as my wife above them all, and that has proved to be a hateful marriage—it has destroyed me. You're not a woman. You're a she-lion. Your nature is more bestial than Scylla, the Tuscan monster."[10]

One of the central themes of the play is the idea that forces exist within us that are fundamental to our psyche but also alien to our rational self-identity. The classicist E. R. Dodds argues that the ancients understood this uncontrollable internal force as a literal demonic spirit, and it only slowly came to be identified with natural rather than supernatural emotions.

Just as in my earlier discussion of morphological monsters, however, the sequence of beliefs did not traverse a simple upward path of antisuperstitious enlightenment. Rather, belief in demon possession alternated in seriousness from one age to the next. Dodds points out, for example, that "people in the *Odyssey* ... attribute many events in their lives, both mental and physical, to the agency of anonymous daemons; we get the impression, however, that they do not always mean it very seriously."[11] But then the much later *Oresteia* trilogy of Aeschylus (525–456 BCE) is populated by a more abundant and seemingly literal host of meddling demons, "more persistent, more insidious, more sinister." By the time we get to Euripides' *Medea* we have a pluralistic expression of natural and supernatural demons at work within the human breast. The Greek mind allows for the possibility, at this time, that a demon can actually use Medea's thumos to kill her children: the literal and figurative expressions of thumos are not mutually exclusive. It is like the case of the hermaphrodite or the abnormal ram's horn: they may be both natural results of "too much matter" (or developmental blockages or what have you) and also portents or messages with more cosmic meaning. Socrates championed antisuperstitious rationalism on most issues, but also claimed to have regular consultations with an internal helpful demon (*daimon*). During these episodes of possession, he would stand quite motionless and seem altogether absent, leaving modern scholars to speculate about the possibility of epilepsy.

Much later Freud would offer a psychological bridge in the form of *projection* to connect the mysterious external world of spirits with the mysterious internal world of passions. In *Totem and Taboo* Freud claims that "spirits and demons were nothing but the projections of primitive man's emotional impulses; he personified the things he endowed with affects, populated the world with them and then rediscovered his inner psychic processes outside himself."[12] In an important sense the objectification of volitions is entirely understandable when the boundaries of inner and outer have not yet been defined.

The important point in all this is that the ancients were trying to work out a language and a way of thinking about internal forces, usually monstrous, sometimes benign. There are things inside us that raise their ugly heads during crisis points in our lives. As Dodds puts it, they "are not truly part of the self, since they are not within man's conscious control; they are endowed with a life and energy of their own, and so can force a man, as it were from the outside, into conduct foreign to him."

The aspect of this ancient demonology that is harder for us to grasp in our own age is that the demons who populate our internal and external world are not just spirits from another copresent dimension that occasionally step into our lives to wreak havoc. These certainly do exist for the ancients, but demons are also *created* by our own misdeeds. They do not just come from a realm of spectator spirits who are watching our behaviors and dispatching just deserts accordingly. Jason makes it clear that Medea has actually created an avenging fury by her own deeds.[13] First she betrays her father and kills her brother; this creates a demon searching for blood vengeance. But this vengeance, in the form of the now slaughtered sons, has struck at *Jason* as well as her.[14] Now Jason curses Medea with another source of trouble: "May the avenging Fury of our children destroy you— may you find blood justice." Uncontrollable forces inside us cause us to murder and misbehave, and the misdeeds cause more uncontrollable forces to return to us like karmic consequences.

For the more educated members of Euripides' audience (Anaxagoras and even Plato were overlapping contemporaries of Euripides), the demonic forces were internalized and identified with psychological faculties such as thumos. Monsters may be harassing us from the external world, but now we must recognize that our own desires and emotions are harassing us from inside as well. Plato's theory of the tripartite psyche may be applied to *Medea* in the sense that even when she *knows* right from wrong (rationality) she is unable to fight the urge for revenge because her thumos has never been properly trained to submit to reason's authority.[15]

The response to this realization of internal monsters is not asceticism and denial of our emotional lives. By and large, Greeks and Romans did not recommend the kind of cave-dwelling yogic responses to desire that their Eastern contemporaries advocated. Thumos, the locus of our passions, was considered more like a blind force, spontaneous and powerful, capable of energizing good deeds but also evil ones if the vitality was aimed in the wrong direction. Another of Plato's metaphors for thumos, besides the lion, is the dog.[16] This is because the dog can be very aggressive with its enemies but gentle and protective of its own clan, including its master. Dogs embody thumos because they are spirited and dangerous but also *loyal* if well trained. The challenge for the ancients was not to renounce one's inner dog, but to cultivate its love for its master (reason). In that way, our chances of becoming Medea-like monsters could be diminished. If passion goes untrained it can become the force that drives one to murder one's children, but it is this same spirited part of our psyche that, if properly trained, makes good mothers protect their children when threatened and drives the courageous acts of warriors who, like Alexander demonstrating monster-killing techniques, protect their comrades, their families, and their countries. It may be appropriate to become *beastly* in some circumstances, but that doesn't mean we have to become *monsters*.

There is an ongoing debate from the Hellenistic era through the early Roman Empire about how much power to accede to passion. Are we really powerless in the face of such monstrous inner drives, or is this just a weak and cowardly characterization built by snivelers who refuse to master themselves? The former Roman slave and Greek Stoic Epictetus (50–130 CE) argued that Medea was not really divided between rational and irrational forces; she may have been pushed and pulled by conflicting impulses, but she could have adapted to things beyond her control. Understanding what is in our control (a rather finite inventory) and what is *not* (a significantly bigger list) and adjusting our emotions accordingly is the basic philosophy of Stoicism.

The classicist Julia Annas characterizes the Stoic interpretation of Medea thus: "We say, Medea could not help acting as she did; she was overcome by passion, so surely she had no real choice. No, says Epictetus; she thought she had no real alternative, but this was wrong. She could have adjusted to her loss, difficult though this would be. 'Stop wanting your husband, and nothing you want will fail to come about,' he says. Everything I do, I am responsible for; there is always something else, I could have done, some other attitude I could have taken up."[17] One cannot accuse Epictetus, who suffered many hardships as a slave, of being out of touch with the anguish of thwarted desire. He must have known it well.

The Stoic consideration leaves us with a good ending point for reflection. It is interesting to notice that while the ancients had sophisticated ideas about the *structure* of the psyche (reason, passion, and appetite) and also had nuanced theories about *developmental* psychology, they had little in their ideas of human monstrosity about the role of bad luck.[18] This point is all the more striking when our own age is dominated by a commitment to the idea that human monsters are made that way by childhood experiences, experiences that they are not responsible for. Amid the explanations of Euripides' karmic demon possession, Plato's untutored thumos, and Epictetus's Stoic theory, one wants to ask, What about the bad stuff that just happens to you? Susan Smith, a modern-day Medea who murdered her own children in 1994, was brutally and regularly molested by her stepfather while growing up. America's first female serial murderer, Aileen Wuornos (subject of the Hollywood film titled simply *Monster*, 2003), also suffered a childhood filled with physical, emotional, and sexual abuse. Many other murderers whose special brand of sadism invokes the "monster" epithet have been victims of terrible violence early in life. It has become simple common sense to immediately ask after the childhood of a criminal the moment we hear about his or her heinous infamy. But that was not the question first on the minds of the ancients.

There was not a big conceptual or cultural space in the ancient world for "victim monsters," people who might be excused from some portion of responsibility or agency. The Stoic response most clearly undermines any victim status of a monster by claiming that even the most abused individual still has power over the fates by dint of rational freedom. According to the Stoics, when you can no longer master yourself, your external world or your internal urges, you still have the gift of suicide.

In his essay "On the Proper Time to Slip the Cable" (in *Epistulae Morales*, epistle 70), Seneca considers it a great consolation that Nature "allowed to us one entrance in life, but many exits." He offers several examples of men who avoided extreme "victimhood" (torture and abuse) by freely choosing their own death. In a rare acknowledgment of barbarian nobility, Seneca tells of a German slave who was being forced against his will into a gladiator contest. Rather than allowing someone else (or the unfriendly Fates) to choose his destiny for him, he elected to "slip the cable." Seneca writes, "He withdrew in order to relieve himself,—the only thing which he was allowed to do in secret and without the presence of a guard. While so engaged, he seized the stick of wood, tipped with a sponge, which was devoted to the vilest uses, and stuffed it, just as it was, down his throat; thus he blocked up his windpipe, and choked the breath from his body. That was truly to insult death!" Seneca follows this with several other nauseating paeans to self-determination, leaving readers feeling positively embarrassed about their own misfortunes and received slights.

Though it is hard to welcome suicide in our current paradigm of thinking, it is nonetheless true that many ancients recommended suicide as a dignified alternative to extreme cases of victimization. No matter how bad things get, you can still slip the cable and avoid both the abuses of a monster and also becoming a monster yourself. It was a way to restore one's humanity in the face of dehumanization. Admittedly, this is cold comfort. But it's interesting that some ancients contemplated their fears of external and internal monsters so carefully as to rejoice in their discovery of the ultimate escape.[19]

2

Medieval Monsters
Messages from God

5

Biblical Monsters

And when men could no longer sustain them, the giants turned
against them and devoured mankind.
BOOK OF ENOCH

IN THE ANCIENT POLYTHEISTIC WORLD, monsters were like free
agents. Neither the gods nor the monsters were omnipotent, so they
fought indefinitely, with humans in the middle. When a person was set
upon by overwhelming forces that brought death and terror into his family or village, he appealed to the gods for help. Gods and monsters existed
equally in a counteracting, dualistic relationship. But when monotheism
became the dominant premise of religious culture, monsters had to be
brought under the omnipotent, omniscient, omnibenevolent God. Monsters needed to be explained within the idea of a universal creator God
who presumably created frightening beasts, deformities, and demons, too,
or at least let them exist. Monsters became intertwined with the theological question, Why did God create evil? As the religion scholar Timothy
K. Beal suggests, monsters became intimately bound up with the theodicy
problem: "Who is more monstrous, the creatures who must live through
this vale of tears, or the creature who put them here?"[1]

GOD'S LACKEYS

One of the ways monsters were recast was as God's lackeys. Monsters
threatened human health and happiness, but at God's bidding; that is to

say, the suffering they inflicted was morally justified by a new concept of a unitary personal God. Satan's experiment with the righteous Job may be the most obvious case of *local* evil taking place in a mitigating context of *global* divine goodness.[2] Satan tells God that the happy and pious Job is only righteous because he is so prosperous. So, in a game to test this hypothesis, with God's consent Satan destroys Job's money, property, children, and health, leaving him a highly confused, mere husk of his former self. God eventually tells Job that humans cannot understand the world as God does and therefore should not try to judge it. God alone is king of all and does not need to answer to his creation. Then God restores Job to even greater wealth, giving him ten new children and extending his life for 140 more years.

Satan's relative power has always been a topic of interest for theologians. Most of his appearances, like the episode with Job, show Satan as a servant (albeit an unpleasant one) to God. But there are incidents, as in Chronicles 21, where Satan appears to act according to his own free will against God: "And Satan rose up against Israel: and moved David to number Israel."[3] This autonomous Satan is sometimes thought to be the result of influences from Iranian Zoroastrianism, a dualistic religion of two equally powerful good and bad Gods, influences that seeped into some monotheistic scriptural narratives. This more sovereign Satan, however, is distinctly heterodox to mainstream Abrahamic monotheism, and, theological flirtations aside, it never became dominant. Even the satanic possession of Judas (Luke 22:3) can be brought in line with orthodoxy if we understand the episode as a step in God's overall sequence of Christian redemption.[4] In this sense, the Satan of the New Testament is entirely consistent with the trouble-making accuser we meet in the Book of Job. As the art historian Luther Link puts it in his survey of devil imagery, "The Evil One is on God's side. He carries out the garbage."[5]

Some of the most well-known monsters of the Bible, Behemoth and Leviathan, also appear in the Book of Job and echo this henchmen theme of God's monster accomplices. They don't actually plot against anyone, but these giant beasts of earth and water, respectively, serve as evidence of God's power and strength; they act as living billboards for God's sublime creativity and awe-inspiring authority. The giant creatures are not opposed to God but represent the more chaotic and frightening visage of God. Behemoth and Leviathan are introduced after Job has finally broken down and complained about his suffering. God, in the form of a whirlwind, tells Job, "Gird up thy loins like a man" (*accinge sicut vir lumbos tuos*). The harsh lesson that follows is obviously drawn from the Jewish Septuagint, but it augurs a very common theme later developed in Christian ethics: that

Symbolic of God's power, the biblical Behemoth appears in the Book of Psalms and Job. Pencil drawing by Stephen T. Asma © 2008.

humans should be humble, not proud. (I will examine this point more carefully in my discussion of *Beowulf.*) Humility, meekness, gratitude: these are the proper sentiments for a puny species like man, and to better understand this frailness Job need only witness the gigantic land monster. "Behold Behemoth whom I made with thee, he eats grass like an ox. His strength is in his loins, and his force is in the navel of his belly. He sets up his tail like a cedar, the sinews of his testicles are wrapped together. His bones are like pipes of brass, his gristle like plates of iron."[6]

The use of Behemoth and Leviathan in the scriptures is highly ambivalent. In some places, such as Psalm 74 and Job 3, Leviathan is described as a frightening monster that threatens order and stability, a giant sea monster that rises from the depths to cause mayhem but who is easily checked by the power and righteousness of Yahweh.[7] In some cases, God is described as smashing Leviathan's head, but in other places, such as Psalm 104 and Job 40, Leviathan is identified as a part of God's wonderful creation, a sublime force that reflects God's overwhelming aspect. In these passages, the giant sea monster is an ally and even a manifestation of God.

It may be impossible to reconcile the various characterizations of Leviathan, especially if they are meant to reflect different and even conflicted human religious sentiments within us. Beal suggests that Leviathan functions as a threat because "the challenge of taking on Leviathan merges with the challenge of taking on God,"[8] and such a challenge would be a foolhardy expression of pride. The idea that God is beyond our weak human faculties and that our minds would be overwhelmed if we tried to grasp him is a common theme in religion, though much of this tendency was toned down by rationalist theologians from Maimonides to Aquinas and beyond.[9] Still, long before the lucid God of the rationalists, there was the incoherent sublime God so prevalent in mythical and mystical traditions in the East and West. That God, symbolized by the frightening monsters of Behemoth and Leviathan, conveys a parallel religious emotion found in many Hindu scriptures. For example, in the *Bhagavad Gita* (ca. fourth to second century BCE) the god Krishna famously reveals himself to the warrior Arjuna in a sublime vision that overwhelms and subjugates him:

> Seeing your infinite form with many mouths, eyes, arms, thighs, feet, stomachs, and many fearful teeth; the worlds are trembling with fear and so do I, O mighty Lord.
> Seeing Your great effulgent and various-colored form touching the sky; Your mouth wide open and large shining eyes; I am frightened and find neither peace nor courage, O Krishna.
> Seeing Your mouths, with fearful teeth, glowing like fires of cosmic dissolution, I lose my sense of direction and find no comfort. Have mercy on me! O Lord of gods, refuge of the universe. (11:23–25)[10]

The notion of God as frightening, a disturbing reality that destroys human perceptual and conceptual equipment, is not entertained to the same degree in Western monotheism as in Hinduism.[11] But in the creatures of Behemoth and Leviathan one finds a glimmer of the Abrahamic God's more horrifying dimension. This dimension is reiterated in the Christian New Testament, when the Book of Revelation unrolls its unique prophecy of monstrous doom. But in Revelation and its prophetic precursor, the Book of Daniel, monsters function more traditionally as enemies to be crushed and overcome. In the prophetic scriptures it's clear that God may have allowed some monsters to exist, and even to have their fun for a while, but the time has come to crush them under righteous foot.

These monsters of the prophetic tradition appear to have no zoological significance whatsoever. The four beasts of Daniel and the dragon and hydra of Revelation are incarnations of the *fallen* state of being: fallen angels in the case of Satan, and fallen men in the case of oppressive Roman imperial power.

THE APOCALYPSE

The Book of Revelation, also called the Apocalypse of John, was written in the early 90s of the Common Era, during the reign of Emperor Domitian. It is a beautiful, frightening jumble of end time forecast, conspiracy history, and veiled sociopolitical manifesto. The description of monsters involves, among other things, a giant red dragon (*ecce draco magnus rufus*, 12:3), a hybrid leopard-bear-lion beast (*et bestiam quam vidi similes erat pardo et pedes eius sicut ursi et os eius sicut os leonis*, 13:2), and a two-horned beast that emerges from underground (*et vidi aliam bestiam ascendentem de terra et habebat cornua duo similia agni*, 13:11). The dragon plays a crucial role throughout the Apocalypse and also down through the ages as a symbolic counterpart to Christian virtue, but it is unclear whether John's influences were Greek or Near Eastern.[12]

The author of Revelation, John of Patmos, spins an elaborate mystical vision of the end of the world and explicitly draws on the earlier prophetic traditions to reinforce and validate the urgency of his call to repentance. His confusing visions entail a trinity of terror that focuses on the central demonic character of the giant seven-headed dragon (*draco*), "who is called the devil and Satan" (12:9). This satanic dragon first appears in a vision, beside a woman who is about to give birth to a child (the messiah). The dragon menaces the woman, waiting to devour the child. But the creature's evil plan is thwarted because when the son is born he is immediately whisked up to God and his throne, and the woman escapes to the wilderness. A gigantic battle ensues in which the dragon and his minions fight unsuccessfully against Michael and his angels, who overcome the dragon with the blood of the lamb. The dragon and his army are hurled down from Heaven and must continue their nefarious ways on the earth, where they persecute "the woman who brought forth the man-child" (*mulierem quae peperit masculum*, 12:13).

Most scholars agree that John of Patmos is providing a coded narrative about the religious persecution of Christians, a persecution that received imperial sanction under Nero's rule (54–68) and may have become acute under Domitian (81–96).[13] The symbolism is further nuanced by the introduction of the two monstrous henchmen, the beast from the sea with seven cat-like heads and the horned beast from the earth, subsequently referred to as the *pseudoprophetes*, "false prophet." In some readings the Roman emperor himself is identified with the satanic dragon; others read the beast of the sea as the emperor, the seven heads symbolizing the succession of emperors (Revelation 17). In the early modern period, Protestants read the beast as the Roman Catholic pope, while the Catholics returned the favor by reading the beast as Luther himself. In any case, the chain of monster command is clear in the scripture: the satanic hydra is the central authority of evil, giving power and strength to the beast from the sea, who in turn is served by the beast from the earth (pseudoprophetes). It is this subservient beast of the earth that famously encourages humans to get "the mark" of the sea beast, the number 666 (*sescenti sexaginta sex*).[14] The pseudoprophetes acts as a kind of public relations manager for the sea beast. The mark of the beast, worn on the right hand or forehead, is an indicator of allegiance to the evil power, a sign of collusion with the wicked temporal world because only by this mark can man have economic commerce. One suspects that this is a coded way for John to express his call to Christians to reject the temptations of acquiescent pagan life under Roman rule. Martyrdom is preferable to submission.

All of this monster activity precipitates the great battle between good and evil at Armageddon, located between Tel Aviv and Nazareth. During this battle the legions of the beast will fight against the righteous and the beasts will be vanquished to the lake of fire. The satanic dragon will be trapped for a thousand years, after which there will be yet another era in which the evil one seduces humankind, the "children of disobedience." The beasts of Revelation, finally vanquished by God, explicitly echo the monsters from the Book of Daniel (ca. second century BCE),[15] and together they show us another important function of monsters in biblical culture. The prophet Daniel dreams of four great beasts that rise out of the sea (*et quattuor bestiae grandes ascendebant de mari diversae inter se*, 7:3); each of them foreshadows the versions in the Apocalypse. The description is truly frightening, in particular that of the fourth beast, and it deserves to be quoted in full.

> The first was like a lioness, and had the wings of an eagle: I beheld till her wings were plucked off, and she was lifted up from the earth, and stood upon her feet as a man, and the heart of a man was given to her. And behold another beast, like a bear, stood up on one side: and there were three rows in the mouth thereof, and in the teeth thereof, and thus they said to it:

Arise, devour much flesh. After this I beheld, and lo, another like a leopard, and it had upon it four wings, as of a fowl, and the beast had four heads, and power was given to it. After this I beheld in the vision of the night, and lo, a fourth beast, terrible and wonderful, and exceedingly strong, it had great iron teeth, eating and breaking in pieces, and treading down the rest with his feet: and it was unlike to the other beasts which I had seen before it, and had ten horns. I considered the horns, and behold another little horn sprung out of the midst of them: and three of the first horns were plucked up at the presence thereof: and behold eyes like the eyes of a man were in this horn, and a mouth speaking great things. (Daniel 7:4–8)

This nightmarish cadre of monsters wages war against the "saints of the most high God," and the "talking horn" on the head of the fourth beast leads the charge. There is considerable disagreement about how to interpret the beasts, but most scholars see them as corresponding to the four empires that threatened and even occupied Palestine between the sixth and second centuries BCE; the lion-eagle hybrid represents Babylon, the toothy bear represents the Median Empire, the four-headed leopard is the Persian Empire, and the egregious fourth beast is the Greek and Macedonian Empire (Alexander the Great conquered Judea in 332 BCE).[16] The monsters win their temporary successes against the righteous, but God is always ultimately victorious and the eventual victory is characterized as *eternal* because God's power is "an everlasting power that shall not be taken away" (*potestas eius potestas aeterna quae non auferetur*, Daniel 7:14).

The stories of these creatures in Daniel and Revelation bring into relief a texture of monsterology that eventually comes to dominate the medieval religious mind. These monsters are symbols of prideful insurgency, and as such must be brought low and be damned by God's overwhelming justice. They are symbols of what men will inevitably become, pawns in various regimes of torture, if they attempt to rule without the guidance and approval of Yahweh. In the Jewish tradition the monsters are incarnations of the inevitable political trouble that arises when gentiles impose upon the chosen people. In the prophecy traditions, monsters are not creatures of natural history but symbolic warnings of a horrifying life without the Abrahamic God (or, in the case of Christians, without his son). They are the symbols of both degenerate paganism and fallen "children of disobedience," those who should know better but have given in to earthly temptation. In Old Testament beast narratives, such as the Book of Daniel, the reckoning is accomplished by Yahweh's greater strength. But in Christian versions, such as in the Book of Revelation, the paradoxical ingredient of

The "Beast" with seven cat-like heads, from the Book of Revelation. From Alixe Bovey, *Monsters and Grotesques in Medieval Manuscripts* (University of Toronto Press, 2002). Reprinted by kind permission of the British Library.

the lamb's blood (Christ's sacrifice) is added as the ultimate weapon in the arsenal.

It may be worth mentioning that these prophetic books of the Bible have themselves been treated in some quarters as monstrous appendages on the sanctified scriptural corpus. In addition to the obvious recent history of suicidal apocalyptic groups such as the American Branch Davidians and the Ugandan Movement for the Restoration of the Ten Commandments of God, one finds warnings about these prophetic scriptures in both Jewish and Christian theology. Maimonides (1138–1204), who is probably the most influential Jewish philosopher of the medieval period, argued that only fools try to calculate the actual end time. To attempt to prophesy a precise coming of the Messiah is a dangerous business, and an untutored public will be led astray by such pseudo theology. From the father of the Christian Reformation himself, Martin Luther

A medieval depiction of hell as a monstrous mouth. From Alixe Bovey, *Monsters and Grotesques in Medieval Manuscripts* (University of Toronto Press, 2002). Reprinted by kind permission of the British Library.

(1483–1546), we hear serious anxiety about allowing the flock to read the potentially dangerous Book of Revelation.[17] Dangerous or not (or perhaps *because* they were dangerous), these biblical monsters were like manna for the medieval imagination and served to simultaneously inspire wonder, provide metaphysical explanations of history, legitimize authority, and foster fear-based morality.[18]

Throughout the medieval era, the scriptures and their subsequent interpretations and pictorial representations slowly build a new version of God. The monotheistic deity becomes the most fearful entity in the medieval imagination, partly because he's capable of staggering violence, but also because he's unknowable and infinitely powerful.

A race of biblical monsters that seem largely forgotten by the moderns but were a source of endless fascination for the medievals is the giants. Most of the speculation about giants stems from a passage in Genesis (6:1–4): "And after that [Noah becoming a father] men began to be multiplied upon the earth, and daughters were born to them, the sons of God seeing the daughters of men, that they were fair, took to themselves wives of all which they chose.... Now giants were upon the earth in those days. For after the sons of God went into the daughters of men, and they brought forth children, these are the mighty men of old, men of renown." This passage, together with other cryptic references to giants (Numbers 13, Genesis 10:8–9, I Samuel 17:4–5), account for a popular theory about giants who roamed the earth prior to the Flood (most of whom died in the deluge, but some of whom may have lived on). Mainstream interpretations of the Genesis text follow the tradition laid down by Jerome and endorsed by Augustine, wherein the "sons of God" reference was interpreted as the offspring of Seth (Adam and Eve's *other* son, besides Cain and Abel), and the "daughters of men" was read as the children of Cain.[19] But a radically different interpretation, further developed in the Book of Enoch,[20] seems to have predated, and even run parallel to, this now standard version.

In this alternative interpretation, the "sons of God" are taken to be angels who fall from grace because they have sex with beautiful human women (daughters of men). The Book of Enoch (7:2) says, "And when the angels, the sons of heaven, beheld them, they became enamored of them, saying to each other, Come, let us select for ourselves wives from the progeny of men, and let us beget children." When these fallen angels, called Grigori or "the Watchers," mated with mortal women, their offspring were giants called *nephilim* (from the Hebrew root *naphal*, "to fall"). The Grigori angels were punished for leaving their rightful place and cavorting with human women, and the giants were then destroyed by the Flood. In fact, the tradition that takes its lead from Enoch suggests that it's the destruction of these mongrel giants, not man's sinfulness, that explains God's true motive for the Flood. In chapter 7 Enoch explains that a kind of war had broken out between the giants and the humans. The giants had "consumed all the acquisitions of men. And when men could no longer sustain them, the giants turned against them and devoured mankind. And they began to sin against birds, and beasts, and reptiles, and fish, and to devour one another's flesh, and drink the blood" (7:4–6). Finally, according to the story, the archangels went to God and asked him to resolve the bloodbath, and the cathartic Flood followed accordingly.

But the giants proved to be a wily breed and crop up from time to time in postdiluvian episodes, both canonical and apocryphal. The Venerable Bede (ca. 672–735), a Benedictine Church father, commented on the famous Genesis passage by saying, "It calls 'giants' men who were born with huge bodies, endowed with excessive power, such as, even after the Flood, we read that there were many in the times of Moses or David."[21] For example, Nimrod, the grandson of Ham and instigator of the tower of Babel, was sometimes interpreted as a giant, and Goliath, whom David unexpectedly defeated with a slingshot, is described as the Philistine Giant. It's worth quoting David's battle speech to the incredulous Goliath: "This day, and the Lord will deliver thee into my hand, and I will slay thee, and take away thy head from thee: and I will give the carcasses of the army of the Philistines this day to the birds of the air, and to the beasts of the earth: that all the earth may know that there is a God in Israel" (1 Samuel 17:46).

Like some other monsters in the Bible, giants symbolize hubris or arrogance. As such, they play the necessary foil to God's righteous demonstrations of superior power. David is only a small boy relative to the giant Goliath, but his faith and courage create a conduit for Yahweh's dispensation of justice. If you trust in the God of Abraham, even giants will fall.

6

Do Monsters Have Souls?

Monsters are not contrary to nature, because they come from divine will.
ISIDORE DE SEVILLE

S T. AUGUSTINE REJECTED the Enoch-based interpretation of Genesis, that fallen angels (Grigori) mated with human women who gave birth to giants (nephilim).[1] But he did not reject this version on the grounds of some general prescientific skepticism. A careful reading shows that Augustine specifically objected to the fallen angels as begetters of giants. Humans of gigantic stature, Augustine observes, actually lived before, during, and after the episode of these fallen angels. By an impressive sleight of hermeneutical hand, he reads "angels" as "messengers" and then interprets these fallen men as just a different ethnic group (the sons of Seth) from the women (daughters of Cain), thereby tossing out the supernatural sex part of the story. The giants are preserved.

Augustine accepts the reality of individual giants and also the possibility of giant races in far-off lands. Moreover, he is convinced that the average pre-Flood humans were larger compared to contemporary humans:

> But the large size of the primitive human body is often proved to the incredulous by the exposure of sepulchers, either through the wear of time or the violence of torrents or some accident, and in which bones of incredible size have been found or have rolled out. I myself, along with some others, saw on the shore at Utica a man's molar tooth of such a size, that if it were cut down into teeth such as we have, a hundred, I fancy, could have

been made out of it. But that, I believe, belonged to some giant. For though the bodies of ordinary men were then larger than ours, the giants surpassed all in stature.[2]

He cites a variety of ancient writers in defense of this general thesis, including Pliny the Younger, who concluded, "The older the world becomes, the smaller will be the bodies of men." Which I suppose is a reasonable theory, albeit unfamiliar, when one is regularly digging larger bones out of the earth than one is encountering in the flesh.

The most marvelous of these giants were thought to be drowned in the Flood, of course, but Augustine reminds readers that giants of some sort will always be around. "Was there not," he asks, "at Rome a few years ago . . . a woman, with her father and mother, who by her gigantic size overtopped all others? Surprising crowds from all quarters came to see her, and that which struck them most was the circumstance that neither of her parents were quite up to the tallest ordinary stature."[3] Giants, in this sense, are part of the natural order of things, rare but unsurprising.

Archbishop Isidore of Seville (566–636), the learned author of the influential *Etymologiae*, reiterated Augustine's views on giants, affirming their probable existence but denying their origin from angel-human coitus.[4] Like other issues in his encyclopedic summary of medieval knowledge, the word *gigantic* is dissected and given etymological analysis. Isidore's analysis shows that the word is derived from the Greek *ge* (earth) and *genos* (kind, or clan), suggesting a race of powerful earth-born men (*terrigenas*).

According to Isidore, giants are just one of the various types of monsters (such as Cynocephali, Cyclopes, and Blemmyae) that exist at the margins of God's creation.[5] But of course anomalies crop up inside the perimeter as well. In his chapter "De Portentis," he corrects the pagan scholar Varro's earlier claim that portentous births are "contrary to nature." "But they are not," Isidore counters, "contrary to nature, because they come by the divine will, since the will of the Creator is the nature of each thing that is created."[6]

MONSTERS AND A CREATOR GOD

Nature is a reflection of God, and like other reflections doesn't contain anything beyond the original source. This intimate relationship, according to Isidore, leads pagans to sometimes refer to God as "Nature" and sometimes just "God."[7] Being a good Christian during an era when intellectuals were still extricating themselves from impressive Greek and Roman philosophy, Isidore sought to improve on pagan ideas of God. The idea that God created the world from nothing (*ex nihilo*) was a relatively recent idea, and it was considered incoherent by pagan intellectuals. Most ancient theories claimed instead that God was the force that gave shape and character to an otherwise unformed, shapeless matter.[8] By these ancient principles God did not *create* matter, which was thought to be contemporaneous with God, he only wrestled it into a coherent system. The explanatory advantage of this viewpoint with regard to monsters is that distorted and malformed beings could be seen as an unfortunate but necessary consequence of "difficult" matter. God tried to make this species perfect, but damnable matter proved recalcitrant during construction.

But a heavier burden of explanation falls to Augustine and Isidore because, if God made matter, then he must have *wanted* these monsters to exist. In Western monotheism God cannot get off the hook by complaining of stubborn, unaccommodating building supplies. Hermaphrodites, conjoined twins, all birth defects, and a slew of monstrous races must be, as Isidore claims, expressions of God's will because nothing, after all, is outside of God's will. The medievals embarked on a rich speculative tradition that tried to articulate what God *wanted* when he made monsters. What was his purpose?

If giants, for example, expressed God's divine will, then what was God up to when he made them? Augustine suggests that giants exist in order to fall. The bigger they are, the harder they fall. Augustine writes, "It pleased the Creator to produce them, that it might thus be demonstrated that neither beauty, nor yet size and strength, are of much importance to the wise man, whose blessedness lies in spiritual and immortal blessings, in far better and more enduring gifts, in the good things that are the peculiar property of the good, and are not shared by good and bad alike."[9] The point of being a giant, then, is to overreach and fail, and in that failure highlight their corruption to others as a cautionary tale and consolation. Notice that Augustine's theory applies to beautiful people as well as the vertically prodigious giants. Based on the same logic, they too will ultimately demonstrate their flawed unenduring rank to the uglier but more spiritually righteous. Extraordinary people, or should I say fabled extraordinary people, are at once flattened into one-dimensional morality lessons by this symbolic approach, a confident approach that applies beautifully to people you'll never actually meet. But this moralizing tendency gets stronger and more pernicious when it spreads eventually to cover other, real races and nations whom you might actually meet.

Giants, of course, were not the only monsters to cause a flurry of medieval theorizing. The old standbys from Pliny's famous text were all on hand to pose Christian integration puzzles. Augustine and Isidore both describe the Cyclopes and the dog-headed men, Cynocephali. Augustine adds a list of favorites from antiquity, including some men with "feet turned backwards from the heel; some, a double sex, the right breast like a man, the left like a woman, and that they alternately beget and bring forth; others are said to have no mouth, and to breathe only through the nostrils; others are but a cubit high, and are therefore called by the Greeks 'Pigmies.'"[10] He goes on to describe the race of men who have two feet but only one leg, the Sciopodes, and also Pliny's Blemmyae, the men who have no head proper but a face looking out from their chest, and who apparently live south of Egypt.[11]

In the late medieval period a text circulated that led many to believe that Augustine had seen Blemmyae firsthand. In a sermon entitled "Ad Fratres in Eremo," Augustine writes, "I was already Bishop of Hippo, when I went into Ethiopia with some servants of Christ there to preach the Gospel. In this country we saw many men and women without heads, who had two great eyes in their breasts; and in countries still more south, we saw people who had but one eye in their foreheads."[12] This passage was popular and considered to be compelling for the credulous, but we now know that it is probably a twelfth-century apocryphal fake. Anyone who was truly familiar with Augustine's monster discussions in *The City of God* would have a hard time reconciling this so-called eyewitness account. Yet the passage was influential in the folk culture of late medieval Europe.

Umberto Eco offers a wonderful speculative description in *Baudolino* of the Sciopodes and Blemmyae. In search of the mythical kingdom of Prester John, Eco's fictional characters encounter the monstrous races. A Sciopod surprises the travelers: "It had a leg, but only one. Not that the other had been amputated; on the contrary, the single leg was attached naturally to the body, as if there had never been a place for another, and with the single foot of that single leg the creature could run with great ease, as if accustomed to moving in that way since birth." Eco fleshes out the medieval descriptions and pictorial traditions by describing the creature's foot as twice the size of a human's, but "well shaped, with square nails, and five toes that seemed all thumbs, squat and sturdy." The monster in Eco's story is handled charitably, as in the Augustinian tradition. The Sciopod is described as being "the height of a child of ten or twelve years; that is he came up to a human waist, and had a shapely head, with short, bristling

The contemporary artist David F. Driesbach portrays some of the monstrous races, including the Sciopodes, the Blemmyae, and the Cynocephali. "Prester John's Land," color intaglio print (1995, 35 ¾ × 23 ¾). Reprinted by kind permission of the artist.

yellow hair on top, a pair of round affectionate eyes like those of an ox, a small snub nose, a broad mouth that stretched almost ear to ear and revealed, in what was undoubtedly a smile, a fine and strong set of teeth." Eco's description of the Blemmyae is also worth quoting because it crystallizes many historical descriptions: "The creature, with very broad shoulders, was hence very squat, but with slim waist, two legs, short and hairy, and no head, or even neck. On his chest, where men have nipples, there were two almond-shaped eyes, darting, and beneath a slight swelling with two nostrils, a kind of circular hole, very ductile, so that when he spoke he made it assume various shapes, according to the sounds it was emitting."[13]

Isidore, who was one of Eco's sources, fuels the natural history of monsters by listing the Antipodes, whose feet point backward, locating their home in Libya. The dog-headed men, Cynocephali, are reaffirmed to live in India, and the Sciopodes are located in Ethiopia. "In the remote east," Isidore explains, "races with faces of a monstrous sort are described.

Some without noses, with formless countenances; others with lower lip so protruding that by it they shelter the whole face from the heat of the sun while they sleep; others have small mouths, and take sustenance through a narrow opening by means of oat-straws; [a] good many are said to be tongueless, using nod or gesture in place of words."[14] He also describes the Satyrs as homunculi with upturned noses, who "have horns on their foreheads, and are goat-footed, such as the one St. Anthony saw in the desert." Here Isidore refers readers to the then well-known legend of the early Christian hermit, St. Anthony, who encountered a strange Satyr in the desert. When Anthony asked the Satyr who he was, the creature responded by saying that he was only a mortal beast, whom locals in their pagan ignorance had mistaken for a spirit or god. The Satyr was excited to learn more about Jesus Christ and the true God, leading Anthony to exclaim, "Woe to thee, Alexandria [a stronghold of pagan beliefs]! Beasts speak of Christ, and you instead of God worship monsters."[15]

This brings us to an important question regarding medieval monsters: Do they have souls? The Latin word for soul, *anima*, and the Greek, *psyche*, have descended to the present, giving us two different aspects of the soul concept. On the one hand, the soul is that which animates creatures; it is the principle of life and distinguishes animals from inanimate objects. But *soul* is also used more narrowly to express the uniquely human psychology, the inner cognitive self. It is fair to say that the ancients stressed the more general meaning, of the soul as the principle of life, whereas thinkers in the medieval world confined their interests to the more narrow sense of the soul as a uniquely human "divine spark."

While Christian, Jewish, and Muslim scholars constructed a primarily religious notion of the soul as allowing one to live on after death, they also grafted this idea onto earlier Greek concepts. From Augustine to Thomas Aquinas (1225–1274) and beyond, Christian philosophers interpreted the Genesis passage in which God makes man "in his own image" as a description of God's creation of the human mind. The human mind, a little fractal form of God's mind, was considered to be the most godlike part of the human being. In *Confessions* Augustine writes, "But that he judgeth all things, this answers to his having dominion over the fish of the sea, and over the fowls of the air, and over all cattle and wild beasts, and over all the earth, and over every creeping thing that creepeth upon the earth. For this he doth by the understanding of his mind, whereby he perceiveth the things of the Spirit of God; whereas otherwise, man being placed in honor, had no understanding, and is compared unto the brute beasts, and is become like unto them."[16] Eight centuries later, in the *Summa Theologica*, Aquinas argues that intellectual creatures are, properly speaking, made in

God's image.[17] In this emphasis on rationality, the Church fathers were following Aristotle's original lead.

In *De Anima*, Aristotle offered a rather naturalized description of the soul and its distribution in the animal kingdom. The soul was a broader concept and applied to all living things, not just the apex of creation. But the Stagirite recognized that souls come in varying styles and degrees. Plants, for example, have "nutritive souls," that is, they have the power to take in food and grow. They differ from rocks and sand and iron by dint of this additional physiological potential. Animals obviously have this power too but represent a new class of creatures in their ability to move around and to feel sensations. This level of soul, up a step from mere growing potential, brings the powers of locomotion and sensation and distinguishes dogs, monkeys, fish, and every other animal from trees and plants. The relation of soul categories is asymmetrical because every animal, every sensate soul, also has the soul capacities, the physiological powers, of a plant, but *not* vice versa. The crowning potentiality of the soul is realized only in the human species, and this is the power to reason. Aristotle has no creation story such as Genesis to explain why this is so; in fact he doesn't seem very interested in the origin of this distribution of the rational soul. He merely empirically describes the natural world as he finds it.

These days most people think about the soul as a thing, a substance of some sort. Whether you're a believer or a skeptic, you probably imagine some rarified nouminous spirit inhabiting the mechanical body. Thinking of the soul as an entity is inevitable when the traditional metaphors refer to the soul as the captain of a ship or a ghost inside a machine.[18] But as we can see in the works of Aristotle, an equally old tradition argued that the soul is more like a *function* than a *substance*, more like a physiological *activity* than a *thing*. This is important with regard to monsters.

For medieval intellectuals, who carried on and modified the ancient philosophies of soul, monsters were just extreme cases of the larger metaphysical question regarding the status of animals. What creatures are capable of redemption? Which have souls, and how do we know? St. Aquinas, for example, concludes that animals do indeed have sensate souls (i.e., can feel pain, pleasure, etc.), but they lack reason. Animals don't innovate and problem-solve in the same way humans do: "That animals neither understand nor reason is apparent from this, that all animals of the same species behave alike, as being moved by nature, and not acting on any principle of art: for every swallow makes its nest alike, and every spider its web alike. Therefore there is no activity in the soul of dumb animals that can possibly go on without a body."[19] Add to this argument the typical Thomist logic: humans regularly contemplate immortal life and crave it, but animals cannot do so because they are trapped in the play of immediate stimuli and cannot apprehend themselves in the far distant future.[20] In other words, without *reason*, a creature cannot attain immortality.

This philosophy gives us a sense of how the scholastic mind understood monsters: if they have souls, then they can attain immortality. But candidates for redemption have a downside: they are capable of sinning. In other words, having a soul implies that one has agency. In what category do monstrous dog-headed men or men with a face in their chest fall?

Augustine's answer is refreshingly charitable: "Whoever is anywhere born a man, that is, a rational mortal animal, no matter what unusual appearance he presents in color, movement, sound, nor how peculiar he is in some power, part or quality of his nature, no Christian can doubt that he springs from that one protoplast. We can distinguish the common human nature from that which is peculiar, and therefore wonderful."[21] Using the Aristotelian criterion, the essential definition of *rationality*, Augustine decides that the monster question is an empirical one. If the creature displays rationality, then it is, despite its horrifying appearance, a kind of human. Entailed in that humanity is the potential for redemption, immortality, and legal and moral standing. This is an impressive tolerance for otherwise repellent creatures.

Perhaps the best evidence for a charitable Christian view of monsters (viewing them as redeemable) is the fact that St. Christopher was himself a Cynocephalus. The dog-headed version of Christopher, a third-century martyr, is not well known among Roman Catholics or Protestants, but he was venerated in the Eastern Orthodox tradition. Before his conversion Christopher was known by the name Reprobus and was said to have come from the land of cannibals and dog-headed people. According to a medieval Irish *Passion of St. Christopher*, "This Christopher was one of the Dog-heads, a race that had the heads of dogs and ate human flesh."[22] Reprobus, a gigantic and fierce warrior from a tribe west of Egypt, was captured by Romans sometime around 300. He appears to have been a Berber from the tribe of Marmaritae, and after his capture he was enlisted to fight for the Romans in a Syrian garrison. Sources are confusing, but he seems to have converted and been baptized shortly after his capture; subsequent to his conversion he refused to abandon Christianity under Roman pressure in Antioch. The *Passion* explains that Reprobus "meditated much on God, but at that time he could speak only the language of the Dogheads." After asking God to give him the gift of speech, "an angel of God came to him and said: 'God has heard your prayer.'" The angel blew upon Reprobus's mouth, and "the grace of eloquence was given him as he had desired. Thereupon Christopher arose and went into the city, and immediately began to stop

St. Christopher, the Cynocephalus. The dog-headed version of Christopher was venerated in the Eastern Orthodox tradition. Pen and ink drawing by Stephen T. Asma © 2008.

the offering of sacrifice. 'I am a Christian,' he said, 'and I will not sacrifice to the gods.'" Authorities in Antioch tried repeatedly to kill him but he proved magically resilient. They tried burning him, skinning him, throwing him down a well, and various other techniques.

The dog-headed Christopher proved to be troublesome company because every Antioch citizen who came in contact with him converted to Christianity. The frustrated authorities then set upon these fresh converts with redoubled zeal, torturing and killing them because they too refused to worship the Roman gods. "Christopher kept encouraging the Christians, telling them that the kingdom of heaven awaited them. And on that Sunday ten thousand three hundred and three of the Christians were put to death." Finally Christopher agreed to his own martyrdom and allowed the executioner to remove his canine head.[23]

The legend speaks a lesson of possible redemption for even the most vile of creatures. Not only is a Cynocephalus saved, but he is sainted and celebrated for his evangelism, devotion, and courage. With popular tales like this floating around in the folk cultures of the medieval era, it is understandable that sophisticates like Augustine could take a charitable view of the beasties.

A monster who converts to Christianity certainly demonstrates, by exercising his higher faculty, the existence of his soul, but another type of monster posed special difficulties for the soul question. When beings appear to be made up of multiple creatures, to be at once unitary and multiple, how should we understand their spiritual status? How many souls, for example, reside in the conjoined twin? In the case of newborn conjoined twins, most of whom would not live long enough to demonstrate the existence of their rational souls, the question of their status weighed heavily on the practical question of baptism. If the monster was truly human, then it needed to be baptized immediately to save it from eternal damnation.

The medieval scholar John Block Friedman has pored over church manuals for parish priests and discovered that some rough-and-ready rules of thumb could be utilized by the baffled clergy. When the offspring *looks* humanoid (form indicating function), then one should treat it as baptizable. When the baby has one head but excessive body parts, then one should baptize it as one soul. When two heads are present, one should treat it as two souls in need of baptism.[24]

This question about the souls of conjoined twins and other monsters continued to fascinate European clergy well into the scientific era. The seventeenth-century magazine *Athenian Mercury* considered the famous Italian conjoined brothers, Lazarus and Baptista. Added to the old question of the rational soul, Christians wondered whether the *bodies* of these extraordinary creatures would also be resurrected on the Day of Judgment.

Lazarus toured all over Europe in the 1630s and 1640s, exhibiting himself for money. His parasitic brother, Baptista, consisting of a head, torso, and leg, emerged from Lazarus's chest and hung upside down. Baptista showed negligible signs of consciousness and did not speak, but he did respond reflexively to pain. According to the *Athenian Mercury* (1691), Lazarus would probably go to beatific eternity alone, without his more deformed brother. The magazine suggested that because Baptista did not demonstrate rationality, Lazarus would surely "rise without him at the Day of Judgment, for there will be no monsters at the Resurrection."[25] And if Baptista should turn out to have a very rudimentary, passive mind, then he will be raised up with the children and imbeciles but housed in a new, perfected body.

The famous Italian conjoined brothers, Lazarus and Baptista. From George Gould and Walter Pyle, *Medical Curiosities* (W. B. Saunders, 1896).

THE DESCENT OF MONSTERS

In addition to all this theorizing about the souls of monsters, theologians were also intrigued by the question of their genealogy: Who or what were the progenitors of these misshapen creatures? In particular, the races of monsters were difficult to square with the biblical Table of Nations. If they were indeed men, then we must conclude that they, like every other human race, were descendants of Adam.

The descent of monsters was usually put in the context of Genesis 9. Two very important themes arise from this chapter. One theme is Noah's lineage: that "the sons of Noah, who came out of the ark, were Shem, Ham, and Japheth... and from these was all mankind spread over the whole earth" (9:18–19). Another theme is the "curse of Ham." In this narrative Noah gets drunk and passes out naked in his tent. Ham accidentally witnesses his naked father and reports it to his two brothers, Shem and Japheth, who quickly walk backward (to prevent seeing Noah's nakedness) and cover him with a cloth. When Noah awakes from his drunken state and "learns what his younger son has done to him" he curses the descendants of Ham, decreeing that subsequent generations of Ham's son, Canaan, will have to be the servants or slaves of Japheth's and Shem's descendants. This influential episode eventually served as a map by which Christians viewed infidel races. By the time of the Crusades the Table of Nations had become a handy template for metaphysically separating the "noble" races from the ever-threatening exotic foreign hordes. Monsters, Jews, races of color, and Muslims all came to occupy a conceptual territory *outside* orthodoxy. The curse of Ham was just one of these many boundary inventions.[26]

On the face of it, the curse of Ham episode makes little sense. A son sees his father naked, and because of this the father damns all subsequent generations to live in servitude. The narrative seems incoherent on both dramatic and theological grounds, and several schools of interpretation arose around this passage. The rabbinic interpretations suggest that Ham actually castrated Noah and was subsequently punished severely, or Ham's son Canaan castrated Noah, or Ham had sex with a dog while on the ark and this led his offspring to be "dusky," or Ham raped Noah, or even that he raped and then emasculated Noah.[27] The Christian interpretations, found in Augustine and Ambrose, among others, are rather more symbolic and perhaps tame by comparison. According to Augustine, Noah's naked state is symbolic of Christ's vulnerability, the Passion itself. Augustine claims that Ham laughs at or derides his naked father, symbolizing the betrayal of Jesus by the Jews (Christ's own family).[28]

Whatever the actual sin was, the cursed party was more obvious. Ham's descendants were people of color (i.e., Africans, but also Asians and eventually Americans), and their plight in life was to be subservient to the favored races (i.e., Semitic descendants of Shem and Indo-European descendants of Japheth).[29]

In addition to these potent claims about the origins of tribal and national difference, we must also recognize the importance of the Tower of Babel story in Genesis 11. Here we find a relatively unified people working together with one language. These descendants of Noah (possibly led on by the hubristic giant Nimrod) decided to build a tower that would reach Heaven and thereby glorify themselves. God responded by striking down the arrogant humans and their tower, leaving them impaired by multilingualism, unable to understand each other.

These Genesis verses came to dominate medieval and even early modern theories about racial and geographical differences. This ethnological story of Genesis, with its Table of Nations, had an influential role in explaining the dispersion of humans and pseudo humans throughout the earth.[30]

The questions of race and monstrosity became even more intertwined in the age of exploration, which we'll turn to presently. But first, let's look at Augustine's influential ideas about monster genealogy.

The fact that Augustine even addresses the question of monster genealogy suggests that it was a point of contention for early medieval scholars. The three options preferred by Christians at the time were that monsters descended from Ham's descendants, or from Adam directly, or even possibly from pre-Adamite races. Augustine remained convinced of a single ancestry, reaching back to Adam. But Augustine and other patristic writers were up against some compelling non-Christian alternative theories about national ethnic origins. Julian the Apostate (331–363), emperor of Rome (of the Constantine dynasty) and a proud pagan, once challenged Christians with a theory of "national theology." Instead of one God and one original man, Adam, from whom all races descended, Julian suggested that each nation had its own origin by the hand of its own specific God. It would be reasonable, on Julian's account at least, to argue that monster races had their own monster gods. Indeed, polytheism easily makes room for monsters. Part of the challenge to monotheism is to persuasively fit "abnormalities" (exotic races and even monsters) into the table of normality.[31]

In *The City of God* Augustine suggests that distant monstrous races and local individual monstrous births are closely interconnected. We have direct evidence of abnormal births, but only hearsay about faraway abnormal races. When we encounter an innocent child born with extreme physical maladies, we might naturally conclude that God is a poor craftsman. But Augustine proposes that monstrous races may exist *in order to* prevent us from drawing this impious conclusion and show us instead that God knows what He's doing. When we realize that our newborn cycloptic child has some parallel with an entire race of Cyclopes, we cannot think of our child as a "mistake" or a "failure." Moreover, he suggests that the logic works both ways. We know that the individual child is not a mistake because of the existence of monstrous races, and we know that monstrous races are not mistakes because individual monsters crop up regularly. "What if God has seen fit to create some races in this way, that we might not suppose that the monstrous births which appear among ourselves are the failures of that wisdom whereby He fashions the human nature, as we speak of the failure of a less perfect workman?"[32]

ALEXANDER'S GATES

As time passed, few followed Augustine's charitable single-ancestry theory for all races, including monsters. Most seemed to prefer the xenophobic uses of monsters, and by the late medieval period mainstream Christians were not only distancing themselves further from the legendary exotic tribes but they were also adding more proximate ethnicities (Jews, Tartars, Moors, etc.) to that reprobate category.[33] In this more dominant mind-set, "their deformed characteristics were believed to be signs of God's displeasure, corroborated by crusading literature that was replete with evidence of projection of monstrous traits upon the enemy."[34] Augustine and Isidore had answered the *whence* and *why* questions by putting monsters *inside* the system of God's benevolent plan, but many later medieval Christians interpreted monsters as threatening forces from *outside* the kingdom of God, opponents to be overcome in the crusade of righteousness. The fact that, philosophically speaking, there is no *outside* of God's plan (as expressed in the first line of the Nicene Creed) doesn't seem to have stopped people from imagining such radical enemies.

The xenophobic idea of dangerous monsters culminated in a popular story about Alexander's gates. The European version of the story, of a barrier erected against barbarian enemies, seems to have first appeared in sixth-century accounts of the *Alexander Romance*, but the legend is probably much older. Alexander supposedly chased his foreign enemies through a mountain pass in the Caucasus region and then enclosed them behind unbreachable iron gates. The details and the symbolic significance of the story changed slightly in every medieval retelling, and it was retold often, especially in the age of exploration.

By the thirteenth and fourteenth centuries, the meaning of Alexander's gates had long since been Christianized and played an important role in both the geography of monsters and the ultimate end-time purpose of the fiends. The maps of the time, the *mappaemundi*, almost always include the gates, though their placement is not consistent. Most maps and narratives of the later medieval period agree that this prison territory, created proximately by Alexander but ultimately by God, houses the savage tribes of Gog and Magog, who are referred to with great ambiguity throughout the Bible, sometimes as individual monsters, sometimes as nations, sometimes as places. In the story of Alexander's gates, a kind of synthesis occurs, in which "Gog and Magog" becomes a label for designating infidel nations and monstrous races, a monster zone, which different scribes can populate with all manner of projected fears.

Mathew Paris was the chronicler of the Benedictine abbey of St. Albans in England from 1235 to 1259, and he drew up a series of influential maps, usually with Jerusalem and the Holy Land as the central focus. In his maps he placed the monster zone of Gog and Magog in northern Asia and populated it with Tartars (multiethnic Muslim populations).[35] The British Hereford *mappamundi* (ca. 1300) continued the tradition of moral geography, placing Jerusalem as the righteous navel, with lesser known territories, some quite deviant, near the perimeter.[36] In addition to the *Alexander Romance*, the Hereford map drew heavily for its source material on the writings of Solinus, a fourth-century author of *De Mirabilibus Mundi* (On the Wonders of the World). The *Mirabilibus* itself drew significantly on Pliny's *Natural History* and therefore repeats the familiar monsters of the ancient world. But now the creatures, including the dog-headed Cynocephali, the Satyrs, the Blemmyae, the cannibal Anthropophagi, and others, are all reconceptualized as players in the metaphysical geography of Christianity.

The Hereford map shows the people of India as exotic, but it does not disparage them. The inhabitants residing along the Nile, however, are characterized as deformed and less civilized. But the full weight of aversion is saved for the northern perimeter of the map, in Scythia, where live the worst monsters, who are shut up behind Alexander's gates. Here we find the Arimaspeans, the one-eyed race of men, together with their enemies, the gold-digging half-lion, half-eagle griffins. But most important, the map warns us that in this region "everything is horrible, more than can be believed" (*Omnia horribilia plus quam credi potest*). The map continues its description: "Here there are very savage men feeding on human flesh, drinking blood, the sons of accursed Cain. The Lord closed these in by means of Alexander the Great.... At the time of the Antichrist they will break out and will carry persecution to the whole world." Here we find two extremely popular late medieval ideas: that the monstrous races are descendants of Cain and that when the end of times comes they will join forces with the Antichrist and persecute the righteous.

The late medieval theorists reach back to a figure after Adam but before Noah in order to isolate the cause of monsters. Recall that Adam and Eve (in Genesis 4) give birth to Cain and Abel, and while both of them make a sacrifice to God, only Abel's blood sacrifice is pleasing to God. In retaliation, supposedly, Cain kills his brother and becomes ever after cursed by God to live on earth marked as an outcast who can't get any of his crops to grow. Cain seems a perfect candidate for monster race paternity.

A twelfth-century German version of this biblical story, called the Vienna Genesis, analyzes the genealogical story more fully.[37] Here we find that Adam's third son, Seth, about whom little is said in the scriptures, is the offspring who "replaces" the physical loss of Abel and the moral and spiritual loss of Cain. It is the pure and righteous Seth who eventually gives rise to the normal human races of the earth, including, significantly, the lineage that gives rise to Jesus. Cain, on the other hand,

The Psalter *mappamundi* (ca. 1225) continued the tradition of moral geography, placing Jerusalem as the righteous navel, with lesser known monster territories near the perimeter. Courtesy of the British Library.

becomes the progenitor fall guy for every subsequent nefarious character and creature.

In the *Zohar* of the Kabbalah the Jewish midrash tradition further develops the Cain story, suggesting that Cain's own depravity was partly genetic. Cain's mother, Eve, fouled the bloodline by having a relationship with the serpent: "When the serpent injected his impurity into Eve, she absorbed it and so when Adam had intercourse with her she bore two sons—one from the impure side and one from the side of Adam.... Hence it was that their ways in life were different.... From [Cain] originate all the evil habitations and demons and goblins and evil spirits in the world."[38] Apocryphal scriptures, legends, and even the pictorial traditions tend to characterize Cain as misshapen, with horns and lumps on his body, and often draped in fur pelts like a feral man. But this story is important for the way that it broadcasts the tendency in ancient and medieval thought to connect sin and heredity, the tendency to explain monsters and evil generally as the result of unholy sexual union or dysgenics. In the late medieval mind, these myriad errant offspring could be localized in one contained place.

The monsters' incarceration behind Alexander's gates is only temporary. They await their imminent release, the medievals believed, and will be upon us shortly. The *Travels of Sir John Mandeville* (published between 1357 and 1371) reveals precisely how this unleashing will finally occur.[42] Mandeville retells the story of a monster zone full of dragons, serpents, and venomous beasts in the Caspian Mountains, but he adds another ethnic group, indeed, what he considers the main ethnic group, to the famous confinement. In chapter 29 he writes, "Between those mountains the Jews of ten lineages be enclosed, that men call Gog and Magog and they may not go out on any side." Here he is referring to the legendary ten lost tribes that disappeared from history after the Assyrian conquest in the eighth century BCE.[40] These Jews, according to Mandeville, will escape during the time of the Antichrist and "make great slaughter of Christian men. And therefore all the Jews that dwell in all lands learn always to speak Hebrew, in hope, that when the other Jews shall go out, that they may understand their speech, and to lead them into Christendom for to destroy the Christian people."

Christian paranoia about Jews is, of course, an old story. Here in Mandeville we find a late medieval anti-Semitic maneuver that linked Jews directly with other monsters behind the gates and also gave Christians reason for increased paranoia about the local Jewry. To Christians, Jews were proximate in-house monsters (the Diaspora) who also had genealogical relations with the most foreign and distant of monsters. Anti-Semitism didn't really need help from Mandeville's like because the pious fury of the formally anti-Muslim crusades (1095–1291 and beyond) had been spilling over to include violence against local Jewry for centuries. The religious zeal of a Christian warrior culture marching to retake the Holy Land from the infidels did much damage to Jews in France, Germany, Hungary, England, Syria, and Palestine. In a demonstration of Freudian aggression theory, Christians who were frustrated in their desires to beat down their Muslim enemies vented spleen on their in-house "foreigners," the Jews. Christian forms of anti-Semitism, which had long demonized Jews for killing Christ, offered ready-to-hand justifications for such massacres, and now Mandeville simply added more fuel to the fire.

It is ironic that Mandeville displays greater tolerance of and appreciation for Muslims (Saracens), the actual targets of the recent crusades, than he shows for Jews. Mandeville claimed that the Muslims, though wrong and dangerous, still had so much theological common ground with Christians (e.g., acceptance of the same scriptures, acceptance of the importance of the same prophets and the importance of Jesus and Mary) that conversion to Christianity was eventually quite possible. The Muslims were monstrous on the surface, but theological solidarity made their redemption imaginable.[41] Why this same charity was not extended to the Jews is somewhat unclear, but it appears to be the result of the long-standing culture of blame that saw Jews as responsible for the crucifixion of Jesus (a putative culpability not shared by the Saracens).[42] More prosaically, the resentment of Christian merchants and ecclesiastics who were defaulting on their Jewish loans often led to ethnic-based condemnations of moneylending. All these demonizations and projections conspired until Jews were eventually expelled from England (1290), France (1306, 1322, and again 1394), and Spain (1492).[43] "Anti-Semitism," according to Judith Taylor Gold, "is the perception of the Jew as a monster."[44]

In the end, Mandeville predicts, a lowly fox will bring the chaos of invading monsters upon the heads of the Christians. He claims, without revealing how he comes by such specific prophecy, that during the time of the Antichrist a fox will dig a hole through Alexander's gates and emerge inside the monster zone. The monsters will be amazed to see the fox, as such creatures do not live there locally, and they will follow it until it reveals its narrow passageway through the gates. The cursed sons of Cain will finally burst forth from the gates, and the realm of the reprobate will be emptied into the apocalyptic world.

It would be unfair to leave the reader with the impression that Mandeville's *Travels* is just an excuse for intolerant prejudices. It is, in fact, only slightly concerned with Jews and Muslims, and is instead a wonder-filled compendium of weirdness. Mandeville's fanciful encounters with giants and freaks led many subsequent real explorers, including Christopher Columbus, to express surprise (and possibly disappointment) at *not* finding such extreme exotica. In chapter 31 Mandeville describes many enormous giants, some more than fifty feet tall, and then tells of an island tribe of people whose women carry venomous snakes in their vaginas. These snakes sting the penis of the man who enters, and he perishes quickly after. To ensure safe entry, newlywed grooms enlist other men as coitus "testers." These and other such descriptions made the *Travels* one of the most widely disseminated books before the advent of printing.

The Christians were not the only ones interested in Alexander's gates. The Qur'an itself tells a story that rehearses many of the features of the Alexander story. In the Cave chapter ("Surat al-kahf") of the Qur'an we learn of a great king, Dhu'l-Qarneyn (He of the Two Horns), whom many secular and Islamic scholars take to be Alexander.[45] The Qur'an tells the following story of how the great king confined Gog and Magog:

> Then he followed a road till, when he came between the two mountains, he found upon their hither side a folk that scarce could understand a saying. They said: O Dhu'l-Qarneyn! Lo! Gog and Magog are spoiling the land. So may we pay thee tribute on condition that thou set a barrier between us and them? He said: That wherein my Lord hath established me is better (than your tribute). Do but help me with strength (of men), I will set between you and them a bank. Give me pieces of iron—till, when he had levelled up (the gap) between the cliffs, he said: Blow!—till, when he had made it a fire, he said: Bring me molten copper to pour thereon. And (Gog and Magog) were not able to surmount, nor could they pierce (it).[46]

Muslims, like everyone else, accepted the existence of barbaric races. The historian Aziz Al-Azmeh even suggests three common markers that Muslims used to diagnose foreign peoples for barbaric status; filth, profligate sexuality (ascribed to Europeans), and unholy funerary rites.[47] In principle, then, the idea of a great king shutting up dangerous uncivilized races behind an iron gate made sense, but the question was, Who were these brutes? Muslims could not and would not interpret the gates as enclosing themselves or the relatively more familiar peoples of the Eurasian steppes, nor did they believe Gog and Magog comprised the lost Jewish tribes. Islamic civilization of the time, unlike European Christendom, was simply too close to the region to accept any facile identification of the monstrous Gog and Magog. During the Patriarchal and Umayyad Caliphate expansions of Islam (632–750 CE), for example, the territories near the legendary gates would likely have been Muslim. When, in the ninth century, Caliph al-Wathiq-Billah sent an interpreter named Sallam to find Alexander's renowned gates, Sallam failed to discover them in the Caucasus but claimed to find them much further inside Asia.[48] This tells us something about the human tendency to keep locating barbarism and monstrosity farther and farther away from oneself and one's own tribes. Instead of naming the ethnic groups inside Gog and Magog, Aziz Al-Azmeh claims, Arab Islamic culture left them unnameable, imaginary place-holders. These unnamed were the antithesis of civilization, and Muslims accepted the idea that their counterhumanity would strike against pious culture once the gates were breached, but the creatures themselves were more anonymous than in the European narratives.

Both Christians and Muslims had deep-seated monster narratives to explain the evil and the uncivilized. The looming threat of their revolution opened the door for numerous hero narratives, tales that defined human virtues.

7

The Monster Killer

No man can follow where God's enemies glide through the fog.
BEOWULF

ONE OF THE GREAT MONSTER KILLERS of all time is the
Scandinavian hero Beowulf. He comes to us in the form of an
Old English manuscript called the Nowell Codex by archivists
but titled *Beowulf* after its main character, which is bundled together with
other famous texts, including *Liber Monstrorum* (Book of Monsters) and
Alexander's *Letter to Aristotle*. Most scholars put the date of this particular manuscript copy around 1100, but the story probably had existed in
oral form for centuries before. The text and the tale are considered British
national treasures, despite the fact that the story is about a Scandinavian
hero fighting monsters in Denmark.

"I HAVE KNOWN MUCH PERIL"

Beowulf is the name of a young warrior from the land of the Geats in
southern Sweden, and his story unfolds sometime around the late fifth
and early sixth centuries. He hears of a troubled Danish king, Hrothgar,
whose subjects and feasting hall (Heorot) are being menaced by a monster
named Grendel. Beowulf offers his services as a monster killer: "I have
known much peril, grim death dangers. Grendel's ravages came to my ears
in my own homeland."[1]

Beowulf and his band of Geat warriors are welcomed with open arms
and a feast by the Danes. A mischievous Dane, named Unferth, calls

The Grendel monster from Robert Zemeckis's 2007 film version of *Beowulf* (Paramount Pictures and Warner Bros.). Image courtesy of Photofest.

Beowulf's ability into question by reporting a story of Beowulf's loss in a swimming competition with his friend Breca. Beowulf sets Unferth straight and establishes his monster-killing credentials, explaining that he and Breca swam side by side for five nights until an "angry sea-flood broke out above us—blackening sky and freezing northwinds forced us apart, towering salt-swells struck between us. Strange sea creatures surfaced around me.... To the deep sea-floor, something pulled me—hard gripfingers hauled me to sand with grappling tight claws. It was granted to me to reach this devil, rush him to sleep with sharp sword-point—swift blade-slashing, strong in my hand, haled him deathward." Beowulf was then attacked by several more sea monsters, all of whom he "sent to hell." So, Beowulf concludes, Breca may have won a simple swimming contest, but he never fought and triumphed over heinous demons of the deep.

We can already see that this is a man's story, told by men, about men, and celebrating manly virtues. Even before the encounter with Grendel we have heroes in chain mail, emptying mugs of beer, and trading stories of violent victories against formidable enemies. The testosterone level only builds as the story progresses.

The monster Grendel, who regularly breaks into the large feasting hall at night to kill and eat the sleeping Danes, is probably the most famous monster descendant of the biblical Cain. He is described as the "kin of Cain," underscoring the medieval tendency to tether monsters to an already established hereditary line of evil.[2] Grendel, like his banished biblical ancestor, lives outside the region of normal society, like a phantom that seems to materialize only in the black of night. He lives in the "cloud misted moors" and "no man can follow where God's enemies glide through the fog."

As night falls, Beowulf and his Geat warriors prepare to ambush the monster by lying quietly in the feasting hall. "Not one believed they would leave Heorot (the hall), take ship once more, seek out their homeland, the known meadows of their native country. Too many stories of that tall wine-hall, emptied of Danes by dark night slaughter, had found their ears." In the quiet black of night, Grendel, "craving a blood feast," suddenly bursts into the hall, ripping the iron doors off its hinges with ease. The beast snares a victim immediately; he "tore frantically, crunched bonelockings, crammed blood-morsels, gulped him with glee." When the beast grabs his second victim, the victim grabs back. The monster is astonished to feel Beowulf's awesome grip upon him. Beowulf's iron fingers pin the beast and prevent any escape. A horrible battle ensues, but Beowulf doesn't let go. It was long established that swords had no effect upon the scaly fiend, but no one was prepared, least of all Grendel, for Beowulf's mortal grip. "Then that giant ravager—rejected by God, marked with murder, measured by his sins—finally conceived in his fiend's mindthoughts that his loathsome body would bear no more." As the monster pulls away in anguish, Beowulf, still refusing to let go, rips off its arm. The defeated monster, "a great death-wound gap[ing] in his shoulder," runs back into the darkness.

The following night Beowulf is presented with many precious gifts in gratitude and the whole hall rings out with drunken celebration. But it turns out that even monsters love their children, and waiting for that night, "slouched through the shadows, searching for revenge—grim murder-fiend Grendel's hell-mother . . . mourned for her child. She was damned to hide in a dark water home, cold wildwood stream, since Cain murdered his only brother-kin, beat down to earth his father's son-child. He was sent for that, marked with murder, from man's company—banished to wasteland. Then woke from his loins misbegotten monsters." Grendel's mother turns out to be an even more dreadful foe, and Beowulf must fight her in the hall and then follow her to her watery lair. In an underwater cave Beowulf tries to crush the "sea hag," but she is too strong. Finding a huge sword in the monster's cache, he manages finally, "with rage in his heart," to slay the creature. Waiting anxiously above water, the Danes and Geats watch "a welling of blood, waves of death gore, rise to the surface." Beowulf emerges victorious, carrying the hilt of the successful sword; the sword itself has melted from the monster's vitriolic blood.

After much celebration Beowulf returns home and eventually becomes the king of the Geats, living happily for many years as a noble ruler. But after fifty years the peaceful interval is broken and Beowulf must rise again to meet a monstrous enemy. A wandering fugitive incurs the wrath of a horrible dragon when he steals a golden cup from the creature's hidden treasure. The dragon takes his vengeance on all men, "spewing flame-murder, blistering mead halls—mountains of hate-fire moved through the land, he would leave no creature alive on the earth, lone night-flyer." After the serpent blasts and sears the land of the Geats, Beowulf "called for a shield." His warriors abandon him out of fear, but a young relative named Wiglaf stays to fight alongside the aging hero. Together the two manage to defeat the giant serpent after a difficult battle, but not before Beowulf is bitten badly by the venomous dragon. "Murderous poison welled within his breast, baleful serpent gall pushed toward his heart. The proud one wandered slowly by the wall—sat by the barrow-stone, lost in life-thoughts." Beowulf finally dies, is cremated, and is buried on a cliff overlooking the ocean.

TOLKIEN'S TRAGIC BEOWULF

I've just committed the mortal sin, according to J. R. R. Tolkien, of summarizing the plot of *Beowulf*. In his influential 1936 lecture "Beowulf: The Monsters and the Critics," Tolkien argued that critics had failed to see the seriousness and the depth of *Beowulf* because they frequently abstracted the simple plot from the actual poem. There seems to be some truth in this. If I say, for example, "*Beowulf* is about this guy who fights three monsters and then dies," I've pretty much covered the plot. Thinking about the poem in this way led many scholars to see it as a historically important linguistic artifact, but otherwise dumb and unsophisticated. It's just a monster fight, after all.

Tolkien showed us that the actual poetry of *Beowulf* was indeed powerful stuff, haunting and eerie on a line-by-line basis and emotionally edifying when taken as a whole narrative. In a passage that unknowingly augurs his own importance as an inspiring writer of monster fantasies, Tolkien defended *Beowulf* and its "low" monsters: "The dragon in legend is a potent creation of men's imagination.... Even today (despite the critics) you may find men not ignorant of tragic legend and history, who have heard of heroes and indeed seen them, who yet have been caught by the fascination of the worm. More than one poem in recent years... has been inspired by the dragon of Beowulf."[3] Tolkien said this just one year before he published *The Hobbit* and began his own cottage industry of thrilling tales.

More than just a champion of the fantasy horror genre, Tolkien weighed in on the substantive debate as to whether the poem was a work of Christian or pagan imagination. The poem is ambivalent about its hero, making him an inspirational figure, but also tragic. His strength and reliability make him a champion, but his pride and conceit make him flawed. Moreover, the poem mixes pagan tropes (e.g., the culture of fame and honor is celebrated, and Beowulf is cremated like a pagan) with Christian tropes (e.g., monotheism is sometimes intoned, and Cain is referred to explicitly). Traditionally, scholars read this ambivalence as a sign that the poem itself was a mongrel offspring, written by a northern pagan steeped in Norse legend, but copied and interpolated by a Christian monk who baptized the text with minor Christian additions. Many scholars still claim that this pastiche theory is the most coherent explanation of *Beowulf*'s ambiguities.[4]

Even if *Beowulf* is a pastiche of Christian revisionism mixed with Norse paganism, it's important to locate the precise nature of the amendments. One change, arguably, is the metaphysical status of the monsters themselves. Recall that Odysseus fights the frightening Cyclops Polyphemus, eventually blinding him and escaping his cave strapped to the belly of a sheep. In his lecture Tolkien quoted the following passage by the *Beowulf* scholar Raymond Wilson Chambers:

> Odysseus is struggling with a monstrous and wicked foe, but he is not exactly thought of as struggling with the powers of darkness. Polyphemus, by devouring his guests, acts in a way that is hateful to Zeus and the other gods: yet the Cyclops is himself god-begotten and under divine protection, and the fact that Odysseus has maimed him is a wrong which Poseidon [Polyphemus's father] is slow to forgive. But the gigantic foes whom Beowulf has to meet are identified as the foes of God.[5]

Like so many other monster scenarios we've examined so far, this point underscores the challenges of coordinating God and evil. In a monotheistic tradition such as Christianity, it's hard to imagine anything, monster or otherwise, that isn't technically "god-begotten." But Chambers expresses a popular folk belief, as alive today as it was when *Beowulf* was copied: that God has enemies. One could retort by remembering Grendel's hereditary connection to Cain, thereby bringing him back under the umbrella of God's creation. But there is a more helpful reading: the relationship between heroes, monsters, and gods can be said to experience a sea change in *Beowulf* if we realize that the important pagan *virtue* of pride is the principal *vice* of Christianity.

Monsters, in both pagan and biblical traditions, have been symbols of hubris; the giants are prime examples. But monster killers and heroes have been celebrated in pagan culture as the strong men of action that are needed to save the family or tribe or village. With some exceptions, such as the famous monster killer Ripley in the film *Alien*, who repeatedly dispatches aliens to hell, most monster killers of the Western tradition are men. Monsters give men an excuse to do the things they were built, by nature and nurture, to do: fight, protect, take, and defend. Men are those useful brutes. Hero pride was a favored impulse in the pre-Christian era, even if it came with flaws of excess and immoderation. But the biblical tradition brought a new ethic: "Blessed are the meek." One could argue, in fact, that the main theme of the Old Testament is *submission* to Yahweh, and the New Testament resounds with the call to humbleness. The hero of Christianity, Jesus, even ends in the ignoble position of suffering on a cross.[6] This is not exactly fertile cultural ground for growing manly monster killers. Norse he-men of Beowulf's era would not have understood this new kind of "victory through humility."

Indeed, a new kind of hero was invented in Christianity. Christian heroes suffer, as do heroes of the ancient world, but unlike the ancients the Christians' suffering *is* their heroism. Victory no longer comes when the hero is standing over the slain monster; it comes in the next life, after one has lived humbly and proven oneself by accommodating large amounts of unjust suffering. Traditional heroes such as Beowulf, Hercules, and Odysseus can be acknowledged for their strength and ability, but their prideful humanism, their attempts to personally bring justice to the world, must be devalued in the new Christian paradigm. According to the Judeo-Christian tradition, we don't *need* monster killers when we trust in the Lord. After all, God, not man, punishes the wicked. Heroic faith replaces heroic action.

One of the most impressive aspects of the character of Beowulf is his embodiment of what Tolkien calls "Northern courage." Beowulf embodies a "theory of courage" that puts the "unyielding will" at the center of heroic narrative. The Norse imagination, filled with the philosophy of absolute resistance, was properly tamed in England, according to Tolkien, by contact with Christianity. The Viking commitment to "martial heroism as its own end" is unmasked by Christianity as mere hopeless nihilism, something to be overcome and remedied. Tolkien says that the poet of *Beowulf* saw clearly that "the wages of heroism is death." The Christian looks back over the course of pagan history and finds that all the glory won by heroes and kings and warriors is for naught, because it is only of this earthly temporal world.

Without Christianity, monster killers are either hopeless existential heroes, trying by pathetic human effort to rid the world of evil, or they are themselves monstrous giants amid a flock of righteous and meek devotees. Hercules, for example, is judged by medieval Christians as an abomination to be dethroned from his traditional place of adulation. The medievalist Andy Orchard quotes Aelfric's tenth-century *Lives of the Saints*, which asks, "What holiness was in that hateful Hercules, the huge giant, who slaughtered all his neighbors, and burned himself alive in the fire, after he had killed men, and the lion, and the great serpent?"[7]

Alexander the Great's ancient heroism was also reconfigured in the medieval era. He courageously kills monsters in the *Alexander Romance* but is also regularly humbled by wise sages who point out his prideful ambition. In the medieval story of Alexander's *Journey to Paradise* he is given a Judeo-Christian lesson in humility. After being surprised by a small mystical jewel that outweighs hundreds of gold coins, he is told by "a very aged Jew named Papas" that the jewel is a supernatural gift. The disembodied spirits who are waiting for Judgment Day (when they will get their bodies back) have offered this jewel to Alexander. Papas tells Alexander, "These spirits, who are enthusiastic for human salvation, sent you this stone as a memento of your blessed fortune, both to protect you and to constrain the inordinate and inappropriate urgings of your ambition." "You are oppressed," he continues, "with want, nothing is enough for you." After more criticism of his vaulting ambition, Alexander is converted to meekness and charity: "At once he put an end to his own desires and ambitions and made room for the exercise of generosity and noble behavior."[8] The new nobility is quite different from the old pagan nobility.

Beowulf is both the last gasp of pagan hero culture and an important breath in the rise of the Judeo-Christian humility culture. The truly Christian monster, the one that has completed the arc that *Beowulf* only initiates, will not really be a monster at all, but only a confused soul who needs a hug rather than a sword thrust. True Christianity seeks to embrace the outcast, not fight him. Christianity celebrates the downtrodden, the loser, the misshapen. Grendel is an outcast, and tender hearts have argued that the people who cast him out are the real monsters. According to this charity paradigm, the monster is simply misunderstood rather than evil. Perhaps God has created the monsters in order to teach us to love the ugly, the repulsive, the outcast.

This has become the preferred reading, for example, of Mary Shelley's *Frankenstein*, and this ethical posture can be seen in some recent adaptations of *Beowulf* as well. For example, Sturla Gunnarsson's 2005 film *Beowulf and Grendel* gives us a Grendel who is actually just a sad outcast, someone Beowulf even pities at one point. The blame for Grendel's violence is shifted to the humans, who sinned against him earlier and brought the vengeance upon themselves. Or consider Robert Zemeckis's 2007 Paramount Pictures version of *Beowulf*, featuring the voices and computer-generated images of Anthony Hopkins, John Malkovich, Angelina Jolie, Crispin Glover, and Ray Winstone as Beowulf. Zemeckis's film follows Gunnarsson's 2005 version in casting Grendel as the sad, misunderstood outcast rather than the evil monster we find in the original. In the film, Grendel is even visually altered after his injury (with CGI effects) to look like an innocent, albeit scaly, little child. In the original *Beowulf* the monsters are outcasts *because* they're bad, just as Cain, their progenitor, was an outcast because he killed his brother, but in the new liberal *Beowulf* the monsters are bad *because* they're outcasts. And while the monsters are being humanized in the new versions, the hero is being dehumanized. When Zemeckis's Beowulf asks Grendel's mother, "What do you know of me?" she replies, "I know that underneath your glamour, you're as much a monster as my son Grendel." The only real monsters, in this now dominant tradition, are pride and prejudice. In the original story Beowulf is a hero. In the 2007 film he's basically a jerk, whose most sympathetic moment is when he finally realizes that he's a jerk. It's hard to imagine a more complete reversal of values.

Friedrich Nietzsche (1844–1900) wrote, "He who fights with monsters should look to it that he himself does not become a monster." Nonetheless he argues in *Beyond Good and Evil* that the pagan cultures of nobility arose out of barbaric, even beastly sentiments of power, strength, and pride. Unlike Tolkien, who was happy to see such will-to-power tamed by Judeo-Christian virtues, Nietzsche missed the old days and wished we would bring back a little bit of our monstrous selves. He would have liked the pagan Beowulf, a tribal-minded monster killer. Reaching back to a pre-Christian notion of nobility, he quotes Norse mythology approvingly:

In honoring himself, the noble man honors the powerful as well as those who have power over themselves, who know how to speak and be silent, who joyfully exercise severity and harshness over themselves, and have respect for all forms of severity and harshness. "Wotan has put a hard heart in my breast," reads a line from an old Scandinavian saga; this rightly comes from the soul of a proud Viking. This sort of man is even proud of *not* being made for pity, which is why the hero of the saga adds, by way of warning, "If your heart is not hard when you are young, it will never be hard." The noble and brave types of people who think this way are the furthest removed from a morality that sees precisely pity, actions for others, and *desinteressement* as emblematic of morality. A faith in yourself, pride in yourself, and a fundamental hostility and irony with respect to "selflessness" belong to a noble morality just as certainly as does a slight disdain and caution towards sympathetic feelings and "warm hearts."[9]

The sign of the Cross, and a little steel, help St. George vanquish a dragon. Pen and ink drawing by Stephen T. Asma © 2008.

Pagan heroes want to be publicly recognized for their acts of heroism; they want honor as payment for their monster-killing services. Beowulf himself says he wants fame. Another medieval hero, the crusader Roland from *La Chanson de Roland* (ca. 1170), is motivated by his desire to have a good song, rather than a bad one, sung about him back home in France. Judaism and Christianity, on the other hand, demote public honor in favor of private honor. According to the Judeo-Christian tradition, prideful men misidentify their proper audience: "They act out the drama of their lives before the audience of their contemporaries rather than before the all-knowing and merciful eyes of God."[10] This mistake makes them prideful giants, impressive in the short term but ridiculous from the point of view of eternity.[11]

8

Possessing Demons and Witches

Be not angry...for it is not he, but the demon which is in him.
ST. ANTHONY OF THE DESERT

WHEN MOST PEOPLE THINK OF MEDIEVAL MONSTERS, they think of demons, witches, and ghosts—in short, supernatural monsters. This kind of monster is perhaps more frightening than what might be called zoological monsters, deformed creatures and exotic races, because of their ability to possess. The idea that monsters can get inside a human being and use him or her for monstrous ends predates the medieval period, flourishes during it, and continues to the present.[1]

ST. ANTHONY FIGHTS THE DEMONS

The story of St. Anthony of the Desert (ca. 251–356) had a huge impact on the development of Christian monasticism. He is sometimes referred to as the Father of Monks, having created a desert monasticism that drew Christian ascetics far away from the urban centers. But his famous fight with monsters in the Egyptian desert also laid the groundwork for medieval thinking about demons and possession.[2]

Anthony was a pious Egyptian boy, born of Christian parents who died when he was around eighteen years old; subsequently, on a religious impulse, Anthony gave away all his property and possessions.[3] He studied with local ascetics, learning how to better discipline his mind and his loins, and eventually mastered the practical difficulties of living without comforts. "But the devil, who hates and envies what is good, could not endure to see such a resolution in a youth, but endeavored to carry out against him what he had been wont to effect against others."[4] The devil began by "whispering to him the remembrance of his wealth...love of money, love of glory, the various pleasures of the table and other relaxations of life," but Anthony remained firm in his regimen of fasting and prayer. So the devil redoubled his efforts to snare Anthony's desires, even taking on the shape of a woman one night and imitating all her beguiling ways. "But he, his mind filled with Christ and the nobility inspired by Him, and considering the spirituality of the soul, quenched the coal of the other's deceit." Anthony then moved to live in a tomb outside the village, where he was attacked by a "multitude of demons" who sliced him into a bloody mess. "He affirmed that the torture had been so excessive that no blows inflicted by man could ever have caused him such torment." But his faith revitalized him and he rallied back. After throwing off the temptations of the flesh, Anthony was revisited by the devil many times, but the devil always shapeshifted to appear as some creature.

> But changes of form for evil are easy for the devil, so in the night they make such a din that the whole of that place seemed to be shaken by an earthquake, and the demons as if breaking the four walls of the dwelling seemed to enter through them, coming in the likeness of beasts and creeping things. And the place was on a sudden filled with the forms of lions, bears, leopards, bulls, serpents, asps, scorpions, and wolves, and each of them was moving according to its nature.

These creatures, together with demonic hounds, attack and torture Anthony, but he insults the devil with audacity, telling him that such shape-shifting attacks are evidence of his weak cowardice. Eventually a ray of light pierces the dark tomb and causes the monsters to disappear. God has intervened, after years of torture. Anthony asks, "Where were you? Why didst thou not appear at the beginning to make my pains cease?" God responds, "Anthony, I was here, but I waited to see thy fight." Convinced that Anthony has the right mettle, God commits to give him support and strength ever after.

Anthony moves farther into the desert now, finding an abandoned fort "filled with creeping things" and taking up residence there. For twenty years he lives in solitude, fighting temptations and creatures, until other pious young men, hearing of his legendary asceticism, begin to join him in the desert. A reluctant role model, Anthony imparts his wisdom to the new desert monks. First, he explains to the neophytes that one must never be afraid of demons. The devil and his minions may have had significant power

The German engraver Martin Shongauer's fifteenth-century print of
St. Anthony's troubles. From Edward Lucie-Smith and Aline Jacquiot,
The Waking Dream: Fantasy and the Surreal in Graphic Art (Knopf, 1975).

in the old days, but ever since Christ came to earth the evil ones have lost
most of their power. After Christ's victory, Anthony explains, the demons
have no power and "are like actors on the stage changing their shape and
frightening children with tumultuous apparition and various forms."

The major weapons of the demons are fear and temptation: "When
they cannot deceive the heart openly with foul pleasures they approach
in different guise, and thenceforth shaping displays they attempt to strike
fear, changing their shapes, taking the forms of women, wild beasts, creeping things, gigantic bodies, and troops of soldiers." But the most effective response to an immediate threat, Anthony explains, is the sign of the
cross. As a long-term strategy against evil, monks have three weapons with
which to do spiritual battle: prayer, fasting, and faith.

Anthony warns his brethren that if they should survive these waves of demonic assault, there will certainly be a final phase of frightening attack. The minions, in their frustration, will finally invoke the "prince of the demons," the devil himself. His eyes will burn like the morning star, his mouth will pour the fire and smoke of a conflagration, and his nostrils will fume like hot coals. But Anthony insists that even this terrifying monster is all sizzle and no real substance. In a fascinating, albeit brief, piece of biblical interpretation, Anthony characterizes the devil as a chump, a two-bit thug. The evidence can be found as far back as the torture of Job. The devil had no real power over Job; it was God who *allowed* every bit of torture of the hapless victim. Anthony's indictment here is strange because although it makes the devil look bad, it makes God look worse. Seemingly uninterested in the theodicy problem, Anthony suggests that the only thing to fear is God.[5]

All this makes sense, according to Anthony, when we realize the true nature of demons, their true metaphysical status. "The demons," he explains, "have not been created like what we mean when we call them by that name for God made nothing evil, but even they have been made good. Having fallen, however, from the heavenly wisdom, since then they have been groveling on earth." They are not inherently rotten, malicious creatures, and they are not imbued with some Manichaean force that rivals God's goodness. They are in fact tragic characters who have made themselves miserable by their rebellion and now seek to make men miserable. The demons envy the Christians. Like circus performers, they have the ability to make spectacles, and this leads pagans to erroneously fear and worship them, but Christians should just despise them.

Anthony admits, however, that the demons have gradations of ill intent, and it behooves one to cultivate a kind of demon radar. He says, "When a man has received through the Spirit the gift of discerning spirits, he may have power to recognize their characteristics: which of them are less and which more evil; of what nature is the special pursuit of each, and how each of them is overthrown and cast out." Because Anthony himself is just such a virtuoso of demonology, he is regularly appealed to for exorcisms.

In addition to demons who shape-shift into frightening phantasms, which are easily banished by a resolute sign of the cross, Anthony acknowledges the phenomenon of real human possession. This is somewhat difficult to square with his persistent claim that demons have no real power. In the second half of the *Life of Anthony* Athanasius tells of many terrible cases of people who have come into the custody of demon spirits. A man named Fronto, for example, had a madness that involved biting his own tongue and injuring his own eyes; a woman from Busiris had mucus fall from her nose that immediately turned into worms once it hit the ground; and "another, a person of rank, came to him, possessed by a demon; and the demon was so terrible that the man possessed did not know that he was coming to Anthony. But he even ate the excreta from his own body." This young man actually attacked Anthony, but the sage said, "Be not angry with the young man, for it is not he, but the demon which is in him." Anthony cured all these cases and many more, but it is unlikely that the man eating his own excrement would have agreed with Anthony's refrain that demons are powerless. For that matter, if they are truly powerless, why would anyone need Anthony's exorcising acumen? The logic here, if there is any, is never quite expressed but can be reconstructed perhaps by saying that demons do not have real power unless you become afraid of them, in which case you grant them entry into the cause-and-effect world. Our *response* to demon attack can either give them causal traction in our world or banish them from it. We are instrumental in the outcome of the encounter.[6]

WITCHES

The early medieval period is dominated by the sort of demonic harassment that plagued St. Anthony, but the later period is given over to those peculiar vessels of demonic ill will, the witches. From the Inquisition of the late Middle Ages to the New England trials of the 1690s, witches were the monsters foremost in the imagination.[7] And more than the imagination, they became players in a new legal bureaucracy.

Heresy hunting was a major interest for two centuries after the Great Papal Schism, an almost forty-year span in the late fourteenth and early fifteenth century when the papacies of Rome and Avignon (and later Pisa) battled for dominance and legitimacy. The Council of Constance in 1414 restored the Roman papacy, but paranoia grew around issues of orthodoxy and authenticity. The official culture of the day saw itself as beset by schismatics, Turks, apostates, heretics, idolaters, and even the Antichrist.

Heresy itself was understood as a kind of "monstrous thinking." The heretic Giordano Bruno (1548–1600), for example, had become too clever for his own good and veered away from the true faith into atheism. Bruno, a hero to many subsequent free thinkers, once frightened Henry III in Paris by demonstrating astounding powers of memory. When Henry accused him of witchcraft, Bruno assured him that his skill was the product of study. Eventually his Pythagorean ideas were used against him by the Inquisition in a trumped-up charge that Bruno had abandoned the Aristotelian-Christian teachings on the soul in favor of reincarnation (metempsychosis). He was judged to be a heretic and was burned at the stake in the Campo dei Flore in Rome. The Bruno case, taken with what follows here on witches, demonstrates how both high-culture academic knowledge and folk culture shamanism fell equally under suspicion by the anxious Church. Rooting out and persecuting witches were common in this culture of fear.[8]

In 1579 a small coven of witches were executed in Abington, England, and a news pamphlet of the time, published in London, set forth some important aspects of witch belief.[9] The pamphlet is titled *A Rehearsal both straung and true, of heinous and horrible actes committed by Elizabeth Stile, Mother Dutten, Mother Deuell, Mother Margaret, fower notorius witches apprehended at Winsore.*[10] We learn that, "among the punishments which the Lord God hath laid upon us, for the manifest impiety and careless contempt of his word, abounding in these our desperate days, the swarms of witches, and enchanters are not the last nor the least. For that old Serpent Satan, suffered to be the scourge for our sins, hath of late years, greatly multiplied the brood of them, and much increased their malice."

The devil and his minions were plaguing innocents with treachery, but also enlisting the service of already prideful, vain, and envious people. Tempted by Faustian desires, marginally corrupt people could be made into irredeemable servants of the demons. "The witch bears the name, but the devil dispatches the deeds—without him the witch can continue no mischief."

The mischief of the four Windsor witches included transforming themselves into various beasts, keeping demonic black cats and other nefarious animals that they fed with their own blood, killing several townspeople (including a former mayor, a landlord, and a couple of butchers) by making effigy pictures of the victims in red wax and sticking pins in their hearts, and reversing a child's hand so that it painfully twisted palm-side up. These and other black magic deeds were attested to by trustworthy neighbors and ultimately confessed to by the accused themselves.

As one might imagine, the evidence for the demonic nature of these women was so paltry and circumstantial that no right-minded adult could take the claims seriously. For example, one neighbor testified to feeling sick after every visit with one of the women and concluded that magic was being used against him. Similarly feeble substantiation was considered compelling to judges and jailers of the time. Still, we must measure this seeming gullibility by the evidential methods of the time, not by our own. Moreover, the power of paranoia in corrupting the search for evidence is not limited to any historical era and has to be admitted as a dominant causal force in all such cases of moral panic.[11] We also have to factor in the possibility that natural *chemical* causes may have given the accused and the accusers some real hallucinations that were difficult, if not impossible, to explain without appeal to supernaturalism. One thinks here, for example, of the impressive link that has been established between the Salem witch trial hallucinations and seizures and the effects of spoiled rye grain. Ergot, a parasitic fungus that produces LSD-type hallucinations and grows on damp grain in storage, can poison whole communities. Many historians and anthropologists believe that such an epidemic broke out in Salem and explains the bizarre and ultimately tragic events, events that could be explained at the time only by resort to metaphysics.[12]

In Windsor, Elizabeth Stile was arrested first and testified against the other witches, which led to their subsequent arrest. When the other witches were taken into custody, they used their powers to inflict revenge on Stile. Mother Deuel bewitched Stile so that "the use of all her limbs was taken from her, and her toes did rot off her feet, and she was laid upon a barrow, as a most ugly creature to behold." In less than one month after their arrest, the witches were executed. This short-order justice epitomized the sort of witch-hunt culture that flourished all over Europe and New England.[13]

In a letter written in 1649 in St. Albans, Hertfordshire, a local citizen reported on the case of two witches recently captured and executed.[14] John Palmer and Elizabeth Knott were found to be colluding in black arts, and Palmer even confessed to being a witch for over fifty years. The report of their downfall includes some telling passages, revealing the shock and original incredulity of the reporter himself: "It had been very difficult to convince me of that which I find true, concerning the wiles of that old Serpent the Devil, for the supporting of his dark dominions, which appears in the subtle trade he drives for the enlarging of his territories; by strengthening himself upon the weakness of his subjects, relapsed men and women." In particular, the devil and his demons target a man like Palmer, who, "rather than keep his station, will trial what the Devil can do for his advancement in knowledge." A man like John Palmer was ripe for conversion to witchery because he had "an inordinate desire to know more than his Maker had thought fit for him to know."[15]

When the witch John Palmer "adjoined himself to the Devil," he received a branding mark on his side, some sort of bizarre tattoo of a dog (inexplicably named "George") and a female figure named "Jezabell." This mark somehow symbolized the unholy compact (tattoos were common for witches), and henceforth Palmer engaged in a variety of magical crimes, including the seduction of Elizabeth Knott, the remote murder of Miss

Pearls by using a clay effigy and hot embers, a "revenge killing" of a horse, the bewitching of a cow, self-transformation into a trouble-making toad, and other, lesser misdeeds. Palmer, like other witches, had incriminated himself with a confession, most probably involving torture.

Two of the principal horrors that witches performed during the medieval era were penis removal and baby stealing. As you might expect, witches are extremely interested in human fornication. One of the most popular witch manuals of the day asks, "Do Witches Employ Illusions to Trick People into Thinking that Men's Penises have been entirely Uprooted from their Bodies?"[16] Another chapter heading is "How They Usually Remove Penises." All of this is described flatly in a manner that suggests a truly commonplace interest on the part of readers, as if the author is addressing a constant cultural refrain of "Whither the penises?"

The good news is that most penis disappearances are only illusions created by witches, but sad to say there are, on rare occasions, real removals. A cautionary tale of a young man living in Ravensburg, Germany, who was "involved with a young girl" is discussed. In time, the young man left the girl; subsequently he "lost his penis." "That is to say," the inquisitor writes, "the art of illusion made him unable to see or touch anything except a body which was flat and even. This caused him much distress." In this case, the young man's imaginative faculty was attacked by a witch, and he was fooled into perceiving his own unmanning. It is a conjuring trick that changes only the man's perception of reality.[17] The inquisitor says, "Thus, [in the case of the missing penis], there is no deception when it comes to the fact of the matter, because his rod is still attached to his person. But there *is* deception when it comes to the sense organ."[18]

While drowning his sorrows at the wine cellar, the young man confided to a helpful woman that his ex-girlfriend must be a penis-stealing witch. His confidant told him, "When a friendly approach does not work in your favor, it's a good idea for you to use violence to induce her to restore your health." Taking this to heart, the man waylaid the ex-girlfriend one night on a dark road and insisted that she "make him sound in body again." She proved quite intractable until he choked her with a towel, whereupon she blurted, "Let me go and I'll cure you."[19] She then touched his crotch and said, "Now you have what you want," and the young man did indeed find himself restored. Which means, of course, that he was no longer hallucinating.

Happily, one's penis does not go missing, the inquisitor assures us, if one is in a state of grace. The best protection against penis-stealing witches is sexual modesty. Witches cannot infiltrate the righteous man's "imaginative faculty" in order to play this trick on him.[20]

Witches Apprehended, Ex-
amined and Executed, for notable
villanies by them committed both by
Land and Water.

With a ſtrange and moſt true triall how to know
whether a woman be a Witch
or not.

Printed at London for *Edward Marchant*, and are to
be ſold at his ſhop ouer againſt the Croſſe in Pauls
Church-yard. 1 6 1 3.

A 1613 pamphlet advertising witch detection tests. A woman is
being dunked in water to determine her status. Courtesy of the
Newberry Library.

Although it is disheartening to *think* you've lost your penis, it's significantly worse to really lose it. True removal is effected directly by the
demons themselves, rather than through the conjuring witches. So how do
you know if your penis has really been removed or just whisked away by
a witch-induced hallucination? The answer, perhaps unsurprisingly, is that
the former case is accompanied by terrible pain, whereas the latter case is
accompanied by "depression." And rest assured that in either case, as with
all such harm, God must have given the green light. If one's penis goes
missing, one can feel confident that one deserved it. Likewise, switching to
a milder example, if a man experiences erectile dysfunction when he wants
to procreate with his wife, then it's quite likely to be the result of harmful
magic. One can't help but speculate whether this excuse proved credible to
the long-suffering wife.

The inquisitors did not confine themselves to men's deep castration and performance anxieties, but found room to foment other primordial fears and apprehensions as well. It may be a platitude to mention that no greater wellspring of irrational fear and worry exists than the emotions surrounding the subject of one's own children. When you first become a parent, charged with the greatest responsibility possible, you discover subterranean deposits of emotional vulnerability in yourself that you didn't know existed. Parents of the medieval era had the inquisitors to help nourish their worst hysterical fears. Besides stealing penises, witches apparently were very interested in stealing babies. Inquisitors claimed, "Midwives who work harmful magic kill fetuses in the womb in different ways, procure a miscarriage, and, when they do not do this, offer newly born children to evil spirits."[21]

There are three ways witches attempt to counter the sacred purpose of procreation. The first, already mentioned, is to render the penis flaccid. The second is to produce a miscarriage or prevent conception altogether. The third is to steal the infant shortly after birth in order to eat it or offer it to an evil spirit. "Those who are indisputably witches are accustomed, against the inclination of human nature—indeed contrary to the temperament of every animal (at least, with the exception of the wolf)—to devour and feast on young children."[22]

The inquisitor of Como, Italy, relates that "a man had lost his child from its cradle and, while he was searching for it, he saw some women who had gathered together during the nighttime, and he came to the conclusion that they were slaughtering a child, drinking its fluid, and then devouring [it]." In response to that event, the inquisitor came down very hard on the local witches, burning over forty-one of them in a single year. One might well ask how all this baby stealing and torturing was possible. The answer is simple: midwives.

Inquisitors took a very dim view of midwifery.[23] No particular compelling reason is given in the text for this hostility. The Dominican inquisitor Heinrich Institoris claimed, however, that penitent witch midwives had confessed to him, doubtless under duress, "No one does more harm to the Catholic faith than midwives. When they don't kill the children, they take the babies out of the room, as though they are going to do something out of doors, lift them up in the air, and offer them to evil spirits."[24]

Besides midwife witches, evil demons themselves got into the business of human procreation. Remember the discussion of incubi that we encountered in St. Augustine, who somewhat reluctantly agreed to the *possibility* of spirits having sex with human women. A millennium later, according to the inquisitors, the possibility evolved into certainty.[25] Demonic spirits transformed themselves into attractive and alluring men and women and then seduced human partners into sexual union. A seductive female demon was called a *succubus* ("bottom," or underneath) and the male, as we've already learned, was called an *incubus* ("top," or above). The succubus was thought to lure a man into her arms, engage him in sex, and then steal his semen after climax. Once the trickster succubus had the precious bodily fluid, she would bring it to an incubus, who would in turn seduce a human woman, only to deposit the stolen semen into her womb.[26] The woman would be impregnated by this demonic insemination process and in time give birth to a doomed child. But the offspring of such a union was not itself a demon nor the child of a demon. It was, properly speaking, the offspring of the man whose semen was originally stolen and the woman in whom the semen was deposited. Something in this unholy process of deception, however, created a child that was more susceptible to demonic manipulation later in life.

THE WITCH HUNTER

The most famous manual for understanding, detecting, and vanquishing witches is the 1486 text *Malleus Maleficarum* (The Hammer of Witches), written by the Dominican inquisitor Heinrich Institoris. This German witch hunter synthesized his own significant experience chasing and persecuting witches, but also set the terms for subsequent generations of pious purifiers. Witches were a particularly odious species of the larger genus of heresy, and the Inquisition was busy at work protecting orthodoxy and the Roman papacy. In a 1484 papal bull, *Summis desiderantes affectibus*, Pope Innocent VIII gave Institoris and fellow witch hunter Jakob Sprenger wide-ranging legal powers to pursue and eradicate witches. The bull was used as a justificational preface for Institoris's *Malleus Maleficarum*.

A witch must be understood as a human being who has become a pawn in the various schemes of evil demons. An act of *maleficium*, or harmful magic, requires three things: the evil demon who acts as a puppeteer, the puppet human (or animal) who works the harmful magic, and God's acquiescence. But the puppetry goes both ways: once the human-demon compact has been sworn, the human believes he is manipulating evil spirits to do his bidding. The witch feels like the puppet master... for a while; we all know that *after* the witch's brief reign a terrible price must be paid. But the deeper theological point is that even *while* the human witch has his or her fun, a kind of satanic victory is being enacted in the microcosmic betrayals of these fallen parishioners.

In the very beginning of the *Malleus* Institoris reveals how sophisticated and complex witch theorizing had become in the Middle Ages. There was, for example, a prevalent psychological view of witchery, which the *Malleus* sought to discredit. Extrapolating from the early theories that we encountered in the story of Anthony, there was a school of thought that saw all evil magic and demon activity as pseudo-real. Emblematic of the medieval disputation style, Institoris considers this before he rejects it. Some people, he says, think witchcraft is illusory because "if there were harmful magic in the world, in that case something done by the Devil would exist in opposition to God's creation. Therefore, just as it is illicit to maintain that a superstitious creation of the Devil surpasses something made by God, so it is illicit to believe that created beings and various things made by God, in [the form] of humans and beasts of burden, can be damaged by things which are done by the Devil."[27] In other words, some theorists believed that the Creation is so inherently good (by definition of God himself), that evil must be illusory or fantastical. Moreover, if the demons actually possessed *creative* power in the world, they would be encroaching on God's exclusive power to create. Werewolves, for example, are briefly mentioned in the *Malleus*, and Institoris walks a fine line between a purely psychological theory of man-wolf transmutation and a realist theory. The realist theory contends that the devil or an evil demon actually changes a man into a wolf; in other words, the devil *creates* a wolf where there was none a moment ago. But properly speaking, only God can create something de novo, and only God has the power to twist one species into another (an essential transformation), so this position is dangerously heretical. If this realist view is too strong, however, the psychological theory is too weak. The whole point of Institoris's *Malleus* is to establish the very real dangers of witches and witchcraft, so it will not suffice to take the "it's all in your head" approach. A man may become deluded and think that he has become a werewolf, Institoris explains, but that delusion is not pure fantasy. The illusion itself is caused by *malefici*, workers of harmful magic. For Institoris, there are occasional physiological hallucinations in the way we would define them today, as groundless subjective fictions caused by the body. But there are many more spirit-based misperceptions. There are good and evil apparitions, sent to us from somewhere, and the trick is to be able to discriminate the sacred from the demonic.

Institoris says that wolves will sometimes "snatch adults and children out of their houses and eat them; and they will run all over the place with great cunning, and cannot be hurt or captured by any skill, or body of men."[28] This might be the result of natural causes, as when packs of wolves experience famine or humans get between a bitch and its pups, but Institoris rejects mundane explanations and says, "I maintain they happen through an illusion [created by] evil spirits when God punishes a people on account of its sins."[29] The man-eating wolves may be real animals, or they may be evil spirits appearing in that shape, or they may be real animals who have been possessed by evil spirits, but they're probably not men who have been transformed into wolves. Institoris tells a story of a man "who used to think he was being turned into a wolf, and at these times he would hide in caves. He went there on one particular occasion and although he stayed there all the while without moving, he had the impression he had become a wolf and was going round, devouring children; and although in fact it was only an evil spirit who had possessed a wolf and was doing this, [the man] mistakenly thought (while he was dreaming) that *he* was prowling around." Eventually this poor fellow became completely deranged by the mental illness, and they found him dithering in a forest. This madness is precisely the sort of effect that evil spirits enjoy, and such confusion, Institoris adds, is what led pre-Christian pagans to erroneously believe that people could actually transform into animals.

ILLUSION OR REALITY?

The *Malleus* argues throughout for this middle way between witchcraft that's too real, and therefore in violation of God's goodness and power, and witchcraft that is not real enough, but purely imaginative. Earlier demonologists, such as Aquinas and the authors of the influential *Canon Episcopi*,[30] argued that the frightening visions and shape-shifting episodes associated with witchcraft were really just dream-like phantasms. If any mischievous manipulation is occurring to a man who thinks he's a were-wolf, or sees his hand spin around on his wrist, or experiences aerial lift-off on a broom, the cause would have to sneak in, according to these more skeptical demonologists, at the physiological juncture where his "imaginative faculty" meets his "interior senses." The imaginative faculty is described as a "treasure house" in each person that stores or preserves visible shapes, such as the images of animals. It's a treasure house of memories. If some evil spirit were to trigger this storage faculty just right, it would flood the perceptual senses and give the person the illusory experience of real external stimuli. A mundane version of this happens all the time, when bodily humors trigger the treasure house in sleep and we subsequently dream.

Institoris breaks with this more prosaic version of witchcraft and offers a clever way to get demons back in their threatening positions. Works of evil, he says, are not just indigestion-like fabrications of the body. They are real and they are happening in the external world; the hand is really spinning, the children are really being eaten by wolves, the witches are really taking flight. But how is it done, if only God has true creative power?

Evil spirits, according to Institoris, do not make something from nothing when they enact their transgressions; that would truly violate the cardinal notion of a monotheistic God. It may seem that demons and their witches conjure monsters and terrors from thin air, but they do not really create in such an absolute manner. Instead, the demons have an amazing understanding of the Book of Nature. They grasp the first principles, fundamental springs, and material trajectories of physical nature itself. Demons were manipulative "scientists" long before this modern sense of the term even existed. They are the ultimate alchemists.[31]

When demons do shape-shifting and other seemingly supernatural marvels, they are not creating so much as altering nature. According to Institoris, the evil ones sift the matter of nature to find the seeds (*semina*) of transformation, and then use these micro-agents as catalysts for their own nefarious inventions.[32] Demons transform nature more by chemistry than by magic. Just as the form of the oak tree exists as a germ in the acorn, so too all of nature is filled with microseeds that, when triggered, alter the perceivable world in significant ways. Demons understand these mechanisms, which are invisible to humans, and they engineer outcomes in ways that look miraculous to us. By this subtle knowledge of nature witches appear to predict the future, but they cannot really do so, as God can. In this way, Institoris explains how demons and witches create mayhem in the world, but he avoids the heresy. Demons simply *alter* nature in ways that scare and frighten us and seem supernatural.[33] Now we finally see why "God's acquiescence" is frequently intoned in the explanation of witchcraft offered in the *Malleus*. The logic is this: even if witchcraft is only altering nature rather than creating it, it's still doing significant damage in the world. Nature is being altered by demons in ways that allow witches to kill their neighbors with clay effigies and pins. And letting insignificant chump demons and their paltry witch covens undo the beautiful divine cosmic plan would reflect very badly on God, unless God was actually giving his permission for this suffering. *Why* he gives his permission to let demons and witches turn some kid's hand upside down is really beyond the speculative power or will of the demonologist. What matters is that the witch's monstrous activity has been theoretically integrated with Christianity.

MONSTROUS DESIRES REVISITED

Metaphysics aside, the fascinating psychological dimension of all this inquisitorial interest in fornication is often given a Freudian interpretation. Sexual repression probably makes sense out of much of the tone of Catholic writings about sexuality and the body, but then one still wants to know more about why the repression developed in the first place. Repression is a tool for handling the always threatening emotional brand of possession. This topic is too vast to engage here, but some brief comparison with the ancients regarding monstrous eros seems useful.

In the same way that desire, in its most primitive form, frightened the ancient Greeks and Romans, erotic urges also plagued the medievals. The *Malleus* portrays almost all such cases of lust as cases of demonic possession or witch manipulation. Whereas the possession language tended toward the metaphorical in many ancient sources, it becomes quite literal in the *Malleus*. The loss of rational control and the fire in the loins seem perennial, but the cause of these symptoms is now clearly identified as Satan and his minions.

Institoris tells a brief story to illustrate the corruption of "those subject to excessive love or hatred." In the diocese of Konstanz, Germany, a beautiful virgin lived simply and piously. A "certain man of loose character" took a lascivious interest in her; in fact he was entirely overcome with the infatuation. "After a while he did not have the strength to conceal the wound to his sanity. So he came to the field where the said virgin was working and, expressing himself decorously, revealed that he was in the net of an evil spirit." She rebuffed his advances; he grew angry and vowed to have her by magical means, if need be. They parted. Sometime later, after an interval of feeling "not a spark of carnal love for the man in herself," the virgin began to "have amorous fantasies about him." By most standards, this eros episode is pretty mild stuff, no real drama to speak of. But even here, when the actors appear to be in relative possession of themselves, Institoris is convinced that demons are squirming in every act of the tepid tryst. The horror of giving in to temptation is averted, thankfully, when the virgin makes haste to her confessor and unloads the terrible burden of her wicked feelings. Confession, together with a pilgrimage to a holy site, sets the girl in order and, more important, smooths the bumpy terrain of her soul so that no demon can find traction there and no male witch can coerce her emotions with magical techniques.

Lack of self-control, here made literal as possession and magical manipulation, is the same monster we encountered before. But the difference between Stoic madness and Christian is that not only can you no longer answer to yourself, tossed and frayed as you are by your own craving, but now you can no longer answer to God. Taming your internal monsters is not only good advice for living well (the Greek *eudemonia*), but now it is also allegiance to the will and plan of the deity.

All this talk of discipline and desire raises an important general question about witches, one that Institoris addresses directly. Granted that they

Demonization and gender. An example of "woman as dangerous monster." Here, in Felicien Rops's drawing *The Organ of the Devil*, we find Satan unveiling the tempting nude female. Sexual liberation has played an ongoing role in the clash of civilizations. From Edward Lucie-Smith and Aline Jacquiot, *The Waking Dream: Fantasy and the Surreal in Graphic Art 1450–1900* (Knopf, 1975).

could be found in either gender, why were so many of the accused witches women? One answer is that women were considered the carnal flashpoints for any man's spiritual journey. Just as God was using demons to punish fallen humans, demons were using women to tempt the fall of priests, monks, and husbands. Women could be highly effective tools in the devil's attempt to dismantle men.[34] But another explanation, more physiological in tone, held that women were more completely dominated by sexual lust; their receptacle natures were always in need of filling, and this made them crave penetration. Institoris says that one part of the woman that "never says 'enough'" is the "mouth of the womb." Consequently, women's amorous condition makes them easy targets for demons who wish to find some way to influence affairs. And this natural lustful condition makes women proficient temptresses without much effort or study. All the other usual stereotypes are trotted out to buttress this view: a woman is more credulous and therefore open to superstition; a woman will talk incessantly in groups and therefore easily transmit the demonic information, creating covens; and "when she hates someone she previously loved, she seethes with anger and cannot bear it," therefore she is quick to engage in the revenge and retribution tactics so prevalent among witches.

DRIVING OUT THE DEMONS

Finally, we must turn to solutions. What can be done about these monsters? How can we defeat the demons and the witches? Witches were tested using trials by ordeal (e.g., carrying red-hot iron, being dunked in water, being pricked) and torture (e.g., stretching and dislocating limbs with ropes and levers, and virtually anything else a sadistic imagination can dream up). How one interpreted the trial by ordeal was rather inconsistent; some accepted a miraculous ability to carry hot iron as evidence of innocence and God's favor, while others (Institoris in some passages) suggested that such lack of injury be taken as satanic protection. When the witch confessed to black arts and named others, she was often exiled, imprisoned, burned, or hanged. When the witch refused to confess such atrocities, particularly after significant torture, she was said to be especially strengthened by Satan and subsequently sentenced to burning or hanging. Not much rehabilitation or healing existed for witches, only degrees of punishment.

Those who were possessed were in a different position. In the case of possession, the person afflicted was not considered to be evil or malicious but set upon, not entirely responsible for his or her actions. In these cases, the person's monstrous behavior could be exorcised and he or she could be restored to fully human status. Interestingly, Institoris notes that when exorcism fails after multiple attempts, the victim may have been misdiagnosed and probably deserves his or her condition as a divine punishment.

A typical exorcism is outlined by Institoris.[35] It's best if a cleric performs the function, but anyone of good character can do it if necessary. First, the afflicted person must be made to confess. Next, a careful search of the home must be made to detect any magical implements (e.g., amulets, effigies), and these must be burned. It is important to get the individual into a church at this point, and he or she should be made to hold a blessed candle while righteous witnesses pray over him or her. This should be repeated three times a week to restore grace, and the victim should receive the holy sacrament. In stubborn cases, the beginning phrases of John's Gospel should be written on a tablet and hung around the person's neck, and holy water should be applied liberally. If exorcism ultimately fails, then either the person is being punished by God and has to be surrendered, or the faith of the exorcist was not strong enough and new administrators might be brought in.

The message of medieval monsterology is that the causes and cures of monsters are spiritual in nature. Human pride may bring them out, but they are metaphysically real. Heroism of the pagan variety will not conquer the monsters. Only submission to God and humility will beat back the enemy.

PART

Scientific Monsters

The Book of Nature Is Riddled with Typos

9

Natural History, Freaks, and Nondescripts

We ought to make a collection of all monsters and prodigious births,
and everything new, rare, and extraordinary in nature.
LORD FRANCIS BACON

I must have the fat boy or some other monster or something new.
P. T. BARNUM

THE HYDRA

IN THE 1730S A YOUNG Carl Linnaeus stood before a monstrous
creature in Hamburg. Legend held that the creature had been killed
several centuries earlier and its stuffed remains looted after the 1648
battle with Prague, eventually becoming the prized possession of Count
Konigsmark. When Linnaeus examined it, the creature had only recently
come into the collection of the burgomaster of Hamburg. Linnaeus, who
later became the greatest naturalist of the modern era (second only to Darwin perhaps), had traveled from his home in Sweden to examine the "curiosities" of the continent, including Jews (who were then banned in Sweden).[1]

The monster of the burgomaster's cabinet, with seven heads, sharp teeth,
frightening claws, and a giant snake-like body, was called a hydra. It was
already a well-known subject of the science of the day because drawings of
it had been included in many celebrated natural history compendia, such
as Albertus Seba's *Thesaurus*. The hydra of Hamburg was just one of many
monsters populating the collections and imaginations of eighteenth-century
Europeans, and it represented the frightening unknown dimension of a

A drawing of the hydra monster that Linnaeus eventually debunked as a taxidermy hoax. From Albertus Seba's compendium *Cabinet of Natural Curiosities,* republished by Taschen Books, 2005. Reprinted by kind permission of Taschen Books.

nature that was permeated with the *supernatural*. For Linnaeus and many other gentile Europeans, Jews and hydras and other aliens represented the sublimely vast and menacing *terra incognita*, an unknown frontier, barely touched by the tiny border where new sciences forged ahead.

When Linnaeus arrived to study the hydra, the burgomaster was in negotiations to sell the monster at a significant profit; even the king of Denmark had made an offer. But Linnaeus's careful eye detected the skilled hand of a deceptive taxidermist. The clawed feet and the teeth appeared to be taken from large weasels; the body was a graft of mammal parts carefully covered in places with various snake skins. Linnaeus believed that the creature had been fashioned by Christian monks to serve as frightening evidence to the faithful that the Apocalypse was imminent. He conjectured that the creature was supposed to be a portentous dragon from the Book of Revelation fabricated to scare the wayward flock.

News of Linnaeus's discovery spread quickly, and the price of the burgomaster's trophy plummeted. Reading the writing on the wall, Linnaeus left town, lest he himself become a taxidermied trophy.

The story of Linnaeus debunking the apocalyptic monster is characteristic of the new scientific era. Science was on the rise, and monsters

A dragon from Ulisse Aldrovandi's sixteenth-century *Natural History of Snakes and Dragons*. From *Dover Pictorial Archive Series, 1300 Real and Fanciful Animals, from Seventeenth-century Engravings by Matthaus Merian the Younger* (Dover Publications, 1998).

were being exposed as hoaxes or were being cleaned up and fit into the new system of uniform natural laws. Linnaeus himself became the great classifier of animal and plant species, genera, families, orders, classes, and phyla. A conceptual grid of hierarchic categories had been laid over the teeming chaos of nature, and a calm order had been imposed on the seemingly infinite diversity of God's creation. But monsters, from Aristotle's time to the present, always disrupt the neat categories of taxonomy and pose irritating anomalies for science. Hybrids and border-crossing beings are fanciful (like the griffin or centaur) but also real (like the platypus and the slime mold), and the scientific demystification happens only slowly and laboriously. The knowledge that unicorns do not belong in legitimate natural history came arduously, by degrees, whereas the platypus, sent to Europe as a stuffed specimen, was long considered a fake because scientists found the weird creature impossible to believe.[2]

Eventually creatures that seemed to exist between taxonomic categories, together with other data sources, led to serious questions about the ontology of species. But all of that came later. In this section I want to discuss the earlier forms of skepticism, the forms that naturalized the animal kingdom by removing it from the moral sphere of medieval spiritualism. Monstrous species, as the extreme fringes of the animal kingdom, were slowly reconsidered under the conceptual lenses of the new life sciences. But human attraction to and repulsion from the grotesque could not be expunged entirely, even with the new rigorous natural history. Fresh marvels, both hoaxes and realities, continued to excite the more sober endeavors of life science.

Woodcut of a sea monster in Konrad Gesner's credulous sixteenth-century natural history. From *Curious Woodcuts of Fanciful and Real Beasts: A Selection of 190 Sixteenth-century Woodcuts from Gesner's and Topsell's Natural History* (Dover Publications, 1971).

The medieval *Liber Monstrorum* (discovered with the *Beowulf* text) is a forerunner of later scientific monster skepticism and a taste of prescientific incredulity.[3] The doubt was strangely selective and seemed aimed more at pagan poets and philosophers, but nonetheless it expressed a nagging question that continued to grow until reaching a crescendo in the seventeenth and eighteenth centuries: Which exotic creatures are real and which are fake?[4]

It did not help matters that in the prescientific era most zoology was explicitly religious and moral. One of the most influential works of allegorical zoology from the early Middle Ages through the early modern era was the encyclopedia of animals known as the *Physiologus*. Of unknown authorship, the originally Greek *Physiologus* dates back to second-century Alexandria but became highly influential several centuries later, when it resurfaced in Latin translation. Together with St. Isidore's later *Etymologiae*, the *Physiologus* inspired a whole tradition of medieval animal allegories, usually illustrated, called "bestiaries." This allegorical tradition often repeated and embellished the same list of creatures; early versions contained animals and legends from the Mediterranean and North Africa, and later versions incorporated the fauna and fables of northern Europe. It bears mentioning that monsters often had their origin in the specific animal threats of a geographic region. In the imaginative construction of a frightening beast, a folk culture will frequently embellish the local predators rather than compose a completely novel monster. The medieval monster folklore of northern Europe, for example, drew heavily on the devouring wolf as an archetype of monstrosity.[5]

Very slowly the allegorical tradition gave way to more objective zoology. In the early seventeenth century the gradual turn from magical thinking to science had major implications for monsters. Francis Bacon (1561–1626), who said, "We must make a collection or particular natural history of all the monsters and prodigious products of nature,"[6] argued that systematic knowledge would surface only after we amassed collections and specimens in warehouses of study, called "Solomon's houses." In his highly influential book *The New Atlantis* (1626), Bacon imagined scientific societies where researchers would work together sharing information and conducting experiments. "The end of our foundation is the knowledge of causes, and secret motions of things; and the enlarging of the bounds of human empire, to the effecting of all things possible."[7]

To this end, real scientific societies began to form in the century that followed Bacon's call for Solomon's houses, including England's Royal Society, France's Academy of Sciences, and the American Philosophical Society. These groups embraced the new empirical epistemology: that knowledge derives from experimental observation rather than scripture and classical tradition. Skepticism had graduated from suspicion of other cultures (e.g., the *Liber Monstrorum*'s distrust of pagan sources) to suspicion of *all* folk superstition. The savants of this era believed that a universal rationality operated below the surface of idiosyncratic cultural bias and could be accessed through careful empirical analysis and mathematics. Bacon argued that science should build itself from the bottom up using inductive reasoning; particular observations come first, then axioms or hypotheses and, once corroborated, laws of nature could then be stated. But concerning monsters and natural history, the work was always fraught with obdurate gullibility.

When we collect monstrous specimens, Bacon argued, we must be careful of men who practice "natural magic or alchemy" and also those who are "suitors and lovers of fables." Gullibility seems to be the norm when cataloguing nature, so he argued that whatever we admit into our new scientific system must be "drawn from serious and credible history and trustworthy reports."

In the tradition of Bacon's skepticism, Thomas Browne (1605–1682) published a compendium of "vulgar errors" called *Pseudodoxia epidemica* (1646) in which he rolled his eyes, so to speak, at the legends of griffins and other monsters.[8] He argued that when the Bible and other revered texts refer to the griffin, they are only referring to a large bird, and that the idea of a hybrid monster has come down to us through hyperbolic

Sketch of a sea-devil in Ambroise Paré's sixteenth-century book *On Monsters*. From Ernst Lehner, *Symbols, Signs and Signets* (Dover Publications, 1969).

embellishment of the original meaning. Furthermore, he suggested that any direct references to the griffin's hybrid status can be shown to be directly or indirectly derivative of the old Aristeas legend of the Arimaspean war with the Griffin, a legend that has no outside corroboration.[9]

The generations of naturalists that followed Bacon and Browne began to emphasize taxonomy, the rational naming and grouping of species. This method began to produce new compendia that, unlike the pell-mell bestiaries that listed animals alphabetically, had some logical organization, grouping animals according to common environment, common morphology, common physiological function, or other criteria. It wasn't enough anymore to pile together a bunch of mundane and fantastical creatures, only to point out their Christ-like symbolism. Naturalists such as Linnaeus, Buffon, Lamarck, Geoffroy, and Cuvier were discovering the inner logic of nature, referring nature to *itself* rather than the deity.

In addition to developing a common language, Linnaeus's Latin binomial nomenclature, naturalists also began to use the pictorial tradition (e.g., woodcuts, etchings, illuminations, pencil illustrations) to sift through the credible and incredible history of animals. If multiple drawings done by different sources of an exotic creature all conveyed a similar shape and comportment, one could feel more confident about those data. If, however, an image only reproduced earlier images (as the bestiaries did) without actual firsthand observation, then those data fell into a dubious category. The gaps in the fence of acceptable knowledge

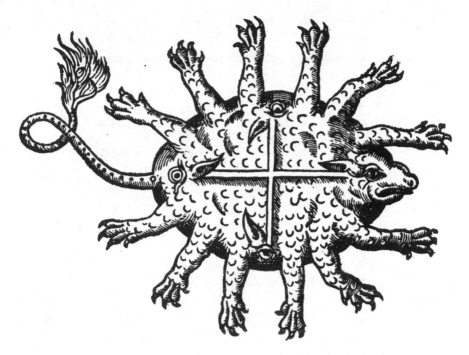

Ambroise Paré's "very monstrous animal that is born in Africa," in his book *On Monsters*. From Ernst Lehner, *Symbols, Signs and Signets* (Dover Publications, 1969).

were closing and leaving monsters and fantastical creatures outside in a kind of limbo.

The unicorn, for example, was a fantastic creature whose pedigree went back to Ctesias and Pliny; it appeared in the Bible (the King James translation), and it regularly appeared as an incarnation symbol in the bestiaries. But Harriet Ritvo points out that as scientific collecting and classifying progressed, the unicorn seemed more and more unlikely. The only physical evidence of such a creature was the horn that populated many early European curiosity cabinets. By the middle of the eighteenth century, however, these long straight horns were successfully identified as the tusks of the arctic narwhale (*Monodon monoceros*). "By the end of the Victorian period 'unicorn's horns' had come, in the eyes of progressive modern curators, to symbolize the dark ages of museology."[10]

As Linnaeus and other sober-minded naturalists deflated taxidermied hoaxes, and other bones and evidence were reduced to more mundane phenomena, the old favorites began to die out. Talk of Cynocephali, Blemmyae, Sciopodes, and Cyclopes faded away. All this science, with its orderly systematizing, certainly managed to expose some monster superstitions, myths, and frauds. But immediately on the heels of the Enlightenment one finds a new and more extreme taste for the fantastical in the form of the disorderly, the exotic, the freakish, the monstrous. In the Victorian era a taste for the abnormal, usually still disguised as "science," burst forth, gorging on all manner of freak show and bizarre spectacle.

RESPONDING TO THE MARVELOUS

One way to help us navigate the various attitudes toward monsters, especially during the birth of science, can be found in the "three levels of response to the marvelous" defined by the historian Madeleine Doran.[11] Around the time that Shakespeare was composing *Macbeth*, the British naturalist Edward Topsell was publishing his bestiary. Nature, at this time, was only half extricated from magical thinking. Shakespeare's plays are filled with exotic creatures, ghosts, and witchcraft,[12] and audiences of the day could enjoy these plays on three different levels.

First, an audience could accept fully and uncritically the marvelous phenomena. This is full-on credulity. When Shakespeare draws back the curtain on the witches of *Macbeth*, or even the humorous characters of Puck and the ass-headed Bottom in *A Midsummer Night's Dream*, the first kind of response is innocent belief. No doubt many in Shakespeare's audience would have accepted the reality of witches, and even the reality of waking up with a donkey's head where one's normal head once perched. A witness to such phenomena, whether it be on stage or in a beer-house traveler's tale, would not flinch from accepting it as true. In this modality, a Shakespearean patron accepts a witch in precisely the same uncritical way that I, at a contemporary play, accept the storyline of a character who's dying from radiation poisoning. The latter is not in my immediate range of everyday experiences, but reports of it are widespread enough in the general culture for me to accept it without hesitation. And we don't have to go all the way back to Shakespeare's day to find credulous responses to witches, demons, and supernatural transformations. Many people today accept the literal reality of demon possession and exorcism, which shows us how these "responses to the marvelous" can be transhistorical categories of belief.

The second mode of response to the marvelous is intermediate, the "entertainment of the possibility without actual belief; it often arises from a conflict between a rational attitude of skepticism and an emotional willingness to believe." Here one humorously protests and even ridicules the believers in witches or werewolves, but then quickens one's pace and furtively clutches one's crucifix while crossing the moor at dusk. Here, too, one loudly denounces the superstitions of the day, but then on another occasion knocks on wood when describing one's good health. The Shakespearean audience would have been well stocked with people of this intermediate variety. They might have mocked or raised their eyebrows at the ghost and witch characters, but they couldn't help feeling the fears and worries that attend such creatures.

The third response to the marvelous is the suspension of disbelief. Here one confidently disbelieves in the marvelous phenomena but willingly plays along with the fiction in order to extract some symbolic or imaginative satisfaction. Shakespearean audiences would have taken this attitude toward the Greek pagan gods and monsters that occasionally made it onto the Elizabethan stage, and we today similarly suspend our disbelief when considering an Elizabethan witch hunt story. The devil, as he appears in Marlowe's *Doctor Faustus*, for example, must have been much more real to the Elizabethans than he is for us. For many of today's fans of the Faust story, the devil is embraced provisionally as response mode 3, but for early moderns he would have elicited response modes 1 and 2. To underscore the transhistorical aspect of these modes: today's evangelical Pentecostal will likely respond to the devil in art, media, and scripture in much the same way as the Elizabethan did.

In Shakespeare's *Othello* the Moor is accused of using witchcraft to lure Desdemona into marrying him. He defends himself by explaining that he simply wooed her with his rich and exotic travel stories. Othello mentions the headless Blemmyae, though not by name, in Act 1, Scene 3:

> Wherein I spake of most disastrous chances,
> Of moving accidents by flood and field
> Of hair-breadth scapes i' the imminent deadly breach,
> Of being taken by the insolent foe
> And sold to slavery, of my redemption thence
> And portance in my travels' history:
> Wherein of antres vast and deserts idle,
> Rough quarries, rocks and hills whose heads touch heaven
> It was my hint to speak,—such was the process;
> And of the Cannibals that each other eat,
> The Anthropophagi and men whose heads
> Do grow beneath their shoulders. This to hear
> Would Desdemona seriously incline:
> But still the house-affairs would draw her thence:
> Which ever as she could with haste dispatch,
> She'd come again, and with a greedy ear
> Devour up my discourse.

The appearance of men "whose heads do grow beneath their shoulders" is included in *Othello* without irony or satire. The Blemmyae are symbolic monsters, indicating the foreign, exotic aspect of Othello himself; only a man of the world would have encountered these far-off creatures. But it is likely that Shakespeare's audience would have *responded* to the headless monsters using modalities 1 and 2, not the suspension of disbelief. Audience members would have accepted, intellectually or at least emotionally, the reality of headless monsters. As natural history progressed in the two centuries that followed, the marvelous monsters shifted (for the most part) into the third modality. Now when an audience enjoys Shakespeare's plays the exotic monsters are merely quaint or symbolic.

The purpose of introducing these three monster modalities is to provide us with a transhistorical way of expressing the diversity of responses or attitudes in any given historical era; one mode may be dominant in the educated classes (e.g., suspension of disbelief) at the same time that another modality (credulity) is strong in the unlettered classes. We might now extend the tripartite model well beyond its original formulation, into the nineteenth-century fascination with nondescripts, freaks, and monsters.

A MISCHIEVOUS TAXIDERMIST

By the early 1800s natural history had come a long way from its wonder-cabinet days. And yet, in this sober era of straight science, we find the hilarious and grotesque nondescript specimens of Charles Waterton (1782–1865). Waterton was born into an upper-class British family in Yorkshire, one that proudly traced its family tree back to Sir Thomas More. But Charles preferred the life of the explorer to that of the Yorkshire gentleman and famously traveled throughout South America (in 1812, 1816, 1820, and 1824), recording observations and collecting specimens. Many of his findings about the tropical flora and fauna of places like Guyana and Brazil were celebrated by the scientific community via Waterton's friendship with Sir Joseph Banks, the president of the Royal Society. Waterton had a reputation for eccentricity, first for being a Roman Catholic in otherwise Protestant England, and then for his habits of walking barefoot in parks and regularly climbing trees well into old age to read Latin poetry.

Waterton described many natural monsters of the tropics, including Camoudi snakes (anacondas) that grew to be "forty-feet long" (local legend putting them at eighty feet), twelve-foot long caimans that "just keep their heads above water, and a stranger would not know them from a rotten stump," and vampire bats that plagued every veined creature of the region.[13] "At the close of the day," Waterton reports, "the vampires leave the hollow trees, whither they had fled at the morning's dawn, and scour along the river's banks in quest of prey. On waking from sleep, the astonished traveler finds his hammock all stained with blood. It is the vampire that hath sucked him. Not man alone, but every unprotected animal, is exposed to his depredations: and so gently does this nocturnal surgeon draw the blood, that instead of being roused, the patient is lulled into a still profounder sleep."

As another illustration of the credulity problem for naturalists, who were regularly faced with exotic monsters that didn't fit into known categories, we should note Waterton's sloth. Certain legends about the sloth had already traveled to Europe, but Waterton debunked the "exaggerated history" of the creature, which included the idea that it was in a "perpetual state of pain," and offered descriptions from the field: "Man but little frequents these thick and noble forests, which extend far and wide on every side of us. This then is the proper place to go in quest of the sloth."[14] When he reported that the strange creature lived its entire life hanging upside-down from tree branches, he was openly mocked by colleagues back home; they found the behavior and the described morphology unbelievable. "When the reviewers impugned his veracity," according to his biographer, J. G. Wood, "he troubled himself very little about them, saying that the creatures which he had described would one day find their way to the Zoological Gardens, and then that everybody would see that he had but spoken the truth."[15]

In addition to taxidermied specimens of many of these exotic creatures, and in a seemingly defiant mocking of his critics, Waterton proffered even more extreme "border-line" creatures. He returned to England with a strange humanoid monster that could not be fit into any known taxonomic group, so it was called a "nondescript." Waterton describes his acquisition of the oddity:

> I also procured an animal which has caused not a little speculation and astonishment. In my opinion, his thick coat of hair, and great length of tail, put his species out of all question; but then his face and head cause the inspector to pause for a moment, before he ventures to pronounce his opinion of the classification. He was a large animal, and as I was pressed for daylight, and moreover, felt no inclination to have the whole weight of his body upon my back, I contented myself with his head and shoulders, which I cut off: and have brought them with me to Europe.[16]

He continued to pique the reader's curiosity by wondering if there were other such creatures skulking through the tropical jungle. After all, another specimen procured by the courageous explorer could confirm the existence of a new humanoid species. "Should anybody be induced to go, great and innumerable are the discoveries yet to be made in those remote wilds." He closes the discussion by acknowledging the skeptics. Some had accused Waterton of creating an elaborate hoax with his nondescript, but he protested that nobody to date had the taxidermy skills to effect such a beautiful fraud. "If I have succeeded in effacing the features of a brute, and putting those of a man in their place, we might be entitled to say, that the sun of Proteus has risen on our museums."

But masterful taxidermy fraud was precisely what Waterton had created. He had built the convincing bust of the nondescript by using the head and shoulders of the red howler monkey. Using his own novel techniques, he shaved the flesh from the back of the animal's face until he had created a thin layer of skin that he could manipulate into all manner of creature. In addition, he found that two skins similarly prepared could be molded together when wet to create the illusion of a hybrid animal. He was a taxidermy genius, and he used his skills to prank his stuffy professional peers and the gullible lay audience. So convincing was his humanoid grotesque that some observers complained that Waterton should not be allowed to kill natives in order to demonstrate his taxidermy skills. But an early reviewer called him out on his mischievous monster, claiming that the nondescript looked suspiciously like a well-known master in Chancery from the House of Commons. "It is foolish," the reviewer said, "to trifle with science and natural history."[17]

As if natural history wasn't troubled enough by real oddities, pranksters like Waterton added confusion to the attempts to order and organize nature. He created other composite hoax creatures, such as the "Noctifer" (part eagle, owl, and heron), and he severely twisted a monkey into a devilish smiling humanoid that he privately titled "Martin Luther After His Fall." Hucksters like Waterton reveal that, in the history of monsters, the scientific cleanup of superstitions only reorients people back to the animal monsters. Religious monsters such as demons and witches eventually submerged below the intellectual cultures of the West, but new zoological cryptids, more in keeping with *natural* monsters of the ancient world, took their place in the imaginations of both official and popular cultures.

FREAKS

The nineteenth century may have been an era of acute hucksterism because it corresponded with the increasingly public mass-media culture, which included print media but also large-scale public museums and fairs.[18] The professionalizing of science had become relatively successful in the eighteenth century, but all that newly acquired and standardized knowledge needed to be transmitted from gentlemen peers to the working-class masses. The marvelous was employed by educators as the hook experience for instruction and edification. The American naturalist Charles Wilson Peale (1741–1827), for example, started a noble edutainment philosophy of "rational amusement" for the masses, but P. T. Barnum (1810–1891) eventually purchased Peale's collection and increased the "amusement" part of the philosophy, gradually relegating the "rational" part to less and less value.

P. T. Barnum, the self-proclaimed "Prince of Humbug," has to be mentioned here, in the context of natural history monsters. His "Feejee Mermaid" alone would qualify him for any discussion of liminal creatures, but that curious specimen was only one of many nondescripts and oddities. After unsuccessful attempts at being a newspaper man, a grocer, and a lottery agent, Barnum entered show business at age twenty-five. In 1835 he purchased and exhibited an African American slave, Joice Heth, as the "nurse of George Washington." He claimed that she was over 160 years old and that she had tended the dying General Washington. She died one year later, but before her demise she made Barnum a decent amount of money and he had glimpsed the potential prosperity of showmanship. He capitalized twice on the Joice Heth scam because he also sold his inside story about the hoax to any newspaper that would buy. In 1840 the *New York Atlas* wrote, "We are now in possession of all the facts, documents, etc. connected with the origin, progress and termination of the exhibition of Joyce Heth, who was palmed upon the public with perfect success, as the nurse of Gen. Washington, aged 161 years! The truth is, she was not eighty years old when she died in 1836! The extraordinary developments and amusing, side-breaking anecdotes connected with this exhibition, illustrates the potent power of HUMBUG and the gullibility of mankind in a most eminent degree."[19]

Obviously the nurse of General Washington (hoax or not) is only a historical curiosity, not a monster. But Barnum's genius was in his recognition that people would stand in line and pay for all manner of curiosities— historical, zoological, or teratological. Throughout his long career Barnum did not bother to separate the historical from the "scientific" or the purely entertaining. Curiosities were curious, no matter what their domain. Sometimes the curiosity was totally bogus, as in the case of Joice Heth, but sometimes the curiosity was a manifestly interesting body or face or creature repackaged and publicized with a bogus narrative. In this blending of natural, historical, and artificial marvels, the spirit of his collecting tendencies ran along the much earlier tracks of European *wunderkammern*.

Monsters, grotesques, and nondescripts simply formed one branch of Barnum's tree of wondrous offerings.

After the success of Joice Heth, Barnum created a small touring circus called Barnum's Grand Scientific and Musical Theatre. In 1841 he became the proprietor of the American Museum in New York, and a year later he hit the jackpot with the "Feejee Mermaid" and "Tom Thumb." The Feejee Mermaid was a taxidermy hoax that must have been somewhat convincing in its day.[20] Its hybrid body, the top half of a monkey fused to the bottom half of a large fish, fooled a reporter at the *Philadelphia Public Ledger*, among many others. After an effusive paean about the gloriousness of living in the "era of progress," the reporter gleefully proclaimed, "The greatest discovery yet made is still to be announced, and it is left for us to make the fact public."

> *We have seen a mermaid!!* Start not and curl your lips in scorn, though concerning a fish it is not a *fish story*. We have seen the tangible evidence exhibited to our senses. Of the existence of that monster hitherto deemed fabulous by all the learned, though religiously believed by every salt water naturalist that ever crossed the Gulf Stream.... The monster is one of the greatest curiosities of the day. It was caught near the Feejee Islands, and taken to Penambuco, where it was purchased by an English gentleman named Griffin, who is making a collection of rare and curious things for the British Museum, or some other cabinet of curiosities. This animal, fish, flesh or whatever it may be, is about three feet long, and the lower part of the body is a perfectly formed fish, but from the breast upwards this character is lost, and it then approaches human form—or rather that of a monkey.[21]

Barnum drummed up public interest in this specimen by first tantalizing newspaper reporters with a phony story about trying to convince "Dr. Griffin" (also a Barnum fraud) to exhibit his astonishing specimen. Barnum invented a "curating drama" and then complained about it loudly, after which he printed posters and fliers, including illustrations of half-nude women, and eventually, when frenzy was high, announced that Griffin had acquiesced.[22] The public, and the media, swarmed.

In the weeks that followed, newspapers vacillated between astonished credulity and skeptical disgust.[23] But Barnum had succeeded in making significant profits, and he planned to make more. In a letter to his friend and Mermaid co-conspirator Moses Kimball, Barnum reveals his new taste for profitable monsters: "I *must* have the fat boy or the other monster [or] something new in the course of this week.... don't fail!"[24]

In addition to bogus taxidermy, Barnum offered a steady stream of real extraordinary bodies to the paying public; some of the most well-known

Chas Eisenmann's photograph of Fedor Jeftichew, the Russian Dog-faced Boy (ca. 1884). From Michael Mitchell, *Monsters: Human Freaks in America's Gilded Age: The Photographs of Chas Eisenmann* (ECW Press, 2002).

were Tom Thumb (Charles Stratton, a midget), the Siamese Twins (Chang and Eng Bunker, conjoined twins from Thailand), and Jo-Jo the Dog-faced Boy (Fedor Jeftichew, a Russian with hypertrichosis, or werewolf syndrome). Current-day sentiments may find it difficult to see Barnum's relationship with his "curiosities" as anything but exploitive, but in fact the relationship between the exhibitor and the exhibits was more complex. Tom Thumb was trained and displayed by Barnum from the time he was four years old, but he eventually became a contracted *partner* with Barnum and a wealthy man as a result, even lending money to Barnum when certain speculations failed. Some curiosities were presented with little dignity (Jo-Jo the Dog-faced Boy was expected to bark like a dog); the Siamese Twins, the Bearded Lady, and William Tillman the Colored Civil War Hero, among others, were respectfully framed and compensated.

Barnum himself was a character of contradictions—in other words, quite human. His letters reveal a mixture of kind-hearted benevolence, awe, and disdain toward his grotesques. As a showman, he appealed to the most sensationalist side of popular audiences, but he also became a teetotaler and implored his audiences in leaflets, posters, and lectures to abstain from drink and to live piously.

One of Barnum's favorite strategies for luring the gazing public was to make the most of the liminal creature, the unnatural intermediate between natural kinds. A particularly significant liminal monster was Barnum's famous "What Is It?" exhibit. This "non-descript," as Barnum promoted him, was a diminutive man with abnormal physical features (real name, Harvey Leach). Barnum describes his new project in a letter to Moses Kimball: "The *animal* that I spoke to you…about comes out at Egyptian Hall, London next Monday, and I half fear that it will not only be exposed, but that *I* shall be found out in the matter. However, I go it, live or die. The thing is not to be called *anything* by the exhibitor. We know not and therefore do not assert whether it is human or animal."[25] But the exhibit failed to draw the British public, and Barnum shelved the idea for over a decade.

The supposed appeal of "What Is It?" was the seemingly timeless interest we have in finding some creature that bridges the human-animal divide, something that mixes the ultimate taxonomic domains. Although Harvey Leach, the first "What Is It?" failed in 1846, Barnum's second "What Is It?" an African American man named William Henry Johnson, worked like a charm after 1860. The idea behind the exhibit had come into better fashion after Darwin's 1859 *Origin of Species* put such matters before the public again. Barnum played up the "missing link" question with his new "What Is It?" suggesting in his ads that the creature was a "man-monkey." His flier describes Johnson as "a most singular animal, which, though it has many of the features and characteristics of both the human and the brute, is not, apparently, either, but, in appearance, a mixture of both—the connecting link between humanity and the brute creation."[26] One wonders if the racist dimension of the exhibit, offering a black man as an uncivilized transitional animal, must have played better to an American audience struggling with abolition and race questions than to the earlier audience in England, where slavery had been abolished a century earlier.[27]

William Henry Johnson (1842?–1926), also known as "Zip the Pinhead," was an African American from New Jersey whose head remained small and severely tapered while the rest of his body developed normally. Some have argued that he was a genuine microcephalic, someone with a neurological disorder resulting in reduced head size, but Johnson's normal intelligence throws doubt on that diagnosis. The normal size of his jaw and nose were accentuated and exaggerated by the steep slope of his forehead,

Chas Eisenmann's photograph of William Henry Johnson, otherwise known as Zip the Pinhead (ca. 1885). Zip is pictured on the left, sparring with a "negro turning white." He worked for both Barnum and Ringling. From Michael Mitchell, *Monsters: Human Freaks in America's Gilded Age: The Photographs of Chas Eisenmann* (ECW Press, 2002).

and this allowed Barnum to make the "biological" suggestion of "missing link" status. Barnum dressed him in a furry suit, told audiences that he had been captured in Africa, and choreographed a show that portrayed Johnson's increasing "civilization."

Johnson drew a good salary from Barnum and eventually outlasted the Prince of Humbug, moving on to exhibit himself with the Ringling Brothers Circus. Altogether he worked as a freak for over sixty years. A year before his death, when the famous Scopes monkey trial was raging, the enterprising Johnson even offered to make himself available to the courts as "evidence" of missing links.

Many of us have seen drawings and daguerreotype images of Barnum's famous attractions, but we also have a unique "moving image" access to one of Barnum's late prodigies, "Prince Randian." Prince Randian was born in the 1870s in Guyana with no limbs, just a head and a short torso. Barnum brought him to the United States and displayed him as the "human

caterpillar." He was eventually featured in Tod Browning's highly controversial film *Freaks* (released in 1932 and banned in the United Kingdom
for more than thirty years), where his onscreen presence is both profoundly
surreal as he wriggles his body through a mud puddle, carrying a knife in
his mouth, and also strangely mundane as he rolls and lights a cigarette
using only his mouth. In real life Randian was an intelligent man who
spoke several languages, lived with his wife in New Jersey, and fathered five
children. He died shortly after Browning's film was made.[28] The film's nar-
rator cryptically underscores the "scientific" view of monsters, as opposed
to the spiritual or moral view, when he says, "But for the accident of birth,
you might be even as they are."

The three audience responses I analyzed when discussing Shakespeare's
monsters seem relevant here, too. One could see a sideshow monster and
respond with credulity, skepticism, or some intermediary reaction. In Barnum-style hucksterism, we have completely fabricated monsters, such as
the Feejee Mermaid, but also real disabled or abnormal individuals who
were cloaked in fabricated exotic narratives. Often those fabricated narratives had implicit (and explicit) moral and political significance, as when
white gawkers were inclined to read some monsters as evidence of a racial
chain of being, an old hierarchy to which social Darwinism had given new,
though spurious, credence. Monsters were intrinsically exciting but also
extrinsically useful in giving audiences a sense of relief and possibly even
gratitude about their own station in life.

Beyond these social implications, the purely fantastic monsters were
also remarkably popular. Even when the press had definitively unmasked
the hoax of some pasted-together specimen, people would line up for a
firsthand experience of the spectacle. Like Shakespeare's Blemmyae, these
"natural history" monsters captured the *hearts* of audiences, even while
their *minds* barred entry to the creatures. Barnum regularly claimed that
the American people "loved to be humbugged," but this was not an insult
so much as a declaration of solidarity. The emotions of wonder and amaze-
ment are highly pleasurable, even when our own senses (and our mass
media) turn out to be lying to us.

10

The Medicalization of Monsters

A woman gave birth to a child having two heads, two arms, and four legs,
which I opened; and I found inside only one heart (which monster is in my
house and I keep it as an example of a monstrous thing).

AMBROISE PARÉ

WE HAVE SEEN THAT THE ANCIENTS interpreted monsters as omens or signs. Whether it was the birth of a hermaphrodite child or a one-horned ram, many believed the event to be a message about future military campaigns, the political wind, or the general social welfare. Monsters continued to function as portents throughout the medieval era and well into the modern. In 1642, for example, a London pamphlet reported on a frightening creature that got tangled up in a fishing net, which set the whole region on edge with worry. The pamphlet heralds, "A relation of a terrible monster taken by a fisherman near Wollage, July 15th 1642, and is now seen in King's Street Westminster. The shape whereof is like a toad, and may be called a toad-fish. But that which makes it a monster, is, that it hath hands with fingers like a man, and is chested like a man—being near five foot long and three foot over, the thickness of an ordinary man."[1]

Between four and five o'clock in the morning, Thomas West was casting for salmon when the weight of his submerged net became unaccountably heavy. Thinking he had hit upon a thick school of fish he happily struggled it to the surface, whereupon he drew back in horror. He saw, in the net, "a fiend, not a fish; at the least a monster, not an ordinary creature." The hefty five-foot creature seemed part giant toad and part man, capable of gulping with its wide toothy maw for prey, but also able to paddle-swim with humanoid arms. The posterior of the beast terminated with a whale-like tailfin. Here the author of the pamphlet breaks off from the reportage and muses on the history and significance of this toad-fish monster: "Now the coming up of this monster into the fresh river, and so nigh the shore, is more than remarkable (never any of this strange kind ever having been seen by any age before)." One exception, the reporter notes, is that Pliny "the naturalist" did describe something like a monster toad-fish, but the beast lived far under the sea. Pliny "never saw or heard of any taken upon any coast save one, which was in the year that Nero (that never-sufficiently detested tyrant) was born." Pliny notates this correlation of the toad-fish and Nero by saying "Monstrum praecessit monstro" (an omen precedes the monster). Pliny "plainly divined that its arrival was ominous, as indeed all histories do with constant consent maintain and write, that all unusual births, either in men or brute creatures, in sea or upon land, especially out of their seasons, have ever been the forerunners and sad harbingers of great commotions and tumults in states and kingdoms, if not mournful heralds of utter desolation." At the end of the pamphlet the author crumbles into a stream of prayers, beseeching the Lord for mercy.

The precise significance of a particular prodigy was often turned to some political purpose. In the Reformation era Catholics and Protestants used monsters to foretell the destruction of their opponents. Martin Luther published a pamphlet in 1523 that discussed a monstrous cow born in Freiburg that year. The calf was born with a thick folded skin around its neck and back, making it appear as if clothed in a monk's cowl. In addition to a woodcut depiction of the "monk-calf," Luther's pamphlet included a woodcut of a "pope-ass" monster (part sea creature, part donkey) suppos-edly caught in the Tiber River a few years earlier. These monsters were taken to be living symbols of the corruption and eventual decay of the Roman Church. The monk-calf was like a typical Catholic monk: pious and humble on the outside, but base and brutish on the inside.[2] Luther claimed that two other monsters, one born without a head and another with inverted feet, constituted omens foreshadowing the death of Freder-ick the Wise.[3]

MONSTROUS BIRTHS

In addition to large-scale social meanings, monsters born of human par-ents continued to indicate moral or spiritual depravity in the specific kin. Without any medical understanding of madness, a British broadsheet from 1652 demonstrates the way aberrant behavior was punished with aberrant issue. The sad story of Mary Adams, a resident of Tillingham in Essex, involves her heretical decline into "wickedness."[4] The pregnant woman began to tell her neighbors that she was the Virgin Mary and that "she was conceived with child by the Holy Ghost, and how all the Gospel that had been taught heretofore was false; and that which was in her, she said, was the true Messiah." Mary's revelation was very badly received by her neighbors, who quickly had her locked up in jail. When she eventually went into labor, she struggled for eight days and nights in great agony. On the ninth day she delivered "the most ill-shapen monster that ever eyes beheld; which being dead born, they buried it with speed, for it was so loathsome to behold; for it had neither hands nor feet, but claws like a toad in the place where hands should have been, and every part was odious to behold." "And as for Mary," the pamphlet continues, "who had named herself to be the Virgin Mary, she rotted and consumed as she lay, being from the head to foot as full of botches, blains, boils, and stinking scabs, as ever one could stand by another." All this was a terrible lesson, the pamphleteer explained, reminding us to stay committed to the true faith. Mary had been a pious member of her community until she began to fall in with the "heretical" Anabaptists. After associating with these fringe believers in adult baptism, her entire life unraveled to its monstrous end.

In 1636 John Sadler wrote a book titled *The Sick Woman's Private Looking-Glass*, designed for women who might be worried about giving birth to a monster. In it he gives us evidence of the conceptual turn that was symptomatic of the era, from a spiritual view of monsters to a materialistic view. Sadler begins by reminding his readers that God can punish parents by giving them deformed offspring: "The Divine cause proceeds from the permissive will of God, suffering parents to bring forth such abominations, for their filthie and corrupt affections which are let loose unto wickednesse, like brute beasts that have no understanding." This explains, Sadler continues, why monstrous or otherwise disabled people are not allowed in temples or churches. God does not want monsters to "pollute" his sanctuaries "because the outward deformity of the body is often a signe of the pollution of the heart, as a curse layd upon the child for the parents incontinency." Then Sadler's discussion makes the naturalistic turn that slowly pivots physicians from the seventeenth century right down to Darwin's age: "Yet there are many borne depraved which ought not to bee ascribed unto the infirmity of the parents. Let us therefore search out the naturall cause of their generation, which . . . is either in the matter or in the agent, in the seed or in the wombe."[5]

John Sadler is symptomatic of the sea change in monsterology, but the man who is usually credited with rescuing monsters from the melodramatic arena of spiritual and moral meaning is his predecessor, the French surgeon and scholar Ambroise Paré (1510–1590). His influence was not enough to effect a complete revolution in monsterology, and he himself was highly superstitious, but he paved the way for future medical scientists to study birth anomalies. In the conceptual history of monsters he certainly represents a turn toward the more naturalistic explanation of extraordinary beings.[6]

Paré's book *On Monsters and Marvels* took a relatively empirical approach to monsters, preferring the collection and dissection of oddities rather than the pursuit of hearsay natural history. In fact, he had little interest in the traditional taxonomy pursuits of the natural history tradition that I examined in the previous chapter. Monster races like the Blemmyae and Cynocephali were of little interest compared with human monstrosity.

Paré's *On Monsters* is really a transitional work, steeped in the superstitions of the day but struggling to extricate itself from dead-end research avenues. One finds all the usual ingenuousness about unicorns, sea creatures, and such, but also an attempt to put some monster legends to rest. For example, the incubi and succubi stories reappear in Paré's work, but now they are reconsidered. Recall that these demonic monsters were thought to lure human men and women into sexual encounters, then steal the male semen and plant it in different women. Paré argues against these legendary monsters in a way that demonstrates his naturalistic approach. He says it is "an absurd thing" to believe that devils can take seed from a man and transport it to a woman to effect a pregnancy: "In order to disprove this empty opinion, I shall say only that seed, which is made of blood and spirit [and] which is apt for reproduction, if transported very little [or slowly], or not at all, is immediately corrupted and altered, and consequently its force is completely extinguished, because the warmth and spirit of the heart and of the whole body is absent from it, so much so that the seed is no longer free of excesses, either in quality or in quantity."[7] The seed must go immediately into the woman or it is useless; this is why men with very large penises are usually sterile, because "the seed, having had to take such a long journey, is already cooled before it is received into the womb." Other, similar stories (such as the case of the woman who got pregnant from her contaminated bath water, and the case of the woman who got pregnant from semen she retrieved from the ground) are equally disproved. But then Paré scolds the reader with some basic erotic metaphysics: "You must not believe at all that demons or devils who are of a spirit nature can have carnal knowledge of women; for in the execution of that act flesh and blood are required, which spirits do not have.... Besides, demons are immortal and eternal; what necessity, then, have they of this reproduction, since they have no use for offspring, in as much as they [themselves] will always exist."

Having shown the unreasonableness of such demonic intercourse, Paré offers an explanation of why some people believe they've had supernatural sexual encounters. Sometimes a person reclining in repose will feel as if he is "being oppressed and suffocated by some heavy load on his body, and it comes principally at night; the common people say that it is an old woman who is loading down and compressing the body."[8] But Paré explains that this sensory experience with a succubus is nothing more than severe indigestion: "The cause is most often from having drunk and eaten much too vaporous viands, which have caused an indigestion, from which [viands] great vapors have arisen in the brain which fill one's ventricles, by reason of which the animal faculty—which makes [us] feel and move—is prevented from coming into full luster by the nerves, from which an imaginary suffocation arises, through the lesion which is created as much in the diaphragm as in the lungs and other parts which are used in respiration." Paré has eliminated the succubi and incubi from the list of real monsters and has relegated them to the realm of misinterpretations.

An even more compelling example of his strategy to reduce supernatural to natural causation can be seen in his analysis of hybrid monsters. Creatures that appear to be half-animal and half-human are not the result of supernatural causation; they are not omens or signs sent to us as coded messages. They are more mundane than that. Paré includes in his book many woodcut images of hybrid monsters: a figure of a child-dog fusion, a goat with a man's face, a pig with a man's face and hands, and more. These sad monsters are no mystery, he explains; they are the result of "sodomites and atheists" having sex with animals. These impure humans "join together and break out of their bounds—unnaturally—with animals, and from this are born several hideous monsters that bring great shame to those who look at them or speak of them. Yet, the dishonesty lies in the deed and not in words; and it is, when it is done, a very unfortunate and abominable thing, and a great horror for a man or a woman to mix with or copulate with brute animals; and as a result, some are born half-men and half-animals."[9]

Other kinds of monstrous births are similarly naturalized, albeit less scandalously, as products of material causation. Working somewhat systematically, unlike Gesner, Topsell, and other taxonomic list makers, Paré begins with definitions of terms and then proceeds to causes. "Monsters," he begins, "are things that appear outside the course of Nature . . . such as a child who is born with one arm, another who will have two heads, and additional members over and above the ordinary."[10] Notice that, despite terminology, Paré is not disagreeing with the much earlier theological naturalism laid down by Isidore of Seville, for he is stating only that monsters deviate from the norm. Well beyond the abnormalities of monsters, however, are the "marvels" and "prodigies": "Marvels are things which happen that are completely against Nature as when a woman will give birth to a serpent, or to a dog." In other words, even the barriers of taxonomic kinds are violated or transgressed. Throughout the book, when Paré describes and discusses these marvels he usually turns to "historical" tales and reports rather than rely on firsthand experience. He further distinguishes monsters and marvels from "maimed persons," "the blind, the one-eyed, the humpbacked, those who limp or [those] having six-digits on the hand or the feet... or any other thing that is against Nature." Notice the strangeness of this category, which contains both congenital defects and accidental wounds. Paré's logic here cannot be entirely appreciated, because he mentions the maimed only briefly and focuses instead on monsters and marvels.

His list of the *causes* of monsters demonstrates his historical cusp status, at once progressive and enlightened but also backward and uncritical. "There are several things," he says, "that cause monsters."

The first is the glory of God.
The second, his wrath.
The third, too great a quantity of seed.[11]
The fourth, too little a quantity.
The fifth, the imagination.
The sixth, the narrowness or smallness of the womb.
The seventh, the indecent posture of the mother, as when, being pregnant,
    she has sat too long with her legs crossed, or pressed against her womb.
The eighth, through a fall, or blows struck against the womb of the mother,
    being with child.
The ninth, through hereditary or accidental illness.
The tenth, through rotten or corrupt seed.
The twelfth, through the artifice of wicked spital beggars.
The thirteenth, through Demons and Devils.[12]

PREGNANT WOMEN SHOULD NOT LOOK UPON MONSTERS

Perhaps the most surprising cause in Paré's list is the fifth item, the imagination.[13] Paré follows his ancient predecessors (i.e., Hippocrates, Aristotle, and Empedocles) in upholding a theory about the role of the mother's imagination at the moment of conception and in early gestation. If a woman in coitus is exposed to frightening or disturbing or simply strong imagery, through either the senses or memory, the offending image may be impressed on her offspring.[14] Paré accepts the reality of a physiological process, one that begins as a disturbing sense impression and ends with a distorted fetus. He offers a few cases to illustrate his point, some of which strain his own credulity and some that seem quite credible to him. Undermining his own embryonic empiricism, he cites the authorities of old. He tells of Queen Persina of Ethiopia, who with King Hidustes mysteriously produced a white baby "because of the appearance of the beautiful Andromeda that she summoned up in her imagination, for she had a painting of her before her eyes during embraces from which she became pregnant." Likewise we are told of a girl who was born as furry as a bear. Her unfortunate state was the result of her mother's "having looked too intensely at the image of Saint John [the Baptist] dressed in skins, along with his [own] body hair and beard, which picture was attached to the foot of her bed while she was conceiving." The potential convenience of this particular explanation is nowhere more evident than in his retelling of a story from Hippocrates. Hippocrates, it seems, saved a young woman from the accusation of adultery "because she had given birth to a child as black as a Moor, her husband and she both having white skin; which woman was absolved upon Hippocrates' persuasion that it was [caused by] the portrait of a Moor, similar to the child, which was customarily attached to her bed." A more contemporary example is offered in Paré's story of a baby born in France in 1517 with the face of a frog. When asked what the cause of this monster might be, the father of the child explained that his wife had been ill with a fever and had taken the curative advice of her friend. The folk cure required the wife to carry a frog in her hand until the frog died, at which point she would be cured of the fever. "That night she went to bed with her husband, still having said frog in her hand; her husband and she embraced and she conceived; and by the power of her imagination, this monster had thus been produced."

Based on these cases Paré the medical man offers some advice. Women "should not be forced to look at or imagine monstrous things" at the time of conception or during the early formation of the child (which takes thirty to thirty-five days for males and forty to forty-two days for females). But once the formation of the child is complete, no images or imaginings will have a detrimental effect on the offspring. These sorts of causal explanations may seem ridiculous to us, but they represent a naturalistic turn in the sense that they opened up possible research avenues. There may or may not have been a discoverable physiological *mechanism* that transmitted disturbing sense impressions to the conceptus, but at least Paré didn't just throw up his hands and say "the devil did it." Invoking the imagination also indicates some sense of psychological effects; psychology can lead to very concrete manifestations (e.g., a deeply troubled woman may miscarry). In this respect, Paré seems to foreshadow psychosomatic theories that flourished during Freud's generation.

Of course, Paré was not a secular humanist, and devilish demons were quite real for him. He did not have an ironic or literary response to the demonic. "Satan's actions," he says, "are supernatural and incomprehensible, surpassing the human mind, [it] not being able to explain them, any more than [it can] the magnet which attracts iron and makes the needle turn." But he goes on to say that we should not fall into a general skepticism about the "principles and reasons of natural things." The human mind may not be up to the challenge of supernatural spiritual riddles, but let us not give up, he seems to suggest, our attempts to grasp the natural world. Here we find an inconspicuous boundary marker in Paré's thinking: the natural monsters are appropriate subjects for medical study, but the supernatural monsters exist in a domain that cannot be penetrated properly by science. The proper response to this latter domain is prayer and piety, not scientific exploration. This important concession to the Church, reiterated by most scientists of the following century, helped to create an autonomous domain for previously forbidden explorations of nature.

MONSTERS AND THE MECHANIZATION OF NATURE

Thinking about monsters as products of embryological processes was part of a larger paradigm shift in thinking about the causal processes of physical material. The century after Ambroise Paré's was marked by astounding advances in what we now call chemistry, physics, biology, and astronomy. Nature came to be regarded as a giant machine that could be analyzed in terms of *material* and *moving* (or efficient) causes, and any appeals to divine *purposes* (teleology) seemed increasingly irrelevant for understanding, predicting, and manipulating the physical world.

Galileo Galilei (1564–1642) helped to bring about this burst of independent science, even though as a forerunner he could not himself benefit much from the shift. He laid greater emphasis on the empirical study of material and efficient causation; he took an agnostic phenomenalist attitude toward any supposedly hidden metaphysical causes; and he explicitly built a safety retaining wall between science and religion. The Bible, he argued, was God's manual for how to live virtuously, but the book of nature was also God's gift, a mysterious puzzle for us to exercise our rationality and curiosity. In his letter to the grand duchess of Tuscany he writes, "Since the Holy Ghost did not intend to teach us whether heaven moves or stands still, whether its shape is spherical or like a discus or extended in a plane, nor whether the earth is located at its center or off to one side, then so much the less was it intended to settle for us any other conclusion of the same kind.... I would say here something that was heard from an ecclesiastic of the most eminent degree: 'That the intention of the Holy Ghost is to teach us how one goes to heaven, not how heaven goes.'"[15]

What did this retaining wall between science and religion mean for monsterology? Simply put, the human body, now conceptualized as an elegant machine, became increasingly anatomized, analyzed, and understood. And the pathologies of that body, the monsters, became an important means by which the new surgeons and physicians could limn the *normal* laws of nature. Natural monsters came under the new umbrella of a mechanistic worldview, and spiritual monsters (e.g., demons and devils) were sent packing, along with the diviners, priests, and theologians, never to return in any significant way to the pages of the natural philosophers.

René Descartes (1596–1650) describes his own astonishment at the mechanical nature of the heart.[16] In the *Discourse on Method* he asks the reader to follow his mechanical analysis, but first, "those who are not well versed in anatomy will find less difficulty in understanding what I am going to say if they will take the trouble, before reading this, to have the heart of some large animal cut open before them."[17] Then he offers a detailed description of the heart, its parts, and its mechanisms, demystifying the formerly miraculous organ of life. "The motion which I have just explained," he insists, "follows necessarily from the mere disposition of the parts of the heart visible to the naked eye, from the heat which one can feel with the fingers, and from the nature of the blood, which one can learn by experiment: just as the motions of a clock follow from the weight, location, and configuration of its counterweights and wheels."

Descartes is trying to establish that the entire body is a machine and its behaviors are mechanical. The machine is animated by subtle fluids and vapors, or animal spirits, as they travel through the apparatus. He speculates that the "nature of the network of nerves and muscles of the human body must be to enable the animal spirits within to move its members, as one sees when freshly severed heads still move and bite the earth although they are no longer alive."[18] This gruesome phenomenon demonstrates, says Descartes, that our bodies can move in complex ways, even "without the guidance of volition." Bodily activity may be more robotic than intentional. "This will hardly seem strange to those who know how many automata or machines can be made by human industry, although these automata employ very few parts in comparison to the large number of bones, muscles, nerves, arteries, veins, and all the other component parts of each animal. Such persons will therefore think of this body as a machine created by the hand of God, and in consequence incomparably better designed and with more admirable movements than any machines that can be invented by man."

It was a short step from Descartes' God-made machine to the idea of a Nature-made machine, which had no need of the God hypothesis. And the savant who took that short step was Julien Offray de La Mettrie (1709–1751). Descartes had kept God in the picture as the creator of the machine, and he had managed to keep the human *soul* insulated from the materialist analysis of the body by formulating his dualistic metaphysics. But now La Mettrie, with his radical materialism, did away with both God and soul. His book *Homme machine* (Man a Machine) reduced human beings completely to mechanical forms and functions. La Mettrie's writings were so scandalous that he had to leave France; he sought refuge in Holland but eventually had to leave even that bastion of free thought to settle in Berlin under the protection of Frederick the Great. At first his ideas were embraced by other *philosophes*, including Voltaire and D'Holbach, but his embrace of hedonism in his later writings led his radical French contemporaries to treat him as an anarchist.[19] It may also have led him to an early grave after a particularly hedonistic binge with some *pâté aux truffe*.

For our purposes La Mettrie is important because there would be no eventual Frankenstein monster without him. Starting from Descartes' conclusion, La Mettrie goes on to say that "the body is but a watch.... a collection of springs which wind each other up," and "the soul is but a principle of motion or a material and sensible part of the brain."[20] He belittles humanity throughout his writings in an attempt to give mankind a more accurate picture of itself, divested of magical spirits and species-centric arrogance. At a time when it was almost unthinkable, La Mettrie argued that other animals, especially the apes, could probably be taught language. "The transition from animals to man," he said, "is not violent, as true philosophers will admit. What was man before the invention of words and the knowledge of language? An animal of his own species with much less instinct than the others." If we taught the "wild man" ape (the orangutan) to speak, "then he would no longer be a wild man, nor a defective man, but he would be a perfect man, a little gentleman, with as much matter or muscle as we have, for thinking and profiting by his education." Life is not *magically* different from the inanimate, and humans are not divinely different from animals.[21]

Though scandalous in his own day, La Mettrie's mechanical approach to biology and cognition eventually became part of the general Enlightenment project to demystify nature and man. The benefit of a scientific approach, philosophes argued, was the elimination of socially divisive superstitions and the recognition of a universal human nature, one that could flourish in the new light of rational social organization. But contained in this optimistic movement was the kernel of its own downfall.

Francisco Goya's (1746–1828) 1796 etching *El sueno de la razon produce monstrous* (The Sleep of Reason Produces Monsters) is both an assertion of and a critique of Enlightenment philosophy. The etching shows a man (probably Goya) who has fallen asleep at his writing table; behind him a writhing group of monsters emerge out of the darkness. Rationalists have claimed it as a statement about the need for constant rational vigilance over the lurking monsters of ignorance and prejudice. Romantics and Counter-Enlightenment figures have seen it as a pessimistic revelation of the inevitability of dark, irrational, and emotional forces in human life. Like the ancient Lucretius, Enlightenment rationalists believed that monsters were not real in any metaphysical sense but simply terrible confusions, misperceptions, and bigotries. Monsters could be eradicated from human psychology and society by good education about the causes and principles of nature. But at the same time that French materialism was declaring rational illumination of the human condition, French society was undergoing the horrors of the Revolution. And subsequent to this, it didn't help the public relations of French rationalism that so many Europeans found themselves bloodied in the Napoleonic Wars. A Counter-Enlightenment movement began to stress the negative consequences of "too much reason," too much science and not enough heart.

FRANKENSTEIN

The year that Goya etched his famous irrational monsters was the year that Mary Shelley (1797–1851) was conceived. So much has been written about the meaning of Shelley's *Frankenstein* that I hesitate to add more, and yet in a book about monsters I can hardly skip it. The Frankenstein creature may be the most famous monster of the past two centuries, and it's important to situate the wretch in his original context. *Frankenstein* is often read as part of the Counter-Enlightenment critique of science; there's good reason for this interpretation because Shelley modified later editions to underscore this stance. But we have to back up, before the critique, and remind ourselves of the novel reasonableness of her generation's interest in animation.

The scientific pursuit of the creation of life is older than alchemy, but in Shelley's era two relatively fresh pathways had been opened for that pursuit. First was the trend of materialism that I've been tracing from Galileo through La Mettrie and beyond, a theoretical position that certainly had its detractors but nonetheless enjoyed more respectability than in previous eras. Second was a wave of new empirical investigations into vitalism, begun by Luigi Galvani (1737–1798), Alessandro Volta (1745–1827), John Hunter (1728–1793), William Lawrence (1783–1867), and others. Shelley was familiar with a growing body of experimental science that demonstrated the underlying electrical and chemical sparks, the animating principles, of organic life. She was aware, for example, of Galvani's bioelectricity experiments, in which he directed an electrical current through a dead frog's body and produced jumping and twitching motions. In the introduction to a late edition of *Frankenstein* (1831) Shelley reveals that a conversation between her husband, Percy Bysshe Shelley, and Lord Byron influenced her creation of the monster story. That influential conversation was about Dr. Erasmus Darwin's vitalistic experiments to bring inanimate matter to life. According to Mary Shelley's account, Erasmus Darwin (Charles Darwin's grandfather) had vivified a piece of vermicelli noodle by using galvanism and other mysterious scientific catalysts. Actually, Darwin did no such thing, and the whole business appears to be a confusion, but it reveals the supposed credibility of the idea of mechanical, nonmiraculous life.[22]

Still, this credibility was more common in the vanguard circles in which Shelley moved than among the more conservative elements of Georgian society. The idea that science could penetrate the mystery of life itself and then manipulate it for its own end transformed from exciting to frightening almost immediately. Whatever her original attitude toward scientific materialism, her book became the principal cautionary tale warning us that science can go too far. The age-old fear of forbidden knowledge was laid over her novel, and her moral indictments of Victor Frankenstein's irresponsible parenting became mixed with growing Romantic criticisms of scientism. Man should not play God.

> It was on a dreary night of November, that I beheld the accomplishment of my toils. With an anxiety that almost amounted to agony, I collected the instruments of life around me, that I might infuse a spark of being into the lifeless thing that lay at my feet. It was already one in the morning; the rain pattered dismally against the panes, and my candle was nearly burnt out, when, by the glimmer of the half-extinguished light, I saw the dull yellow eye of the creature open; it breathed hard, and a convulsive motion agitated its limbs.[23]

Mary Shelley apparently added the moralizing antimaterialist tone to *Frankenstein* in later editions; her friend Professor William Lawrence had been suspended from the Royal College of Surgeons because of his radical materialism and controversial book, *Lectures on Physiology, Zoology and the Natural History of Man*, and fearing that her own book might be withdrawn Shelley tempered her original 1818 edition.[24] Dr. Frankenstein's already Faustian qualities could now be enlisted in a more generic indictment of Baconian science.[25]

The intellectual hubris of Victor Frankenstein was a result, in part, of his poor education, which was heavy on intellectual scientific analysis but lacking in the humanities. His own natural analytic tendencies could have been cultivated in a healthier direction if only he had balanced them with more literature, poetry, music, and moral study.[26] These faults make the doctor slightly robotic and soulless, like his son the monster. To that extent, parent (Victor) and child (monster) stand as literary embodiments of the Romantic warning from Johan Georg Hamann that "the tree of knowledge has robbed us of the tree of life."[27]

The Frankenstein monster embodies many of the themes I have already discussed (hybridity, liminality, outcast status, etc.), but also crystallizes another recurring monster theme; in fact, the title of the book has actually become a shorthand way of describing any human creation that has unintended consequences, from atom bombs to cloned sheep.[28] The monster is that unpredictable, uncontrollable force that cannot be reasoned with or persuaded. It's an incarnation of Nature itself, upsetting our optimistic project to tame and use her.

What's wrong with materialism and too much science? The answer, in part, is reductionism. The monsters of this literature are creatures that have been *reduced* to their parts alone. They are dehumanized humanoids, brutes that sometimes walk and talk like us but ultimately lack the mysterious heart and soul ingredients to make them human. Their creators demonstrate their own cleverness and Promethean pride, but though human knowledge might be able to compose life itself, it cannot, it seems, compose it well. Something essential is always missing.

While the Romantics were exploring the monstrous dimensions of materialism, many scientists, astounded by their own successes in medicine and physiology, were staying the course of the mechanical philosophy. At the same time the Romantics were depicting imaginary monsters and scolding science, methodical researchers such as John Hunter and Etienne Geoffroy Saint-Hilaire were exploring the real monsters of embryology.

The result of scientific reanimation. Boris Karloff, the most famous twentieth-century visual representation of Frankenstein's creature, in James Whale's 1931 *Frankenstein* (Universal Studios). Photo courtesy of Jerry Ohlinger.

JOHN HUNTER'S MONSTERS

Surgeon, natural historian, and monsterologist, John Hunter cast a long shadow over British science. In some ways Shelley's character Dr. Frankenstein could have been modeled on him.[29] Hunter's work on organic transplantation (e.g., growing human teeth on top of a rooster's head and grafting cock testicles inside hen abdomens) laid the conceptual groundwork for stitched-together Frankenstein-type monsters.[30] The fact that John and his brother, William, went to body-snatching extremes to procure corpses for dissection also seems quite inspirational for a good monster story. But my interest in Hunter is best confined to his embryological monster theories.

Hunter collected many specimens of monster fetuses, which he preserved in glass bottles of distilled alcohol. He did not confine himself to human specimens but went far and wide into the animal kingdom to find similarly distorted bodies. In the same way that his physiological cabinets were designed to show the more universal animal functions of digestion, circulation, and respiration, his cabinets of monsters and malformations sought to display the underlying laws of abnormal growth. To that end, he grouped many different species of monster specimens together and looked for patterns or tendencies that would reveal the logic of monsters.[31]

By arresting and dissecting developing animals, in particular chicks, Hunter came to formulate some important ideas about metamorphosis. When one examines the structures of a developing chick, for example, one finds transitional stages that seem to correspond with the adult anatomical structures of other species: first the chick is worm-like, then it appears to have a tail, later it loses the tail, and so on. Hunter observed, "If we were capable of following the progressive increase in the number of the parts of the most perfect [developed] animal, as they were formed in succession, from the very first state to that of full perfection, we should probably be able to compare it with some one of the incomplete animals themselves, or every order in the Creation." He goes on to say, "If we were to take a series of animals from the more imperfect to the perfect, we should probably find an imperfect animal corresponding with some stage of the most perfect."[32]

Following Ambroise Paré, Hunter understood that monsters had their own rules of logic. They were not chaotic departures from the norm; they swerved from normality in predictable and repeated ways. Long before genetics, Hunter's metamorphosis idea sought to acknowledge that some kind of internal code was being impressed on the developing embryo.[33] Embryos were not preformed, but they certainly had some constraining code in the germ. Monsters might be caused when there is a corruption or breakdown in this code. Like a baked cake that collapses because the recipe is flawed, monsters diverge because the code is flawed. Hunter seemed to prefer this idea to the competing theory: that the code is fine, but the ingredients and the cooking go badly; that is, changes in the uterine environment derail normal growth. Trying to articulate his view, he writes, "I should imagine that Monsters were formed Monsters from their very first formation, for this reason, that all supernumerary parts are joined to their similar parts, as a head to a head; etc., etc."[34] Indeed, Hunter possessed a monster in his collection, called the Bengali Boy, that looked in every way like an ordinary boy except that he had another head growing upside down on the top of his functioning head.

Hunter was suggesting that a multilegged or -armed or -headed monster will have its monstrosity develop at the same time that the healthy legs or arms or head are forming in utero; in other words, an extra leg won't get added at the last minute of gestation or well before the usual leg-building time. All this led him to think that the cause of a congenital malformation exists in the original germ of the animal.

For Hunter, the corruption of the germ code can be species-specific, as when a bird develops "scissors beak," but it can also be generic and apply to many taxa. Hunter dissected many chick embryos and described the usual formation, from the internal heart outward to the lungs and then eventually to the skin of the abdomen that grows over the internal organs.[35] Occasionally, however, the skin fails to form around the organs, and the result is a monstrous chicken that lacks abdominal parietes (walls). While this case clearly applies to the birds that he was directly observing, he also ventured a more general extrapolation. "There is reason to believe," he writes, "it is the same in other animals; for in some Monsters in the Quadruped, we have no abdominal parietes. This state of deficiency in the parietes of the abdomen has all its degrees; some much more, others less."[36] In this way Hunter helped us to see that Nature composes diverse animal forms, but not as a specialist micromanager, fitting every species with unique equipment; instead, Nature utilizes a common bag of supplies (the common physiological systems) and tinkers with unique designs on top of those common structures and functions. In the end, Hunter organized his many monster specimens (which can still be seen at the Royal College of Surgeons) into four categories: monsters from preternatural situation of parts, monsters from addition of parts, monsters from deficiency of parts, and monsters that combine the addition and deficiency of parts, such as hermaphrodites.

Hunter provided incredible sophistication to the naturalistic approach to monsters, an approach that includes the teratologists Aristotle and Paré. None of Hunter's predecessors nor his peers dissected, investigated, and preserved as many humans and animals. His work constitutes a bridge from the mere promise of monster science to the reality.

GEOFFROY SAINT-HILAIRE'S TERATOLOGY

Across the Channel, the French anatomist Etienne Geoffroy Saint-Hilaire (1772–1844) was further refining the logic of monsters; his son Isidore instituted the use of *teratology* to describe the new science. His explanation of cyclopic babies illustrates his overall approach to embryology and anatomy. Geoffroy worked in a scientific environment dominated by Georges

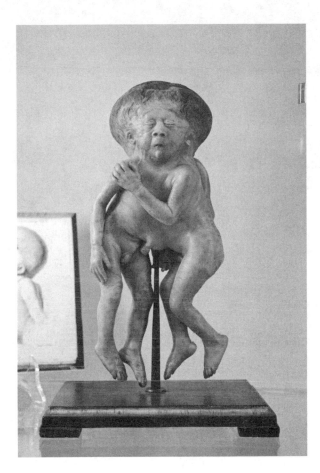

A conjoined twin, with two bodies sharing one head. Photo by Joanna Ebenstein © 2008. Reprinted by kind permission of the artist and the Museum of Anatomical Waxes "Luigi Cattezneo" (Museo Delle Cere Anatomiche "Luigi Cattaneo"), Bologna, Italy.

Cuvier and other naturalists who believed that animals were built perfectly to fit their environment, their particular "functions" or "conditions of existence." Carnivores, for example, were perfectly adapted to find prey (they possessed keen perceptual equipment), to catch prey (powerful locomotive equipment), to eat prey (sharp teeth, claws, etc.), and to digest prey (short digestive tracts, etc.). In other words, studying the anatomy of animals led to finding the ingenious matches between features and functions. Against this reigning philosophy, Geoffroy began to argue that animals from very different conditions of existence still seemed to possess similar body plans. Humans, bats, moles, and whales had very different functions and environments, yet they still seemed to have the same blueprint for a bony pentadactyl forelimb. Geoffroy spent his career throwing these weird patterns, or archetypes, into the faces of function-minded anatomists like Cuvier, daring them to explain the similarities by appeal to good functional design. Using a materialist approach, he did not think of these archetypes

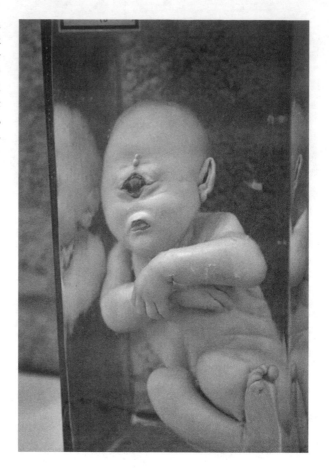

A cyclops specimen from the Vrolik collection. Photo by Joanna Ebenstein © 2008. Reprinted by kind permission of the artist and the Vrolik Museum, University of Amsterdam.

of anatomy as transcendental Platonic essences instantiated in different animal kinds. Instead, he argued that inductive observation of many body types revealed converging natural laws of growth. The regular patterns, or archetypes, occur because diverse animals (moles, humans, whales, etc.) are built according to the same sequential building processes.

Common body plans, such as having two forelimbs, two hind limbs and other tetrapod traits, were the result, Geoffroy argued, of generative laws. One of these generative laws of growth he called the law of *soi pour soi*, or "like attracts like." He argued that this embryological law of attraction of similar parts was the underlying impetus for organ formation and general animal composition. This same law also explained why things could go monstrously wrong. The law of attraction of similar parts was employed to cover the recurrent stable forms (normality) and the anomalous malformations. A child born with cyclops syndrome was explained by Geoffroy as a case of soi pour soi. If an external force should accidentally arrest the development of the olfactory organ (perhaps the result of blocked blood flow in the embryo), then the gap between the two eyes would be bridged by the two structures because of soi pour soi. With the olfactory barrier removed, two eyes would fuse into one.[37]

Against Hunter's claim that monsters were errors of metamorphic code, Geoffroy argued that monsters like the cyclops were produced by external causes, accidents to the fetus forming in utero. He tested his epigenetic hypothesis by subjecting many incubating chick embryos to violent trauma and extreme temperatures. Though he mostly just killed chickens, he did manage to produce deformed monster chicks, some without eyes, for example. These experimental results, together with his philosophical anatomy, led him to a general epigenetic view of monster formation.[38] Monsters were departures from normality, but they further demonstrated the regularities of generative laws. Furthermore, their deviation represented a somewhat predictable derailing of these generative laws, brought on by violence of some kind to the fetal organism. Studying monsters told us something about embryology, but also something about the developmental morphology underpinning the taxonomical classifications of life. In the same way that monsters cannot be explained as "designed" for specific functions, so, too, other (normal) morphological patterns seem to exist without any such teleological explanation. These last points will prove more significant when we get to Darwin's revolution.

THE MATERIALISTIC APPROACH TO EMBRYOLOGY was gaining ground in the early nineteenth century, but it still offended many who saw the generation of life as one of the last "miraculous" territories left. Theologically minded naturalists had found the preformationist view of embryology more palatable because it suggested that all normal beings were successfully unrolled out of the procreative process just as the Creator had designed them: the seed person grew in utero but preserved the Designer's essential format. Monsters, according to this preformationist view, were rare glitches in this unrolling process; they were perfect in their seed form, but some external force had spoiled the translation. This view denied purpose and design to the monsters but maintained it for every normal creature. Nature was still teleological, and monsters were only an exception. Epigeneticists such as Geoffroy, Hunter, and William Lawrence began to throw doubt on this basic assumption. Lawrence summarized the conventional apprehensions and then, like La Mettrie before him, dismissed any sanctimonious twaddle:

> Regarding this business [embryogenesis] as the work of God, and having already assumed that all his works are perfect, they [the preformationists]

maintain that the young animal is originally perfect, and degenerates into a monster through the action of external forces. More accurate observation discloses to us in this affair merely the operation of secondary causes, and exhibits to us the production and development of the fetus as the result of vascular action in secretion and nutrition: in short, however his pride may be offended at hearing it, the simple truth is, that man, considered at the epocha of his first formation, and with respect to his corporeal frame, is a secretion.[39]

WILLIAM LAWRENCE
AND THE HEADLESS CHILDREN

If man is a secretion, then he is not ideal at the *beginning* of embryogenesis but only at the *end*—and even then he is not perfect or ideal, but serviceable. Some of these secretions vary in extreme ways and end up as monsters; the rest of them vary to a lesser degree and end up as virtually everyone else.[40] Perhaps Lawrence's most surprising claim, eventually developed further by Darwin, is that all of us deviate from the norm; for this reason he would not bother to "draw very accurately the line of distinction between varieties and monstrous formations, which differ rather in degree than in kind."

Lawrence argues that malformations can actually shed considerable light on the logic of life itself. For example, studying two preserved fetuses in John Hunter's collection, Lawrence saw that a fetus could develop to a penultimate stage of development but lack a heart. Counterintuitive though it seemed, a human fetus could complete its formation (with minor morphological imperfections) without a rather essential vital organ. Lawrence underscored the importance of studying embryological monsters in order to unlock some of nature's hidden secrets: "Monsters, in which considerable parts are wanting, seem peculiarly likely to assist in the prosecution of physiological researches. If we never saw animals, except in a perfect [fully developed] state, we could not form just ideas of the comparative importance of the different organs." In fact, Lawrence argued, we would be led astray if we studied only the normal and the completed organisms. Because the heart and brain are so essential to the finished human, we might conclude that they are foundational for the developmental logic. But heartless fetal monsters are joined by equally surprising cases: the brainless and headless fetuses.

Acephalous (headless) fetuses were, and are, more common occurrences than one might imagine. Often the brain case is missing altogether and a truncated face terminates upward into a soft mass, sometimes covered by a smooth membrane. The neck is very short, making the reduced head

Terminal craniofacial anomalies like those studied by William Lawrence. Photo by Joanna Ebenstein © 2008. Reprinted by kind permission of the artist and the Museum of Anatomical Waxes "Luigi Cattezneo" (Museo Delle Cere Anatomiche "Luigi Cattaneo"), Bologna, Italy.

sit almost directly on the shoulders, but hair often grows at the base of the cranium formation and "the body is well formed in every respect, and generally reaches the full size." Lawrence explains, "These children generally die very soon after they come into the world; but they have sometimes lived for many hours, cried, sucked, &c."[41] The astonishing thing is that they should make it this far in the first place.

The lesson Lawrence draws from these cases is that there are two different physiologics to the human animal. Previously, scholars assumed that the complex organs (e.g., brain, heart) that play such a vital role in the functioning of the baby must also be essential to the construction of the animal in utero. But "the monsters just described," Lawrence says, "prove that this is not the case." We find instead that bones, cartilage, ligament, membrane, organs, cellular substance, intestines, and more can all be formed and become operational by the actions of the vascular system alone. A blood vessel system, Lawrence concludes, builds the body, and monsters have revealed this logic not only for themselves but for all humans. After birth, of course, a new logic kicks in and vital functioning cannot be sustained without a heart and a brain. Poetically stated, the monster points the way to scientific truths but pays the price with its life. All humans deviate or vary slightly, but when the variation is extreme they become monsters and nature spontaneously aborts them. If they should somehow survive this natural editing, then, Lawrence says, "the hour of their birth is with them generally the hour of their death."[42]

Lawrence lays to rest three very popular misconceptions about monsters. Regarding the theory that a mother's imagination can corrupt the fetus, he asks what sort of mechanical process could operate from the mother's imagination down to the womb, where it would then have to destroy the normally developing head and reconstruct a new monkey head or whatever. Furthermore, there is extensive evidence that women can suffer serious disorders (e.g., diseases, amputations) with no ill effect on the fetus, so frights and imaginings seem far too weak for fetal reconstruction. Next, he counters the theory that extreme monsters, such as the headless children, are caused by blunt or acute traumas to the mother's gravid abdomen. For one thing, a majority of cases of unfortunate offspring are born to women who suffered no such violence. For another, if the heads were caved in or broken in half we should discover some excess matter in utero and some bruising or signs of trauma.[43]

Lawrence also criticized speculative monsterology. Too many naturalists conducted their work by saying to themselves, and their readers, that "it seems *reasonable* that x should follow after y, therefore it must be the case that x follows after y." Lawrence's generation had grown tired of such teleological speculations, and he pressed embryologists to restrain their imagination when ignorant of the facts.[44] Theorizing that these "illogical" things can't be happening simply because they upset our deep assumptions about a rationally designed nature only stalls our empirical understanding of real biology.[45]

II

Darwin's Mutants

Mr. Owen suggested to me that the production of monsters...presents an analogy to the production of species.
CHARLES DARWIN

It may be advantageous to turn to non-functional, grossly maladapted, teratologies when studying the properties of internal factors in evolution.
PERE ALBERCH

AS FAR BACK AS THE ANCIENT Greek philosopher Empedocles, monsters have been considered possible jumping-off points for the evolution of new species. As we saw in part I, Empedocles speculated that prehistory contained a nightmarish environment of animated body parts, crawling around and clumping together until some accidental hybrids finally produced viable procreators. Nobody in Darwin's era held quite so crude a theory, but it was entirely reasonable to consider the mysteries of species generation (transmutation or evolution) in light of individual generation (embryology). If monsters were individual deviations from the norm, then maybe they were the key to understanding species deviation. Did mutations in the individual lead to new branches on the phylogenetic tree?

MONSTERS AND TRANSMUTATION

In Darwin's time high stakes were involved in issues of teratology. Every animal was seen as an example of God's designing acumen, and because God was thought to be omnipotent, his animal designs should be absolutely perfect. Recall that it was difficult for medieval theologians to reconcile the existence of monsters with the omniscient, omnipotent, and omnibenevolent God. In that era, the problem was mostly about how to reconcile evil and evildoers with God's obvious authority over the cosmos. Now, in Darwin's era, the evil had largely gone out of the monster concept, but monsters continued to challenge assumptions about God's ultimate authority over nature. Why would the perfect craftsman create (or allow) the imperfect craftsmanship implied by teratology?

The natural theologians tried to show that nature was elegant, economical, and rational, a perfect incarnation of God's blueprint. During the 1830s a popular series of books called the Bridgewater Treatises endeavored to show how nature's beautiful adaptations proved the existence of a divine architect. But it was becoming increasingly difficult to maintain this optimism when paleontology was uncovering massive evidence about extinct genera. Why would God retract whole orders and families of his beautiful creation? Were these "mistakes" in God's overall plan? Was it even possible for God to make a mistake?

In addition to the theological threats from paleontology, the new work in embryology and morphology was also discovering some disconcerting truths about ontogeny. Natural theologians had built a professional industry on the demonstration of useful traits: the eye is designed perfectly for seeing, the canine tooth for tearing flesh, the neck of the giraffe for reaching higher foliage, and so on. For a mole, which lives underground, digging through dirt, normal eyes would only create an unhealthy nuisance; lo and behold, the Designer has seen fit to perfect the mole by withholding its eyes. But to this cheerful party of hand-in-glove correlations between structure and function came uninvited observations from anatomy. On closer analysis there appeared to be many structures that are *not* perfectly adapted to function. Recall Geoffroy's and Hunter's recognition that many animals with radically different life conditions nonetheless seemed to have similar structures; one finds a common pentadactyl forelimb structure, for example, in humans, whales, moles, and bats. Why would the Designer use the same structure for flying, digging, swimming, and grasping?

Homologies between different kinds of creatures did not sit well with natural theologians who saw each species as independently created by God. By the time Darwin was writing in his notebooks, the atheistic implications had been fully drawn out and emphasized against the more pious adaptationists. Significant anatomical structures did not have any obvious purpose in nature, and these anomalies threw doubt on the more general assumption that nature had been divinely designed. The morphologists, in contrast to the adaptationists, argued that a mole's paws, a whale's flippers, a human's hands, and a bat's wings all had similarities because nonpurposive materialistic laws of embryological growth were shaping them. Radical anatomists, taking their start from Geoffroy's ideas, began referring to the theologically minded Bridgewater Treatises as the "Bilgewater Treatises."[1]

Monsters became part of the rallying cry of the radical atheists against a perfect, purposeful nature. Mutants and homologies theoretically conspired to undermine the Panglossian adaptation ideology of natural theology. Against this growing tide of atheism, Darwin's colleague Richard Owen hatched two "curative" solutions. Owen argued that the structural homologies, emphasized by the morphologists, should not be seen as evidence against a divinely designed nature. Rather, these deeper unities underneath diverse species are actually transcendental archetypes: God's blueprint plans for the animal kingdom. Owen eventually described an ideal vertebrate archetype that could be detected like a Platonic Form embedded in every snake, fish, monkey, and man. This clever move allowed natural theologians to concede that not every structure is perfectly adapted, but now this counterevidence that morphologists claimed as blind, nonpurposive laws could be seen as just *more* evidence of a divine hand in nature.

Now we can appreciate Owen's second theoretical move: the idea, contra Geoffroy, that monsters are triggered by *internal* germ causation. Owen revitalized Hunter's theory of monsters as an alternative to the blind view of nature that the radicals were preaching. If monsters, or pathological structures, are caused by anomalous conditions in their external environment, then changes in nature are accidental. Chance and contingency are the distressing implications of an exogenic theory of monsters. In other words, one child is born with two arms, but if we dial up the heat significantly (according to an exogenic view), we might end up with another child having four arms. Pure chance, not purpose, seems to be behind nature's processes. To combat this accidental view, Owen argued that monsters resulted from preset changes in the germ, and this made room for the idea that monsters were purposefully caused.[2]

Owen offered a clever rescue, one that made sense out of the increasingly undeniable empirical data of transmutation, but also saved a role for God's design. The rounded jigsaw skulls of vertebrate animals, for example, may originally have been a monstrous deviation from an ancestor, a teratological alteration of rostral vertebrae. But, according to Owen, such a monstrosity was preprogrammed by God and had led to an evolutionary jump, called *saltation*, a new kind of genus or order. The logic of monsters is synthesized with the idea of morphological archetypes if we consider that the homologies we see (the common body plans) are like footprints of the previous saltational monster jumps. God uses monsters to install his evolutionary designs over time, and the archetypes reveal to us some of those installation points.

Darwin's *Origin of Species* was published in 1859, but long before that he was privately scribbling his theories in red notebooks. After his long journey on the HMS *Beagle* (1831–1836) he returned to London with a veritable treasure trove of exotic specimens, preserved animals, and strange fossils. At the same time that he was secretly writing notes to himself about transmutation, he was working with a variety of British naturalists to analyze, describe, and name his specimens. One of these new London friends, introduced by the famous geologist Charles Lyell, was the curator and anatomist Richard Owen. At the time, Owen was in charge of John Hunter's collection, which was housed in the Royal College of Surgeons. Owen worked to describe Darwin's specimens (including a giant sloth species that Owen named *Mylodon darwinii*), but he also exposed Darwin to the teratological interests of Hunter's work.

It is clear from Darwin's notebooks of the late 1830s that he became fascinated with the monsters in Hunter's collection and Hunter's opaque teratology theories. One idea that he underscored, even calling it "Hunter's Law," was that monsters varied according to laws.[3] In particular, specific anomalies seemed to happen during certain times of gestational development. The unnatural positioning of limbs or organs happened during a certain week range, and the addition of digits or limbs happened during another range, and so on. These correlations were both species-specific and more generic. Darwin agreed with Owen, Hunter, and the Geoffroys that monstrosity had a law-like logic, but he was more interested in the implications of this for evolution than for embryology.[4]

Remember, Hunter thought monsters were already malformed in the germ code, but Geoffroy claimed they were the result of external mechanical influences of temperature or pressure. Owen sided vigorously with Hunter.[5] At first, Darwin absorbed this whole debate and, following Owen's suggestion, entertained the idea of monsters as launching points for species transmutation. But how, he still wondered, could such a launching point produce the amazing fit between a species and its environment? The theological solution seemed too incredible.

NO MONSTROUS JUMPS IN NATURE

In Darwin's notebooks we see him sifting his way through these teratological issues, keeping the workable bits from his predecessors but ultimately finding his own way. He starts from the premise, pushed for by William Lawrence and other forerunners, that monsters are part of a larger biological phenomenon called *variation*.

But why do we recognize, he asked, that an albino is a monster variation, but a white-colored Arctic animal (e.g., an ermine hare) is an adaptational variation? Or similarly, why is a dwarf plant a monster in a temperate region but an adaptation in an alpine region? We have such variations as a six-fingered hand passed down from a parent (or even appearing de novo), but *not* related to the habit, function, or specific environment of the animal. Darwin says that some cases are obvious and easy to determine, such as when we discover nonfunctional traits: beetles, for example, "with wings beneath soldered wing-cases."[6] In those cases the oddities are inherited but they are not (at least currently) useful adaptations. But in the tricky cases, the only way of determining if a specific variation is an adaptation is to see if a subgroup of the larger family has a unique trait correlated with a unique habit of life. In other words, one would have to observe a subgroup of finches, say, with larger beaks, living successfully in a unique ecological niche away from the otherwise similar family of finches.[7]

Contrary to Owen, Darwin came to the conclusion that most monstrous variations were either too extreme for replication or just unrelated to environment (a characteristic they shared with most variations). However much Owen wanted to see macromutations as a first step toward new kinds of populations, empirical evidence from breeders and naturalists suggested otherwise.[8]

Darwin observed that hybrids either revert quickly to one of the parent types, or they do not reproduce at all. They fail utterly to spread their dramatic new traits to offspring; instead, such traits are lost in the next generation (if another generation is even possible). "An animal," he writes, "is only able to transmit those peculiarities to its offspring, which have been gained slowly." He continued to demonstrate his favorite rule, *Natura non facit saltum* (nature does not make sudden jumps), by pointing out that "mules have their whole form of body gained in one generation, so it is impossible to transmit them [to a subsequent generation]."[9] Departures that are too far from the parents will always disappear quickly because "what has long been in the blood, will remain in blood." Consequently, only slight variations, not monster jumps, will be passed down and possibly build up new populations gradually over time. So, although monsters are forms of variation, Darwin realized that they are not relevant variations for the transmutation issue. Monsters are either embryological mutants that cannot reproduce, or they reproduce (like six-fingered men) but don't fit as adaptations, or they result from hybridism but again fail to reproduce.

By provisionally entertaining the monster theory of species transmutation, Darwin was able to better hone his own thinking about evolution. It was shortly after considering the mechanism of monster jumps that he famously discovered the economist Thomas Malthus's theory of population reduction and applied it "not only to population and depopulation, but extermination and production of new forms."[10] The idea that environmental pressures could slowly shape the distribution of minor mutations and thereby adapt the populations to their conditions of life led Darwin to his mechanism of natural selection. The year 1838 was the turning point for Darwin; before that, he thought of monsters as a reasonable catalyst for evolution, but after the discovery of natural selection he rejected the role of monsters.

Monsters continued to intrigue Darwin in his mature writings, including *Origin of Species* and *The Descent of Man*, but they never again seemed compelling as nature's primary mechanism of transmutation. In fact, he often pointed out that the only way monsters continued to thrive, reproduce, and even become subspecies was through the reckless arts of human breeding (artificial selection). Considering the odd differences between the greyhound, the bloodhound, the bulldog, and the Chihuahua, Darwin wrote, "Domestic races of the same species . . . often have a somewhat monstrous character," in the sense that "they often differ in an extreme degree in some one part, both when compared with one another, and more especially when compared with all the species in nature to which they are nearest allied."[11] The unfortunate creation of freak animals is because "man selects only for his own good; Nature [by contrast] only for that of the being which she tends." Unlike natural selection, which results from multiple causes such as food supply, weather and geological conditions, disease, and competition inside and outside the species, humans breed animals in ways that do not maximize the health and fitness of the animal.[12]

The argument of the *Origin of Species* moves from conscious artificial selection to unconscious natural selection, but stylistic metaphors led some subsequent naturalists to try to put "consciousness" back into natural selection. Darwin's occasional anthropomorphic or theomorphic metaphors got him into trouble because many people used them to justify their hope that a divine hand was guiding natural selection, and he had to denounce this interpretation for decades after.[13]

Remember that Owen's monsters were possible mechanisms by which some design, some teleological direction, could be built into evolution. For Darwin, there is no teleological direction in nature. Once he hit on natural selection of chance micromutations, he didn't *need* any designing force in nature. He could explain the amazing adaptations of animals to environment without any need for conscious craftsmanship.[14] Darwin's nature did not need a designer, nor did it need sudden saltational jumps to create new species. Additionally, Darwin was unimpressed by Owen's ideal archetypes, and as the years wore on the two men grew further apart as naturalists and as friends. Suggesting that common body plans were the result of divine archetypes put Owen behind the times rather than in the vanguard.[15]

Just as homologies demonstrate ancestry rather than divine ideas, so, too, some monsters demonstrate ancestry rather than potential new species. Recall Darwin's description of humans born with werewolf syndrome, long hair covering their entire body and face. In *The Descent of Man* he considered cases of werewolf syndrome together with humans who are born with tails and suggested that both kinds of monsters are evidence that human beings are descended from animal ancestors. He included them in a battery of substantiating phenomena, all grouped together in chapter 1, "The Evidence of the Descent of Man from Some Lower Form." He offered the anomalous case of a tailed human as an atavism of our pre-human ancestral connection to primates and therefore a compelling bit of evidence for evolution. But the human werewolf monster is "a more curious case." Darwin argued that the hairy human anomaly is connected to a completely normal state of intrauterine fetal development. Around sixteen weeks after conception, all humans start to form fine hairs covering the body, called *lanugo* (Latin for "downy"). Shortly before birth the fetus sheds this lanugo and swallows it; it mixes with bile and mucus and becomes part of the meconium (the first bowel movement of the baby). Darwin didn't know some of these facts, but he did know that lanugo was part of normal embryological processes. And he suggested that perhaps human werewolf syndrome was a case of "arrested development," a teratological retention of a normally abandoned hair growth process. Darwin did not tarry on this topic, leaving it (placed in the same chapter with other "evidence of descent") as merely suggestive of evolution. But strictly speaking, if the werewolf syndrome is a monstrous arrested development of embryological process, then it is *not* really evidence of ancestral descent in the same way that human tails might be.

In the case of both hairy monsters and tailed monsters, Darwin recognized the importance of teratologies, but not as sources of new evolutionary pathways. They are not causes; they are either vestigial remnants that demonstrate the *fact* of evolution, or they are cases of arrested development that reveal more to us about the mysteries of embryology.

Despite Darwin's reining in of monsters, they remained provocative for many biologists, and more than one theory of evolution vied for allegiance in the late nineteenth and early twentieth century.[16] The botanist Hugo de Vries (1848–1935), for example, proffered a popular alternative to Darwinism called the "mutation theory of evolution." "It must be obvious," de Vries wrote in *Species and Varieties: Their Origin by Mutation* in 1904, "that this theory of natural selection leaves the question as to how the changes themselves are brought about, quite undecided. There are two possibilities, and both have been propounded by Darwin. One is the accumulation of the slight deviations of fluctuating variability, the other consists of successive sports or leaps taking place in the same direction."[17] De Vries, who developed an early genetics hypothesis, performed breeding experiments on plants and decided that Darwin had been too hasty to dismiss the role of macromutational jumps.

A monstrous plant, the Nepaul barley (a variety of *Hordeum vulgare*), came under de Vries's careful study, and he drew significant conclusions from its morphology. In the botanical world, flowers rarely grow directly out of the leaf of a plant, but Nepaul barley not only had the odd case of a flowered leaf but also a second, smaller floret growing above the first. This freakish morphology had no use, according to de Vries, and constituted "perhaps the most obviously useless structure in the whole vegetable kingdom." Nevertheless, he explained, the mutation was as completely hereditary as any of the most elegant adaptations in nature. "Therefore," he concluded, "it is one of the most serious objections to the hypothesis of slow and gradual improvements on the sole ground of their usefulness."[18]

This idea, that evolution occurs by sudden leaps without intermediaries, found its strongest supporter in Richard Goldschmidt (1878–1958). A controversial biologist, Goldschmidt made his reputation first in Germany by working on genetics and sex differentiation in gypsy moth varieties, and then in the United States (after fleeing the Nazis) by working on fruit fly mutations. His objections to the emerging "Mendelian-chromosomal theory" of genetics caused him to miss the boat of the dominant neo-Darwinian synthesis of natural selection and Mendelian genetics, called the *new synthesis*. But his mutation experiments led him to emphasize the importance of development, timing, rates of reaction, and function in ways that make some aspects of his biology seem more prescient than his peers acknowledged.[19] Goldschmidt coined the phrase "hopeful monsters" to refer to macromutational jumps that might, in time, form successful new

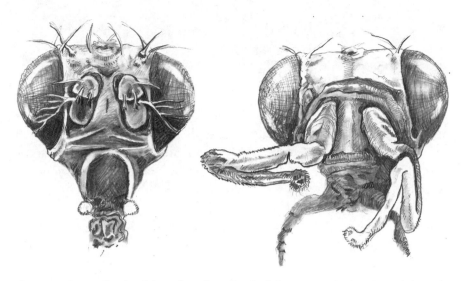

Compare the two heads of these fruit flies. On the left is a normal specimen; on the right the mutant fly has grown legs in the place of antennae. Pencil drawing by Stephen T. Asma © 2008.

species. The idea of viable large-scale saltation was completely out of step with the neo-Darwinian biology of the 1930s and 1940s.[20]

Imagine a fruit fly (*Drosophilia melanogaster*) with arms growing in place of wings, or a fly whose wings were transformed into halteres (the balancing appendages on either side of the body), or a fly with legs growing in place of antennae (aristapedia). These and many other monstrosities increased in frequency when Goldschmidt shocked his embryonic flies with temperature changes. In fact, he found that mutations increased by six times if he administered such shocks. Now admittedly, a monster with legs in place of antennae is not terribly "hopeful," but the basic jump of macromutation revealed by such experiments led him to suggest that hidden building mechanisms, such as segmentation, could somehow shift and thereby alter the organism's phenotype. To use an analogy, if you think about micromutations as small-scale changes in the spelling of words on this page, Goldschmidt's macromutations were more like transformations in the rules of grammar itself. Tweaking the grammar produces more dramatic effects in the overall result. Simple micromutations could not, in Goldschmidt's view, rack up the major transformations that evolution seemed to require, whereas mutations in the grammar of development (eventually called homeotic mutations) seemed a better candidate.

When biologists want to understand an animal, they must *reverse-engineer* it. Like a mechanic who wants to learn how an unfamiliar engine came to be built, the biologist must infer the causal mechanisms that shaped the anatomy of an individual or a population. This can be exceedingly difficult to do, especially when very different causal stories are consistent with the animal's present morphology. Is the particular shape of a fish's lobe fin entirely the result of a strong environmental selection pressure, or is it best understood as the effect of internal laws of growth? By analogy, if one is reverse-engineering an unfamiliar vehicle, it may be the case that the oddly shaped exhaust pipe was developed as an adaptation for occasional submersion in water, but it might also be shaped this way simply because an enlarged catalytic converter forced the pipe into a unique position, and its successful submersion ability is just an accidental consequence.

Because the morphological traits of an animal are usually useful and functional in a specific environment, it is hard to determine the internal nonfunctional material laws that may have shaped the traits independently of environment pressure. The developmental biologist Pere Alberch (1954–1998) created a new movement in the 1990s when he proposed "that it may be advantageous to turn to non-functional, grossly maladapted, teratologies when studying the properties of internal factors in evolution."[21]

Because monstrous deviations from normal development are usually poorly adapted when compared with their parents, they will be selected against. "This is a useful property because if, in spite of very strong negative selection, teratologies are generated in a discrete and recurrent manner, this order has to be a reflection of the internal properties of the developmental system." Like Goldschmidt, Alberch experimented with fruit flies. He found that the imaginal disks (tissues in the larval fly) could be manipulated to produce monsters, but the transformations were not chaotic: "For example, if a prospective genital cell makes a mistake, it will most likely produce a leg or a head-antenna tissue type....It will never give rise to a wing or a thorax." From these and other experiments Alberch concluded that mutations, whether natural or lab-induced, undergo a finite set of transformations. These limited trajectories, or developmental patterns, were not, he argued, sufficiently appreciated by neo-Darwinians, who tended to see mutation as unpredictable and almost infinitely potential.

In humans, for example, we have many cases of two-headed teratologies, but not three-headed. There is no good evidence of a single body axis that trifurcates at the anterior end into three heads.[22] Alberch surveyed the historical reports and concluded that the only seemingly reputable report of a three-headed child (from the Italian physicians Reina and Galvagni) appeared to be a case of a conjoined twin with two distinct spinal chords and a further parasite head built on the axis of one of the doubled spines. Double monsters (conjoined twins) divide and branch in the same three or four discernable ways, whether they are men, cows, or fish. Alberch also pointed out that cyclops teratologies exhibit the same morphological aspects, regardless of the particular species or higher taxa in which they occur. Monsters come to the rescue for biologists who want to isolate internal causes, but Alberch saw himself as returning the favor, raising monsters from their demoted Darwinian status. He claimed that his interest in teratology "contrasts with the bad reputation that monsters have traditionally enjoyed in the Darwinian literature." From a Darwinian perspective, teratologies are not adaptive variations, so they are "evolutionary dead ends" and "unworthy of study." But Alberch and his subsequent school of typologists treated monsters as "model systems to study the patterning generated by developmental properties." This approach to monsters continues to pick up steam and flourish today, but Alberch claimed that he was not a proponent of the "hopeful monsters" thesis of biologists like Goldschmidt. "I do not contend," Alberch said, "that teratologies are variation with evolutionary potential. In fact, I assume them to be lethal in most cases."

Stephen Jay Gould extrapolated on Alberch's research and showed how teratology can be profitably linked to evolutionary questions.[23] Consider the pentadactyl hand of tetrapods. Gould pointed out that the earliest known tetrapods, from the late Devonian period (390–340 million years ago), were incomplete fossils, but paleontologists in the 1930s reconstructed their limbs as five digit forms (assuming the orthodox view of pentadactyl homology). Surprisingly, however, more recent paleontological discoveries have shown that the earliest tetrapods had seven and sometimes even eight toes and fingers. It appears now that five digits was not an original vertebrate structure, but probably represents a later stabilization of form, one that still sits at a significant branching limb of the phylogenetic tree. But then Gould introduced some of Alberch's teratology to interesting ends.[24]

Before Alberch's research it was thought that the formation of the forelimb followed a central axis, with digits forming outward from some theoretical middle-line origin. Alberch showed that the order of the limb and digit formation followed a pattern of construction from back to front: the pinky finger is built first and the thumb is last (in the feet, the little toe is first and the big toe is last).[25] This was surprising and counterintuitive. Gould pointed out that, under Alberch's revision, "the array of digits

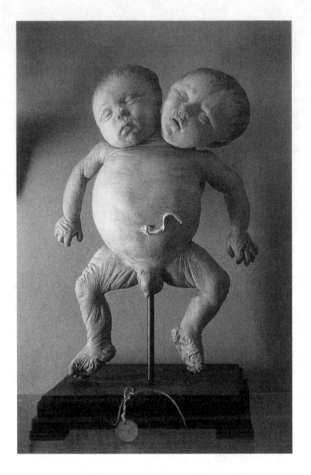

A conjoined twin, with two heads sharing one body. Photo by Joanna Ebenstein © 2008. Reprinted by kind permission of the artist and the Vrolik Museum, University of Amsterdam.

becomes a sequence of timing: Spatial position is a mark of temporal order. Back equals old; front is young." Confirmation of this theory came from independent phenomena suggesting that many animals who grow extra digits (monstrous polydactyls) do so by failing to shut off the normal sequence, thereby adding an extra digit after the "youngest" digit.[26]

Why does this have evolutionary significance? We may not know for sure when or why a mutation arose that fixed the pentadactyl structure for modern tetrapods. The answer to that may lie in the impenetrable swamp of evolution's historical contingency. But we now know that evolutionary change can happen to entire embryonic patterns, not just individual microvariations. If we extend Alberch's limb logic to phylogeny we have new tools for understanding evolution. Gould wrote, "Evolution can reduce the number of fingers by stopping the back-to-front generating machine at five. What we now call digit one may only be the stabilized stopping point of a potentially extendable sequence."[27] Why five digits survived when eight did not is a question for natural selection. But how five and eight digits were originally built is an issue of development, not selection.

Monsters with supernumerary or missing digits help us to see the causality at work in normal animals. Monsters demonstrate internal constraints, but monsters themselves are extreme cases and therefore deleterious. Smaller scale mutations in these same constraint systems, however, can play a role in evolution.

Do these developmental jumps indicate violations of Darwin's *natura non facit saltum*? The jury appears to be out on this question. Gould seemed to think that there was, in this new logic of monsters, a kind of vindication of sorts for Goldschmidt's "hopeful monster" idea.[28] Orthodox neo-Darwinians claim that all macromutations are produced by micromutations (harkening back to Darwin's claim that species are nothing but stabilized varieties), but Gould wanted to include macromutation as an additional evolutionary mechanism. Despite the jitters produced by these comments among the creationist set, it seems Gould was correct when he argued that such theoretical and empirical discoveries are healthy refinements of Darwinism, not death knells. "Hopeful monster" became a rhetorical banner for biologists who wanted to emphasize development more than natural selection, but nobody except the most marginal characters were willing to throw out the dominance of natural selection, the undisputed adapting force in nature.

EVO-DEVO

Within the past few years this whole business of "hopeful monsters" has become paramount again, in the new science of *evo-devo*, "evolutionary developmental biology." In recent years biologists have discovered the empirical genetic evidence for the developmental constraint systems that the monsterologists Geoffroy, Owen, Goldschmidt, and others could only theorize about.

Biologists who were working in the 1990s on cracking genetic codes assumed that major phenotypic differences between species would be reflected in major gene pool differences. It seemed reasonable to suppose that we'd find very different genetic ingredients in the molecular makeup of the different animal species; tiny Darwinian mutations would have slowly accumulated diverse pools of DNA information, and hundreds of millions of years of changes would have resulted, neo-Darwinians believed, in very unique genetic codes for humans, mice, and insects. But such was not the case.

In 2001 a provisional map of the human genome was completed, and it surprised everyone. Contrary to expectations, humans turned out to have only around 25,000 genes—about one third the predicted number. And like another in a long history of scientific blows to our collective ego, we also learned that humans and mice had roughly the same number of genes. Even nematode worms were genetically closer to us (quantitatively and qualitatively) than we ever expected.[29] So if the phenotypic diversity of the animal kingdom is not the direct result of genotypic diversity, then it's not the genetic stuff that causes all the diversity.[30] Biologists began to appreciate the fact that gene *expression* is as important as the genes themselves. An expression system of on/off timing switches has a huge role to play in the morphology, physiology, and even taxonomy of species. Neo-Darwinians had erroneously treated development as if it were just the medium for unrolling the message, but in fact the medium *is* the message. Two similar gene pools could have different switching patterns, and two radically different animals could subsequently result. Expression, we now know, is largely controlled by special timing switches, called homeotic genes. To return to my beleaguered cooking metaphors, DNA is like the ingredients of a cake, and homeotic genes are like the recipe that dictates how much and when the ingredients should be added.

Monsters return in this new investigation because, as always, their various abnormalities help biologists detect the relevant expression mechanisms, both abnormal and normal. The biologist Scott Holley, for example, is currently studying zebra fish monsters in the Department of Molecular, Cellular, and Developmental Biology at Yale University.[31] He and his colleagues are exploring the ways that early genetic events can transform limb and body morphologies across vertebrate species. Zebra fish, especially teratological versions, are a relatively new model for studying the formation of the spinal column; humans and fish, for example, have the same genetic process for segmenting vertebrae,[32] and certain spinal teratologies of the zebra fish appear to unfold similarly in certain cases of human spinal birth defects. So progress in our understanding of the fish may help us prevent or ameliorate spinal deformities in humans.

The focus of Holley's research is to understand how the genes *express* in the segmentation process (somitogenesis) of the vertebral column. The anterior and posterior axis of the forming fish begins to divide into repeated elements, called somites, which will eventually become vertebrae. Cells transcribe the gene and build the spine downward from top to bottom. The cells build the spine by dividing through mitosis and also by migrating in a distinct downward, then outward pattern. But this building process is regulated further by a "segmentation clock," a universal biological timing system that can now be observed across vertebrate species. The growth is pushing downward, but regular oscillations are traveling upward toward the anterior of the developing fish, creating repeated wave-fronts. The waves constitute ebbs and flows of transcription activity. The wave-front, which travels one cell diameter every five minutes, tries to make somites (prevertebrae) everywhere, but the regulating clock gates the activity and thereby creates the necessary gaps between vertebrae. All of this is a complex feedback system of signals which ensures that enough, but not too much, material is growing, but also being channeled correctly. Embryogenesis is a remarkable dance of dynamic cell division, migration, and tissue complexification, but still a relatively stable process if you back up to observe the level of body plan morphogenesis.

Professor Holley's group has isolated some specific zebra fish mutations in which the on/off switches are not working; the gates are not regulating properly. Malfunctions in the segmentation clock can produce too many or too few vertebrae, or lead the organism to build a spine with too much cell migration and not enough mitosis. The same mutation causes abnormal formation of the vertebral column in fish, mice, and humans.

Professor Holley himself is not particularly concerned with the evolutionary implications of his research, but one can see how the proponents of macromutation could get very excited about it. Small adjustments in the segmentation clock could result in significant changes to the overall length of the body. And these switching systems are not just concerned with anatomical construction; they also regulate the postpartum or postovum growth and aging mechanisms of organisms. Neoteny, for example, is the retention of otherwise juvenile traits well into the adult phase of an animal's life span.[33] Evo-devo biologists suggest that such adjustments to maturation rates (inter- and intraspecies) could be the result of mutations in the regulating homeotic genes. These timing mutations would be selected for or against, just like smaller variations, depending on whether they conferred advantage to the organism.

In 2006 the Swiss ichthyologist Maurice Kottelat discovered the tiniest fish in the world, the size of a fingernail clipping, living in the acidic peat swamps of Sumatra. This monstrous fish is a mosaic of mature and immature phenotypes: it has a juvenile larval body with mature gonads and pelvic fins. It is as if the sexual equipment of an adult was found on a newborn. It is unclear *why* such a mosaic would be selected for and preserved, but the mechanics of *how* mutations of aging occur are slowly becoming clearer.

Evo-devo biologists love these weird and murky interfaces between homeotic genes, embryogenesis, and species transformations. Theirs is still very much an emerging field of study, but we have some impressive data so far. Homeotic genes regulate the development of an embryo by regulating smaller scale gene sequences, often acting like repressor molecules that bind onto specific DNA sites and block RNA transcription and subsequent protein production. Some regulating genes, such as Pax genes, are conserved over many species and orders, acting like little tool kits capable of building their same products in whatever context they appear. When the Pax genes that help build eyes are transplanted from an insect to a mouse, or vice versa, they start to build eyes in these radically new environments.

Eight of these homeotic controlling genes are called Hox genes; they can be found in most animals as the controlling system of body morphology. These eight Hox genes are so embedded in the deep grammar of life that biologists believe they've been at work in our collective gene pool for over half a billion years. It is possible that these Hox gene systems cause many of the homologous body plans that Richard Owen previously obfuscated by evoking transcendentalism. If these Hox genes turn out to be the real archetypes, then Geoffroy, with his "generative laws," may have been more correct even than Darwin, with his thesis of contingent shared ancestry.

IN LIGHT OF EVO-DEVO, what more can we conclude about the nagging question of hopeful monsters? The scientist Sean B. Carrol seems confident that the "specter of a 'hopeful monster'" has finally been banished by evo-devo.[34] In support of the neo-Darwinian modern synthesis, Carrol claims that the gradual (nonsaltational) micromutations, together with the sifting effect of natural selection, are all that is needed to explain evolution—no appeals to jumps, leaps, sports, monsters, or macromutations are necessary. "Evolution of homeotic genes and the traits they control has been very important," Carrol explains, "but has not occurred by different means than the sorts of mutations and variations that typically arise in populations. The preservation of Hox genes and other tool kit genes for more than five hundred million years illustrates that the pressure to maintain these proteins has generally been as great as that upon any class of molecules. Instead, the evolutionary tinkering of switches, from those of master Hox genes to those of humbler pigmentation enzymes, typically underlies the evolution of form." In short, Carrol claims that macroevolution is entirely explained by microevolution.

In the United States, where all evolutionary issues are still battling with ridiculous creationist claims, it is easy to understand why biologists want to present a unified Darwinian front against the looming threats of irrationality. My suspicion is that some of the current reemphasis on gradualism is due to this perceived need to cut off pathways to special creation or various miraculous evolution theories. But the idea, loathed by Darwinians, of nature jumping is not inherently incoherent. The objection that Darwin originally had, and that all biologists still rightly have, is to the idea that a jump could somehow *foretell* the best adaptive direction (the potentially helpful trait) and then modify accordingly to meet the niche demands. Nature cannot see that wings or extra vertebrae would be really helpful to a specific rodent and thereby accelerate an anatomical jump to wings or extra vertebrae. The reason Darwinians are so riled up by the mention of saltation is that it has historically been connected to the idea of a purposeful Nature (e.g., by Owen, Asa Gray, de Vries, neo-Lamarckians). If we strip saltation from this unfortunate teleological association we find nothing prohibitive about the idea that macromutations can strike out and take their chances, just as micromutations do, in the domain of natural selection. The vast majority of mutations, micro and macro, would be deleterious (or neutral) in the face of environmental pressure, but occasionally they might offer a slight advantage to their possessor. In any case, in a historical science such as evolution theory, which must rationally reconstruct events from deep time, the idea of successful nonteleological macromutations is at least as coherent as gradualism in the reconstruction of phylogeny.

In the end, some of the recent debates about monsters in biology are more semantic than substantive. If you decide to define monsters or teratologies as variations too extreme to reproduce viable offspring, then of course you're not going to find any monsters acting as launching pads for evolutionary pathways; you've begged the question in your definition. But if you define monsters as extreme morphological deviations and leave it at that, the issue of whether or not there are "hopeful monsters" becomes a more empirical point.

Inner Monsters
The Psychological Aspects

12

The Art of Human Vulnerability

Angst and Horror

Presently, I heard a slight groan, and I knew it was the groan of mortal terror.
It was not a groan of pain or of grief—oh, no! It was the low stifled sound
that arises from the bottom of the soul when overcharged with awe.
EDGAR ALLAN POE, *THE TELL-TALE HEART*

THE WORD *HORROR* COMES FROM the Latin verb *horrere*, to "stand on end" or bristle. The term is often used today to designate an artistic genre that began with the gothic literature of Shelley (*Frankenstein*, 1818), Polidori (*The Vampyre*, 1819), and Irving (*Sleepy Hollow*, 1820) and continues to the present with such authors as Stephen King and filmmakers George Romero, Sam Raimi, and Wes Craven. But *horror* has also found its way into ordinary language as the name of the ineffable emotion that one experiences when one is afraid of something unfamiliar; for example, a monster, or perceived monster, induces an experience that's somewhat different from the fear provoked by a snarling dog. Horror is both the human emotion and the artistic genre designed to produce that emotion. It is the subjective arena in which we usually encounter monsters.

We are moving in our story from anxieties about external monsters to anxieties about inner monsters. Obviously, earlier eras felt the drama of inner alienation, but the nineteenth and twentieth centuries dredged the depths of the unconscious more deeply and tried to map their findings. In this chapter I want to analyze some of those psychological mechanisms that *respond* to monsters. In this way we'll have better insight when we turn to the unique creatures ahead.

There seems to be some undeniable cognitive component to monster fear.[1]
Is a headless horseman particularly scary when compared with a mous-
tache-less man or a hatless man because we've never experienced such an
anomaly, or because we have some instinctual understanding that heads
are essential for human life, so that the headless monster is an instance of
multiple "category jamming," both morphologically incoherent and also
transgressing the categories of animate and inanimate?

The philosopher of horror Noel Carroll invented the term *category jamming* and makes an argument that fits nicely with findings from developmental psychology. Experiments demonstrate that animals and humans
respond to their earliest experiences by internalizing a cognitive classification system based on the creatures they regularly encounter. After a
certain time, however, the classification system "solidifies" into a cognitive framework, and any subsequently strange and unclassifiable encounter
produces fear in the knower.[2] Categorical mismatch makes the knower
very uncomfortable. Carroll arrived at his own mismatch theory by notic-
ing that most horror monsters are *disgusting* as well as threatening.[3] He
argues that human beings seem especially disgusted by "impurity." Things
that we find impure and consider to be abominations are usually interstitial entities, in between normal categories of being. For example, blood,
feces, spit, snot, and vomit all blur the usual categories of *me* and *not me*, or
human and *not human*. Pushing this idea of transgressing categories further, Carroll extends the unsettling aspect of interstitial awareness to our
experience of monsters in horror genres. The argument is made more compelling by the fact that so many monsters are depicted as truly disgusting.
One thinks of the mucus-like slime oozing off most aliens, the gelatinous
blob monsters, the undulating goopy transformations of shape-shifters,
or the viscous twisting of monster reproduction. Carroll thinks that it is
this cognitive slippage invoked by monsters that explains why we are both
repelled by and drawn to horror films and novels. The fascination produced
by categorical mismatches is the solution to the paradox of why we seek
out an experience that is at least partly unpleasant.

ANGST AND FEAR

H. P. Lovecraft (1890–1937) is a name synonymous with horror, and
many connoisseurs of the genre consider him the rightful heir to Poe's
distinguished mantle. His stories, such as the "The Call of Cthulhu," were
sometimes published in the pulp magazine *Weird Tales* during his lifetime,

but his influence has been acknowledged by many, including Jorge Luis Borges, Clive Barker, Stephen King, Neil Gaiman, and even a small army of heavy metal bands.

In "The Call of the Cthulhu" Lovecraft describes a giant sea monster sleeping at the bottom of the ocean until accidentally awakened by foolish men. Allusions to Leviathan abound, but also the legends of the Kraken, the ship-smashing giant octopus or squid feared by northern sailors since at least the seventeenth century. The monster appears to draw on imagery from Alfred Lord Tennyson's 1830 poem "The Kraken" in which Tennyson describes the beast's "ancient, dreamless, uninvaded sleep." Tennyson's poem, it bears mentioning, also influenced Jules Verne's 1870 novel *Twenty Thousand Leagues under the Sea*. Lovecraft's monster Cthulhu is described as a green, sticky, mountain-size creature, with an "awful squid head," "writhing feelers," and "flabby claws." When the monster's head is rammed with a ship, it bursts with "a slushy nastiness" like a "cloven sunfish," but then recomposes and regenerates of its own self-organizing power.

Lovecraft was a master at giving us these blood-curdling monsters, but it is the emotion of eerie dread he excels in producing that I want to examine here. In his 1927 *Supernatural Horror in Literature*, Lovecraft argues that good horror evokes a unique subjective emotion, which he refers to as "cosmic fear."[4] There is something in the horror experience, he claims, that resonates with a deep, instinctual awe of the unknown. "The one test of the really weird," he explains, "is simply this—whether or not there be excited in the reader a profound sense of dread, and of contact with unknown spheres and powers; a subtle attitude of awed listening, as if for the beating of black wings or the scratching of outside shapes on the known universe's utmost rim." Lovecraft suggests that all human beings have an instinctual awareness (some more refined than others) of the paltry state of human understanding, especially when compared with the almost limitless domain of the strange and unfamiliar. That sense of fragility and vulnerability is a major aspect of this "cosmic fear" that horror triggers in us.

The same year that Lovecraft published *Supernatural Horror in Literature*, the German philosopher Martin Heidegger published his magnum opus, *Sein und Zeit* (Being and Time). From quite a different starting place, Heidegger, Jean-Paul Sartre, and other existential writers argued that there is a radical kind of human experience, which is like fear but in a way deeper. Heidegger calls this radical dread *angst* (anxiety). Fear, he argued, is different from angst, because fear is a response to a definite, identifiable threat. One will have a fearful response to an assailant in a dark alley, an approaching aggressive animal, or a felt earthquake or other natural disaster. But angst is the response to an indefinite threat; the danger is nowhere in particular and yet everywhere. Like Lovecraft's "cosmic fear," Heidegger's angst is an ineffable emotion of metaphysical proportions. Angst doesn't make me aware of a particular threat, but draws me out of my ordinary utilitarian ways of operating in the day-to-day world and makes me aware of my existential quandary: Who and what am I? "Being-anxious," Heidegger says, "discloses, primordially and directly, the world as world."[5] It places human beings into a face-to-face crisis with their own authentic potentiality. Angst is that unsettling philosophical sense that you, and every other thing in the world, are just dust in the wind.

It is remarkable that thinkers as diverse as Lovecraft, Heidegger, and (as we'll see) Freud were all trying to articulate a similar range of oblique irrational subjective experiences—dark, unsettling experiences that could not be discursively communicated except in the poetic and visual expressions of artists. When the horror genre pushes past the simple fear-based narrative of a monster chasing a victim and instead constructs an eerie world of foreboding, it seems to cross over into this more metaphysical pessimism of cosmic absurdity. Cosmic fear or angst or despair suggests, even if only temporarily, that the world *lacks* the secure structure and meaning that we ordinarily assume it to have. Every horror film, and there are a lot of them, that gives us a false ending of heroic triumph over the monster, but then shifts the camera to an unstoppable legion of such monsters now on their way to wreak further havoc challenges our deep sense of a just moral fabric to the universe. The same can be said about monsters like Lovecraft's Cthulhu or Hercules's Hydra, who take a beating, even seem to be obliterated, but then reassemble their odious slime bodies into new and improved tentacles, claws, morphologies, or even clones. Both existentialism and horror, in their emphasis on human vulnerability, are critiques of rationalist Enlightenment-based modernity.

The description and theory of a cosmic fear, with its threatening "unknown spheres and powers…on the known universe's utmost rim," might be traced back to Immanuel Kant's concept of *the sublime*. Sometimes we have an aesthetic experience that is both painful and pleasurable, and Kant calls this the sublime. Kant's favorite examples usually involve huge, unintelligible magnitudes, such as contemplating the infinity of the universe as you peer out at the night sky, or experiencing some overwhelming natural disaster from a safe distance. If I am asked to think of the *whole universe*, I understand very well the request and I have some sort of *idea* of the whole universe, but I cannot actually *imagine* it. I imagine parts of it maybe, or I imagine some giant amorphous blob of matter contained in a larger empty space, but both of these are failures or frustrations of the imagination to follow through on the idea. "Hence the feeling of the sublime," Kant explains, "is a feeling of displeasure that arises from the imagination's inadequacy, in an aesthetic estimation of magnitude, for an estimation by reason, but is at the same time also a pleasure" because we experience (in this frustration) that *reason* itself has interests which are above and beyond our usual modes of experience and understanding. "In presenting the sublime in nature," Kant states, "the mind feels *agitated*, while in an aesthetic judgment about the beautiful in nature it is in *restful* contemplation."[6] All this becomes part of Kant's larger project, which is to make room for the higher truths of ethics and religion (i.e., the moral law and the big ideas of God, freedom, and soul) that cannot be discovered directly by the common modes of human knowledge, but that can be inferred from these universally unattainable tasks or yearnings of reason.[7]

Kant was optimistic that whatever lay beyond the range of our frustrated minds was good (was God, actually), albeit inaccessible to our understanding. Other philosophers didn't share that comfort. The German philosopher Arthur Schopenhauer (1788–1860) developed Kant's philosophy further (some say he corrupted it) by suggesting that our own experiences with desire, craving, and striving, even in their brutal and cruel forms, are more in touch with reality (the *noumenon*) than are our logic, reason, and science. Art, according to Schopenhauer, has the unique ability to raise the usually submerged machinations of will to the surface, so we can see the world and ourselves in their naked primordial state of suffering. Art has the power to show us the suffering of the will-dominated real world, but also to break our servitude (if only temporarily) to the omnipresent will.[8]

Friedrich Nietzsche (1844–1900) extended Schopenhauer's pessimism further and argued that the will-to-live is derivative of an even more primordial force, which he called the will-to-power. Nietzsche looked at the world as an expression of psychological forces, prince among them the psychological drive to be powerful. Underneath the day-to-day phenomenal realm (we go to work, find mates, have children, do art, fight wars, etc.) is the deeper truth of competing volitions and hidden motives. And this will-to-power is not simply human, but is the spring inside all nature.

As we move from Nietzsche to Freud, we arrive at a mature, gloomy tradition of darkness, both metaphysical and psychological.[9] For pessimists, reality is not a well-lit orderly place with occasional corners of shady superstition. Instead, reality is a sinister, haunted world of ill will, with fragile glimmers and flickers of human knowledge and safety. "The horror. The horror," Kurtz says in Conrad's *Heart of Darkness*. Even the Darwinian view of nature as "red in tooth and claw" was incorporated into Victorian pessimism. Like Schopenhauer (but out of a very different tradition), the evolutionist T. H. Huxley believed that "the ethical progress of society depends, not on imitating the cosmic process, still less in running away from it, but in combating it."[10] Mirroring that external struggle and insecurity is the pessimistic internal world of monsters: desires, cravings, fears, anxieties so powerful as to make us feel alienated from our very selves.

Freud tempered the speculative flights of the philosophical pessimists and treated the dark and hidden *thing-in-itself* as a feature of human psychology rather than a cosmic metaphysical force. Confining himself to the human experience, he argued that the veil of conscious representations (the realm of the manifest) concealed an enormous reservoir of emotional drives and impulses: the *unconscious* (the latent realm). Like Schopenhauer and Nietzsche, Freud claimed that the irrational, emotional, and instinctual dimensions of man were more powerful and constitutive than conscious rationality. He contended that disparate and seemingly unrelated events in our conscious life (behaviors and beliefs) are in fact tied together and coherent in the pseudo logic of the unconscious. We can access this deep reservoir of instinctual desires and fears only indirectly, through clues provided in dreams, hypnosis, art, linguistic slips, and so on. It may be safe to say that the unconscious becomes the twentieth-century home of the monsters. Having worn out their welcome in religion, natural history, and travelers' tales, the monsters settled into their new abode of human psychology.[11]

FREUD

In 1919 Sigmund Freud wrote an influential essay titled "The Uncanny" ("Das Unheimliche"). In it he explored the spooky literary conventions of fiction writers (e.g., E. T. A. Hoffmann) but also derived a larger psychological category, the category of feeling strange, not at home, not secure, not quite right.[12] Freud defined the uncanny as a feeling that is somewhat familiar but also foreign. It is a form of emotional and cognitive dissonance: "It is undoubtedly related to what is frightening—to what arouses dread and horror."[13] The scholar of religion Timothy Beal says, "Monsters are personifications of the *unheimlich*. They stand for what endangers one's sense of security, stability, integrity, well-being, health and meaning."[14]

In his essay Freud discusses some dominant elements of horror: severed limbs, disembodied spirits, evil doppelgangers, and the fear of being buried alive. These fears are explained by his psychoanalytic theory, which proposes that one's early psychological life (the psyche) is dominated by the narcissistic pursuit of pleasure (the pleasure principle), whereas one's later psyche is more accommodated to a world indifferent to one's particular ego satisfaction (the reality principle). You come into the world

Sigmund Freud, pioneer in the science of monstrous feelings. Courtesy of Photofest.

wanting everything, but in short order you are dealt the repeated blows of the reality check: you are not the center of the universe. Repression, an internal punishment, is the mechanism by which the early narcissism is reeducated, overcome, and subsumed into the later psyche. Such repression begins externally, in the form of parents disciplining the child's cravings and behaviors, but soon the disciplinary authority takes up residence inside the child's mind, becoming the conscience.[15] The original desires and cravings of Id and Ego do not, according to Freud, evaporate and disappear, but instead submerge below the conscious surface into the deep fathoms of the unconscious.

Why are we so disturbed by horror stories of cloning and doppelgangers generally? Why are "evil twin" scenarios so commonly feared?[16] The idea of another version of yourself, Freud argues, is a thinly veiled expression of your desire to extend your life. The desire to live on and not perish, to never terminate, is made manifest in the form of a fantasy about another you.[17] Reality reminds us on a daily basis that we will die and everyone we love will die. So the universal urge to live forever must be repressed as we grow up. This repression means that the desire must be transformed from positive to negative. In order to grow up one must negate one's urge to live forever.

As mature adults we have, practically speaking, overcome our infantile desire for immortality, but, like everything that's repressed, the craving has only gone deep underground into the unconscious. The doppelganger, as another self, was loved in our original psychological phase, but during repression it came to be regarded with suspicion, fear, and loathing. Evil twins, clones, and supernatural doppelgangers are experienced as uncanny rather than just fearsome because they simultaneously stimulate the older unconscious familiar feelings *and* the newer negative feelings of terror. It seems clear that this Freudian explanation applies equally well to our ongoing fascination with zombies.[18]

Severed arms that crawl, jump, and choke their victims regularly inhabit our nightmares and our horror novels and films. Freud writes, "Dismembered limbs, a severed head, a hand cut off at the wrist…feet which dance by themselves…—all these have something peculiarly uncanny about them, especially when, as in the last instance, they prove capable of independent activity in addition." Ultimately Freud thinks that fears of severed body parts are coded instances of castration anxiety.

In an essay entitled "Medusa's Head," Freud takes on the Greek monster myth. Recall that Medusa was originally one of the three Gorgon sisters, and her frightening, fanged, snake-haired visage could turn men to stone. The hero Perseus, using a mirrored shield to safely look at Medusa, killed the monster by decapitating her. Perseus made use of the head as a weapon, turning enemies to stone, before finally offering it to Athena, who in turn placed it on Zeus's shield as a talisman. Freud ties this common Western monster to his psychoanalytic theory, in particular the castration anxiety. The severed head is just the manifest representation of the latent fear of castration, but the Medusa head is also a "mitigation of the horror" because the snakes symbolically replace the penis. Moreover, the Medusa head, which turns men to stone, symbolizes the psychological retort to emasculation by signifying rock-hard erect potency.[19]

Whether or not Freud's *explanation* of the uncanny is correct, few would dispute the phenomenon. In fact, in our day of computer animation and robotics, there is renewed interest in the uncanny because the attempts to create virtual humans have stimulated new ways for us to feel strangely familiar and unfamiliar at the same time. Masahiro Mori, a Japanese roboticist, noticed a common phenomenon that he calls the "uncanny valley," referring to the feelings of empathy that viewers have toward virtual protagonists.[20] If a robot or video game avatar looks humanoid we tend to have more empathy toward it. One could plot an empathy curve upward from the abstract creatures of an arcade game like Pac-Man to the more humanized creatures of Super Mario Brothers and Halo. Apparently viewers will report empathic feelings for increasingly humanoid features, but when the illusion is quite close, a drop-off in empathy occurs. When a replicant or an avatar is very close to human, but not quite exact, a distinct feeling of strangeness or creepiness rises. The phenomenon is called an uncanny valley because the empathy rises again dramatically once the representation crosses some mysterious incremental line into a more perfect depiction. The sensation indicates that "almost human" is more creepy and unsettling than a cartoonish or exaggerated representation of human. This would apply equally to the soulless eyes of otherwise well-rendered CGI characters and the particularly loathsome pseudo humans of the zombie genre.

Freud's general point, that we have anxiety after discovering that we are *not* God, is still compelling. Our narcissism is so satisfying when occasionally sated, but it grossly overexaggerates our power and control in the wider world, where it is eventually subdued by the inflexible and nonnegotiable aspects of reality. There are forces out there (Freud uses the Greek word for "necessities," *ananke*) that are stronger than us and overpower us (the weather, gravity, politics, fathers, etc.). Monsters can act as symbolic projections of all these frustrations rolled into one beast, or kind of beast. Like ananke, the monster is usually intractable and cannot be reasoned with. It is a symbol of opposition and therefore a great justification for our aggressions, something we can love to hate. When it cannot be conquered (like the elusive serial killer, the entrenched political tyrant, or the alien onslaught of science fiction stories) it demonstrates our limits, it curbs and checks our narcissism. But when the monster is conquered, as when St. George slays the dragon, Theseus kills the Minotaur, Dracula gets staked, or Perseus decapitates Medusa, it symbolically returns our narcissism and reaffirms, albeit temporarily, our infantile power.

For Freud, the dark well of reality, which cannot be successfully processed by the intellect, is the unconscious, and this deep well holds our myriad repressed desires in a state of suspended animation. But they are occasionally awakened in dreams, horror movies, and altered states of consciousness and given momentary freedom in the realm of conscious awareness. Freud's theory of the uncanny and Lovecraft's cosmic fear share a common ancestor in Schopenhauer's pessimistic notion of an overwhelming hidden force, which in turn owes its mutated descent to Kant's sublime. In all these theoretical progeny one finds a common, though sometimes inarticulate investigation of human vulnerability. We are all impermanent ephemera.

Whether you are confronting God in a religious ecstasy or confronting the onslaught of unstoppable monsters, you feel *helpless, powerless* by comparison. You identify with the film's or the novel's characters as they face the radically uneven and unfair power proportions. That awe-ful emotion, which I've been describing as a radical vulnerability, is the common reservoir from which religion and horror mutually draw. I take this sense of vulnerability to be the phenomenological seed experience that gives life to the diverse posited metaphysical causes (e.g., the will to power, the noumenon) as well as the relevant psychoanalytic conjectures of Freud and the more vague speculations of Lovecraft. I'm not interested in defending one of these over another, although my tendency is to prefer less metaphysics rather than more. But I believe that all these diverse approaches, especially from Schopenhauer onward, are correct in their stress on the more emotional, instinctual, prelinguistic, noncognitive aspects of horror. Against Carroll's rather intellectual view of horror as cognitive category jamming, this other tradition (especially Freud) gives us the more sensual or gut-felt aspects of horror.

Furthermore, in defense of the sublime or cosmic thesis, I would suggest that an overwhelming sense of the sublime need not be tied to a theological entity like God, or even a mystical otherworldly force. The inexorable laws of nature alone will do nicely to crush my own egotistical sense of power in the world, and I don't need to read the universal uncontrollable forces as being transcendental or wholly other. This is why, I think, the biological monsters created by H. R. Giger in Ridley Scott's film *Alien* are so horrific: we are as helpless (at least in the first three acts) in the face of these natural selection machines as we are before any traditional deity (or at least the common narratives about those deities). Like Sartre, who redefined hell as "other people," we can redefine awe-ful, nonnegotiable reality as *nature* itself. In this way, the metaphysical tendencies of earlier "vulnerability thinkers" like Schopenhauer are tamed and naturalized, such that they are consistent with the Freudian notion of an inevitably constraining reality principle.

The most far-reaching idea of monsters during the twentieth century is probably Freud's mature theory of aggression as an internal force that makes narcissism look charming by comparison. I take up the monsters of aggression extensively in the next chapter, but for the remainder of this chapter I should like to illustrate further some of the subjective states of vulnerability that emerge in the imaginative realm of modern horror.

Maybe Freud is correct when he argues that uncanniness is caused by a return of the repressed, or perhaps some future breakthrough in neurobiology will reveal an "uncanny" neural network in the brain. But causal stories aside, there seems to be relative consensus about which writers, film directors, and other artists are good at producing the mysterious emotion. David Lynch, for example, seems to top most people's lists of creators of the creepy and eerie. If he had done nothing but direct *Eraserhead* (1977) he would go down in the annals of spooky weirdness, but that proved to be just the start of a long career of highly disturbing films. *Eraserhead* is an impossible film to summarize, and its nightmarish surrealism has to be experienced to be believed, but suffice it to say that the film involves a mutant baby, a severed head that gets turned into erasers, a freakish woman living in a radiator, and a troubling vivisection on said mutant baby. The director Stanley Kubrick was apparently quite taken by the spookiness of Lynch's film, and even showed it to his cast of *The Shining* to put them in the proper uncanny mind-set.[21]

Lynch has given us a catalogue of memorable films and television shows, including *The Elephant Man* (1980), *Blue Velvet* (1986), *Wild at Heart* (1990), *Twin Peaks* (1990–91), *Lost Highway* (1997), *Mulholland Drive* (2001), and *Inland Empire* (2006). Playing with surrealist techniques that date back to Dali and Buñuel, but also forging his own cinematic language, Lynch gives us an abundance of cosmic fear. His films are filled with psychopaths, severed body parts, vomit, blood, and characters whose motives seem as mysterious to themselves as they plainly are to the audience. Lynch seems interested in mining the ineffable micro-weirdness of mundane objects and events for their deeper, buried, unconscious root systems. As David Foster Wallace wrote, trying to crystallize the Lynchean aesthetic, "Quentin Tarantino is interested in watching somebody's ear getting cut off; David Lynch is interested in the ear."[22]

Lynch's films seem to be direct explorations of the permanently oblique unconscious, especially when compared with other creepy filmmakers, such as Tim Burton. By comparison, Burton's gothic films are nostalgic references to the uncanny through the mediating lens of the horror genre's earlier films (e.g., the Hammer Horror films of the 1950s–1970s). Burton's films, which include *Edward Scissorhands* (1990), *Sleepy Hollow* (1999), and *Sweeney Todd* (2007), are self-conscious and self-referential about the horror genre, whereas Lynch's films are more directly evocative of the uncanny itself. When asked in an interview if it is necessary that he understand something if he's going to film it, Lynch replied confidently, "No, not one bit. The reverse is true."[23]

There are monsters in Lynch films, some metaphorical (e.g., Frank Booth in *Blue Velvet*) and some misunderstood (e.g., John Merrick in *The Elephant Man*), but I've been trying to suggest a more abstract concept of monstrous throughout this chapter, one that Lynch illustrates well in his work. The angst that Heidegger claimed to have *no specific object* (unlike fear) and the cosmic fear that Lovecraft tried to articulate seem to me to be obscure but palpable expressions of a dispersed, diffused monster. The mundane and ordinary things of the world have been infused with an alienating, monstrous quality. Perhaps the most obvious and patent example of this immanent, not imminent, threat can be found in the short films of the Brothers Quay.

Stephen and Timothy Quay are identical twins and filmmakers, born in America but living in England; their films include *Street of Crocodiles* (1986), *The Cabinet of Jan Svankmajer* (1984), *In Absentia* (2000), and *The Piano Tuner of Earthquakes* (2005). They seem to have taken the uncanny aesthetic, which one finds in directors like Lynch, and pushed it to degrees of abstraction hitherto unexplored. In many cases, characters and stories are completely gone, but through the genius of the Quays' animation sensibility the audience is often angst-ridden and uneasy at the repetitive twitching of a hair or a spoon or a calligraphy quill or some other mundane object. In an interview the Quays said, "What happens in the shadow, in the grey regions, also interests us—all that is elusive and fugitive, all that can be said in those beautiful half tones, or in whispers, in deep shade."[24]

TORTURE PORN

Leaving aside these more subtle examples of uncanny horror, we need to acknowledge the mainstream film explorations of vulnerability, particularly the recent genres "splatter-punk" and "torture porn." One might take the recent celebrations of torture in horror films, and the box-office popularity of such horror, as suggestive evidence for a Freudian understanding of the genre. We seem to have mysterious tastes and predilections inside us, which get satisfied only by indulgence in the grisly and macabre. Freud may have given us a new language for understanding this taste for the grotesque, but the taste itself is very old.

In Plato's *Republic* the human attraction to the grotesque is taken to be more evidence that the psyche houses a multifaceted set of desires and powers, sometimes working in confederation and sometimes at odds. "There is a story," Socrates explains,

> which I remember to have heard, and in which I put faith. The story is, that Leontius, the son of Aglaion, coming up one day from the Piraeus, under the north wall on the outside, observed some dead bodies lying on the ground at the place of execution. He felt a desire to see them, and also

a dread and abhorrence of them; for a time he struggled and covered his eyes, but at length the desire got the better of him; and forcing them open, he ran up to the dead bodies, saying, Look, ye wretches, take your fill of the fair sight.[25]

Serial killers have probably always existed, and maybe they've always been fascinating and entertaining to those of us at a safe distance, but it seems fair to acknowledge a new grand-scale media celebration of such killers. Of course, public fascination and hysteria reached fever pitch with nineteenth-century monsters like Jack the Ripper, the famous slasher of Whitechapel, and the alluring mystery of Jack the Ripper was, and is, matched by the alluring grotesqueness of his disemboweling techniques.[26] These days we have extensive media coverage of, and corresponding public appetite for, real serial killers, such as Jeffrey Dahmer, Charles Manson, John Wayne Gacy, and Ed Gein, as well as the popular fictional characters Norman Bates, Sweeney Todd, Hannibal Lecter, Freddy Krueger, Leatherface, and Michael Myers.[27] Are we drawn to these gruesome stories and images, as Plato's Leontius was drawn to the executed corpses piled up near the port of Piraeus? Why are so many of us repelled, disgusted, and morally outraged, but also willing to lay out cash to see psychotic murderers hang people on meat hooks, sever limbs, and eat their innocent victims?

After the relatively high-brow cinematic forays into gothic horror in the 1990s, such as *Bram Stoker's Dracula*, *Interview with a Vampire*, and *Mary Shelley's Frankenstein*, the first decade of the twenty-first century settled into a new focus on "torture porn" and "splatter-punk" horror, usually stressing the monstrous serial killer as the central protagonist. Recent examples include *Dawn of the Dead* (1978, 2004), *Turistas* (2006), *Hostel* (2005), *Hostel II* (2007), *The Devil's Rejects* (2005), and *Saw* (2004) and its many sequels. These films usually involve extended graphic depictions of sadism and cannibalism.

Some critics, including the creator of *Buffy the Vampire Slayer*, Joss Whedon, have claimed that torture porn debases, by taking something away from, the people who view it.[28] Stephen King defended the genre, particularly *Hostel*: "Sure it makes you uncomfortable, but good art should make you uncomfortable."[29] "You screw, you die" is the message of slasher films, according to the conservative critic E. Michael Jones.[30] "The moral of all horror films" is that "sexual sin leads to death." The narrative of earlier slasher and later torture porn films is numbingly predictable: erotically charged young folks experiment with sexuality, libido rises, and sexual ecstasy is replaced with a violent climax of blood and death. Contrary to Freudian repression theory, Jones suggests that horror films are playing

The monsters from the sequel *Texas Chainsaw Massacre 2* (Warner Bros.). Image courtesy of Jerry Ohlinger.

out a different subtext, a deep morality tale just below the surface of the filmmaker's and the audience's conscious awareness.[31] "All monster stories," Jones explains, "beginning with *Frankenstein*, the first of the genre, are in effect protests against the Enlightenment's desacralization of man." By which he appears to mean that modern scientific secular ideology has reduced humans to animals (or even machines), and sexuality has become just another animal function without sacred status (in marriage). Horror narratives, according to Jones, remind us of our betrayal of morality and reinforce a timeless ethic (more keenly felt before the Enlightenment) of sexual moderation: "If you violate sexual morals, you will be punished by death, and the city will be destroyed; tampering with sexual morals is a threat to civilization." In Jones's conservative account, horror gives us a virtual tour of the consequences of "leftist" sexual liberation.[32]

Though from a very different perspective, some liberal monsterologists also see civilization hanging in the balance. But now the danger comes not from too little self-control but from too much. Too much repression can cause neurotic individuals and societies, so horror films come to the rescue to release the pent-up pressures. The director of *Hostel*, Eli Roth, has defended his sadistic films on what appear to be Freudian grounds.

Interviewed frequently in the media, Roth argues that horror films tend to crop up more when the country is undergoing severe social stresses; the Vietnam era produced the original *Texas Chainsaw Massacre, Last House on the Left*, and others, and the post-9/11 and Iraq war era also corresponds with an influx of violent horror films. (In contrast, according to Roth, the Clinton era produced fewer such films.) Political correlations aside, Roth argues that human fear and anxiety are held in check during our day-to-day functioning, but sometimes we need to exorcise these troubling emotions. Horror films allow us the opportunity to scream and release anxiety in a cathartic manner;[33] according to Roth, they have a therapeutic effect. "There are soldiers in Iraq," Roth explains, "that write me and tell me that *Hostel* is one of the most popular movies in the military."

> They love it. I wrote back and asked, "Why on earth would you watch *Hostel* after what you see in a day?" And he wrote back and said that he was out during the day with his friends and they saw somebody's face get blown off, and then they watched the movie that night with about 400 people and they were all screaming. But when they're on the battlefield, you have to be a machine. You can't react emotionally. You have to tactically respond to a situation. And these guys are going out every day seeing this horrible stuff, and they're not allowed to be scared. But it all gets stored up, and it's got to come out. And when they watch *Hostel*, it's basically saying, for the next 90 minutes, not only are you allowed to be scared, you're encouraged to be scared because it's okay to be terrified.[34]

Roth does not explicitly invoke Freud in his explanation, but that is only because the theory of the repressed and released Id has now attained the paradigm status of common sense. But if torture porn encourages a purging of anxieties, it certainly adds new, previously unimaginable images of vulnerability to the audience's experience. When they encounter a grisly corpse, the father warns his son in Cormac McCarthy's postapocalyptic novel *The Road* (2006), "Just remember that the things you put into your head are there forever."[35] It remains to be seen whether or not the fears and anxieties that torture porn takes out of viewers by catharsis is superseded by the new fears it puts in.[36]

A compelling alternative to this theory of horror, the catharsis of dangerous inner drives, is the idea that slasher and monster films are just subspecies of the traditional morality tale. The anthropologist Claude Levi-Strauss argued that myths, whether ancient or cinematic, have very similar sociocultural functions. The purpose of the mythic narrative is to make the world intelligible, to use magical means to resolve the contradictions of life. Perhaps this general point can be applied to the horror genre.

In many myths, heroes overcome monsters as a mechanism by which we resolve our anxieties about injustices in the world. Our daily experience is filled with bad guys who are winning and prospering while good guys are losing and suffering. Our films are cultural narratives that bring in justice where it otherwise seems fugitive. On this account, horror movies must end with a profound reckoning for the monsters, otherwise the "restoration of justice" thesis cannot hold. Of course, many horror films do indeed end with a final triumph of good over evil and may stand as evidence for this thesis. In addition, the popularity of first-person shooter video games such as Halo, wherein the gamer can fight monsters directly and blast virtual justice into place, seems to be evidence for a very satisfying moral application of aggression. Nefarious aliens and zombies populate a whole genre of "survival horror" video games, such as Resident Evil, and draw a large market of young men who want to punish monsters themselves. Why leave the meting out of justice to Hollywood stars when you can do it yourself?

CREEPING FLESH

Although much more could be said about the relationship between horror monsters and human vulnerability, I wish to briefly describe one other significant trend. The monsters of horror are ostensibly external agents of menace, but positioning them in the context of philosophical pessimism and Freudian psychology has, I hope, rendered their subjective inner dimension apparent. Freud explains the logic of *projection* in a way that explicitly connects the inner and outer monsters. "Phobias," he explains, "have the character of a projection in that they replace an internal instinctual danger by an external perceptual one. The advantage of this is that the subject can protect himself against an external danger by fleeing from it and avoiding the perception of it, whereas it is useless to flee from dangers that arise from within."[37]

In twentieth- and twenty-first-century horror we have a relatively new aesthetic focus on the subjective revulsion and terror of the flesh—in short, the terror of all things biological. After Darwin we have a radically different theoretical picture of nature, and when we combine this with our age of time-lapse photography, electron microscopy, and penetrating nature documentaries, we have a new and chilling sense of biological suffering.[38] Reflect for a moment on the *Rhizocephala* or "root-headed" barnacle that lives its life feeding inside crabs and other crustaceans. This complex organism attaches itself to the shell of the crab, bores a hole through the shell, and deposits a tiny seed of itself into the crab's body, whereupon the outside attachment falls off the host's shell and the seed begins to grow inside. Next the seed begins to spread throughout the crab in a series of complex root systems, often infiltrating, like a creeping vine, every limb of the crab. This root system castrates its host (thus precluding the crab's continuation of the gene line), stops the crab's molting cycle, and keeps it alive, all the while feeding off it, for years. Or consider the tarantula hawk, a giant wasp (*Pepsis*) that hunts tarantulas as a food supply for its larvae. The wasp paralyzes a tarantula with its powerful sting, then bites off its legs for easier transport and carries it back to a burrow, where it lays an egg on the spider's paralyzed body. When the wasp larva hatches, it feeds slowly on the still living tarantula, even carefully avoiding at first the consumption of working vital organs to guarantee extended freshness. Not even the most inventive Hollywood writers can spin tales this fantastic, yet it is the bread and butter of biology.

Predator-prey and host-parasite relationships are more detailed and documented than ever before. The contemporary imagination is flooded with images of the macabre side of nature, and our own bodies seem to be battlegrounds for viruses, bacteria, and other immunological nightmares. Not all the monsters inside us are psychological, but of course the sense of vulnerability stemming from this new biology is psychological.

Should we thank the *E. coli* in our gut that helps us to digest? Should we alternatively blame the virus that is breaking down our immune system and spreading through the host population? These organisms are not evil or noble creatures, intentionally wreaking havoc or health; they are simply doing what comes naturally, surviving and reproducing. This is not meant to sound callous or insensitive, for it is obvious that our struggle with other organisms matters a great deal to us, causing real despair. But from the more general evolutionary perspective, this drama is value-neutral.

Many science fiction horror films explicitly recognize this metaphysical position and build it into the deranged scientist character, who respects the adaptive power of the alien creature even as it devours his comrades and himself. The increasingly detached Dr. Carrington of the film *The Thing* (1951) proclaims a number of dialogue gems, many of which have echoed throughout this genre's films, including "There are no enemies in science, only phenomena to study." In a soliloquy to the alien at the end of the film, Carrington gushes about the superiority of this magnificent monster species, whose adaptive powers are far beyond our own. The alien responds to this admiration, of course, by bludgeoning the good doctor.

Legions of mad scientists from sci-fi monster stories act as personifications of the Darwinian metaphysic. Our culture betrays its uneasiness with the Darwinian paradigm by making these characters slightly insane

The original "thing," part animal, part vegetable, all sinister. From Howard Hawk's 1951 classic *The Thing from Another World* (RKO, Turner Broadcasting). Image courtesy of Jerry Ohlinger.

and definitely dangerous. These mad scientists understand the value-neutral character of natural selection; they understand that humans have no exalted place and are not insulated from a process that might eventually lead to their extinction. And they understand that this process knows nothing and cares nothing about the human tragedy that may result. The aliens of these films are destroying and even torturing human lives, but always inadvertently. Human suffering, in this genre, is an unintended outcome of the predator's natural survival and reproductive techniques. It is this quality of innocence preceding the aliens' destructive consequences that invokes the peculiar admiration of the scientists in these films. It also prevents us from applying the old lexicon of "evil" to these monsters.

Recent horror, from Lovecraft to Cronenberg to H. R. Giger, tries to give us a subjective participatory experience of vulnerable flesh rather

The aesthetic created by H. R. Giger for Ridley Scott's 1979 *Alien* (20th Century Fox) continues to set the tone for a whole genre of films interested in exploring the vulnerabilities of post-Darwinian biology. Image courtesy of Jerry Ohlinger.

than just a spectator's observation. The films make our skin crawl. The influence of evolutionary and paleontology data is clear in earlier bio-horror such as *King Kong* (1933), *Godzilla* (1954), and *Them* (1954),[39] but a creepier focus on nauseating reproduction, disease, injury, and decay seems to have risen to dominance in the last quarter of the twentieth century. David Cronenberg's 1979 film *The Brood* and Ridley Scott's 1979 film *Alien* are good examples of this disturbing mixture of reproduction anxiety, parasite monstrosity, and human vulnerability. The scene in which Scott and Giger's chest-bursting alien appears, "fanged, phallic, and fetal," seems to have shaped over three decades of subsequent monster aesthetics.[40] Was the film itself shaped by larger social anxieties surrounding abortion and reproductive rights during the 1970s? Are the current films and novels about apocalyptic, monstrous disease epidemics the result of contemporary anxieties over biochemical warfare? Do Americans feel more vulnerable after 9/11 and now seek to exorcise those emotions via torture porn? One suspects that the correlations are not entirely accidental.

THE MORE HARDCORE FREUDIAN ARGUMENT eschews specific sociopolitical contextualization. In every civilization, emerging adolescent sexuality is always fraught with intense repression pressures, so that new and powerful libidinal impulses cannot be straightforwardly fulfilled. According to Freud, the urges themselves and their hard-won containment involve a high degree of aggression. In this view, torture porn is just an increasingly efficient catharsis of built-up adolescent sexual energy; thus it is unsurprising that the target demographic audiences for such films are teenagers.

MY GOAL IN THIS CHAPTER HAS BEEN TO EXPLORE the recent emphasis on the subjective emotional and cognitive aspects of monsterology, aspects that parallel the rise of psychology and underscore the philosophy of human fragility and vulnerability. Monsters make up a significant part of the frightening underbelly of modernity, whether they are only hinted at in the uncanny experience or are chasing us with chainsaws. Monsters of contemporary horror are not like their medieval counterparts, who were more like God's henchmen. That older paradigm held out the inevitability of monstrous defeat by divine justice, but the contemporary monster is often a reminder of theological abandonment and the accompanying angst. Nor are the more recent horror monsters like the monsters of the Enlightenment, products of human superstition that can be conquered by the light of reason. Monsters after Schopenhauer, Nietzsche, and Freud are features of the irrevocable irrationality inside the human subject and outside in nature.

13

Criminal Monsters

Psychopathology, Aggression, and the Malignant Heart

You're presenting him like a monster, and he wasn't. He was anything but a monster.

JESSICA BATY, REFERRING TO STEVEN KAZMIERCZAK, HER BOYFRIEND, WHO WENT ON A SHOOTING RAMPAGE AT NORTHERN ILLINOIS UNIVERSITY IN 2008

MONSTERS IN THE HEADLINES

AS CHANCE WOULD HAVE IT, the week I sat down to write this chapter my alma mater, Northern Illinois University, was all over the national news. On Valentine's Day 2008 I turned on the TV and immediately recognized the building where I had once had an algebra class. Now people were being carted out of it on stretchers. A CNN news crawl at the bottom of the screen reported that eighteen or more people had just been shot in Cole Hall at NIU.

Over the next few days some facts came to light. The shooter's name was Steven Kazmierczak. He entered a geology lecture carrying a pump-action shotgun in a guitar case and three handguns in his belt. From the stage he began shooting into the audience, killing five people and wounding twenty others. Then he shot himself.

Kazmierczak was a former student of criminology at NIU, and he had impressed his instructors with his sophisticated research and writing. By all accounts, he was an exemplary student. Apart from some relatively tasteless tattoos based on the horror movie *Saw*, Kazmierczak bore no marks in his personal life of any impending deviance. His girlfriend, Jessica Baty, whom he lived with, was so unaware of any threat that she perceived the early report of his heinous deed as the result of mistaken identity. "He was anything but a monster," she said a few days later. "He was probably the nicest, most caring person ever."[1]

In 1999, after Eric Harris and Dylan Klebold killed thirteen people and injured twenty-three others at Columbine High School, *Time* magazine published a cover with photos of the killers and the headline "The Monsters Next Door." Harris and Klebold saw themselves as avengers, paying back jocks and princesses for a high school career of humiliation and persecution.

In December 2007 Willie Kelsey was charged by authorities in Dekalb County, Georgia, with breaking into a home and shooting two children in their beds while they slept. "Willie Kelsey is one of these individuals that when you look at his record and you look at who he is, he's just a monster among us, and thank God we got this monster off the street," said Police Chief Terrell Bolton. In the face of such appalling inhumanity, one can't help but grow philosophical, and Chief Bolton continued, "Anytime you live in a society where you can't shut your doors at night and expect peace and tranquility while you sleep and somebody come in and shoot two of your children, I don't know how else to describe anybody like that. He's a monster among us."[2]

While we're touring some staggering examples of deviance, consider the appalling aberration of the British sex offender Paul Beart, who in April 2000 sadistically tortured to death a waitress, Deborah O'Sullivan. Beart first assaulted his victim on the street and dragged her behind a wall, where he bit off her face and ripped open her torso with his bare hands. He also burned her with a lighter, smashed her with a trash can, broke her arm, strangled her, and sexually assaulted her.[3] For the likes of Paul Beart, even the horrible label "monster" seems much too polite and dignified.

The same revulsion seems appropriate for the Austrian Josef Fritzl, whose crime was discovered in the spring of 2008. The Austrian newspaper *Die Presse* called it the "worst and most shocking case of incest in Austrian criminal history."[4] Seventy-three-year-old Fritzl had begun raping his daughter Elisabeth when she was only eleven, and when she was eighteen he imprisoned her in his basement fallout shelter, where he kept her for twenty-four years. Worse yet, he fathered seven children with Elisabeth, three of whom (ages nineteen, eighteen, and eleven) lived their entire lives locked in the basement with their mother; three others lived upstairs and one died at birth. He did all this while living normally upstairs with an unknowing wife; Fritzl claimed that the upstairs children had been left on his doorstep by their long lost "runaway" daughter Elisabeth. Newspapers referred to Fritzl as the "monster who kept his daughter in a dungeon."

The "monster" epithet is applied liberally these days to a wide variety of criminal deviants, but there is no entirely accurate profile of the modern criminal monster. By all accounts Steven Kazmierczak was nothing like the socially inept, megalomaniacal loner Cho Seung-Hui, who killed thirty-two people at Virginia Tech in 2007. And while Cho apparently claimed some sick solidarity with the Columbine killers, it seems that only the "monstrous acts" themselves unify the otherwise diverse members of the psychopathic club.

Still, the parameters of the monster epithet are not infinitely malleable, and one can assume that ordinary language users are somewhat coherent in their application of such labels. Often the label is applied to those criminals who transcend the usual or traditional motives for violent crime. Sometimes the criminal is difficult to understand because his rageful behavior is so extreme, but sometimes our bewilderment is based on the absence of *any* motive whatsoever. A criminal who kills for economic gain or for romantic revenge is odious to be sure, but at least he's understandable in principle. Such a villain is certainly a tragedy, but still a distant relation in the human family. The label of monster, on the other hand, is usually reserved for a person whose actions have placed him outside the range of humanity.

LEOPOLD AND LOEB

On the south side of Chicago on May 21, 1924, Nathan Leopold, age nineteen, and Richard Loeb, age eighteen, abducted Bobby Franks, age fourteen, and murdered him with a chisel. They drove to a swampland near Hegewisch and stuffed the boy's body into a conduit pipe under a railroad embankment. After the thrill kill, Loeb, the respectable son of the vice president of Sears and Roebuck, toyed with unsuspecting detectives by volunteering all manner of helpful theories and possible suspects. Eventually the body was discovered, as were Leopold's nearby glasses. The glasses, together with the discovery of a matching typewriter used by Leopold to create a bogus ransom letter, led to the arrest of the affluent boys. In the introductory essay for Leopold's later book, *Life Plus 99 Years*, the writer and creator of Perry Mason Erle Stanley Gardner explains, "Society looked upon Leopold and Loeb with revulsion and horror. Coming from good homes, they had committed a murder apparently just for the thrill. The two boys were considered monsters."[5]

Nathan Leopold (1904–1971) and Richard Loeb (1905–1936). Pencil drawing by Stephen T. Asma © 2008.

When Leopold reflected back on their murder, he tried to convey the complex and contradictory nature of his friend Loeb. Leopold idolized the charismatic Loeb and marveled at his dual capacity for generosity and warmth on the one hand and cold-hearted brutality on the other. "How could a contradiction like that," asked Leopold, "live in one body? I'd read Stevenson's *Dr. Jekyll and Mr. Hyde*, of course. And with his literary wizardry, Stevenson had made it sound almost plausible, at least while you were reading it. But even Stevenson had made the personalities alternate. Here [in Loeb] was a man in whom Jekyll and Hyde coexisted at one and the same moment."[6] It is a testament to the evocative power of the monster metaphor that even the murderer himself must appeal to it in order to explain his partner.

In Stevenson's novella *The Strange Case of Dr. Jekyll and Mr. Hyde* (1885), Jekyll creates a potion that, once consumed, separates the good and evil inside him. Stevenson gives us a melodramatic scenario of a split personality, but one that presages the alienated or fractured Freudian self. Jekyll represents the socialized ethical self, while Hyde emerges like the Id incarnate to engage in aberrant lust binges and murder sprees. Stevenson explains, "Even as good shone upon the countenance of the one, evil was written

A promotional poster for the 1931
film *Dr. Jekyll and
Mr. Hyde* (Universal Pictures).
Image courtesy of Jerry Ohlinger.

broadly and plainly on the face of the other. Evil besides (which I must still believe to be the lethal side of man) had left on that body an imprint of deformity and decay."[7] Eventually the monster inside Jekyll overcomes the good doctor, and Hyde's deviant debauchery becomes uncontrollable. In the end, facing discovery and the threat of justice, Hyde kills himself. But Stevenson bequeathed a powerful allegory that would provide a dramatic formulation of the psychoanalytic ideas to come.

In 1924 the publisher of the *Tribune* offered Freud $25,000 to come to Chicago to analyze Nathan Leopold and Richard Loeb, but Freud declined. The invitation was certainly sensationalistic, but even if it was only partially sincere we still recognize the infant stages of forensic psychotherapy and a cultural validation of the belief that a science of the mind can tell us how human monsters are formed.

Freud's refusal did not dissuade the defense team, led by Clarence Darrow, from enlisting a small army of "the brand-new Viennese psychiatry" experts, five principal analysts and about a dozen auxiliaries. It is no accident that professional mental pathologists of this era were called "alienists," trading on the notion that insane people were especially estranged or alienated from themselves.[8] But in Freud's conceptual secularization of evil, all of us, not just Leopold and Loeb, are only so many steps away from the extreme cases of monstrous killers. All of us are a little alienated. Darrow strategically chose to plead the boys guilty instead of the expected plea of not guilty by reason of insanity, and he built his argument around the idea that the precocious boys were tragically confused by the heady intellectualism of amoral Nietzschean philosophy and other such dangerous medicines, imbibed too young for healthy result.[9]

The psychoanalytic approach to Leopold and Loeb's crime stressed the continuity rather than dissimilarity between the healthy and the unhealthy psyche. Erle Stanley Gardner's first sentence in the introduction to Leopold's book makes a boldly unifying declaration of boyhood narcissism: "There comes a time in the history of every bright boy when a constantly increasing influx of knowledge, the recognition of growth in his own powers of reasoning make him feel he is able to outwit the world if he chooses."

Would Freud's own analysis of Leopold and Loeb have produced a different outcome? Doubtful. The judge, John Caverly, claimed that the entire brilliant defense, with its elaborate psychiatry, had no real influence on his decision to spare their lives in the sentencing phase; they were simply too young to hang. But the whole scenario gives us an opportunity to reflect upon a new kind of psychologized monster. How do Freud's ideas about aggression and psychopathology explain certain kinds of twentieth-century monsters?

RAGE AND AGGRESSION

A highly imaginative artist, according to Freud, might give expression to deep psychological truths, even in the form of jokes and humor. In a sinister but playful mood, Freud quotes the Romantic poet Heinrich Heine's description of the good life:

> Mine is a most peaceable disposition. My wishes are: a humble cottage with a thatched roof, but a good bed, good food, the freshest milk and butter, flowers before my window, and a few fine trees before my door; and if God wants to make my happiness complete, he will grant me the joy of seeing some six or seven of my enemies hanging from those trees. Before their death I shall, moved in my heart, forgive them all the wrong they did

me in their lifetime. One must, it is true, forgive one's enemies—but not before they have been hanged.[10]

This bit of gallows humor helps us, Freud thinks, to recognize a true aspect of ourselves, an aspect that usually lies submerged under the surface of the more sunny socialized image. He argues that "men are not gentle creatures who want to be loved, and who can at the most defend themselves if they are attacked; they are, on the contrary, creatures among whose instinctual endowments is to be reckoned a powerful share of aggressiveness." My neighbor, Freud says, is not just a potential helper or sexual object, but also a prospective target for my aggression. I am tempted to "exploit his capacity for work without compensation, to use him sexually without his consent, to seize his possessions, to humiliate him, to cause him pain, to torture and to kill him. *Homo homini lupus* (man is a wolf to man)." With neighbors like this, who needs monsters?

Freud derived his pessimism from *experience* via the headlines of current newspapers, plus his own personal familiarity with anti-Semitism, and also from a Darwinian view of the human animal.[11] We must have a fair share of aggression in our "instinctual endowments," else we would never survive the severe challenges of living to adulthood (e.g., avoiding predators, outstripping competitors, fighting enemies). In his structural model of the psyche, Freud calls this selfish, instinctual, amoral aspect of the self the "it," the Id (*das Ich*).

Rage is a powerful force that, along with other socially deleterious impulses, lives like a frustrated virus in the dark cellars of the Id. The Ego (the "I") emerges slowly in the postuterine life of the baby and forms a node of conscious awareness, a locus of self-identity. Later, the toddler internalizes the values and mores of the external society (the nuclear family), regulating its own behavior by internal conscience rather than parental punishments. But unfortunately it all goes wrong sometimes. When conditions are right, the viral rage escapes the usual Superego subjugation and vents its terrible energy on hapless victims.

Freud explains that we all have a "policeman" in our head if our parents do a decent job of raising us. A child's basic mix of love and fear toward the parent is utilized in the earliest forms of discipline. If the parent scolds the child after some infraction, the child will feel the direct fear of the parent (especially if struck), but also the fear of the loss of parental love. These two fears combine to form a powerful motive to accommodate the wishes of the parent. The move from external control (parent) to internal (conscience) happens when a more mature child encounters reasonably consistent and just punishments from the parent. The natural aggression that a child points outward toward his or her external punisher can turn back upon the self when the parent remains a lovable (nonabusive) and consistent force in the child's life. When the child's aggression turns on his or her own behavior and desires, it provides the repressive force requisite for self-mastery and the formation of conscience. If a child is brought up by an unloving and overly strict parent, the child's own aggression stays trained outwardly on the abuser and subsequent surrogates, failing to turn inward. But if the parent is overindulgent and too lenient, the child's aggression has nowhere to go but inward, causing an overly severe Superego.[12] Thus abusive parents create outwardly rageful offspring, and indulgent parents create inwardly rageful, self-punishing offspring. In reality, of course, human character formation is much more complicated than this, but Freud's explanation continues to be highly influential in our understanding of psychological pathology. After Freud, monstrous murderers and abusive people could be theoretically dissected and understood through an examination of their own childhood. Metaphorically speaking, one's childhood is the parent of one's adulthood.[13]

Given our aggressive nature it's a miracle we don't have more violent crime and even extreme serial-killer pathology. Most of us manage to acquire a second nature, which writes a new program over the original caveman program. Monstrous crime such as rape and murder can be seen as the unfortunate byproduct of failed socialization, failed psychological accommodation to social realities. In the history of ideas it is not long after this psychologizing turn that criminal responsibility or agency begins to seep out of the individual and into the larger societal context, but that discussion will come in the next chapter.

I noted in part I the monstrous nature of rage in the case of Medea, who killed her own children. In some ways Freudian theory only modernized and formalized the penetrating insights of the ancients, but no one has yet successfully moved this discussion out of the *metaphorical* domain of knowledge. Indeed, the arts, rather than the sciences, still are more accurate in their treatment of powerful emotions such as rage.[14] Psychologists remain divided, for example, about a clear taxonomy of alienating emotions. Is rage always an impulsive expression, without calculation, planning, forethought? Is it explosive, like a mysterious animal that bursts out of a human being? Or is it merely the last culminating violent gesture in a long series of mental meditations on one's own wounded pride? Is ego consciousness quietly fomenting rage for long stretches before rage finally sheds its cognitive tutor and makes its own terrible way?

In many monstrous crimes the cognitive picture that an offender has of himself is a significant component in the pathological emotionally charged behavior. In 2004 a British teenager, Brian Blackwell, used a claw hammer to beat and stab his parents to death in their Merseyside home. Then he went on a £30,000 holiday spending spree using his parents' money, including a three-night stay in the Presidential Suite at New York's Plaza Hotel. In his mind, he somehow deserved this. His defense argued successfully that Blackwell suffered from narcissistic personality disorder, claiming that he had a grandiose sense of self-importance and suffered from fantasies of limitless power, brilliance, and success. The radical cognitive misperception of his own status in the world was used as a lever by the defense to get Blackwell a lesser charge. Rage is intimately connected with indignation, which is intimately connected to subjective notions of justice. The emotional shades into the intellectual, and vice versa. One aspect of narcissistic monsters is their inability or unwillingness to confront existence and accept it on its own terms. Healthy, socialized human beings learn to live with and even accept some degree of anxiety, frustration, hostility, and aggression in their lives (in their romantic lives, their role as parents, children, siblings, schoolmates, office colleagues, etc.). Of course, even for a healthy person, there's a limit to the amount of frustration one can and should bear, but the poorly socialized person finds that limit very nearby.

The sociologist Jack Katz, who masterfully analyzes the criminal mind in *Seductions of Crime*, points out that many murderers see themselves, at least at the moment of slaughter, as righteous avengers. "What is the logic of rage," Katz asks, "such that it can grow so smoothly and quickly from humiliation and lead to righteous slaughter as its perfectly sensible (if only momentarily convincing) end?"[15] When an individual feels either humiliation or rage he simultaneously has a feeling of powerlessness, as though something or someone has forced or compelled him. He feels victimized by forces outside himself in the case of humiliation, and by forces inside himself in the case of rage. The spouse who feels repeatedly humiliated by her partner may feel, according to Katz, as though her very *identity* is being broken and degraded by the other person. Rage promises to rebalance the situation.

The logic Katz discovered is more topographic than syllogistic, but it is evidenced in ordinary language. Humiliation lowers one; it makes one feel small. Humiliation reduces, diminishes, lessens, shrinks, dispirits, depresses, and casts down. Rage reverses this downward trajectory: rage rises up, blows up. "It may start in the pit of the stomach," Katz explains, "and soon threaten to burst out of the top of your head." The rageful are cautioned to keep their lids on and not to blow their tops. In response to humiliation, rage might be said to be a psychological ascent (with terrible consequences).

Two people, both dead, really know whether or not O. J. Simpson killed his wife and her friend in that *other* famous "trial of the century."[16] Simpson was acquitted in his criminal case in 1995 but found guilty in his civil trial in 1997. The popular and even academic discussions of the Simpson murder case were remarkable in their avoidance of the issue of monstrous rage at the heart of the case. Questions of racial justice and injustice expanded geometrically and crowded out any real reflection on the more mysterious question: How angry do you have to be to cut off somebody's head? Whether or not Simpson committed the murders, such rageful acts usually betray monstrous levels of frustration and fury.[17] The forensic psychologist Stephen Diamond goes so far as to say that, although anxiety is a strong facet of neurotic modernity, rage is the major problem of our times: "The preeminent problem in contemporary psychopathology is not anxiety, but repressed anger and rage."[18]

Rage is only one aspect of the aggressive Id. The Freudian view of crime is similar to Plato's description in the *Republic*. As we saw in part I, we are all capable of the most disturbing deviance, and evidence of our innate depravity can be found in our sadistic and forbidden dream life. The criminal monster is just the waking dream, the nightmare realized. The psychopath is simply acting out all the taboo fantasies that the rest of us have learned to control. Plato says that the deranged man has lost his powers of self-discipline and let loose the inner beast: "You know there is nothing [this beast] won't dare to do at such a time, free of all control by shame or reason. It doesn't shrink from trying to have sex with a mother, as it supposes, or anyone else at all, whether man, god, or beast."[19] Incest is one of the monstrous, albeit primordial, urges that must, according to Freud, be subjugated and transformed into more socially healthy expressions of libido. Like violent rage, lust for one's own family members must be chained by socialization on a very short leash. Freudian monsters come into being when those chains are poorly fashioned, become too slack, or break altogether.

MONSTROUS DESIRE REVISITED

One of the most imaginative artistic representations of Id forces unchained from the fetters of socialization and sublimation is the classic 1956 Hollywood film *Forbidden Planet*. This science fiction film is an allegorical meditation on a world wherein our natural pleasure-principle narcissism is given free rein, unchecked and unrestrained by the social greater good. We may want to overcome our repressive constraints, but we must be careful about what we wish for. Our naïve quest to attain happiness through greater power and libidinal expression is tantamount to the opening of Pandora's box.

Loosely based on Shakespeare's *The Tempest*, *Forbidden Planet* gives us a desolate "island" in the form of planet Altair IV, sixteen light-years from earth. Instead of Prospero and Miranda, we have Dr. Morbius and his daughter, Altaira, who are the only surviving members of the earlier *Bellerophon* expedition. A new spacecraft and crew, led by Commander John Adams, arrive on the forbidden planet to investigate the mysterious disappearance of the *Bellerophon*. They find Morbius and his daughter living in a kind of paradise, aided by Robby the Robot. After repeated warnings and attempts to turn back the new crew, Dr. Morbius reveals that all his colleagues from the *Bellerophon* were vaporized years ago and he now spends his time researching the long lost indigenous civilization of Altair IV, the Krell.

While a romance begins to heat up between the innocent beauty Altaira and the commander, the overly protective Morbius grudgingly reveals amazing technologies of the extinct Krell. A brain-boosting machine, called the "plastic educator," proved highly dangerous, but after brief usage it increased Morbius's IQ significantly. Gradually it comes to light that the plastic educator is somehow connected to a massive underground machine, a twenty-mile cube powered by thousands of nuclear reactors. This vast and ancient machine, originally built by the Krell, has been mysteriously maintaining itself and generating power for hundreds of thousands of years. Despite all this advanced technology, the Krell, Morbius explains, perished long ago in one violent night of devastation.

The plot thickens when Chief Engineer Quinn, from the new crew, is mysteriously murdered, ripped limb from limb, by an invisible monster. Despite its invisibility the new crew is able to infer some of the creature's physical properties and determine that it is a horrific chimerical beast.[20] When the monster returns the following night to wreak havoc, it disappears at the precise moment that Dr. Morbius awakens from a nightmare, clueing us in on the connection between the good doctor's dream life and the prowling beast that threatens the crew, especially the love interest of his sheltered daughter.

In light of these threats, Commander Adams and his crewmate Dr. Ostrow decide to explore the mysterious Krell technology more thoroughly. Despite the warnings, Ostrow tries on the brain-boosting plastic educator and learns the secret connection between the machine, Dr. Morbius, and the invisible monster. The knowledge is too much for him, however, and Ostrow perishes in the experiment, but not before he reveals the truth. The Krell had originally built the powerful machinery as

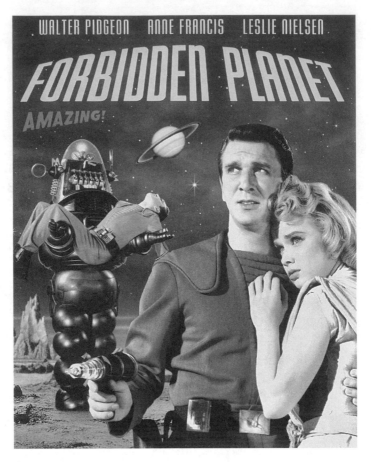

Forbidden Planet (MGM), made in 1956, capitalized on Freudian ideas about the monstrous Id. Image courtesy of Photofest.

a wish-granting technology: if the Krell could but think it, the machine would realize it. The advanced intellectual sophistication of the Krell, however, merely veiled the deeper and darker instinctual realities. "But the Krell forgot one thing," Dr. Ostrow cries to the commander. "Monsters, John! Monsters from the Id!" Their own internal monsters were unleashed that fateful night thousands of years ago, and the entire race was wiped out by those fearsome incarnations.

The commander realizes that Dr. Morbius, through his much earlier experiments with the plastic educator, now has the Krell technology wired into his own Id. Every disaster, from the original destruction of the *Bellerophon* to the new attacks, has been a manifestation of Morbius's own subconscious desires. When Altaira confesses her love for Commander Adams and her desire to leave her father, Morbius's monstrous Id attacks the crew again. In a sequence that demonstrates the estranged or foreign nature of the unconscious, the doctor does not recognize the monster as his own. But when he comes to fully grasp the truth, he throws himself at the monster, saving his daughter, redeeming himself, and destroying the monster and himself in the process.

In his later writings Freud reified the Id drives even further, eventually reducing the myriad human impulses to two major forces: Eros and Thanatos, the love and death drives.[21] More than just romantic attraction, Eros is a metaphysical principle of centripetal force. Eros gathers disparate things together, seeking unity and wholeness, and human love is just one example of its fusion activity. Thanatos is not just a drive for human death, but also a centrifugal force of destruction. Thanatos seeks to break down living holistic unities into inanimate broken bits. Eros builds up, Thanatos tears down.

Erotic relations, according to Freud, are always mixed with some share of Thanatos, either in the explicit aggression of mastery and sadism or in the unconscious pursuit of *le petit mort* (the little death) of orgasm. One could argue that monsters in literature and film are, among other things, personifications of Thanatos, artistic expressions of subconscious psychological impulses. Perhaps the pleasure we receive from artistic monster violence is more than just a holiday for our own aggression; perhaps it is also an expression of our Shiva-like desire to obliterate and annihilate order and coherence.

Another, less metaphysical but no less Freudian explanation of monsters is tied to the issue of homosexuality. In the twentieth century both fictional monsters and real criminal pathologies found a new explanatory framework in the form of repressed sexual orientation. Freud argues that the sexual life of civilized man is tragically impaired because the socially sanctioned heterosexual relation is only a fraction of our actual sexual urges. "Man is an animal organism," Freud explains, "with an unmistakable bisexual disposition." But society, and more so in Freud's day, frowns on any sexuality that breaches the parameters of heterosexual monogamy, leaving some people in painful conditions of frustration and stress. Freud writes, "Every human being displays both male and female instinctual impulses, needs and attributes; but though anatomy, it is true, can point out the characteristic of maleness and femaleness, psychology cannot. For psychology the contrast between the sexes fades into one between activity and passivity, in which we far too readily identify activity with maleness and passivity with femaleness, a view which is by no means universally confirmed in the animal kingdom."[22]

Using this prism of repressed sexuality, some theorists of heinous crime have argued that monstrous acts result from the final explosion of long contained homosexual frustrations.[23] Repression and abuse of gay teens, the journalist Anthony Chase argues, is largely responsible for some of the school massacres that have been on the rise since the 1990s.

> I recall the feelings of hatred and fantasies of revenge I harbored as a teenager in the rural Hudson Valley, where certain classmates tormented me because they thought I was gay. The arrival of my adolescence was urgently convincing me that when bullies called me faggot, they were right. My good grades, the leads I got in plays, and the encouragement I received for artistic ability could not compensate for the fear I felt as my sexuality became more and more real. Those memories return to me each time I hear that yet another teenage boy has taken a gun into a high school and opened fire, leaving his community terrorized and bewildered. I do not feel bewildered. The memory of my own revenge fantasies, Bosch-like in their terror, return to me vividly, even now, 30 years after my days at Van Wyck Junior High School.[24]

Chase marshals a surprising list of massacres from the late 1990s in which the murderers were boys who had been regularly teased and labeled gay. He points out that media representations of the murderers as monsters only closes off attempts to understand the troubled boys, implying that monsters cannot really be explained. Extrapolating on Chase's point, we notice that such labeling of criminals as monsters leads us away from recognizing neurotic and intolerant aspects of our larger culture, aspects that might be implicated in the causal story of monstrous crime. Obviously most people somehow manage to survive being called gay in high school, and they don't decide to send a cadre of school jocks to their doom. But these factors of sexual orientation frustration, abusive stigmatizing, and the surge of adolescent libido clearly need to be added to the other causal ingredients (e.g., easily accessible guns, bad parenting, drugs) when trying to understand these recent massacres.

In addition to power struggles and repression, we have the demonization of ethnicity and religion. The religion scholar Judith Taylor Gold uses an interesting Freudian logic to connect sexual repression to the anti-Semitic treatment of Jews as monsters.[25] She argues that both the horror monster genre and pornography (enjoyment of which cuts across all economic and social classes) suspend or violate normal moral conventions. The fantasies of horror and porn place us in a world outside (or before) normal laws of nature and society. They are breaks from civilization, from law and order, and they symbolically recreate primitivism, including our primitive sexuality, incest; the older Count Dracula drinks the blood of his younger female victims, for example, and the porno industry recreates countless explicit and symbolic incest fantasies. Following Freud, Gold speculates that incest was the original primitive sexuality, but then, as humans "multiplied and diversified into groups—tribes and families—incest became anathema...to the very foundations of social structure and order."[26] Like other tempting impulses that must be inverted into abominations through repression, incest must be rejected. The urge to incest is a monster inside us, always threatening to reassert itself. In horror and pornography we allow a brief, symbolic, and benign reassertion of that primitive monster because we allow alien forces to break down order. But anti-Semitism and other forms of xenophobia are attempts to regain order. They are psychological projections of our own fears (of incest) onto external agents. Foreigners and outsiders are symbols of freedom and primitive, precivilized reality. So, psychoanalytic logic goes, the outsider, in this case the Jew, must be persecuted as a surrogate for our own internal depravity. Anti-Semitism, according to Gold, seeks to "purge the monster within [incest] by murdering the monster without."[27]

In spite of its ingenuity, I confess that this Oedipal aspect of Freudian logic is simply too sly for me. The links in the argument are a bit too tenuous and the evidence seems truant, but more important the phenomenon of prejudice that "incest repression" purports to explain is better explained by another, more empirically grounded Freudian mechanism, the one I've already articulated: aggression. The "convenient other" of anti-Semitism and other forms of prejudice are understandable as expressions of the human tendency to carve the world into friends and enemies. "Nothing seems more natural," says the Freud scholar Peter Gay, "than the ease with which humans claim superiority over a collective Other. It is an immensely serviceable alibi for aggression."[28] The drive for *power* over others seems to me more intuitively clear, although (to give the Oedipal theorists their due) that might be because incest is at a lower, more socially repugnant level of the subconscious.

In any case, this returns us to the question of criminal monsters like Leopold and Loeb. The emotions and behaviors I have been discussing—rage, sadism, revenge, homophobia—all share the unifying nucleus of *power*. Losing control and being victim to inner Id powers is readily recognized as monstrous, from Medea to Morbius. But obsessive pursuit of greater power and control is equally monstrous, leading to megalomania. When Nathan Leopold, referring to his and Loeb's murder of Bobby Franks, asked "What was the motive for the crime then?" he had to admit that Loeb had some charismatic power over him: "My motive, so far as I can be said to have had one, was to please Dick. Just that—incredible as it sounds. I thought so much of the guy that I was willing to do anything—even commit murder—if he wanted it bad enough. And he wanted to do this—very badly indeed."[29] When he tries to articulate Loeb's motives he admits that no simple reductionist explanation will suffice, but he turns generally, like a good Freudian, to Loeb's childhood. He claims that Loeb was raised by an intensely strict and critical governess who gave him an inferiority complex and led him to pursue later power trips. Loeb, according to Leopold, had an exaggerated need to prove himself, to demonstrate his own power.

COLD DETACHMENT

The idea that monsters of the Id lurch out from repressed inner depths makes sense of certain kinds of narcissistic personality disorder, but it also bears a lineage with earlier Romantic views of evil. Criminal monsters, in this view, have a *Sturm und Drang* drama to them and seem like secularized versions of the earlier, theologically grounded evildoers. Despite all these ways that the Id might be responsible for violent crime, we must now turn to another psychological version of the twentieth-century monster. It is true that rage and other uncontrollable emotions lead to monstrous crimes, but a new kind of monster emerges in the twentieth century, one that, on the contrary, doesn't seem to feel any emotions at all.[30]

This emotionless robotic deviance was in fact the more dominant characterization of Leopold and Loeb, in part because Clarence Darrow's defense proffered such a picture. In his trial summation, Darrow referred to Nathan Loeb as "an intellectual machine, going without balance." Erle Stanley Gardner said that the detached boys lacked some important "moral vitamins."[31] Leopold, in his autobiography, described his accomplice as utterly without scruples: "He wasn't immoral; he was just plain amoral—unmoral, that is. Right and wrong didn't exist. He'd do anything—anything. And it was all a game to him."[32] Under the constant scrutiny of the press and detectives, Leopold confessed to feeling like a laboratory experiment. "I suppose," he recalled telling reporters, "you can justify this as easily as an entomologist can justify sticking a bug on a pin. Or a bacteriologist putting a microbe under his microscope." But this badly expressed quip was taken to be a reference to the murder itself, so the legend of Leopold and Loeb as unfeeling experimenters became even stronger.[33] I am more interested in the large-scale and changing cultural meanings of "monster" than I am in Leopold and Loeb proper, so I take it as significant (regardless of its accuracy) that the concept of robotic unemotional deviance played so successfully in the public media and imagination.

Serial murderer John Wayne Gacy (1942–1994). Pencil drawing by Stephen T. Asma © 2008.

John Wayne Gacy (1942–1994) was an American serial killer who raped and murdered thirty-three boys in the 1970s. Gacy, who worked part time as a clown, ensnared young men and boys with bogus magic tricks, eventually trapping and murdering them. He kept the dead bodies near him for many days and then buried them in the crawl space under his home. The journalist Michael Harvey was able to interview Gacy many times after the "killer clown" was caught and imprisoned. Harvey, a lawyer as well as a journalist, uniquely gained Gacy's confidence because he offered to discuss the legal issues of the case. Harvey spent long hours speaking with Gacy on the phone and in person at the prison. In the end he was the last journalist to speak to Gacy, the night before he was executed by lethal injection. He told me that Gacy had a noticeably cold, detached way of relating to other people: "Gacy very much wanted to depersonalize his victims. He would speak in a monotone as he described the specifics of a particular crime or victim. His eyes would flatten out and empty of any sort of emotion. I think he saw his victims more as objects—like a newspaper or a coffee cup—rather than as people. He would even go so far as to refer to a victim sometimes with the impersonal pronoun 'it,' rather than 'he' or 'him.'"[34]

The Canadian psychologist Robert Hare is probably the foremost authority on psychopathology and crime and is the creator of the widely used Psychopathy Checklist, a diagnostic tool that measures a subject's degree of psychopathology and tendency toward violent behavior. In his book *Without Conscience: The Disturbing World of Psychopaths among Us*, Dr. Hare profiles a variety of extreme and moderate psychopaths, arriving at a cluster of symptoms that include deceitfulness, egocentricity, grandiosity, impulsivity, manipulation, and, most important, lack of conscience and lack of empathy.[35]

"The world of unfeeling psychopaths is not limited to the popular images of monsters who steal people's children or kill without remorse," says Dr. Hare. "After all, if you are bright, you have been brought up with good social skills, and you don't want to end up in prison, so you probably won't turn to a life of violence. Rather, you'll recognize that you can use your psychopathic tendencies more legitimately by getting into positions of power and control. What better place than a corporation?"[36] Dr. Hare's research, from serial killers to corporate psychopaths, only underscores that most deviance occurs in the form of a spectrum rather than binary categories. Of course, many people might think of their boss as a psychopath, but special odium is rightly reserved for violent offenders. "The association between psychopathy and violence should not be surprising," according to Dr. Hare. "Many of the characteristics important for inhibiting antisocial and violent behavior...are lacking or deficient in psychopaths."[37] Perhaps it will be unsurprising, then, to find that only 1 percent of the overall population is psychopathic, but around 25 percent of the overall prison population is afflicted.

Empathy, the ability to identify with another person's feelings, is significantly missing in people who commit heinous crimes. The science fiction writer Philip K. Dick was intrigued when he read about the utter lack of empathy among Nazis. In large part, Dick's novel *Do Androids Dream of Electric Sheep?* is an exploration of dehumanization. "Although it's essentially a dramatic novel," Dick explained, "the moral and philosophical ambiguities it dealt with are really very profound."

> [The story] stemmed from my basic interest in the problem of differentiating the authentic human being from the reflexive machine, which I call an android. In my mind "android" is a metaphor for people who are

physiologically human but behaving in a nonhuman way. I first became interested in this problem when I was doing research for *High Castle*. I had access to prime Gestapo documents at the closed stacks of California at Berkeley, and I came across some diaries by S.S. men stationed in Poland. One sentence in particular had a profound effect on me: "We are kept awake at night by cries of starving children." There was obviously something wrong with the man who wrote that. I later realized that what we were essentially dealing with in the Nazis was a defective group mind—a mind so emotionally defective that the word human could not be applied to them.[38]

Blade Runner (1982), the highly regarded film version of Dick's novel, centers around the main character, Rick Deckard (played by Harrison Ford), and explores these questions of our humanity. Deckard makes his living as a bounty hunter in the degenerating techno-environment of futuristic Los Angeles. His job is to hunt down and kill (retire) "replicants," artificial humanoids that have been manufactured as slaves on space stations and are indistinguishable from human beings. This makes them highly dangerous if they should make their way back to earth; hence the need for a small cadre of exterminators ("blade runners"), including Deckard. Replicants are manufactured with short life spans (e.g., four years) and they are given memories, language, and general intellectual skills to maximize their particular slave functions. The plot of the film tracks Deckard as he, in turn, tracks four fugitive replicants who are trying to reach their maker, a genetic engineer and corporate mogul named Tyrell. The premise is philosophical, as these rather likable creatures are on a mission to beg their God to grant them a little more life. As we get to know these characters, other philosophical issues emerge.

Replicants act as metaphors for the kinds of cold, robotic deviants I've been discussing. In the same way that we can wonder about the humanity of the Gestapo officer or the psychopath Paul Beart, the film *Blade Runner* meditates on replicant contenders for human status. Actually, since *human* is a zoological term, the real question is: What are the defining traits of a *person*? And what are the entitlements or rights that *personhood* entails? These questions go back to *Frankenstein* and earlier. Beyond simple sensations of pain and pleasure, we tend to think of emotions as crucial ingredients for being a person. *Blade Runner* offers us replicants with varying degrees of emotional life (pain, hopes, disappointment, desire, etc.). Does something deserve basic rights and respect when it is capable of feeling emotions?[39] But not just any feelings will suffice. We recognize certain emotions in animals and yet we do not reward them person status (in fact, we continue to devour them heartily). There seems to be an unspoken premium placed on the emotional levels of sophistication. Fear, for example, is widely prevalent in the animal kingdom, but *empathy* is an emotion that seems very rare except in the human species. Empathy is the power to place oneself in the position of someone or something else and intimately feel the emotions or motives of that other person or thing.[40]

In the film, blade runners are equipped with a special device, the Voight-Kampf test, which enables them to distinguish androids from nonandroids. The device measures the changes in the subject's pupils when asked increasingly difficult questions, and the questions are designed to elicit empathy responses to scenarios of animal and human suffering (the eye as the window to the soul is a repeated theme throughout the movie). The film suggests that some of the replicants, the character Leon, for example, are rudimentary in their emotional equipment, and this can be easily detected through the empathy test. When Leon is asked what he would do if he came across an overturned tortoise suffering in the sun, he cannot empathically process the scenario. Other characters, such as Roy, evolve emotional sophistication that eventually reaches the level of empathy. The climax of the film, in fact, can be read as a transfiguration of replicant Roy to fully human Roy by the empathic act of saving the life of a fellow sufferer (Deckard). Actually an even deeper transfiguration is implied because Roy saves not only a fellow sufferer, but his enemy.[41]

Interestingly, the U.S. military has created a device that looks very much like the Voight-Kampf test, and they use it to scan the eyes of Iraqi men. It has been extremely difficult for U.S. soldiers to differentiate friends from insurgent enemies while fighting in Iraq. The eye scanner is designed to take subtle biometrics rather than detect empathic responses, but the use of such a litmus test on enemies is somewhat unsettling.

At least two points are interesting about the empathy test used in *Blade Runner*. First, we have a kind of deus ex machina or cop-out resolution of the Cartesian problem. How do you know if the thing next to you is a human or an automaton? Give it the empathy test, and if it fails, it's an android.[42] Second, and more interesting, the suggestion that the different replicants have different levels of emotional sophistication (some bordering on real empathy, some completely void) implies that they are different levels of person.

This reflection takes us beyond the film, for we can legitimately ask this same question of the people around us. There appear to be levels of empathy in human beings, from highly sensitive individuals to cold-blooded psychopathic killers. Does having less empathy mean being less human? When we talk of the emotionless individual, we say that he is "cold," perhaps even "inhuman." Is compassion for other beings a defining feature of what it means to be human? Does the inability to feel someone else's suffering make one less of a person and more like a machine or a monster?

THE CAUSES OF PSYCHOPATHOLOGY

Advances in brain science have lent greater credence to the idea that severe deviance has a biological basis. Dr. Igor Galynker of Beth Israel Medical Center scanned the brains of twenty-two pedophiles and found that they all had below normal activity in the temporal lobe. There are rare cases of men with tumors in their temporal lobe region acquiring a taste for sex with children, having the tumors removed, and subsequently losing the deviant urges.[43]

The old chicken-and-egg question remains, however; one can always ask whether brain anomalies cause events, or whether events (such as early abuse) cause brain anomalies.[44] In some cases, young children who experience violent abuse replicate that abuse as adults, but it remains unclear whether genetic heredity is simply unfolding from genotype to phenotype over generations, or whether the early violent experiences create an unconscious need for revenge (the return of the repressed), or whether childhood abuse actually rearranges the brain in such a way that later callous behavior is more likely. With regard to psychopaths, there seems to be some evidence for all of these causal scenarios.[45]

Dr. Kent A. Kiehl, a psychiatrist at the Olin Neuropsychiatry Research Center in Connecticut, studies the relationship between psychopathology and the brain. According to Kiehl, psychopaths do not fail cognitively so much as fail compassionately: "Psychopaths do know right from wrong, they can tell you right from wrong. They just don't care."[46] Dr. Kiehl believes there is compelling evidence that psychopaths have abnormal paralimbic systems. The paralimbic system consists of several structures and coordinates emotion and long-term memory. People with damage to their orbitofrontal cortex, a part of the paralimbic system, display increased impulsivity and selfishness; those with damage to the amygdala, another part of the paralimbic system, become cold-hearted and lose their natural fear of threats. Experiments using photographs confirm that people with a damaged amygdala cannot identify dangerous people as dangerous. As Dr. Melvin Konner puts it, "Without an amygdala we are too trusting and bold in approaching people who look dangerous to others."[47] When subjected to brain scans, psychopaths display some of the same diminished brain activity in these paralimbic areas that injured subjects display. Other tests confirm that areas of the brain that ordinarily process or read facial expressions are crippled in psychopaths; notably, the ability to process fear-ful faces is diminished, according to Dr. Nicola Gray of Cardiff University's School of Psychiatry.[48] Not only is it harder for psychopaths to read threatening faces, but more significantly, it is harder for them to interpret the faces of people who are afraid. If a psychopath is neurologically less responsive to my pained face (and other indicators), then he might be less likely to stop hurting me if we end up in conflict.

These cases of diminished brain activity in specific loci give us a glimpse into the places where empathy breaks down. Psychopaths may be perceiving other people in purely morphological ways, without sensing much of their inner life (pain, joy, etc.). When most normal people cause pain to another person or just witness it, they have some sympathetic pain themselves. This does not appear to be the case with psychopaths. This has led some researchers to wonder if psychopaths, like some autistics, have a reduced ability to attribute mental states (intentions, beliefs, desires, emotions, etc.) to other people and to understand that others experience subjective states that are different from their own. In other words, the failure of empathy may be a result of a weakened theory of mind.[49]

That psychopaths can be highly intelligent and calculating but heart-less is the subject of Ralph Adolphs's research at the California Institute of Technology.[50] Dr. Adolphs recruited thirty men and women to answer fifty carefully crafted questions involving ethical dilemmas. Six of the subjects had lesions on their ventromedial prefrontal cortex (VMPC), a region just behind the forehead; twelve of the subjects had other types of brain damage, and the final twelve had no brain damage whatsoever. The ethical quandaries were broken down into two categories: personal and impersonal. In the personal quandaries, subjects were asked "lifeboat" questions, such as, If you had to harm your friend in order to save a large number of other people, could you do it? The cold calculation of utilitarianism (the greatest good for the greatest number) tends to run counter to our natural attachments to people we know. Part of us naturally privileges our own people because we have strong emotional ties to them, whereas strangers (no matter how many) are abstract; we are not emotionally invested in them. Yet even harming a stranger in order to save other strangers usually causes a high degree of aversion in subjects; most normal people hesitate because they feel compassion for the individual who must be sacrificed. While all the other test subjects showed great anxiety and hesitation at the idea of harming a person in order to save others, the people with VMPC lesions were quick and decisive in their decision to sacrifice an individual for the common good. The researchers argued that abnormalities in the VMPC result in lower levels of empathy and compassion.

These biological approaches to psychological tendencies are not strictly reductionistic. For example, the sociobiologist Linda Mealy argued that a form of psychopathy could be genetically passed down, but only an abusive environmental situation might trigger its expression.[51] Many people may have dormant psychopathic genes that get triggered only by high-stress hormonal environments. If a child grows up in an abusive home, he may produce the high degree of steroid hormones that trigger psychopathic gene expression, whereas a stable, nurturing family environment might indefinitely gate or prevent psychopathic gene expression.

The journalist Michael Harvey, who spent time with John Wayne Gacy and several other heinous murderers, reminds us of the developmental component of psychopathy:

> The common link that binds together most serial killers can be found, perhaps not surprisingly, in childhood. If you dig deep enough, you will find that most serial killers experienced sexual abuse or some other sort of significant physical and mental abuse at the hands of an adult, usually a parent or some other person acting in a position of trust. Often, this abuse is coupled with neglect and general indifference exhibited by other adults who might have been in a position to stop the abuse or otherwise comfort the child who was the subject of the abuse. A typical scenario would be a father who is abusive and a mother who is cold and distant.[52]

In chapter 8 I spent considerable time discussing medieval demon possession. The demon monsters of that more theocentric era were slowly transformed by the medical model into diseases. Nowadays *sin* and *possession* have become laughable terms in the official culture of mental pathology. But Carl Jung, in his 1927 *Structure and Dynamics of the Psyche*, suggested that we have actually gained little with our new scientific nomenclature of mental illness. "Three hundred years ago," Jung writes, "a woman was said to be possessed of the devil, now we say she has hysteria. Formerly a sufferer was said to be bewitched, now the trouble is called a neurotic dyspepsia. The facts are the same; only the previous explanation, psychologically speaking, is almost exact, whereas our rationalistic description of symptoms is really without content."[53]

The point here is that, for the psychopath, no breakdown of his condition into brain chemistry even begins to get at the actual felt experience he's undergoing. From the phenomenological or psychological perspective, demon possession is a more accurate way of describing the horrible feeling of an uncontrollable invisible force pushing you to do something against your will. The feeling of being controlled by something foreign to oneself is probably the same, no matter what era one lives in. The superstitions of the earlier age are now metaphysically ridiculous, but the subjective experience is better captured by reference to unnatural agencies than to neurotransmitters.[54]

JUDGING AND MANAGING THE MONSTERS

"There is absolutely no doubt that people do monstrous things," says Judge David P. Brodsky. "Don't get me wrong. I mean, it's unbelievable, the things I've seen. There are some sick people out there, who cross the line in no small way. But if we're going to be a civilized society, then we have to struggle with the real complexities of crime, and not the cartoon versions of 'saints' versus 'monsters.'" In 2008, I interviewed Judge Brodsky, who was an attorney for the Public Defender's Office in Lake County, Illinois, for over two decades and who now works as an associate judge in the Ninth Judicial Circuit Court of Illinois. He thinks the media, with their simplistic "monster" labels, are partly to blame for overdramatizing criminals and closing off real understanding: "The media has an invested interest in fostering these dehumanizing labels—it makes for 'good TV,' it creates ratings and profits." Add to that the fear-mongering of politicians who are "tough on crime" and you have a recipe for public misperception, a picture of crime and punishment that bears little resemblance to reality. "One of the other problems," Brodsky says, "is that mass communication, by its very nature, tends to oversimplify a message. So when [reporters] cover crime, the complexities are eliminated and criminals get transformed into 'monsters.'"

"I can safely say," he states, "that I've seen the worst. My colleagues and I in the criminal justice system are some of the select few that really know what a shotgun can do to the human body, or what a butcher knife can do. But no, I've never doubted the *humanity* of the criminals. In fact, I usually see the opposite. More often, someone has already been labeled a monster by the state or the media, and then I discover lots of humanity." Usually complex factors lead to violent crimes, and though that complexity doesn't make the crimes less tragic, our understanding of these factors helps us to see the human being behind the vitriol. "Here's a trivial example, off the top of my head," Judge Brodsky offers.

> When I was a defense attorney, we had this teenage kid, who the prosecution was making out to be "monster." He was part of a group of skinheads who had been arrested after a fight at the beach. He was not at the fight and was not arrested for that. His mates beat two girls. The girls were lesbians and these skinheads were charged with a hate crime. The boy was

mentally disabled, and the skinheads were the only kids who would accept him as a friend, so that's really why he was a skinhead. Anyway, he goes to his friends' hearing and after the hearing, as the skinheads are being led away in custody, he gives his buddies the Nazi salute. The prosecutor happens to see this and gets really offended, halting the next case and bringing what he saw to the attention of the judge. He has the kid arrested and they hold him in contempt of court, and they basically demonize him in the heat of the moment. Much later the charges were dropped, because he was not in violation of the law. But it's a simple example of how complexities are passed over for *caricatures* of good and evil.

To my mind, there's a difference between a person who does monstrous *deeds* and a monstrous *person*. For example, we represented a guy—a very sweet and normally gentle guy—who's a delusional paranoid schizophrenic. One day he killed a kid, chopped him up, and buried him in his backyard. He did a very monstrous thing. But I know this guy, and he is definitely *not* in control of his actions. He's not a monster. Now, he was a clear-cut case of insanity—even the state had to recognize it, but unfortunately most such cases involve people who are further along on the continuum and that makes it harder to determine the issues of free agency.

Brodsky acknowledged that many of the murder cases he's seen involved relatively isolated explosions of rage. People perceived themselves to be in some desperate, trapped, or affronted state, and then violently lashed out with ruinous result. That doesn't make them any less culpable for their actions, but it diminishes the tendency to label them monsters. These cases of explosive but relatively uncharacteristic fits of rage (often triggered by drug use) and the capricious actions of the certifiably insane are monstrous *deeds*. But what about the just plain evil? "Well, 'evil' is a lot like the word 'monstrous,'" Brodsky replied,

in the sense that I'd use it to describe specific actions, but not people.[55] And I'd probably not even use that term because of its many religious connotations. When I was a defense attorney, I had my clients referred to as "evil" hundreds of times—it's very common in a trial. Sometimes in the enhancement of a statute, the prosecution and even the legislator will use the language of "brutal and heinous" or "shockingly evil" to describe the acts, and I guess there really is something being communicated by this language. They're trying to indicate that what they want to punish is the *malignant heart*.

Malignant heart is a term that appears in many state laws defining the charge of murder. The term is often used to help demarcate murder proper from manslaughter. The State of California, for example, retains the language of "malice aforethought," but under section 188 of the California Penal Code malice is divided into two forms: express and implied. *Express* malice exists "when there is manifested a deliberate intention unlawfully to take away the life of a fellow creature." Malice may be *implied* by a judge or jury "when no considerable provocation appears, or when the circumstances attending the killing show an abandoned and malignant heart."

Perhaps a criminal monster is one who *chronically* acts from a malignant heart. In that case the difference between a monstrous action and a monstrous person can be detected by the mark of recidivism or recurrence. The law recognizes, albeit with a very high burden, the insanity defense, and even recognizes voluntary intoxication as grounds for denying a malignant heart. A malignant heart suggests that a person's crimes were not so much *situational* as character-based.[56] One criminal act by itself, even a brutal one, is very difficult to read. If that act is a single page in a whole book of weird and crazy behaviors (attested to by credible witnesses), it would indicate something quite different from a case of built-up rage (e.g., the Columbine massacre), and that kind of brutal act would look different still against the backdrop of a repeatedly mean and abusive pattern of behaviors.

IN THIS CHAPTER I HAVE articulated the major contours of a twentieth-century view of criminal monsters. Instead of fading away in the light of clinical, pharmaceutical, and psychological theory improvements, the concept of monster has kept going strong, doing significant work for us. Although the term *monster* is overused and often obfuscates important complexities, the more professional semantic contenders, such as *psychopath*, are not exactly great leaps forward. Even the law is still using wonderful terms like *malignant heart*. We are still very much at the *descriptive* phase of the science of the criminal mind, not yet at the underlying *causation* phase. Some people like to point to the astounding complexity of the brain and the nature-nurture dialectic to undermine the quest for scientific certainty. But perhaps it's not the complexity of a criminal mind that makes many of us despair of scientific comprehension. Perhaps instead, when we think about the horrific crimes of our day, we lose the desire to comprehend.

Monsters Today and Tomorrow

14

Torturers, Terrorists, and Zombies

The Products of Monstrous Societies

Situational forces can work to transform even some of the best of us into
Mr. Hyde monsters, without the benefit of Dr. Jekyll's chemical elixir.
PHILIP ZIMBARDO

XENOPHOBIA AND RACE

A FTER THE MODERN-DAY MEDEA, Susan Smith, drowned her children in 1994, she went to authorities claiming that an African American man had stolen her car and driven off with her children. America was all too willing to accept this bogus story, and tearful entreaties and national manhunts ensued for almost two weeks, until Smith confessed to driving her kids into a lake. The carjacking, kidnapping black monster tapped into a barely submerged tear in mainstream America.

In 1899 Stephen Crane wrote a short story titled "The Monster." In this sad novella, a small-town doctor named Trescott almost loses his son in a house fire, but a black man named Henry Johnson bravely saves the boy's life. In the rescue, Johnson is horribly burned and deformed by the fire, but he lives and eventually rejoins society. Society, however, is not ready to receive him. His casual appearance at a neighbor's home causes genuine terror and flight; his attempt to sit quietly in the town square brings the jeers and taunts of children. At one point he is thrown in jail and a mob forms simply because the town is so frightened of his appearance. Dr. Trescott, who gratefully took Johnson under his care and protection, begins to feel the sting of social rejection himself. The novella ends without resolution but with the suggestion that Trescott and his family will share Johnson's pariah status interminably. Henry Johnson may be interpreted as a symbol of the monstrous black male, a creature composed largely of projected fears and anxieties. Dr. Trescott represents the attempt to see beyond such demonization to the humanity of the black man, and he is punished for his goodwill by the mob, which clings to its convenient enemy.

The story is even more poignant when we consider it in light of the 1892 lynching of Robert Lewis in Port Jervis, New York. Stephen Crane's brother William was a judge living in Port Jervis; on June 2 he heard a mob forming in the street outside his house. Robert Lewis had been accused of raping a white woman named Lena McMahon, and his police wagon was attacked by a vengeful mob on its way to the jail. Lewis was dragged to East Main Street and a rope was thrown around William Crane's front tree. When Crane rushed out of his house "the body was going up" and he saw that "the negro's hands were tied and his elbows were crooked." Crane shouted, "Let go of that rope!" and the crowd quieted slightly, letting Lewis's body descend somewhat. "Again I shouted," Crane explained at the inquest, "and gave a jerk on the rope and it came loose in my hands and the negro fell into the gutter on his back. I pulled the rope down from the tree and loosened the noose from his neck and took it off."[1]

Crane then enlisted the help of a nearby policeman to "protect that man." But the mob began to grow bold again and move in on Lewis and his few protectors. "I could see that he was alive," Crane reported later. "He was gasping for breath and his whole body was quivering. His face was covered with blood and I did not recognize him." A doctor emerged, and after a lightning-quick examination suggested to Crane that Lewis would survive if they could get him to a hospital. At this point a member of the mob, Robert Carr, stepped forward and shouted, "He ought to be hung." Crane recounted that "the crowd then took up the cry, 'hang him!' 'don't let the doctor touch him!' hang all the niggers!'" At this point a fight broke out, a struggle to get possession of the rope. Crane resisted, but the crowd was too strong and the noose ended up around Lewis's neck again. Crane said, "The next I saw of it, it was over the branch of the tree again. I sprang to the tree and caught hold of the rope and tried to pull it down but there were too many at the other end." Crane was overpowered and Robert Lewis was lynched a second time.

As in many other lynchings, this vigilante justice appears to be as symbolic as it is literal. In his essay "The Dramaturgy of Death" Gary Wills argues that most public executions of criminals throughout history have been motivated by obscure emotional impulses rather than rational theories such as deterrence. The community sees the killing as a kind of cleansing. Lynch mobs, for example, project impure traits onto a surrogate monster

Demonization and race. The Ku Klux Klan lynches the black character "Gus" (played by actor Walter Long in blackface) in D. W. Griffith's inflammatory film *The Birth of a Nation* (1915). Image courtesy of Photofest.

or further vilify real criminality so that it stands for all things impure and then seek to destroy and cleanse the impurity. Wills explains that "forms of extrusion require society's purification by destruction of a polluted person. Unless society or its agents effect this purification, the pollution continues to taint them."[2] As the scholar Elaine Marshal describes the lynching of Robert Lewis, a single black man becomes a stand-in for the impurities that social prejudice accuses the entire black male population of embodying: "For the crowd Lewis is more than 'a negro' in this scene; he becomes '*the* negro,' the faceless representative of the whole 'race.' That is the clear import of the transition in the mob's cry from 'hang *him*' to 'hang *all* the niggers.'"[3]

The myth of the black monster has had a prosperous career in the twentieth century, first in the Jim Crow era of public lynchings, then in the reactions to the civil rights struggle, and now in the well-known statistics that one in every twenty black men over the age of eighteen is incarcerated in the U.S. prison system.[4] But the myth itself is very old. Recall that the medievals tended to blend the extreme monstrous races (e.g., Blemmyae, Sciopodes) with the foreign ethnicities of Africa, India, and the Middle

East. Debra Higgs Strickland points out that "Ethiopians were often idealized as a pious and 'blameless' people in the writings of the ancient Greeks, such as Homer. But in European Christian eyes, Ethiopians were monstrous principally owing to their black skin, which was considered a demonic feature."[5]

One of the main reasons black-skinned people were more maligned in medieval Europe than in Mediterranean antiquity is that there were fewer of them around to serve as counterevidence to the unchecked gossip and fear-mongering; very few Africans lived in Europe before the twelfth century. But as I traced earlier in my discussion of the Christian Table of Nations, there were theological prejudices at work as well. "Black was a color," explains Strickland, "associated with evil, sin, and the devil, especially in patristic writings. For example...St. Jerome stated that Ethiopians will lose their blackness once they are admitted to the New Jerusalem, meaning that their external appearance will change once they become morally perfect."

By this point we have already seen many of the negative associations that a hostile imagination can produce for any perceived other (e.g., unclean, barbaric, sexually illicit, spiritually deformed). Demonizing or monstering other groups has even become part of the cycle of American politics. The social construction of an enemy is built into the generational dynamic of a melting-pot democracy. According to the sociologist James A. Aho, any sample of American history will reveal a redundant dynamic between three generations: those currently in power, a second generation that's waiting to take the reins, and the children of the first group. The first group rules for approximately fifteen years, "focusing on the foreign or domestic enemy that provides it, by negation, with that generation's identity as 'good Americans': niggers, fags, papists, spics, commies, nips, Nazis, huns, Satanists, or dope-crazed sex fiends, all drawn from the storehouse of American demonology."[6] But because these "enemies" are largely collective projections and not real causes of social ills, the policies aimed at fixing them fail. The next generation, disgusted by the empty posturing of the first, eventually comes into power and replaces the elders with "visionaries" who can penetrate down to the true causes of social problems, and those true causes tend to be identified as the policies of the predecessors. But the third generation, the children of the first, get their turn at power thirty years after their parents. That third generation, Aho claims, now begins "reciting publicly the myths of evildoers first heard at the feet of their now-deposed fathers." And the cycle starts over.

Obviously race has played a large role in this sociopolitical dynamic. Seeing other races and ethnicities as monstrous has not just helped cynical domestic politics, but has also aided much of the international warfare

Demonization and race. David Lean, the director, and Alec Guinness, the actor, received many charges of anti-Semitism after their grotesque portrayal of Fagin in the 1948 version of *Oliver Twist* (Independent Producers). Unflattering shots of Fagin were edited out of the film before it was released in the United States. Image courtesy of Photofest.

of the twentieth century. The Jews were reconstructed as monstrous vermin by the Nazis, the Vietnamese were reconstructed as soulless gooks, and according to one U.S. soldier, Mike Prysner, the Iraqis and Afghanis are regularly referred to by military personnel as "camel jockeys," "towel heads," and "sand niggers."[7] A Vietnam veteran in the documentary *Faces of the Enemy* says, "You're trained as a soldier to see your enemy as an abstraction. You have to. The soldier's most powerful weapon is not his weapon, but his idea of the enemy."[8]

In the medieval era the monstrous races were conceptualized as cursed by God, but such theological thinking became less available to Westerners in the nineteenth and twentieth centuries. After Darwin, race became a predominantly scientific issue, but this only meant that some prejudices took on a new nomenclature. Anthropology in the early twentieth century was still assuming the old hierarchy of races, but now the bogus declension was supposed to be a product of evolution rather than theological fiat. Underneath the new anthropology was a deeper debate about the nature of the *self*.

The influential philosopher Descartes argued that the human self or soul was completely independent of the body. Like a diamond in a dung heap, the real me maintains its purity inside my transient material body. To the question Who am I really? the rationalist Cartesians answered, The soul or the mind, which has no gender, no class, no race. But the empiricists of the following generation, including John Locke and then David Hume, argued against this idea, claiming that there is no such inner diamond mind; in fact, there is nothing in the mind that is not first in the senses (*nihil in intellectu nisi prius in sensu*). Unlike the Cartesian *internalist* view, *externalist* empiricism held that if the body can be affected by its particular environment, then so can the mind.

Some think that the Cartesian internalist view, with its genderless and raceless pure self, represents a kind of theoretical bar to racism. This has a certain plausibility. Edward Said, for example, claims that the racist stereotypes of Orientalism rest on the presupposition of empiricist theories of self. He suggests that racism is fueled by the empiricist belief "that mind and body were interdependent realities, both determined originally by a given set of geographical, biological, and quasi-historical conditions."[9] Noam Chomsky points out the racist tendency toward social manipulation buried in empiricist theory. "The principle that human nature, in its psychological aspects, is nothing more than a product of history and given social relations removes all barriers to coercion and manipulation by the powerful."[10]

According to empiricist theories of the self, the contents of consciousness, the inner life, is in large part conditioned by the external environment. In this tradition, the ideas of the soul or mind are simply internal copies of bodily sense impressions. A constant thread through such empiricism is Locke's claim that confused minds result from erroneous conflations of impressions. Any interesting epistemology must account not only for our knowledge but for our more abundant ignorance. So, Locke claims, "whole societies of men" are worked into "universal perverseness" because unrelated experiences "of no alliance to one another, are, by education, custom, and the constant din of their party, so coupled in their minds, that they always appear there together" and become confused as one idea.[11] This position would later support racial theorists such as the empirically oriented American Jeffersonians.

The early anthropology of the American Philosophical Society, whose inner circle included such thinkers as Thomas Jefferson and Benjamin Rush, centered around whether Indians, blacks, and whites were members of the same species. The empirically oriented philosophers argued that the races had a common origin, but the current "depravity" of Indians and blacks was a result of poor environment: unhealthy external conditions resulted in internal retrograde souls. Rush, for example, stated, "The weakness of the intellects in certain savage and barbarous nations...is as much the effect of the want of physical influence upon their minds, as a disagreeable color and figure are of its action upon their bodies."[12] A post-Darwinian expression of this same external model of racial causality can be found in Edward Drinker Cope's 1883 assertion that "every peculiarity of the body has probably some corresponding significance in the mental, and the cause of the former are the remoter causes of the latter."[13]

The metaphor of external causation did indeed allow theorists to indulge in justifications for prejudice. However, the explanation of racial variations via empirical environmentalism is not in itself inherently pernicious. Obviously it's a dangerous blunder to argue from one's environment to one's skin color to one's morally significant mental status, but the externalist metaphor has also been the driving force behind some arguments for the fundamental unity of humankind and the moral equality of all races. The advantage of thinking of the mind (and race) as environmentally produced is that it eliminates dangerous forms of essentialism. Normal or abnormal, mundane or monstrous—no group was essentially fixed or eternally different; they simply had different geographical biographies. Of course, this racial relativism was not applied fairly in many cases. Jefferson himself conveniently suggested that although Indians are certainly capable of the most refined capacities of our species, Negroes may not be so capable; thus a certain theoretical justification for American slavery could remain in place. Obviously, this was a perniciously inconsistent application of the theory. But if applied consistently the environmental theory can legitimate a moral egalitarianism in the face of racial variation.

If race is simply a response to particular external stimuli, then given enough time (and the geological revolution finally convinced us that there is enough time), an environmentally transposed black population and white population would eventually take on each other's traits. For if we take Darwinian natural selection seriously, we must recognize that there is no trait that is so *essential* that it cannot become, in time, *accidental*, and even nonexistent. And there is no trait that is so accidental that it cannot become, in time, essential to a race or species. That is to say, the age-old concepts of essence and accident are exploded. Unfortunately, many such theories were still wed to the ancient idea of a hierarchical *scala naturae* and presupposed that one could "improve" the savage (raise him to the "higher" white or European level of the ladder) by altering his environment.

By contrast, a Cartesian model of the self, mixed with prejudice, becomes an odious framework for thinking racial differences to be eternal and forever fixed.[14] Indeed, such a framework was articulated in American polygeny theory, whereby internal selves were expressed through external racial characteristics. Naturalists in the nineteenth century divided roughly into two camps: the polygenists, who argued for several distinct origins of the races, and the monogenists, who argued for one origin for all humankind. Prior to Darwin, the inquiry centered around whether there was *one* Adam and Eve or *many* (multiple creations). After Darwin, the discourse shifted slightly to inquire into whether the species had one origin with several evolved racial variations, or whether each race constituted its own species, having only a very remote connection to others. Polygenists, both before and after Darwin, embraced the internalist or essentialist idea of fixed races. The African descendant, the Native American descendant, and the Caucasian descendant all represented fixed kinds of diverse entities, taking their diversity from some innately bestowed respective essence (usually granted by God). American polygenists, such as Dr. Samuel George Morton, were very popular prior to the Civil War because their internalist metaphor left no room for change in the contemporary racial hierarchy. An internal soul immune from environmental conditions was said to eternally define the slave, from ancient times to the present.

The polygenist idea of races as originally and essentially distinct was a harbinger of the Nazi ideology. The Nazis rejected monogenism because the idea that all races had a common origin lent itself to the democratic contention that Jews, blacks, and Aryans were essentially brothers and sisters, descendants of common parent stock. The polygenist doctrine of eternal divisions between races made it easy to think of the souls of other races (if they had them) as fundamentally other. Thus no amount of external environmental influence could alter the essence of the Jew or the Asian. George Mosse describes this Nazi opposition to the monogenist theory that all races evolved from one source: "As National Socialism and the Volkish movement claimed that the German race was perfection incarnate, that its greatness was immutable, the idea of racial evolution and progress had to be rejected."[15] Adolf Hitler himself invoked this theme of eternal racial identity and rejected the empiricist view of the self when he stated, "A man can change his language without any trouble—that is, he can use another language; but in his new language he will express the old ideas; his inner nature is not changed. This is best shown by the Jew who can speak a thousand languages and nevertheless remain a Jew. His traits of character have remained the same, whether two thousand years ago as a grain dealer in Ostia, speaking Roman, or whether as a flour profiteer of today, jabbering German with a Jewish accent. It is always the same Jew."[16]

INSTINCTUAL XENOPHOBIA

Why do we transform other groups, whole races, into monsters? This is an important question. The kind of theoretical explanation that I've been sketching may be ascribing more *rational* decision-making behavior to racists than really occurs. All such arguments tend to take the form *because it is economically or socially advantageous to see other races as inferior, we elect to see them as inferior.* The argument implies some sort of conscious decision making, or at least a social calculation. But the treatment of other races as monstrous may be more *instinctual.*[17] Specifically, it may be the result of xenophobia, a neurotic exaggeration of an otherwise low-level but ever-present instinctual fear. Fear and anxiety are ubiquitous in humans; they are reported to be the most common emotions in our dream lives. Just as some psychiatric disorders may be intensified modulations of ordinary feelings like fear, so, too, whole societies may suffer from intensified fears, especially if their mass media stimulates such feelings. Treating strangers as monsters may be the neurotic cultural response of a paranoid society. Being afraid is a given part of the human condition, as is suspicion about people and creatures that are different. But if widespread fears are systematically trained upon another population, it won't be long before that population really is a threat because their subsequent feelings of defensiveness and victimization are surefire paths to hostile countermeasures.

"Us-versus-them thinking comes remarkably easily to us," says the primate biologist Frans de Waal.[18] He finds the demonization of others to be strong in primate communities as well: "There is no question that chimpanzees are xenophobic." Jane Goodall described some chimp aggression toward out-group members as so violent and degrading that it was clear that the chimps were treating their enemies as members of some other species. De Waal also describes such behavior: "One attacker might pin down the victim (sitting on his head, holding his legs) while others bit, hit, and pounded. They would twist off a limb, rip out a trachea, remove fingernails, literally drink blood pouring from wounds, and in general not let up until their victim stopped moving." Chimps, like humans, can perceive their enemies as monsters and then respond with torture and other forms of excessive brutality. Perceived monsters bring out monstrous reactions.

A community of chimps in Gombe National Park in Tanzania demonstrates some interesting xenophobic behavior. In the beginning it was a large group of chimps who socialized with each other and functioned like a unified clan. Over the years, however, the group split into northern and southern subgroups. Eventually the two groups began to fight with each other and define each other as hostile out-groups. "Shocked researchers watched as former friends now drank each other's blood," de Waal writes. Biologists extend the point to human hostilities, such as those of the Hutus and Tutsis in Rwanda and the Muslims, Serbs, and Croats in Bosnia. De Waal speculates that when groups feel a sense of common purpose, they suppress their aggression toward other in-group members. But remove that common purpose, and look out. "Both humans and chimps are gentle, or at least restrained, toward members of their own group, yet both can be monsters to those on the outside."

So strong is the xenophobia in chimps that researchers fail whenever they attempt to introduce new members into a clan. If they bring ex-captive chimps, for example, to a wild clan, the new chimps are always met with violence, and the integration experiment usually has to be aborted. On the other hand, such tribalism appears to carry strong bonds of loyalty. When de Waal introduced two males to a group at the Yerkes Primate Center, he was surprised to observe two females approach and defend one of the newcomers, Jimoh. The other chimp was received with the usual violence, but not Jimoh. The two females groomed him and protected him from the other hostile chimps. Sometime later de Waal discovered that fourteen years earlier, Jimoh had been in another institution with the same two females, who recognized him and now protected him as one of their own.

MONSTROUS CIVILIZATIONS

Here at the beginning of our century we find much of the explicitly racial xenophobia being replaced by talk of a "clash of civilizations." The political scientist Samuel P. Huntington prognosticated a future drama between post–cold war world powers in his influential and vaguely paranoid essay "The Clash of Civilizations," where he argued that, after the cold war, international politics would move out of its Western phase (i.e., the battles between liberal democracy, fascism, and communism) and become the clash between Western and non-Western civilizations: "In the politics of civilizations, the peoples and governments of non-Western civilizations no longer remain the objects of history as targets of Western colonialism but join the West as movers and shapers of history."[19] Western nation-states, Huntington argued, must align with each other in order to be strong and resilient in the coming clash with the East.

The idea that foreign cultures are threatening because their cultural values exclude or compete with one's own is certainly contentious, but it is, rightly or wrongly, a dominant position of late. With almost three thousand innocent Americans killed on 9/11, the wars in Afghanistan and Iraq, the war on terror, the Patriot Act, repeated embassy and subway bombings, and so on, many people on either side of the East/West divide feel anxious about the new out-groups. These new monsters are hard to pinpoint and isolate. Such a creature has no corporeal body to fight or dismember; it has no lair to infiltrate, no specific skin color, no national boundary. It is everywhere and nowhere. Global terrorism has given us all fresh opportunities to be afraid, both reasonably and unreasonably. We are in a new culture war now, one that nourishes its hostile imagination every day with the real blood of East/West conflict.

Xenophobia goes both ways, of course. Islamic fundamentalism constructs a specific American monster. We are seen as godless, consumerist *zombies*, soulless hedonists without honor, family, or purpose.[20] Ayatollah Khomeini famously referred to the United States in a 1979 speech as "the great Satan." Along with disgust at U.S. imperialism, some fundamentalist Muslims conceive of average Americans as docile cogs in a monstrous secular machine that seems to be grinding forward to subdue every corner of the globe. In their eyes, we are a viper pit of sexual immorality. In some Saudi textbooks students are told not to befriend Jews or Christians because "emulation of the infidels leads to loving them, glorifying them and raising their status in the eyes of Muslims, and that is forbidden."[21]

An environment lacking in basic needs (employment, food, shelter, etc.) can produce a dehumanized populace, but an environment with too much wealth and prosperity can also dehumanize. Americans appear zombie-like because their raison d'être appears to be the consumption of goods and pleasures, making us seem more attached to plastic surgery, reality television, and giant SUVs than to family, honor, and integrity. Some American films and novels have explored this critique of consumerist monstrosity, not from an outsider cultural perspective but from within it. Bret Easton Ellis's 1991 *American Psycho* and the 2000 film of the same name explore, among other things, the dehumanizing effects of a sick capitalist society. A privileged wealthy investment banker unravels into a vicious serial killer, but even more chilling is that he doesn't seem to feel anything, as if his lifestyle of acquisition and hedonism has neutralized his humanity. Films like *American Psycho* and *Donnie Darko* (2001) explore the idea that *American culture itself* is the source of horror.[22] From the perspective of some fundamentalists of the Muslim world, American individualism looks less like a point of pride and more like a form of selfish infantilism. To some extent,

The Spartans stand momentarily triumphant in front of a mountain of dead Persian "monsters" in the 2006 film *300* (Warner Bros.). Image courtesy of Jerry Ohlinger.

this view of Western pleasure zombies just rearticulates Aldous Huxley's *Brave New World* version of our future.

Conversely, some Americans tend to stereotype Muslims as wild-eyed jihadi primitives who seek to destroy our modern and tolerant way of life.[23] The mutual animosity is not new. In 1664 an illustrated pamphlet titled *The Monstrous Tartar* became very popular in England. It portrayed a frightening Muslim soldier, supposedly taken prisoner in Hungary. He is depicted as having a three-foot-long crane-like neck and is posed with bow and arrow, ready to oppose the good Christian cause. With only slightly more sophistication, we in the West have continued down to the present with this fabrication of monsters. In 2007 Hollywood released its fictionalized version of the battle of Thermopylae, titled *300* after the number of Spartan soldiers who stood their ground against thousands of invading Persians in 480 BCE. This famous battle, chronicled by Herodotus among others, stands as a symbolic tribute to the power of military training and efficiency (the Spartans) over sheer numbers and unskilled aggression (Xerxes' Persian army). More recently, it has also stood as a symbol of the freedom-loving West defending itself against Eastern autocracy.

The visual representation of the Persians in *300* is straight from monster movies. The screen thunders with giant, snarling, twisted and deformed creatures, all bearing down on the buff Spartan heroes. These bad guys, according to the film, are the ancestors of modern Iran, and they drool and bark their way through the film with little resemblance to the human race. Dana Stevens opened her review of the film on Slate.com by saying, "If *300*, the new battle epic based on the graphic novel by Frank Miller and Lynn Varley, had been made in Germany in the mid-1930s, it would be studied today alongside *The Eternal Jew* as a textbook example of how race-baiting fantasy and nationalist myth can serve as an incitement to total war."[24] The Iranian scholar Touraj Daryaee wrote, "In a time when we hear the sirens of war over Iran (Persia), it is ominous that such a film as *300* is released for mass consumption. To depict Persians/Iranians as inarticulate monsters, raging towards the West, trying to rob its people of their basic values demeans the population of Iran and anesthetizes the American population to war in the Middle East." Continuing his connection to contemporary policy, Daryaee sarcastically says, "This way Bush, Cheney, and other 'compassionate' conservatives can more easily rain their precision guided missiles down on the heads of my parents, family members and other Iranians, establish Abu Ghraib detention centers, and perhaps take revenge for the death of the 300 Spartans in antiquity and finally bring democracy, peace and a better way of life to the East."[25]

Samuel Huntington suggests that the clash of civilizations is a relatively new break with older, more ideologically oriented animosities, such as communism versus capitalism. But I would argue that civilization xenophobia is only the latest skirmish in the ongoing ideological warfare. In fact, to call it the "latest" is to disregard the history of demonization. Even before we felt contempt for different races, Westerners felt contempt for barbarian cultures. In that sense, the new xenophobia is the old xenophobia. The strangers of the ancient world were not strange because of their skin color or their exotic geographic location. They were strange because their culture was alien, and they were feared and loathed accordingly.[26]

Some more recent accusations of monstrous societies include the following well-known variations: Godless communism creates nihilistic, immoral monsters; rabid capitalism and consumerism create hedonistic zombies (Karl Marx actually referred to capitalism as a "vampire" sucking the blood of the labor class); theocracy creates uncritical fanatical zealots. We know these are monstrous societies, the logic goes, because they produce monstrous results: genocide, terrorism, and torture.

What's seemingly new, conceptually speaking, is that after the heyday of *internal* Freudian aggression theory, the pendulum has swung and we now have radical social constructionism—in plain English, extreme *nurture* over nature. Systems are evil, not people. It is society or ideology that churns out monsters; the blame is diffused to the larger social system.[27] This view fits nicely with liberal postmodern ideas about *structural* rather than *individual* responsibility, but it also sits well with neoconservative arguments that we must alter the cultures of theocracies and monarchies everywhere in order to create freer, happier, decidedly nonmonstrous individuals at home and abroad. We live in a time when it is reasonable to think of monsters as socially conditioned or constructed.

PATHOLOGICAL SOCIETIES

In the 1960s Hannah Arendt articulated a new kind of monster. In *Eichmann in Jerusalem: A Report on the Banality of Evil* she gives us a picture of Adolf Eichmann, the Nazi architect of the Holocaust, as a calm, almost robotic psychopath. Eichmann was not so much an anti-Semite as an unfeeling, detached career man looking for the most expeditious path to professional success. He lacked empathy, just like the psychopaths I discussed in chapter 13. Arendt points out that "it would have been very comforting indeed to believe that Eichmann was a monster," but "the trouble with Eichmann was precisely that so many were like him, and that the many were neither perverted nor sadistic, that they were, and still are, terribly and terrifyingly normal."[28]

Thinking about Arendt's description of Eichmann, the social psychologist Stanley Milgram framed the notorious Nazi within his overall theory of situational evil. Most people, Milgram argued, would do heinous immoral acts if certain social expectations were placed on them. Recall from the introduction that Milgram asked test subjects to administer painful electrical shocks to other subjects. He was surprised to find how many subjects were willing to follow orders no matter what the cost in human suffering. Milgram concluded that people become torturers and abusers when they are inside specific dehumanizing social frameworks. Individual monsters are extensions of monstrous institutional systems.[29]

Earlier ages recognized the unhealthy group dynamic of mobs. In the seventeenth century Thomas Browne saw large crowds as enemies of reason, virtue, and religion, "a monstrosity more prodigious than the hydra." In the twentieth century theorists expanded this image to include schools, prisons, the military, corporations, churches, and other potentially corrupting organizations. The psychologist Philip Zimbardo conducted a well-known prison experiment at Stanford University in 1971 using college students to role-play guards and inmates. Even though the assignment of specific roles was entirely random and reflected no culpability on the part of the "inmates," the experiment revealed a very rapid descent into sadistic abuse by the "guards." Eventually the experiment had to be halted, but not before it demonstrated to Zimbardo that a kind of overwhelming power exists in certain situations, a power that can sweep away an individual's better judgment.

Dr. Zimbardo updated his original findings in a recent book titled *The Lucifer Effect: Understanding How Good People Turn Evil*, applying his situational theory to the notorious case of torture in Iraq's Abu Ghraib prison.[30] The fact that seemingly normal American soldiers engaged in torture and degradation techniques on Iraqi detainees offers more evidence, Zimbardo thinks, for his view that abuse and aggression are not the results of inner character flaws. The torture at Abu Ghraib was not, as the Bush administration maintained, a result of a few bad apples spoiling the bunch. It was instead, according to Zimbardo, the result of a "bad barrel" corrupting any apples put into it.[31] It was an institution that pressured soldiers to gather intelligence by any means necessary, and this "end justifies the means" philosophy gave interrogators carte blanche in their treatment of the detainees.

Unlike the Freudian view of monstrous behavior, which focused on the deformities of the individual's inner psyche, the new paradigm sees a "Lucifer effect" in the external structures of social interaction. Zimbardo writes, "Situational forces can work to transform even some of the best of us into Mr. Hyde monsters, without the benefit of Dr. Jekyll's chemical elixir. We must be more aware of how situational variables can influence our behavior."[32] This viewpoint of criminality and deviance was only starting to show itself in the days of the Leopold and Loeb murder, when Erle Stanley Gardner said "society itself was partly responsible" and "we are only beginning to realize that the sole cause does not lie entirely with the juvenile."[33] Now this societal view (some might call it a *structural* view) has become standard operating procedure. In fact, so common is this new view of monsters that many contemporary deviants go straight to it when explaining their own depravity.

Ted Bundy killed more than thirty people in the late 1970s, although some (including Bundy himself) put the figure much higher. He also engaged in sexual assault and necrophilia. Hours before he was executed in 1989, Bundy gave a final interview to the evangelical leader James Dobson in which he blamed pornography for leading him astray. Bundy went so far as to say that every other ne'er-do-well he had met in prison during his ten-year stretch had also been inspired to evil by pornography and violence in the media: "Those of us who have been so much influenced by violence in the media—in particular, pornographic violence—aren't some kind of inherent monsters. We are your sons, and we are your husbands. We grew up in regular families."[34]

In addition to conservative structural views about dehumanizing media and popular culture, liberals have taken up structural views of their own, sometimes to ridiculous effect. Recall the Northern Illinois University shooter Steven Kazmierczak, who killed five others and himself and also injured eighteen in a lecture hall. Days after it happened, Mark Ames, the author of the book *Going Postal*, published an essay on the lefty online syndication service Alternet titled "NIU: Was the Killer Crazy, or the Campus Hopeless?" The title alone represents a question about heinous crime that would not, maybe could not have been asked a few decades ago.[35]

Silly, too, but telling, is the extreme structuralism to which Eldridge Cleaver (1935–1998) appealed when trying to explain his own career as a serial rapist. Cleaver is well known as an influential member of the Black Panthers (lesser known is his volte-face as a Reagan Republican in the 1980s), but before all that he was in prison for rape. In the mid-1960s he ingested enough Marxism while in jail on drug possession to bend its explanatory framework into service for other criminal transgressions. He saw himself as a victim. He and other criminals were in fact responding to a broken social system of institutional racism. Society, not the criminal, was the monster, according to Cleaver. Beyond just the degradations of the class struggle, the most insidious threat, for Cleaver, was the socially constructed set of ideals and values in our culture. Above all other such sinfully engineered ideals was "The Ogre": "I discovered, with alarm, that The Ogre possessed a tremendous and dreadful power over me, and I didn't understand this power or why I was at its mercy. I tried to repudiate The Ogre, root it out of my heart as I had done God, Constitution, principles, morals, and values—but The Ogre had its claws buried in the core of my being and refused to let go. I fought frantically to be free, but The Ogre only mocked me and sank its claws deeper into my soul."[36] This horrible monster, according to Cleaver, was "the white woman." In his poem "To a White Girl" he expressed his mixed emotions, saying that he both loved and hated the "white witch" and saw her as a "symbol of the rope and hanging tree." In response to this torment Cleaver became a rapist as "an insurrectionary act." By raping white women, he felt he was getting revenge for the ways that black women had been defiled by white men during the slavery era. Cleaver thus desperately tried to dress up his deviance in the clothes of righteous indignation and political revolution.[37]

Setting aside these more extreme and unconvincing applications of the structural theory of monsters, we must concede the wisdom in more balanced approaches to the idea of monstrous societies. One cannot deny that certain social environments can bring out the worst in people.

MONSTERS FROM THE OPPRESSED CLASSES

The ghetto is often characterized as a Darwinian jungle of kill or be killed. Indeed, certain impoverished pockets in Chicago, Los Angeles, Baltimore, Philadelphia, and elsewhere have barbaric murder rates. In July

2007 then senator Barack Obama pointed out that nearly three dozen Chicago kids had been murdered so far that year, and that figure was higher than the casualty numbers of Illinois soldiers serving in Iraq during the same time.

Many argue that violence becomes a way of life. If you cannot adopt the violent lifestyle, you will be victimized by it. A violent criminal in Franklin, a high-security prison, said, "Normal to me is the jungle. They talk about callousness and lack of empathy, but, please, what the fuck is empathy? Where I come from, if I knock you down, you stay down. It's not normal to come up and kill you stone dead because I want your money, but that is normality for me. At the end of the day, all of us sitting here are monsters, whether we're armed robbers, child molesters, or killers—we're monsters."[38]

Xavier McElrath-Bey, a Chicago native who grew up in the tough "Back of the Yards" neighborhood, an area originally made famous by Upton Sinclair's *The Jungle*, prefers to allude to William Golding's *Lord of the Flies* when he describes his hood. He joined a gang when he was only eleven years old, and by the time he was thirteen he had been arrested nineteen times.[39] When I met Xavier he had been out of prison for a few years, released after serving thirteen years of a sentence for murder. After serving almost half his life in prison and earning a college degree there, he had unique insights into contemporary criminality. "I don't believe there are bad kids," Xavier said, "just bad socialization." When kids become teenagers, he explained, their norms and values naturally shift from those of their parents and family to those of their peer group. In his violent neighborhood, that meant becoming a gang member. "Gang life gave me a sense of purpose and meaning," he said. The hood is a volatile and exciting place, where a young man can forge strong social ties and rise through the ranks of hierarchy and respect. The cost is a life of violence and paranoia, but it seems worth the price when you are young and successful in the lifestyle. Xavier said that he didn't really think much about the people he was hurting, because whenever he was caught he never had to face his victims. In all his court proceedings, he heard only about "the people" or "the state" versus Xavier; he felt that he was simply breaking an impersonal law upheld by an impersonal system and an antagonistic police force.[40] Just as psychopaths lack empathy for others, here we see some of the consequences of *systems* that lack empathy or prevent empathic responses.[41]

Desperate environments create desperate measures. Thug life looks monstrous by the standards of polite society, but it was hatched and nursed in a world where it has distinct advantages. According to this view, social injustice and oppression create a violent aggressive criminal culture as a response.[42] The basic logic of this view can be seen in a different context when we consider suicide bombers. The point here is not to draw a facile comparison between ghetto criminality and suicide bombers, for they are different sorts of characters. But in today's monsterology, they are both considered major threats to stability and they are both subjected to structural explanations. The claim that suicide terrorists are just evil monsters who freely choose to murder innocent people is alive and well. But the common belief today is that structural stresses (economic, political, ideological) *create* monstrously deviant individuals. How true, or perhaps more important, how useful is such a belief?

A study of the writings and pronouncements in the *Al-Qaida Reader* reveals no unified complaint against the United States, no specific charge that rallies and justifies suicide bomber retaliations.[43] Instead one finds a litany of localized grievances and a random body of complaints against U.S. domestic and international policy, mostly lifted from our own internal media critiques. Osama bin Laden, for example, surprisingly takes an angry interest in the refusal by the United States to sign the Kyoto agreement addressing the environmental implications of global warming, and even objects to U.S. campaign-finance laws that unfairly advantage the wealthy.[44] Reza Aslan, a scholar of Islam, interprets the pastiche nature of these grievances as evidence of a general Al-Qaida strategy to *invent* a clash of civilizations, an invention that George W. Bush's administration was all too willing to assist in constructing. But Aslan thinks such a dramatic clash is fictional, a way of illegitimately putting one face on myriad local dissatisfactions, such as Iraqi anger at the U.S. military occupation, Palestinian anger at Israeli policies, Taliban anger at the Musharraf-Bush alliance in Pakistan, and mujahedeen anger in southern Thailand. Even if there is no one grievance that explains suicide bomber attacks on innocents, socioeconomic theorists detect common threads of poverty and lack of education. According to this view, suicide bombing results from the radical despair of crushing poverty and the humiliation of subaltern status, and therefore constitutes an insurrection by the oppressed classes. In some cases the oppressive power is domestic, but more often it is a foreign power. The 1998 militant Muslim "Declaration on Armed Struggle against Jews and Crusaders," which was signed by bin Laden and Ayman al-Zawahiri, argued that it was the duty of every Muslim to fight the United States and the "satanically inspired supporters allying with them."

This interpretation of terrorism as a rebellion suggests that a removal of oppressive forces and policies will result in the end of suicide bombing. It is no stretch to see that such a view of aberrant behavior corresponds generally to Zimbardo's doctrine that situational forces can transform any-one into a monster. In this view, monstrous behavior becomes "rational" in the sense that it can be correlated with, if not predicted from, specific social conditions.

One of the major objections to such a view is the simple fact that a majority of the world's poor do not blow themselves up in order to kill innocent people. In other words, the explanation is neither necessary nor sufficient. Another damaging objection is the increasing data indicating that suicide bombers are *not* as poor nor as uneducated as previously believed. The Princeton economics professor Alan Krueger has gathered data on hate crimes and terrorism since the early 1990s and claims that "the available evidence is nearly unanimous in rejecting either mate-rial deprivation or inadequate education as important causes of support for terrorism or participation in terrorist activities. Such explanations have been embraced almost entirely on faith, not scientific evidence."[45] Analyzing data from the Pew Research Center's 2004 Global Atti-tudes Project in Jordan, Morocco, Pakistan, and Turkey, Krueger found the opposite of the received view: people with higher education were much more likely to see suicide bombing as justifiable. In a study of Hezbollah martyrs (*shahids*), Krueger analyzed the life histories of 129 deceased shahids, again with surprising results: compared with the general Lebanese population, Hezbollah suicide bombers demonstrate a lower degree of poverty and a higher degree of education. Similar studies have found high levels of college education among Al-Qaida members as well.[46]

But perhaps the general structural viewpoint may be maintained if we add the unique ideological ingredients of moral righteousness and afterlife rewards for martyrdom.[47] A religious fanatic might more readily kill inno-cents in a suicide mission if his ideological system allows him to deny the innocent status of his victims. In the same way that some ideologies allow one to redefine terrorists as "freedom fighters," so, too, some ideologies allow one to redefine innocents as "infidels."

Religious ideologies often dehumanize those who do not fit inside the sanctuary of orthodoxy. Some critics have argued that Islam itself is intol-erant, pugilistic, and incapable of conciliation with modernity. Ayaan Hirsi Ali, a Somali Muslim apostate, assessed the tragedy of 9/11 as a tragic consequence of Islam itself: "True Islam, as a rigid belief system and moral framework, leads to cruelty. The inhuman act of those nineteen hijack-ers was the logical outcome of this detailed system for regulating human behavior."[48] In this view, social and economic status does not matter so much as ideas about destiny, metaphysics, and theology.

Osama bin Laden. Image courtesy of Photofest.

MONSTERS OF IDEOLOGY

In 2006 Pope Benedict XVI raised the dander of many Muslims by quoting a medieval Byzantine emperor who referred to Islam as "evil and inhuman." Despite Benedict's claim that the disparaging comments were a quotation and not his own view, the language of a "new crusade" was resuscitated in public discourse. Osama bin Laden himself was quick to embrace crusade terminology, both in chastising the pope for stirring the pot and in promising to return the aggression. "The response will be what you see and not what you hear," bin Laden said, "and let our mothers bereave us if we do not make victorious our messenger of God."[49]

Clerics and devotees from many different religions have bathed God's message in blood and given credence to the theory that monstrous actions such as suicide bombings are produced by monstrous religious beliefs. One critic of religion, Sam Harris, has continued an old tradition, from David Hume to Bertrand Russell, in calling for an end of faith. In his best-selling book *The End of Faith*, he argues that suicide bombers would be almost unimaginable without the fanatical religious beliefs to motivate and justify them: "Subtract the Muslim belief in martyrdom and jihad, and the actions of suicide bombers become completely unintelligible, as does the spectacle of public jubilation that invariably follows their deaths; insert these peculiar beliefs, and one can only marvel that suicide bombing is not more widespread."[50] Recently Christopher Hitchens, Ayaan Hirsi Ali, and Martin Amis have lent their voices to the accusation that Islamic fundamentalism is an ideological cult of death.[51]

The philosopher Daniel Dennett offers a provocative analogy for understanding the suicide bomber's religious devotion, one that underscores the *inhuman* aspect of the influence of ideology. Certain kinds of parasites need to get into the stomach of a cow or sheep to successfully mature and complete their life cycle. To accomplish this relocation, the fluke enters some hapless ant and, by manipulating its navigation system, causes it to crawl to the top of a grass stalk. A cow comes along and eats the ant as part of its grass diet; the fluke has thus successfully entered the cow, using the ant as a vehicle. The ant obviously comes out of this process rather badly; it is simply manipulated by the parasite and loses its own chance for reproduction and longer life. Dennett points out that this whole manipulative process can be found in religious devotees: "We often find human beings setting aside their personal interests, their health, their chances to have children, and devoting their entire lives to furthering the interests of an *idea* that has lodged in their brains."[52] Like any successful organism, religion seeks to promulgate itself (in this case, its memes rather than its genes), and it uses individual believers to make more of itself. For humanists like Dennett, religion is like a seething monstrous mother, pulsing in her lair and spilling out parasitic spores and tentacles to subdue host organisms.

One of the major reasons ideologies seem potentially dangerous, whether they are religious or social or economic, is because they occupy a space in human thinking that is highly influential but also unverifiable. In the religious case, idealistic beliefs are not just difficult to corroborate or check against experience, they are sometimes explicitly and proudly anti-empirical and antirational. God's incomprehensibility, a monstrous magnitude, was examined in chapter 12 in my discussion of the tradition of the sublime. Here in the contemporary critique of ideology and religion we have another rehearsal of the secular idea that going outside of reason and empirical proof leads one to monstrous territory. Just as the early cartographers announced on the uncharted sections of their maps "Here Be Monsters," critics of ideology want to paint the same warning. Monstrosity is that which exists outside rational coherence. If zealots choose to embrace that monster, then monstrous consequences will follow.[53]

All this illustrates a shift in the way we think about monsters. Instead of solitary freaks born of evil parentage or pathological genetics, we think of them as churned out by abstract alienating systems, social and ideological machines that cannot feel the beating hearts inside them. This is one of the major themes of Franz Kafka's stories and has become so commonplace a characterization of modern *organization* that we now refer to such crushing bureaucracies and philosophies as "Kafkaesque." Modern organization alienates us from each other and from our own self, reducing our humanity and tilting us toward zombie status.

DECONSTRUCTING MONSTERS

Social constructionism is the name we give to a loose confederation of ideas about the artificial nature of human knowledge and, by extension, the constructed nature of reality itself. Previously, we thought of the categories species, race, and gender as *natural*, as concepts that pick out features of the real world. The real world was thought to be composed of distinct things and properties, and our languages and sciences were thought to capture those realities in a net of essence-defining descriptions. Social constructionism, on the other hand, suggests that such linguistic categories are more like social conventions, fabricated mostly by the powerful for the purpose of sustaining their power advantage. In recent years we have come to apply this same constructionist logic to everything. We have arrived at the moment in history (presaged dimly and occasionally in earlier ages) where we can say, "One is not born but rather becomes a monster."

In our age of postmodernism (a radical form of social constructionism), it is a good time to be a monster. The monster is but another subspecies of the other, and like all marginalized, subordinated groups, the monster can finally let its hair down and glory in its *difference*. Postmodern theory seeks to deconstruct the dominant social constructions of normative boundaries and rewrite or rebuild them with losers as winners, walk-on extras as main characters, and deformed outcasts as principal luminaries. There is no grand narrative, no universal human nature, no objective reality, no Enlightenment truth to be captured by reason. The politics of difference, which issued from the denial of traditional norms, is a good milieu for monsters.[54]

We saw in the modernization of Grendel and Beowulf how *evil demons* can be recast as *misunderstood victims*. But here, in the contemporary paradigm of postmodernism, the relativism of values seeps even deeper. Formerly we were interested in what makes a person *be* a monster; now we are more concerned with what makes a person *seem* a monster.[55] Relativism, at least in the social sciences and humanities of the academy, is the reigning monsterology of our day. There are no real monsters, only oppressive labels and epithets.

It is ironic that the current champions of neo-Enlightenment liberal values (Hitchens, Hirsi Ali, etc.) consider the superstition that lies *outside rationality* to be the monster, whereas the postmodern deconstructionists consider *rationality itself* to be a repressive and totalitarian monster, forcing everything into a procrustean fit. Fans of the theorist Jacques Derrida, the father of deconstructionism, have suggested a secret history of Western thought, a history of the outcast, including the ultimate philosophical "outcast": the *nothing*, or negation. Reason seeks to map reality, but what about the obscure territories that fall outside of the map? These unreasonable gaps in knowledge have been waiting in the secret darkness of Western thought, occasionally peeking through in moments of skepticism and suspicion, waiting until the deconstructionists came along to unleash them into the machine of logos.[56] Individual monsters (Frankenstein's creature, Jeffrey Dahmer, Dracula, the Blob, etc.) are violations of normal rational taxonomy, but also the general *idea* of the monster is, for deconstructionism, like a conceptual place-holder for all things unclassifiable and a celebration of the irrational.[57] Deconstructionism clears a path to new freedoms and diversity. When everyone is a monster, there will be no monsters.

Interestingly, as soon as the postmodern embracers of irreducible pluralism and diversity staked their ideal ground of a monsterless, otherless beatitude, their putative enemies, the rationalists, seemed to be growing horns, fangs, and tails. We cannot get rid of monsters, no matter how righteously tolerant we get.

My own sympathies, which are probably obvious by now, lie with the neo-Enlightenment liberals.[58] Yes, some monsters have turned out to be wrongfully accused and others have been conjured entirely by politicians and priests, but that doesn't mean there is no such thing as monsters. The understandable desire to avoid the lamentable witch hunts of our history, both recent and ancient, has led many relativists to abandon the term and the concept of monster altogether, seeing it as an outmoded relic.

In 2006 in Kandahar, Afghanistan, four armed men broke into the home of an Afghan headmaster and teacher named Malim Abdul Habib.[59] The four men gathered Habib's wife and children together, forcing them to watch as they stabbed Habib eight times and then decapitated him. Habib was the headmaster at Shaikh Mathi Baba high school, where he educated girls along with boys. The Taliban militants of the region, who are suspected in the beheading, see the education of girls as a violation of Islam, a view that is obviously not shared by the vast majority of Muslims. My point is simply this: If you can gather a man's family at gunpoint and force them to watch as you cut off his head, you are a monster. You don't merely *seem* to be one, you *are* one. A relativist objection here sounds coldly disingenuous.

The relativist might finally counter by pointing out that American soldiers at Abu Ghraib tortured some innocent people, too. That, I agree, is true and astoundingly shameful, but it doesn't prove there are no real monsters, it only widens the category and recognizes monsters on both sides of an issue. Two sides calling each other monsters doesn't prove that there are no monsters. In the case of the American torturers at Abu Ghraib and the Taliban beheaders in Afghanistan, both epithets sound entirely accurate.

15

Future Monsters

Robots, Mutants, and Posthuman Cyborgs

It's obvious that every effort is being made in these years to replicate a human
being and forge armies of them. It might take two centuries, but it does seem to
be what we humans are hell-bent on doing.

NORMAN MAILER

MUTANTS AND ROBOTS

WHEN GODZILLA MADE HIS FIRST FILM appearance in
1954 he created a sensation and a whole new "giant monster" (*kaiju*) genre. Soon audiences would thrill to the likes of
Mothra, Rodan, King Ghidorah, and Gamera. The original film *Godzilla*
was actually considered to be high art in Japan, compared frequently with
the great films of Akira Kurosawa.[1] American audiences experienced a
recut version and a less compelling plot line. In the original film, Japanese
fishing boats are mysteriously destroyed off the coast of Odo Island, and
old legends about a monster god named Godzilla begin to circulate among
the natives. Soon specialists and reporters are called in, and the gigantic
creature rises out of the water to begin a rampage of local villages and
eventually Tokyo itself. Scientists determine that the monster is actually an
ancient dinosaur that has been revived and mutated by underwater atomic
tests. Further investigation reveals that Godzilla is suffused with radiation,
giving him almost immortal powers of resilience and a deadly atomic ray
that he breathes like fire. After he passes through a city, the survivors of

Science and hubris once again give birth to monsters. Godzilla lays waste, in the original 1954 Japanese production of *Godzilla* (Toho Company, Ltd.). Image courtesy of Photofest.

his attack find themselves suffering from radiation poisoning. Dr. Daisuke Serizawa is the reluctant creator of a superweapon, called "the Oxygen Destroyer," and he is enlisted to use the terrible device against Godzilla. Serizawa resists deploying the weapon on the grounds that, once such devastating power is witnessed, every government will pursue it to ruinous result for the whole planet. Finally he yields and personally dives into the sea with the weapon to exterminate Godzilla. As he successfully unleashes the weapon against the monster, he also cuts his own lifeline and dies with the only knowledge of the weapon, thereby preventing further exploitation of the odious invention.

This is a stunning plot when we consider that it was created only nine years after the real atomic bombings of Hiroshima and Nagasaki. Moreover, in 1954 a Japanese fishing boat was exposed to massive radiation contamination by American testing on Bikini Island. The crew and the vessel, *Daigo Fukuryu Maru* (Lucky Dragon 5), were outside the supposed danger zone, but the blast was much bigger than expected, and the crew received deadly radiation poisoning. The film *Godzilla* entered popular culture at a moment when Japanese outrage against nuclear weapons was at fever pitch, and the terrible tragedy of a mere decade before was still fresh in public consciousness.

This masochistic dimension of monster stories is already contained in *Frankenstein* and in the Christian and pagan traditions. Monsters, according to this logic, frequently come to take revenge on deserving individuals and even cultures. God or fate dispatches terrible creatures to dispense the wages of sin. Human arrogance is repaid by chaos and destruction. In some ways, the religious or cosmic aspect of monster vengeance is still retained in the secular masochism of environmentalism. Godzilla is our own fault, just as "the creature" was Dr. Frankenstein's fault. Just as global warming is our fault. Of course, pollution is indeed a serious threat, as are the many other environmental problems we face. The many television, film, and literary plots revolving around the environment confirm that it ranks as one of our worst fears. Interestingly, doing something to ease the threats often requires an admission of our own complicity in bringing them about.[2]

If, as Freud suggested, technology is our prosthetic attempt to become God, will we inadvertently become a monster god? And if we're not actually becoming God, are we still playing God too much, with all this new power to manipulate nature, splitting atoms, genetically engineering food, robotically enhancing our bodies, chemically enhancing our minds, and designing our babies?

The current advances in robotics have led many people (and scores of Hollywood films) to envision a time when a race of artificial slaves will rise up and overthrow their human masters.[3] The imagined scenario raises all kinds of interesting questions about free will and the evolution of self-agency in a digital system. It also rehearses ethical questions about slavery, questions that have all too real and painful associations with our recent national history. But with regard to the monsters issue, it really turns on the fear we have that something we control will twist around and start to control us.

Before he was governor of California, Arnold Schwarzenegger was best known for playing an unhinged robot in three *Terminator* films. The original 1984 film, by James Cameron, has spawned one of the most lucrative franchises in robot-loathing history, including a Niagara of films, books, games, and comics. The story begins in the not too distant future, when robots rule the world. An artificial intelligence computer, named Skynet, evolves enough nefarious intentionality to pursue the annihilation of humankind. John Connor, a rebel human, develops an effective resistance movement called Tech-Con. As the tide turns toward human emancipation, the machines create a robot assassin, a terminator, to go back in time to kill John Connor's mother before John is born. If we set aside the ludicrous time-travel aspect of the story, we have the always emotion-ally satisfying battle between man and machine. The *Matrix* series is yet another mythos about the dehumanizing power nascent in computers and robotic machines and our fears of being turned into mere nodes on a stag-gering digital grid (the old fear of reductionism).

A nice variation on the imagined future of human slavery is the 2008 Pixar film *Wall-E*, which humorously envisions a time when machines have made life entirely too comfortable for humans. In this vision of our future, humans have become so immersed in virtual reality that they do not really walk or stand up or even interact with each other. Humans have become infantilized by convenience-enhancing technology, and they live almost entirely in the digital simulacrum. Generations of life lived on comfy chairs sipping fattening drinks has actually modified the human body; everyone is rendered an obese blob, incapable of physical activity, and their inte-rior mental lives have been hijacked by the manipulations of mass-media consumer interests. The technology-based dehumanization is not one of oppressed slavery, but deadening anesthesia. The computers conspire against the humans when they eventually seek to reclaim their humanity.

Isaac Asimov famously framed the anxiety about robot autonomy when he imbued all his fictional robots with the "three laws of robotics."[4] In his 1950s stories Asimov gave us a more nuanced version of robots, one that diverged from the usual *Frankenstein* story of terrible comeuppance. Robots were programmed with the following laws: (1) a robot may not injure a human being, or, through inaction, allow a human being to come to harm; (2) a robot must obey orders given to it by a human being, except where such orders conflict with the first law; (3) a robot must protect its own existence, except where such protection conflicts with law 1 or 2. These rules produce some fairly sympathetic robots and some interesting scenarios that Asimov explored in his series, but the worst-case scenario, robot insurgence, has been the preferred version of our AI future.

All this makes some highly dubious assumptions about the emergence of conscious intentionality and free will in artificial intelligence. But lest we shrug it all off as sci-fi nonsense, we should take note that robot drones are already fighting battles in Iraq and Afghanistan. American uncrewed aerial vehicles (UAVs) and robot tanks have already been crucial soldiers in battles in Fallujah and in the Tora Bora caves. In fact, by 2015 the U.S. Department of Defense projects that one-third of its fighting force will be robot vehicles, and by 2035 they expect to have autonomous humanoid robots climbing onto the battlefield.[5]

Autonomous robots will be free-standing rather than cabled directly to a human operator. They will operate according to hierarchically stacked rules of behavior programmed by Boolean binary logic. Insect-size robots, and even some small humanoids, are already functioning according to this algorithmic intelligence in laboratories at MIT, Honda, the Space and Naval Warfare Systems Command, and Sony. They navigate difficult terrain by quickly processing logically programmed on-off directives; if blocked by a wall, they move left, then right, until the blockade is passed. Micro versions of these rules govern the adjustments of each robotic foot or tread. Likewise, most robots have already been successfully equipped with rules that instruct them to repower themselves when they run low on energy, giving them a kind of self-sufficient *nutrition* system. In addition to nutritive systems, many artificial organisms have been programmed to *reproduce*, either physically building others like themselves or digitally copying themselves, as in computer viruses. This means they have waded into the stream of chance variation and natural selection. They are evolving.

Dave Bullock spent time in 2008 with the Navy's new MDARS-E armed robot and was unnerved by its sophisticated tracking ability.[6] After the Navy lab in San Diego explained to Bullock that their robot could track anything that moves, they assigned Bullock as the target for a demonstration. "Told that I was the target," Bullock reported, "the unmanned vehicle trained its guns on me and ordered, 'Stay where you are,' in an intimidating robot voice. And yes, it was frightening." The technical director at the lab, Bart Everett, assured Bullock, "We're not building Skynet," a reference to the malignant supercomputer in the *Terminator* films. But the new levels of robotic autonomy are provocative.

True autonomy exists when an agent can problem-solve beyond the parameters of preset programming. Many cognitive scientists doubt that this kind of free will can really emerge out of progressively more complex Boolean rule systems, but an increasing number of such scientists and philosophers are wondering if human autonomy isn't just a very complex version of this digital processing. In this view, the difference between artificial and human intelligence is one of degree, not kind. Even simple insect robots and computer entities act in surprising and unpredicted ways when their programmers put them into novel environments. String enough of this novel problem-solving behavior together and the machines begin to seem like biological systems.

A simple example comes from Steven Levy's book *Artificial Life*. Levy describes a common occurrence, a programmer who is surprised by the adaptive resources of his creation. When Mitchel Resnick designed a small robot to follow a straight line on the ground, he set the creature rolling without actually programming a protocol for when it reached the end of the line. "We wrote the program and it was following this line," explained Resnick. "And all of a sudden it struck me that I had no idea what was going to happen when it reached the end of the line.... When it got to the end of the line it turned around and started following the line in the other direction! If we had *planned* for it to do something, that would have been the ideal thing for it to do."[7]

True robot *autonomy* may not be a realistic fear in the near future, but robot manipulation by an enemy force of human hackers is entirely realistic. A good hacker could access the control system and turn missiles, robots, whatever, back at us just by rewriting the target protocols. In this case, the monsters are not the robots and computers themselves, but these machines become the inflexible tools of human oppressors.

The uniquely frightening aspect of robot-based political and social control is that such mechanical police do not have empathic emotional checks on their behaviors. Will robots be able to follow the rules of the Geneva Convention, for example? No amount of screaming, crying, or human desperation will touch the heart of a robot policeman because, of course, it has no heart. One hopes that even the most hardened human soldier or police officer can be touched in the throes of warfare by the pained entreaties of human suffering. Although, as I've argued earlier, this is precisely the assumption (of natural human empathy) that many human monsters invalidate. Human monsters demonstrate their lack of empathy regularly. Perhaps robot soldiers, programmed with citizen-saving protocols, won't do any worse than flesh-and-blood warriors.

CYBORGS

According to a recent issue of *Nanotech Report*, a newsletter analyzing investment opportunities for this cutting-edge technology, "Nanotechnology is about rebuilding mother nature atom by atom!"[8] This is a dramatic way of pointing out that such technological advancements as the Scanning Tunneling Microscope and such processes as nanolithography have allowed us to manipulate nanoscale structures in ways previously unimaginable. We might, in theory, be able to design chemical programs that disassemble molecules or even organisms into their atomic parts and then rebuild those parts into better organisms or even different organisms. For example, we may be able to create populations of nanobots (little chemical factories) that will eventually live inside the blood stream, releasing insulin into the veins of diabetics to control their blood glucose levels.

The U.S. National Nanotech Initiative, established by President Clinton and continued by President Bush, has already received 6.5 billion dollars in funding for nanotech research.[9] Originally formulated as a thought experiment by Richard Feynman, this cutting-edge attempt to manipulate micronature has recently brought together government, academia, and corporations like DuPont, IBM, and Sony, to name a few. Optimists like Marvin Minsky believe that the new technology will usher in a new and improved posthuman species.[10]

In this age of cloning, nanotech, genetic engineering, and neuropharmacology, a new breed of posthuman philosopher is emerging. It is not just the fiction writers and filmmakers who are intoxicated with the idea of transcending our human limits. A handful of forward-thinking, slightly lunatic artists, scientists, and cultural theorists are exploring the increasingly fuzzy boundary between technology and the biological body. *Posthuman* (or *transhuman* in the United Kingdom) refers to the idea that we will eventually transcend our frustratingly finite flesh. But we won't have to wait for an *afterlife* to achieve this liberation; we will attain it by the application of new technology. Technology, these theorists believe, will usher in a superior life for our species; we will no longer be limited by the spatial and temporal constraints of our corporeal self. For many theorists, this transhumanism is already well under way.

Nick Bostrom, an Oxford professor and the founder of the World Transhumanist Association, has predicted many significant transformations in the near future. In a lecture at the Technology, Entertainment, and Design Conference in 2005, Bostrom predicted that we humans will soon be able to expand our palette of sensory faculties, rearrange our body morphology, and even alter our hormonal makeup to ensure that love will not fade over time.[11] Erectile dysfunction drugs have already allowed men to stave off aging and performance anxiety; soon they will be able to tweak their chemistry to stay faithful and happily partnered. Bostrom believes that the new technology will allow us to alter our basic nature in ways that will enhance our experience—indeed, enhance our lives.

Kevin Warwick, a professor of cybernetics at the University of Reading, states, "I was born human. But this was an accident of fate—a condition merely of time and place. I believe it's something we have the power to change." To that end, he has implanted microchips in his body that communicate to computers in his lab, which respond by flipping on lights and opening doors when he approaches. He and his wife, Irena, plan to get his-and-hers implants that will send signals back and forth between computers and their nervous systems. Soon, he says, they will attempt to download and swap digital versions of their personal sensations and emotions. Warwick describes his wife's intentions: "The way she puts it, is that if anyone is going to jack into my limbic system—to know definitively when I'm feeling happy, depressed, angry, or even sexually aroused—she wants it to be her."[12]

The distinction between our physical self and our cyberself, stretched in all directions by Internet nodes and ubiquitous microprocessors, will blur irreversibly some day, the posthumanists explain. Our bodies will be accessorized with hardware and software improvements, our minds ready for uploading and downloading. Our intellectual aspirations will no longer be hindered by the wet sacks we currently call home.

In the next few years, the French performance artist Orlan will conclude her decades-long work-in-progress titled "The Reincarnation of St. Orlan" by having a team of plastic surgeons construct the largest nose that her face is capable of supporting. Under a local anesthetic, Orlan will lecture on postmodern theory, reading from Baudrillard, Kristeva, and Lacan, while surgeons flay her face and perform her rhinoplasty. She has already done this sort of surgery ten times. In New York Orlan had plastic structures implanted under the skin of her forehead so that it would approximate that of Leonardo's *Mona Lisa*. In another operation she had her chin reconstructed on the model of Botticelli's *Venus*. While these operations are performed she is dressed in outlandish costumes and her audience asks questions of her via fax machine, phone, and e-mail. When the surgeries are completed, the excess bits of skin and fat are stored in jars for display at future performances.

Orlan is not an escaped mental patient. She is a respected member of the international art community, displaying herself and her work at the Pompidou in Paris and touring England with a show titled "This Is My Body, This Is My Software." She is supported by grants from France's Ministry of Culture and the Getty Research Institute in Los Angeles. The art world has embraced this controversial play of nature and technology with open arms.[13]

To some viewers Orlan is blasphemous. Some critics decry her project, claiming that it is playing God to rearrange the face or body that God gave her. Is she transforming herself into a monster? Perhaps there is something sacrosanct about the natural state of affairs. Then again, it seems far too late to raise such a nostalgic objection. The natural state of affairs is already increasingly the product of human intervention. Our tomatoes are genetically engineered to ripen sometime after the apocalypse, our corn is genetically designed to detassel itself, frogs are designed with see-through skin for anatomy students, and human beings walk around with pig-valved hearts and pharmacy-bought psyches. As prosthetic gods, we lengthen and strengthen our arms and legs with machines. We expand our vision and the other senses with amplifiers. We alter our biology and psychology with synthetic chemicals. But the idea that technology makes us more god-like is premised on the assumption that we will be able to maintain *control* of the augmentations, that our human *will* can continue to retain its mastery over the mechanical and digital equipment. If it slips away from us, if the tools become constraints

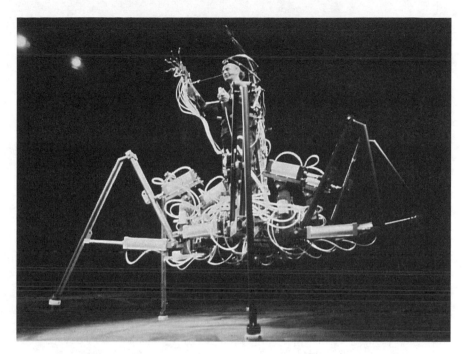

The Australian artist Stelarc finds ways to fuse his own body with robotic technology. From his Web site www.stelarc.va.com. Reprinted by kind permission of the artist.

rather than emancipators, then we may be in for unprecedented forms of alienation. Technology may alienate us from ourselves, dehumanizing us and turning us into self-made monsters of a new sort altogether.

Japan has been refining the cyborg "robo-roach" for over a decade. Microrobotics teams and biologists, like those at Tsukuba University, have successfully outfitted cockroaches with microprocessors and replaced their antennae with pulse-emitting electrodes. The scientists can actually control the movements of the roach, making it turn left and right and move forward and backward. Here, then, is the real-world manifestation of our worst fears. Are we creating technology that will eventually put us in the place of these hapless roaches?

The artist Stelarc (Stellos Arcadiou) takes a different approach to the interface between biology and technology. This performance artist, who is funded by an Australian Council Craft Board Fellowship, fuses his own body with electrical and digital technology. According to his official Web site, "He has used medical, robot and virtual reality systems to explore, extend and enhance the body's parameters. In the past he has acoustically and visually probed the body—amplifying his brainwaves, heartbeat, blood flow and muscle signals and filming the inside of his lungs, stomach and

The artist Stelarc plays with cyborg technology. He pushed the robotic camera down into his stomach to create a sculpture inside his body. From his Web site www.stelarc.va.com. Reprinted by kind permission of the artist.

colon. Having defined the limitations of the body, he has developed strategies to augment its capabilities, interfacing the body with prosthetics and computer technologies."[14]

One of Stelarc's early works was his "stomach sculpture." He first built a finger-size capsule sculpture that contained a camera. Next he fasted for a day to clear his gut, and then he piped this capsule down his gullet, tethered to a flexidrive cable and external control box. Once inserted into his stomach, it moved about and lit up LEDs by external control.

Again the burning question: Why do this? And again no clear answer is forthcoming, though the artist's statement is provocative:

> The idea was to insert an artwork into the body—to situate the sculpture in an internal space. The body becomes hollow, with no meaningful distinctions between public, private and physiological spaces. The technology invades and functions within the body not as a prosthetic replacement, but as an aesthetic adornment. One no longer *looks* at art, nor *performs* as art, but *contains* art. The hollow body becomes a host, not for a self or a soul, but simply for a sculpture.

In Stelarc's "Ping Body" performance, audience members in Paris, Helsinki, and Amsterdam were electronically linked through a performance

Web site (with a video feed) to the main performance site in Luxembourg, where Stelarc stood with wires and circuitry dangling from all parts of his body. These wires, which were muscle-stimulation contacts, were fed into a central computer, and audience members from around Europe were invited to manipulate Stelarc's body from their remote sites. There is something phenomenally strange about this. A person stationed thousands of miles away can push a button and make another person's arm go up in the air.

One of the reasons it's difficult to make sense of Orlan and Stelarc is their clever confusion of the means and ends relationships. When technology serves an engineering purpose or solves a practical puzzle, its role as a tool is clearly defined. As I write this line on my word processor, the computer technology slavishly follows the parameters that lead to effective typing and storing of data. The computer is a means to my goal of writing a book. But in Stelarc's "Ping Body" performance, the technology is almost an end in itself. He is literally playing with technology rather than pressing it into service for some preset goal. The parameters are not clear because the function of the technology is not clear. What will come of Stelarc's technological achievements is difficult to say, though we can bet that electric-organic cyborg fusions and remote-control manipulation will not go unnoticed by people with very definite ends in mind (e.g., the military).

So, too, in the case of Orlan, the means-end distinction is blurred. Plastic surgery and implantation is a technology that's becoming cheaper, more widespread, and more acceptable to popular culture; the public now expect celebrities to be accessorized in this way, and many well-to-do teenagers get new body parts as graduation presents from their parents. When we compare Orlan and Cindy Jackson, for example, the means-end distinction becomes highly relevant.

Cindy Jackson is an American woman who holds the world record for most plastic surgeries, around thirty operations, to transform herself into that cultural icon of beauty, the Barbie doll. When she was thirty-four her father died and left her a sizable inheritance, which she straightaway began to invest in her future face. She had surgery to remove the bags under her eyes, she had implants put into her cheeks and lips, and she had her chin chiseled, her eyes enlarged, her makeup colors permanently tattooed onto her face, her jaw broken and sawed shorter, and more.

Most people recognize a significant difference between Orlan and Jackson. Both employ the same cutting-edge medical technology (pun intended), but though the means are comparable, the ends or goals of the two differ greatly. When asked why she has been reconstructing herself to look like Barbie, Jackson replied that she does it for the power: "I used to seek pleasure from men and now they seek it from me.... This is the ultimate feminist statement. I refuse to let nature decide my fate just because I missed out on the genetic lottery."[15] Orlan, on the other hand, has a different goal; it is more abstract, more philosophical, less personal, and indeed less understandable than Jackson's. But for all that, intellectuals and connoisseurs seem quite sure that Orlan's goals are more legitimate. The use of plastic surgery is vaguely respectable in Orlan's case because her goals are *artistic*, whereas in Jackson's case, they say, the practice seems just sad. I feel less confident about this tidy distinction. Perhaps they are both artists, but one of them has not realized it yet. Orlan has expressed interest in meeting Jackson, but she refuses and is confused by the "artist" designation that some want to bestow on her. Can you be an artist and not know it? Unclear. Can you be a kook and not know it? Doubtless.

As we have seen repeatedly, monsterology is an ironic field of inquiry, and here we find another example. Monsters are symbols of the disgusting, with their decaying flesh, mottled limbs, and rotting, putrefying tissues and organs. In short, monsters are thumbnail sketches of our own destiny. It is our human fate to slowly fall apart and to cause revulsion in younger, healthier witnesses. If we think about the limping, moldering state of most imaginary monsters, we can see our own elderly selves in much exaggerated form. In this view, part of our odium for monsters can be understood as fear and loathing of our own mortality. Cyborg research and development will certainly have great benefits for those of us who become injured or otherwise find ourselves in need of sophisticated prosthesis, but we can also see an emotional meeting place of posthuman philosophy, cyborg research, and mundane plastic surgery—namely, the all too human urge to escape aging and death. In our attempts to live forever or at least ensure that we're, like, totally hot, we may be hybridizing ourselves into new *uncanny* territory, where the cure looks worse than the disease. On the other hand, human beings who have freely chosen cosmetic surgery have a remarkable ability to avoid anything like *regret*; I suspect that Michael Jackson, for example, is entirely happy with his uniquely engineered visage. And one can imagine a thoroughly accessorized human head, floating in a vat, feeling sincerely that his radical new weight-loss amputation program was indeed well worth it all.

DISEMBODIED MINDS

The idea of a head floating in a jar or perched in a pan dredges up the memory of many bad B-movies, among them *The Brain That Wouldn't Die* (1962), *Who Is Julia?* (1986), and *The Incredible Two-Headed Transplant* (1971). But bad horror films aside, the assumption of most posthumanism is that the human mind, and therefore self-awareness, can be theoretically and metaphysically divorced from the body. It's only a couple of short steps, it would seem, from rebuilding human bodies with computer and robot parts (cyborgs) to downloading a human mind into a digital and robotic substrate. Extreme forms of posthumanism contend that one's mind, one's *self* is capable of disembodied (or at least transplanted) existence. In part, this view is descended from a strong tradition of Platonic and Cartesian dualism in the West, but it has taken on more credibility lately because of the computer model of consciousness.

As we've already seen, a dominant premise in the science of artificial intelligence is that a person—a being with intellect, self-awareness, and self-interest—might come to exist in a nonbiological substance. Alan Turing (1912–1954) suggested that if a computer *acts* as intelligently as a human, then we must concede the probability that it *is* displaying intelligence; in other words, if it *looks* like intelligence, it *is* intelligence. He proposed a thought experiment, the Turing test, in which human interrogators in one room ask questions and converse with computers and real humans who are hidden in another room. Interrogators are not privy to which conversations are human and which are algorithmic. If a human participant identifies a computer conversation as a human conversation, then the computer's intelligence has crossed over into real intelligence. A computer that deceives a human subject could be said to have passed the Turing test, and there would be no grounds on which to deny it some agency. Now, add to this assumption (thinking *is* as thinking *does*) the fact that mental activity appears to be a product of brain electrochemistry and you have a platform for arguing that mind is just a software program of functions running on a hardware foundation, the brain.

Films like *2001: A Space Odyssey* (1968), *Colossus: The Forbin Project* (1969), *Ghost in the Shell* (1995), *The Matrix* (1999), and *AI* (2001) imagine the possibility that a conscious mind could reside in a digital format. But more than just fiction, we have had impressive real cases of chess-playing computers and neural-net machines that learn and adapt. Fears about AI fall into the camp of *monsters of our own making* because they once again promise the classic "playing God" transgression. Against this dominant paranoia about AI monsters is a group of philosophers and cognitive scientists who think it's much ado about nothing. I tend to agree with them, although I reserve some trepidation. I seriously doubt that anything like a human mind could arise or be transplanted into a nonbiological body, although I concede that an unconscious problem-solver, very different from an animal mind, could exist and flourish in the future without direct human control. And perhaps this is enough of a concession to raise the fears of the robot pessimists. Maybe it's the dissimilarity that's so troubling. But I want to suggest that such intelligence will be radically unlike any human or animal that evolved in a biological body. Our minds, I suspect, are not downloadable.

The spike against reductionist computer models of mind is not a retreat to mystical or occult ideas of immaterial souls. Instead, we have to dig deeper into the actual biology of mind to see that it is not easily extricated from the body in the way that digital dualists imagine. Yes, animal minds are information processors, but only in the context of much richer interests. At the ontogenetic level we have to recognize that mind develops in an environment that is simply saturated with *feeling*. From before birth, experiences are loaded with values, positive, negative, neutral, and a thousand gradations and mixtures of these. The representational modeling of the world that infants begin to develop is already value-laden. Information registers *as such* only in a context of rudimentary interests, and these interests grow in force and complexity as the organism develops. These interests seem too subjective, too feeling-based, and too multidimensionally complex to be retranslated into binary zeros and ones.[16] Computational models treat the mind as if it were a calculator whose operations are overlaid with epiphenomenal feelings or sentiments. But the mind is *of* the body, not just *in* the body. The little detached cognitive calculator does indeed seem to exist in our later developed, mature mental circuitry, but it grew out of more bodily instinctual problem-solving systems (e.g., autonomic and reflex systems regulate our body temperature, digestion, heart rate, sexual stimulation, motor skills, and other biological forms of intelligence). It's hard to imagine anything like an animal mind without including a nervous system of some sort, and some sort of life history (i.e., a childhood) to organize the values and the information into a coherent hierarchy. Thinking grows out of feeling.[17]

At the phylogenetic level problem-solving intelligence evolved in steps, and every new innovation needed to interface with the older organic structures. Human intelligence is a Rube Goldberg machine of complex input-output pathways. As Daniel Dennett points out, we cannot divorce the informational message of intelligence from the medium in which it evolved. The building materials of mind, the organic transducers and effectors of perception and cognition, influence the kinds of information that can be received, communicated, and controlled. Long before humans had big brains they had elaborate functional systems for *receiving* information (olfactory chemical systems, etc.), *processing* that information (a primitive hind brain, etc.), and *reacting* to that information (fight or flight). Our more intellectual capacities of the neocortex have been built on and through the older control systems. Mind is the entirety of these inter-penetrating pathways, all of which connect to body. Dennett says, "The new systems had to be built on top of, and in deep collaboration with, these earlier systems, creating an astronomically high number of points of transduction."[18] We can't ignore these interpenetrations when we consider isolated control systems such as intelligence; these systems are not really isolated in the evolved organism. All this does not make AI impossible, but it does remind us that mind is heavily physiological, not just medium-neutral information.

PLAYING GOD: BIOTECHNOLOGY

As we've seen, hybrid creatures have always been somewhat troubling for our epistemological categories or taxonomies of nature, but also for our emotions. How should we feel about liminal beings? Zombies are between the living and the dead, hermaphrodites between the male and the female, chimeras between different animal species, and so on. But we now live in an unprecedented technological era that allows us to engineer many more boundary crossings than we ever imagined. Darwin has bequeathed a world of graded continua between kinds, rather than fixed and perma-nent essences. And biotechnology has given us the tools to move creatures around on these continua.

The human body has become more plastic and open to manipulation than ever before. A dramatic case can be seen in the recent surgical rec-reation of a six-year-old severely brain-damaged girl named Ashley. Her parents elected to have her body redesigned in order to keep her small and easily transportable. A team of doctors administered a two-year regi-men of intense estrogen, which closed her growth plates and shrank her height by over thirteen inches. In addition, Ashley's uterus was removed to guard against future menstrual cramps, and also pregnancy if she were to be raped. Finally, Ashley's breast buds were removed because she "has no need for developed breasts since she will not breast feed," her parents argued, "and their presence would only be a source of discomfort to her."[19] Ashley's parents refer to her as their "pillow angel" and believe that their modifications have improved the quality of life for their daughter. Critics think that transforming people into permanent children is a major violation of human rights. Is it okay to cultivate our children's bodies as we might cultivate a bonsai tree? My goal is not to offer an ethical judgment on this complex case, but simply to point out that we can expect to see more of this somatic redesigning in the future. For years parents have been giving growth hormones to their short children to improve their social standing, so we can imagine other body modifications on the horizon. Manipulating the size, shape, and maturity of humans is just the start.

In July 2008 a person who was living as a man, Thomas Beatie, gave birth to a healthy baby girl. Beatie, who was born female, had previously undergone hormone therapy and breast removal surgery in order to live as a man, eventually marrying a woman named Nancy. Beatie had retained his ovaries and uterus, and when his wife could not conceive a child, the couple elected to artificially inseminate Beatie. A pregnant Beatie explained to Oprah Winfrey that when the child was born, he would function as the father or masculine parent and Nancy would function as the mother. In a manner of speaking, Beatie started as a female, became a male, reverted to a female, and became a male again. His explanation is simple and compelling: "I feel it's not a male or female desire to have a child. It's a human need. I'm a person and I have a right to have a biological child."[20]

Biotechnology now allows humans to transform their own gender identity. Transgendered people, those who do not fit neatly in one of the conventional male or female categories, have always been members of the human family. But advances in chemical therapy and surgery have allowed for unprecedented somatic modifications of gender. Being a boundary-crossing transgendered person is entirely comfortable for many people, while others feel strongly that they were assigned the wrong gender at birth. Those who feel trapped in the wrong kind of body and seek to realign their somatic gender with their inner sense of identity are sometimes referred to as transsexual, to differentiate them from transgendered people. Hormone therapy and surgical reconstruction are ways for some transsexuals to correct the original misalignment of psyche and body.[21]

The meaning of gender-bending technology is not obvious, however, and depends largely on one's background beliefs. Changing one's gender is monstrous, for example, only if one first accepts the idea that gender categories are relatively fixed and that original gender assignments are correct. God makes you either a man or a woman, some argue, and changing one's status is tantamount to violating God's plan.[22] But religious conservatives are incorrect if they think that secularists are happy to flout natural categories and make up any gender reality that suits them. If one accepts a Darwinian view of a gender continuum that is mutually constituted by hormones, genetics, and environment, then reassignment surgery is not a monstrous violation of nature but a nudge back into the correct category. Contrary to a relativism of gender, even Darwinian secularists accept the reality of gender specification. But unlike conservative theists, they make room for biological accidents. Biotechnology, in this view, is just a way to improve the lives of those who suffer in the wrong body, so to speak, no different from corrective lenses for the visually impaired.[23] On the other hand, the far left has a different set of background beliefs and sees all forms of identity, including gender, as socially constructed, not biologically based. The only thing monstrous, in this view, is treating gender as if it were natural.

Beyond the ontogenetic and phenotypic manipulations of gender, we can now also transform and hybridize the genetic makeup of animals and plants. We have not succeeded in creating entirely new species by hybridization and genetic manipulation, but we might well do so in the near future. At present we are focused on transgenic manipulations, such as increasing productivity in farm animals and crops and using livestock to produce medicines and nutraceuticals. Starting with tomatoes, many crops have been genetically modified to increase yield, resist insecticides, or last longer on the store shelf. Soybeans, corn, potatoes, cotton, sugar cane, and rice have all been genetically modified, often by splicing in genes from other species. Fish genes have been put into tomatoes, jellyfish genes into rabbits, and firefly genes into corn.

The J. Craig Venter Institute has recently announced the creation of a species of new, partially synthetic bacteria, *Mycoplasma laboratorium*. Synthetic biology is pursuing such biotechnology in hopes of creating new biofuels and new environment-cleaning organisms. Agribusiness and large pharmaceutical corporations have been investing heavily in biotechnology for the past two decades, but Freeman Dyson predicts that a new age of decentralized noncorporate genetic engineering will dominate in the next generation. A more playful biotech future will arise, Dyson argues, when do-it-yourself genetic engineering kits become available for your average dog breeders, reptile enthusiasts, orchid amateurs, and every other kind of biohobbyist: "Domesticated biotechnology, once it gets into the hands of housewives and children, will give us an explosion of diversity of new living creatures, rather than the monoculture crops that the big corporations prefer. New lineages will proliferate to replace those that monoculture farming and deforestation have destroyed. Designing genomes will be a personal thing, a new art form as creative as painting or sculpture."[24]

This is a bold vision of our biotech future, exciting and a little frightening. Dyson envisions a time in the near future when kids will play genetic games with real eggs and seeds, trying to create the prickliest cactus or even the cutest dinosaur. The ethical question of whether or not we should pursue this future is one that Dyson explicitly brackets off and suggests we let our grandchildren decide. I tend to think, on the other hand, that letting our grandchildren decide the ethical issues will be too late in the game.

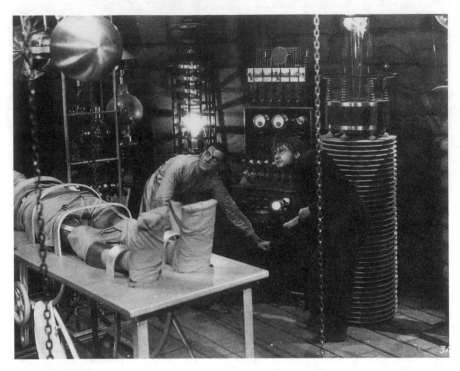

Promethean potential. Today's biotech possibilities make Dr. Frankenstein and Igor look like mere fledgling gods. From *Frankenstein* (Universal Pictures, 1931). Image courtesy of Jerry Ohlinger.

Many religiously minded thinkers will find Dyson's sanguine picture of kids playing with genetic kits horrifying. But even secularists like myself would want us to think long and hard about appropriate limitations on such biotechnology. What will become of all the trial-run creatures that don't turn out quite as the experimenter hoped but nonetheless now live and breathe in a liminal limbo? How will we control the garage-lab creations of dangerous microorganisms and new invasive species? Who will *regulate* all this new and dangerous creation, or will we pursue an ungoverned free-market model and let the survival-of-the-fittest mechanisms sort it all out?

One of the major concerns I have about playing with genetics is Darwin's old concern, only magnified. Recall that Darwin believed that the only real monsters were the ones that humans had bred for ignorant aesthetic purposes. Natural selection has a tempo that weeds out unhealthy variations, whether or not they are aesthetically interesting. But artificial selection has given us bleeding diseases in Dobermans, respiration problems in bulldogs, cancer in boxers, eye lid curling in shar-peis, aorta problems in golden retrievers, and more. Imagine a very fast tempo biotech breeding program that is motivated by human interests rather than the health interests of the animals and plants themselves. Now imagine such misguided breeding programs for every pet species.

Every gene codes for multiple traits. The same gene, turned on or off at different times, can control many diverse phenotypic traits, a phenomenon called *pleiotropy*, from a Greek phrase meaning "many influences." The upshot is that when we think we are altering one trait with our biotech kits, we are also altering many hidden traits. A real case of such unintended genetic consequences occurred when breeders selected for a corn trait but ended up inadvertently devastating the entire strain. A gene that caused corn to lose its own tassel was selected for, but breeders did not understand that this same gene created a susceptibility to southern corn blight, and major crop destruction resulted.[25]

The astronomical complexity of ecological relations seems like a good reason to be extremely careful with biotech engineering. The interconnections of animals and plants are so elaborate that one wonders if we could control all the variables. Organisms have evolved symbiotically. Not only would a slight change in a predator have major consequences for the prey animals (and vice versa), but many organisms live symbiotically inside each other. Humans and cows, for example, can't even digest many foods without intestinal and ruminant bacteria that live in their gut. Cows have bacteria, protozoa, and even fungi living in their digestive tracts, and these help them break down the cellulose in their food. A slight genetic modification in these microbes might spell disaster for the larger mammals that serve as hosts.

Perhaps these worries are only the typical Luddite anxieties, and the positive will outweigh the negative. It may well be that biotech science will be green and solve our problems of soil erosion, greenhouse gases, pandemics, food shortages, fish and forest depletions, and fuel shortages. Dyson says, "Once a new generation of children has grown up, as familiar with biotech games as our grandchildren are now with computer games, biotechnology will no longer seem weird and alien."

Francis Fukuyama is skeptical about the social world that biotech will inevitably create. In his book *Our Posthuman Future*, he predicts that genetic engineering will be used by wealthier parents as a new form of well-intentioned eugenics. The upper class will use biotechnology to make their children smarter, healthier, and more attractive: "If wealthy parents suddenly have open to them the opportunity to increase the intelligence of their children as well as that of all their subsequent descendants, then we have the makings not just of a moral dilemma but of a full-scale class war."[26] We should not, according to Fukuyama, make a new posthuman nature because our current one, flawed though it may be, has finally found a home in the hard-won social environment of liberal democracy. We finally have a good match between human nature and politics; the personal and the political successfully actualize each other's potential.

Using biology to improve social and political life was tried by the Nazis, and we would do well to avoid that terrible nightmare in the future. But, according to Fukuyama, pretending there is *no* human nature or that it is infinitely malleable led to the socialist utopias of the twentieth century, wherein families, money, religion, and education were all dismantled and recreated for the greater good. Although Fukuyama distances himself from knee-jerk religious objections to biotechnology, he nonetheless seems to share the same fears about reductionism. If we think, as posthumanists do, that humans are really just composed of material causes and there is nothing sacrosanct about their current composition, we will be more likely to play God with our social reality. Such utopian perfectibility movements have had a terrible track record. Yes, biotech can give us new personalities and powers, but only by taking away others; we'll have pharmaceutical freedom from depression, but reduced creativity. According to Fukuyama, our very souls are at stake. As moral monsters, negligent about our duties and responsibilities, we will inadvertently create biological monsters.

Historically, however, religious views about technology have not always followed the usual *Frankenstein* anxiety pattern. We are often led to believe that one is either a secular, Godless technophile or a God-fearing technophobe. But many religious thinkers have interpreted technology as a tool that the Creator has given to mankind to help bring about a brighter future.[27] Francis Collins, the head of the Human Genome Project, offers a contemporary version of this view when he says, "God, if it's the God that I worship, created the universe and all the laws that regulate it, and gave us this incredible gift of an intellect. And I, like Galileo, don't think that he gave us those abilities in order for us to forego their use. And so I think God kind of thinks that science is pretty cool!"[28] From this perspective, biotechnology is God's work. On the other side of the divide, I've already suggested that secular Darwinians can be very anxious and fearful (because of plieotropy and ecology, etc.) about the future uses of biotechnology. So both sides of the sacred-secular divide are more interesting than the usual caricatures.

ARE MONSTERS IN THE EYE OF THE BEHOLDER?

In our "you're not the boss of me" culture, we're hard-pressed to pass a value judgment on the posthuman modifications that others adopt. If someone wants to make herself into a cyborg, who am I to roll my eyes? If I want to genetically engineer my baby to have specific phenotypic qualities, who are you to prevent me?

In earlier paradigms of monsterology, all hybridization and the mixing of forms was considered insidious, and such hybrids (e.g., hermaphrodites, conjoined twins, manticores, griffins) were treated with suspicion. But after the Darwinian revolution, and especially after the New Synthesis, we came to understand that deviation, variation, mixing, and even hybridization are mechanisms of all biology; underneath the stable species forms are hidden twists and turns of micromutation. In one sense, fusion, mishmash, and hodgepodge are the techniques of evolution. Darwin's associate John Herschel even referred to Darwin's chance variation and natural selection as the "law of higgledy-piggledy."

Our cultural comfort with variation and pastiche-based biology has only increased with the recent successes of biotechnology. Now we can more quickly and severely alter the bodies of animals and ourselves, just as natural genetic evolution has been doing over time. Once again, however, the postmodernists have jumped from a positive embrace of *difference* and blurred boundaries to the idea that no norms exist. How can we impose a teleological direction on our future biotech selves, our posthuman future, when all the old candidates of essentialism (e.g., God's plan, fixed human nature) are now dead? We're all becoming cyborg monsters after all, the postmodernists say, so we must learn to embrace and celebrate the change. The latest paradigm has reversed the ancient paradigm: now *all* hybrids, *all* variations are good.

But there is a middle way. Yes, the puritanical and essentialist tendencies that led premoderns to suspect variation should be resisted, but it doesn't follow that every hybrid or biotech pastiche must now be affirmed. As we remake ourselves and the planet with biotechnology, we are not totally rudderless in our navigations. Biotechnology has put us in the unique position of actually composing our biological future. Our generation is like Dr. Frankenstein standing over a table of miscellaneous limbs and organs, only we're on the table, too. We can decide what sort of hodgepodge creature will emerge. And the cultural death of God has not robbed us of rational grounds for composing a new teleology for our species.

We saw that from the time of Aristotle the monster concept has functioned as an opposing term to whatever has *purpose*. Nature, according to previous eras, has an orderly and observable developmental pattern: acorns grow into oak trees, humans give birth to humans, and generally speaking anatomical structures fit physiological functions. The fully completed or actualized state of a natural process (e.g., attaining oak tree status) was considered to be the end goal, or the purpose, or the *telos* of the process.

Monsters are the things that never fulfill their purpose or never make it to their goal, either because the development was accidentally arrested (by internal or external causes) or because matter confused or retarded the realization of form or because some moral impurity deformed the creature's true potential. Whatever the particulars, monsters were cases of development that missed their targets.

But we now live in a Nature different from that of previous ages. Biotechnology shows us that we don't know what the *purpose* or teleology of an animal species is (including ourselves), and we are increasingly capable of creating a new one. The old teleological goals for man—"to love God" for the theists, "to attain rational freedom" for the philosophers—were helpful in the sense that specific goals help one assess specific means. In previous eras one could assess how one was doing on the road to the natural goal, modifying one's behavior or growth along the way. Naïve and puerile as it sometimes was, one had a comforting map to navigate through life.

Of course we don't *know* the purposes of nature anymore because *there are no purposes of nature*, unless one wants to include the trivial Darwinian truism that animals seek to propagate themselves. If there are no preset (a priori) goals that humans are on their way to becoming, then biotech gives us a fresh opportunity to voluntarily assign ourselves some. We may decide, for example, that the reduction of needless human suffering is worth pursuing on a global scale, and biotechnology may have a role to play as a means to that end. More specifically, married people might decide to take up Nick Bostrom's suggestion to engineer more monogamous affection between each other by pharmaceutically increasing certain hormone production.

Moreover, the idea that we no longer have any firm foundations from which to critique some societies or individuals as monstrous is again the result of melodrama, perhaps from those who cannot overcome the despair of our posttheological paradigm. For example, it seems entirely reasonable to argue that spending all of one's time, money, and energy on recreating one's face and body through biotech procedures has negative consequences for the obsessed individuals and the societies they live in. To think of them as monstrous is certainly too harsh a judgment, or maybe "self-made tragic monsters" is an apt designation. I only want to suggest that there are still reasonable criteria and norms from which to make helpful value discriminations. First, there is nothing wrong with wanting to be beautiful, but there is significant empirical evidence that external modification does not actually deliver any of the inner satisfactions that such people crave. The cosmetic procedure is often a *category mistake*, a misidentification of the cause of one's suffering (though I hasten to add that extreme mutilations from disease or wounds suffered in military service are indeed debilitating, and the quality of life for those afflicted is much improved by external modifications). Second, despite all the perfectionist rhetoric of the trans-humanists, trying to actually stop and reverse aging is still akin to trying to square a circle. Flesh is inherently impermanent, and trying to make it permanent remains in the realm of pipe dreams. Third, given the fact that human beings have great creative potential in the fine arts, in social diplomacy, in philanthropy, in scholarly pursuits, in craftsmanship, and in the sciences, it's a sad fact that spending one's energy capital on rhinoplasty actually *prevents* the actualization of so much other great potential. In the same way that a life of television watching essentially prevents a young child from doing so many other wonderful things, so, too, the life of cos-metic attention is like a slow leak in the faucet of human potential. And what is said here about the individual is only magnified when we consider the larger *societies* of cosmetic obsession. Obviously, there are much more extreme abuses of biotechnology, such as governments developing biologi-cal germ warfare, but those only demonstrate more effortlessly that our powers of normative judgment are entirely intact after the death of tradi-tional teleology.

As we chart new teleologies with biotechnology, two things seem cru-cial. First, choices for such directions must be the result of democratic process, not autocratic statecraft. Politicians should not impose the norms of the future; we've already seen what kind of monsters that sort of project produces. Second, I would argue that a major source of data for setting our future direction has to be biology. The idea that human norms and *values* have nothing to do with the biological *facts* of our existence is an idea that has foundered and played itself out. Learning more about our emotional, physiological, and cognitive powers, limitations, and tendencies will help us chart a clear-eyed biotech course, one that steers between the Scylla of denial and Luddite avoidance and the Charybdis of gung-ho abandon.

Whatever form this new era of nonteleological nature takes, we can be sure that the concept of monster does not lose its semantic power by exten-sion to everything. Previous eras saw monsters as oppositions to an other-wise teleological nature; now that we've rejected such an idea of nature, the postmoderns are cheerfully folding us all under the monster umbrella and celebrating the end of rational discrimination itself. But *monster* is as useful in ordinary language as it's ever been. Moreover, the family resemblance of *monster meanings* has had significant integrity over the ages. It may not have the connotations of abject failure that it previously held, because tele-ology is not what it was, but it is still used to define the relatively *unhealthy* aspects of our social, psychological, cultural, and biological environments. The term and the concept of monster are still very useful.

Epilogue

One does not become enlightened by imagining figures of the light, but by making the darkness conscious.

CARL JUNG

THE IDEA THAT WE PREVIOUSLY BELIEVED in monsters but now we don't is a comforting illusion. In May 2008 eleven elderly people accused of being witches were dragged from their homes and burned to death by a mob in western Kenya.[1] Down the coast, in Malawi, witches are believed to be cannibals who possess supernatural powers and use their unholy skills to harass, kill, and feed on the meat of their dead victims. Witch hunting has led to many vigilante killings and even large numbers of state-enforced incarcerations.[2] The tendency is to assume that such supernatural extremism is the result of illiteracy, yet the Malawian writer Pilirani Semu-Banda claims that "the witch-hunting activities are occurring in towns and cities where most people are educated." Adding to the indigenous African traditions of witchcraft, Roman Catholicism, which is the religious majority in Malawi, has contributed its own monsterology tradition. Father Stanislaus Chinguo, chairman of the Catholic Commission for Justice in the Blantyre archdiocese, told Semu-Banda that witchcraft is real and the Church is working on solutions to meet the challenge head-on, including the renewal of exorcism practices.

Closer to home, in fact in my own hometown of Waukegan, Illinois, a woman confessed in April 2008 that she murdered her six-year-old daughter because the child was possessed by a demon. Nelly Vazquez-Salazar admitted to killing her daughter, Elizabeth, after the young child woke the mother in the middle of the night. The mother had been in consultation with Elizabeth's grandmother in Mexico because the child had recently been sleepwalking. Both mother and grandmother had come to the conclusion that the child was possessed.[3]

Lest we think that such supernatural monsters are currently confined to the developing world and immigrant groups, we must recognize that large populations in the American Bible Belt are still literally haunted by demons and regularly employ exorcism as a defense. In June 2008 a Texas high court ruled against a woman who was seeking damages against the church that allegedly injured her during her exorcism.[4] Laura Schubert claimed that she was pinned to the floor for hours and received minor injuries and psychological trauma from her 1996 exorcism. In the 2008 decision Justice David Medina wrote that finding the church liable "would have an unconstitutional 'chilling effect' by compelling the church to abandon core principles of its religious beliefs." So in effect, exorcism is recognized and protected by the law.

Contemporary cultural interest in monsters is still very strong. Most people reading this book are probably not overly worried about witches in their neighborhood or possessed family members. But other monster manifestations are of keen interest, even to the jaded and cynical hipsters who look down their nose at gullible bumpkins. My own students, who sometimes fancy themselves a part of the intellectual elite of American culture, are obsessed with cryptozoology, serial killer murderabilia, and monster-killing video gaming.

Nessie, the Loch Ness Monster, may be the most famous cryptid purported to exist. Photos began emerging in the 1930s, and since then there have been more than four thousand sightings of the Scottish leviathan. The monster is such a tourist draw that it is estimated to bring twelve million dollars into the Scottish Highlands every year. The credulity index for cryptids continues to be shored up by truly amazing discoveries in real paleontology. In February 2008 a fossil of a record-breaking fifty-foot-long sea monster was discovered by a Norwegian team of paleontologists. This gigantic Jurassic pliosaur had dagger-like teeth the size of cucumbers and a mouth large enough to consume a small car. In December 2007 fossil experts in Germany found the largest bug ever discovered, a monstrous sea scorpion that measured more than eight feet long. Bigger than most crocodiles, the *Jaekelopterus rhenaniae* acted as a superpredator, chopping up fish and other arthropods with giant spiked claws. Our imaginations are obviously fired up by these wonderful fossil discoveries, and though the creatures are long extinct they continue to hold out the tantalizing possibility of monsters living in remote regions. Even without any serious commitment to the reality of cryptids we still demonstrate a playful mania for monsters and marvels. "Mythic Creatures: Dragons, Unicorns and Mermaids," which is traveling from 2007 to 2012, has drawn huge crowds in New York and Chicago and is reported to be the most popular exhibit in decades at the American Museum of Natural History.[5]

One of the more interesting examples of monster fascination in our contemporary culture, especially among the hip and sardonic set, is the collecting of murderabilia. Serial killers are so fascinating that their personal belongings and their "artistic" creations are fetishized and turned into highly valuable commodities that are traded and purchased by collectors of the macabre. The Internet has fueled a significant underground industry for monster property. Paintings by John Wayne Gacy, Henry Lee Lucas, and Richard Ramirez (the Nightstalker) and personal items of Charles Manson, among others, have all become hot commodities. When the journalist Michael Harvey visited my college class as a guest lecturer, he brought one of Gacy's original clown paintings to class. Recall from chapter 13 that Harvey was the last journalist to speak to Gacy the night before he was executed by lethal injection. Gacy gave him several paintings as a gift. When Harvey allowed my students to pass around the creepy painting they could barely contain themselves, and most of them took cellphone photos of the painting as a souvenir. I can't pretend that I was above the weird sensation of horror and excitement, loathing and thrill, as I held the ominous picture.

It's not clear that the average collector can even articulate why he or she collects such ghoulish material, although some superstitious curators claim that owning a murderer's possessions is like having a talisman protecting them from misfortune. My own view is that murderabilia is just one more attempt, albeit circuitous, to de-monster our world. We live in a consumer culture, and consumption not only fulfills desires but also is a means of imposing order and control. Commodifying a horror is one way of objectifying and managing it. Just as a more religious culture might bring its spiritual paraphernalia and its priest class to bear on a monstrous threat, a consumer culture brings its *capital* to bear. If monsters (in this case, serial killers) churn the stomach, horrify the heart, and boggle the mind, we respond with whatever powers we possess. Buying a monster memento brings the unintelligible creepiness into the light of a quotidian transaction.

Other bourgeois approaches to monsters can be seen in our developed secular society. A whole new horror genre has emerged, for example, in our prosperous culture. The film theorist Barry Grant noticed a tendency in some movies to capitalize on our fears about losing wealth and status.[6] Films such as *Fatal Attraction* (1987), *Single White Female* (1992), and even

Crimes and Misdemeanors (1989) can be read as economic horror films, in which the monsters bring financial ruin and middle-class catastrophe.

Middle-class monsters may not be as supernatural as the monsters of old, but they still harass their victims and keep them awake late at night. Since my son was born, I have watched an enormous amount of daytime children's television. I'm not proud of it, but there it is. Entire cable networks are devoted to kids' cartoons, and several times an hour the programming is interrupted to show commercials to the assumed audience. The demographers are convinced that two populations are watching these shows: kids and moms. For the kids, commercials range between unicorn dolls and racing cars, but for the moms the ads are astoundingly one-dimensional. In the relatively safe world of middle-class America, the one reliable phobia to which advertisers can appeal is poor hygiene. Every housewife's phobia about germs is seized on and celebrated with Oscar-winning special effects. Only Brand X cleaning solution, represented as a purifying acid of goodness, can annihilate the invisible monsters. Computer animation has been enlisted to create seething green, tentacled hordes of bacterial monsters that crawl up out of the toilet bowl to overcome one's precious children or grow ominously as an evil fetid gas from the kitty-litter box or seep up from the kitchen drain, with slimy fangs and pulsing tissue, to infect one's whole family. One must remain equally vigilant about the creatures throbbing on the shower floor and those festering in the carpet. The animated representations of these threats to hygiene are increasingly taken directly from the drawer of monster movie special effects. The toilet bowl monsters look far more menacing than anything in premillennial horror films.

The monster concept also continues to do significant work in our contemporary political sphere. In 2008 Barack Obama's foreign policy advisor, Samantha Power, referred to Hillary Clinton as "a monster" and promptly lost her job. Any word that causes you to get fired is still carrying some heavy connotative baggage. George W Bush regularly referred to the bills proposed by Congress that he intended to veto as "monstrous pieces of legislation." And 2007 saw the beleaguered Karl Rove casting himself to various media outlets as a character in the monster epic *Beowulf*. While Capitol Hill was pressing for Rove's resignation, he told Chris Wallace on Fox News, "Let's face it, I mean, I'm a myth. You know, I'm Beowulf, you know, I'm Grendel. I don't know who I am, but they're after me."

I INCLUDE ALL THESE DIVERSE ANECDOTES to illustrate that both the literal and the symbolic uses of monster are alive and well in our contemporary world. One will search in vain through this book to find a single compelling definition of *monster*. That's not because I forgot to include one, but because I don't think there is one. I am a proponent of a cognitive science position called prototype theory, a theory that began with Ludwig Wittgenstein's idea that conceptual and linguistic meaning is more like "family resemblance" than we previously thought. In earlier theories, from Aristotle to logical positivism, we assumed that every instance of *bird* or *dog* or *bed* or *monster* must satisfy an abstract essential definition. For example, if I want to know whether this thing before me is a *circle*, I see whether it fulfills the essential definition of a plane-sided figure with all points equidistant from the center. Wittgenstein, however, noticed that most things were not connected by a common definition, but instead shared overlapping similarities. His classic example of the *game* demonstrated that although some games share properties (e.g., baseball and football both use a ball, chess and tennis employ two competing sides, golf and poker and charades have certain overlaps), no one defining criterion can be said to capture all games. Instead, we link all these activities together through overlapping similarities, in the same way we recognize that Carol, Edward, Daniel, and David are all members of the same family, some sharing a similar nose, others sharing similar hair, others similar eyes, but none of them with all the same features or properties.[7]

In more recent cognitive science circles this way of thinking about categorization has come to be called prototype theory.[8] When I say or think *bird*, some more or less determinate bird comes into my mind's eye; it looks more like a robin than an albatross or a penguin. For many people, a robin-like bird is the conceptual prototype of *bird*, and other birds are closer or further away from that prototype. The duck, falcon, and ostrich can be conceptually mapped in varying distances from my prototype image of a bird. Each bird fulfills some of the criteria of bird (e.g., has feathers, flies, is oviparous and beaked), but none of them fulfills all the criteria. There is no *definition* of bird that wouldn't eventually leave some bird out.

The term and the concept of *monster* is a prototype category. Like *bird*, there may be environmentally specific archetypes for a clan's central threat, and we might even draw up a general taxonomy of types: "crawlers" (spider-type monsters), "slitherers" (snake-like monsters), "collosals" (giant creatures), "hybrids" (mixed-species creatures), "possessors" (spirits, specters, etc.), and "parasites" (infectious blood-suckers, etc.). But functionally speaking they probably appear and reappear in our stories and in our artwork because they help us (and helped our ancestors) navigate the dangers of our environment. The monster archetype seems to appear in every culture's artwork. This suggests that stories about monster threats and heroic conquests provide us with a ritualized, rehearsable simulation of reality, a virtual way to represent the forces of nature, the threats from other animals, and the dangers of human social interaction.

In this book I have been touring the map of related properties or qualities that we call monstrous. Each era expresses different fascinations with monsters—medieval Christians focused on demons, the Gilded Age had a penchant for freaks—but some prototypical qualities unite the family of monsters, albeit loosely. We have seen throughout this book, for example, that most monsters cannot be reasoned with. Monsters are generally ugly and inspire horror. Monsters are unnatural. Monsters are overwhelmingly powerful. Monsters are evil. Monsters are misunderstood. Monsters cannot be understood. These recognizable monster qualities coalesce into cultural prototypes, such as Frankenstein's creature and St. Anthony's demons, and they reflect the fears of specific eras. But they also reflect more universal human anxieties and cognitive tendencies, the stuff that gives us human solidarity with the ancient Greeks, the medievals, and, as would be seen in more comparative histories, Asians, Middle Easterners, Native Americans, and others.

By now the reader has surely noticed some continuities over historical epochs. Yes, certain aspects of monsters are historically provincial and relative, irrevocably situated in context, but some show perennial persistence. One notices, for example, the recurrent way that inner monstrosity is supposed to manifest itself on the physical body of the creature; *evil* and *ugly* are enduring correlations. Pliny the Elder argued that physiognomy reflected one's moral character, and monsters looked ugly for that reason. The Victorian criminologist Cesare Lombroso continued the long-standing connection by arguing that malformed faces betray atavistic, savage characters. Even the recent Hollywood film *300* has been criticized for portraying enemy Persians as repulsively ugly. The correlation of moral character and physical morphology is an enduring aspect of monsterology.

Consider some other repetitions in monster history. The hugely popular tradition of a monster zone, articulated in the legend of Alexander's gates, is alive and well today. Recall that Alexander's gates were supposed to contain the worst monsters that Christianity and Islam could imagine. The monster zone was a real feature of medieval and Renaissance geography. J. R. R. Tolkien's fictional Mordor continued the tradition of an enclosed land of monsters always threatening to overcome their containment. And though the literal gates have fallen away, our contemporary news media report daily on the mysterious and impenetrable "tribal zone" in northern Pakistan. Military and news media cannot penetrate the difficult region where Osama bin Laden and his "evil horde" reside. The tribal zone has a rich connotative life, one that draws on centuries of mythmaking, xenophobia, and a genuine human need to map the headquarters of evil.[9]

Another recurring leitmotif of monsterology has been the question of how we meet the threat. Usually monsters are for fighting. We examined the way that heroes, from Alexander to Beowulf, define themselves by how they meet the monsters in the field. Thomas R. Pynchon gives us a heroic picture of modern technophobia, a picture that underscores the idea that monsters may come and go, but what they represent persists. Luddites, Pynchon suggests, should be respected because they're fighting the machines on our behalf: "When times are hard, and we feel at the mercy of forces many times more powerful, don't we, in seeking some equalizer, turn, if only in imagination, in wish, to the Badass—the djinn, the golem, the hulk, the superhero—who will resist what otherwise would overwhelm us?"[10] The Badass does not negotiate or try to reason with monsters because monsters cannot be reasoned with. The Badass is an imagined force with the power to meet the overwhelming monster force. Whether the monsters are the giant serpents of Alexander's letter to Aristotle or the robot assassins of sci-fi, they similarly threaten annihilation and need aggressive combat in response.

Yet another recurring theme in our natural history of monsters has been the prototype of demonic possession. From Medea's murderous loss of control to the demon possessions of the *Malleus Malificarum* and the monsters of the Id, we have yearned to express one of the greatest human fears: the loss of freewill agency. The phenomenological experience of losing one's self is familiar enough to anyone who's had too much to drink, who's played the fool in love, who's felt humiliated and then rageful, or who's lived in a metaphorical or a literal state of slavery. The "empirical data of freedom" (a truant experience for some philosophical systems) might be best described negatively as how one feels when not compelled by this list of coercions— or positively described, the feeling of being somewhat in control. Monsters of demonic possession are imaginative expressions of this loss of control. The specific face of the monster will vary from culture to culture, but the universal dimension seems undeniable.

NOTES

INTRODUCTION

1. The coelacanths are closely related to lungfishes. They were believed to be extinct since the end of the Cretaceous period, but a live specimen was found off the east coast of South Africa in 1938. Since then they have also been captured in the Comoros, Indonesia, Kenya, Tanzania, Mozambique, and Madagascar. Giant squids were thought to be mythical, but we now understand them to be real members of the *Architeuthidae* family. They can grow to be as large as forty-four feet long, although some reports go as large as sixty feet. In 2004 a group of Japanese researchers from the National Science Museum of Japan documented the behemoth in its natural deep-ocean habitat, and in December 2006 the same team caught a small specimen (twenty-four feet) off the Ogasawara Islands. The team leader, Tsunemi Kubodera, conjectures that there are many giant squid living very deep and providing a large part of the sperm whale's substantial diet. In "Where Wonders Await Us," Tim Flannery writes, "Studies of squid beaks taken from the bellies of such whales reveal that for the great majority of squid families, the very smallest squid eaten by the whales exceeds in size the largest example ever caught by a scientist" (*New York Review of Books*, December 20, 2007). Also consult the writings of Richard Ellis, a giant squid expert, including *Monsters of the Sea* (Lyon's Press, 2006) and *The Search for the Giant Squid* (Penguin, 1999).
2. Quoted in Flannery, "Where Wonders Await Us."
3. The Bible refers to sea monsters regularly. See Psalms 74:13, Genesis 1:21, Isaiah 51:9, Job 41, and the apocryphal Book of Enoch. Thomas Hobbes famously uses the giant sea monster as a metaphor for his discussion of the social commonwealth in *Leviathan* (1651). Remember also Proteus from Homer's *Odyssey*, and of course Herman Melville's *Moby-Dick* (1851).
4. More detailed comparisons can be found in Darwin's *The Expression of the Emotions in Man and Animals* (Murray, 1872).
5. Charles Darwin, *The Descent of Man*, in *Darwin*, edited by Philip Appleman, 2nd ed. (Norton, 1979).
6. Tim Flannery, "Queens of the Web," *New York Review of Books*, May 1, 2008.
7. For a similar evolutionary approach, see David Jones, *Instinct for Dragons* (Routledge, 2002), in which he traces our dragon mythophobias to prehistoric fears of raptors, large cats, and snakes.

8. In their book *The Evolution of Ethics* (1985), Michael Ruse and E. O. Wilson argue, "Our minds are not tabulae rasae, but moulded according to certain dispositions. These dispositions…incline us to particular courses of action, such as learning rapidly to fear heights and snakes, although they certainly do not lock us, ant like, into undeviating behaviour." In *The Modularity of Mind* (MIT Press, 1983) and elsewhere, the philosopher Jerry Fodor surveys the thesis that the mind may be more "modular" than we previously thought, and strong phobias may be evidence of one of these modules, each module being like a hard-wired, preset computer that evolved for guiding human thinking and behaving. Fodor maintains the primacy of a general adaptive intelligence (an open information system) and does not want to *reduce* the mind to these modules, but theoretical room has been made to include these modules in the wider frame of our cognition model.

9. When Darwin read Plato's theory of innate ideas, as articulated in the *Phaedo*, he scandalously updated the ancient doctrine by suggesting (in his notebooks) that we think of these deep concepts, such as Justice and Beauty, as successful descendants of our ancestral "monkey" minds. See Notebook M, 1838.

10. The Hunterian collection, named after the naturalist John Hunter (1728–1793), is housed in the Royal College of Surgeons in Lincoln's Inn Fields, London.

11. Though it also needs to be pointed out that many "freaks" marketed themselves and profited nicely from the cultural institutions of curiosity. For example, Charles O'Brien (the "Irish Giant"), General Tom Thumb (Charles Sherwood Stratton), Chang and Eng Bunker (the Siamese Twins), and many others all capitalized on their unique gifts and benefited financially.

12. Milgram began the study in 1961, around the time of Eichmann's trial in Jerusalem, but a full analysis can be found in his 1974 book *Obedience to Authority: An Experimental View* (HarperCollins).

13. See Martha C. Nussbaum, *The Fragility of Goodness: Luck and Ethics in Greek Tragedy and Philosophy* (Cambridge University Press, 1986), chapter 13. In a later work, *Hiding from Humanity* (Princeton, 2006), Nussbaum cautions against the tendency to import moral disgust into the legal domain. Criminalizing those who disgust us is common but unfair and illustrates a neurotic impulse toward purification on the part of society rather than a legal transgression on the part of the accused.

14. Which is why the Greeks believed that one cannot be considered happy until one's life is over. For example, see Aristotle's definition of *happiness* in the *Nicomachean Ethics*, book I, part IX.

15. In the indoctrination propaganda of the time, Angkar became a looming abstract Big Brother to the young boys who were essentially abducted into Khmer Rouge service. Khmer people grew to fear Angkar, to love Angkar, to kill for Angkar, or at least to pretend to. See John Marston, "Democratic Kampuchea and the Idea of Modernity," in *Cambodia Emerges from the Past*, edited by Judy Ledgerwood (Northern Illinois University Press, 2002).

16. The damaging agricultural policies of the early Khmer Rouge, inspired by Mao's Great Leap Forward, were disastrous and left tens of thousands of people starving, ill, and exhausted. People were being forced to perform Herculean manual labor efforts to recreate the countryside with new dams and expansive field plots, but it was too much too soon for a labor force that was already weak and famished. Pol Pot and Angkar interpreted this failure as a corruption and betrayal from within and set about a paranoid witch hunt that resulted partly in the S21 catastrophe.

17. See Sam Keen's PBS documentary *Faces of the Enemy* (originally airing in 1987; re-released on DVD in 2004) for an eerie sequence in which Keen sits down for a meeting with a death row inmate, David Rice. Keen confronts Rice, who violently murdered a family, and struggles to articulate his changing perception of the criminal.

18. Around the time of the Han Dynasty (206 BCE–220 CE), the dragon's appearance consolidated into its familiar form, having a snake body, the scales and tail of a fish, stag-like antlers, the face of a camel, the ears of a bull, eagle-like talons, the feet of a tiger, and the eyes of a demon. Often it is portrayed with a flaming pearl under its chin.

19. *Frankenstein*, vol. 3, chapter 3.

20. Long before Christian and Jewish versions of the animated giant, we had the pagan giant bronze man, Talos. He served King Minos as the guardian of Crete, running around the island three times a day and throwing giant boulders at ships that might be trying to invade. His body was made of bronze and his blood was liquid lead. Jason and Medea, who sought to land at Crete, tricked the giant and caused him to fall off a cliff. The fall caused the nail that closed Talos's vein to fall out and his lead blood drained away.

21. For example, many biologically oriented science fiction stories invoke and exploit the host-parasite relation in compelling ways. But such a notion of monster can be found, not just in imagination, but in Nature Herself. Consider the disturbing host-parasite relationships of *Ichneumonidae*, or the digger wasps, for example, and their various prey (usually caterpillars). These wasps lay their eggs inside the tissues of living caterpillars, and when the larvae hatch out they eat the still living caterpillar from the inside out. What is perhaps even more gruesome is that the wasp paralyzes the caterpillar so that it cannot move, but its continual metabolic process keeps its body fresh for consumption. It's a shuddering thought to consider that the hapless caterpillar can feel itself being slowly eaten alive and can do nothing about it.

22. Animism, contrary to most Western portrayals, has its own empirical foundation, one that may be every bit as rational as ours. Animism can be defined as the belief that there are many kinds of persons in this world, only some of whom are human. For an animist it is crucial to placate and honor these other spirit-persons. But it's important to remember that the daily lives of people in the developing world are *not* filled with the kinds of independence, predictability, and freedom that we in the developed world enjoy. Frequently you do not choose your spouse, your work, your number of children; in fact, you don't choose much of anything when you are very poor and tied to the survival of your family. In *that* world, where life really is capricious and out of your control, animism seems empirically corroborated.

23. See Teresa A. Goddu, "Vampire Gothic," *American Literary History* 11, no. 1 (spring 1999).

24. Mark Johnson and George Lakoff, "Conceptual Metaphor in Everyday Language," in *Philosophical Perspectives on Metaphor*, edited by M. Johnson (University of Minnesota Press, 1981). Also see Johnson and Lakoff's important *Metaphors We Live By*, 2nd ed. (University of Chicago Press, 2003). Many people read Johnson and Lakoff as social constructionists who see these deep metaphors as malleable cultural products, liberating us from the deterministic tenor of the evolutionary psychologists. But Johnson and Lakoff are clear that our metaphors of thinking emerge out of our bodily existence, and so it seems but a short step to unify the philosophy of metaphor with the biology of evolution. Even if language (and its deep metaphors) should be studied as an irreducible autonomous reality, the reasons for doing so are largely methodological, and there's no reason to believe that biology and cognitive linguistics cannot be two sides of the same coin. The monster may eventually turn out to be a discursive entity that *shapes* our thinking and communicating, but also a mental module that has *been shaped* by our evolutionary history.

25. In "Monsters as (Uncanny) Metaphors: Freud, Lakoff, and the Representation of Monstrosity in Cinematic Horror," *Other Voices* 1, no. 3 (1999), Steven Schneider

argues that Lakoff's *conceptual* metaphors are more productive starting points than purely *linguistic* metaphors because they allow for the obvious image- or visual-based monster metaphors that we encounter in film and other pictorial media.

CHAPTER 1

1. This and all other quotations from Alexander's letter are taken from two versions (a tenth-century Italian-Latin version and an Old English version from the same codex that preserves *Beowulf*) compiled by Richard Stoneman in *Legends of Alexander the Great* (Everyman, 1994). Although these are late versions, they draw on much earlier Greek versions from pseudo-Callisthenes' third-century *Alexander Romance*.

2. For compelling arguments against the long-standing acceptance of a scientific exchange of information between Alexander and Aristotle, see James S. Romm, "Aristotle's Elephant and the Myth of Alexander's Scientific Patronage," *American Journal of Philology* 110, no. 4 (Winter 1989): 566–75. Romm is doubtful of Pliny the Elder's claim in book VIII of *Natural History* that "King Alexander the Great had a burning desire to acquire a knowledge of zoology, and delegated research in this area to Aristotle, a man of supreme authority in every branch of science."

3. Alexander invaded India in 326 BCE. His actual letter is lost, and most information regarding it comes from the Medieval Latin and Old English translations. Nonetheless, independent ancient sources (Ctesias from Knidos, Megasthenes, etc.) bear out the fact that many of the assumptions and credulous claims of these later versions are indeed symptomatic of ancient Greco-Roman attitudes. See Rudolf Wittkower, "Marvels of the East: A Study in the History of Monsters," *Journal of the Warburg and Courtauld Institutes* 5 (1942): 159–97.

4. From book VII of the Zoology section of Pliny's *Natural History*, translated by John F. Healy (Penguin Books, 2004).

5. Dennis R. Proffitt, "Embodied Perception and the Economy of Action," *Perspectives on Psychological Science* 1, no. 2 (2006).

6. The Roman philosopher Lucretius (99–55 BCE) famously attempted throughout his book *On the Nature of Things* to debunk superstitions. He offered natural materialistic explanations for seemingly supernatural events.

7. Barbara Ehrenreich, *Blood Rites: Origins and History of the Passions of War* (Metropolitan Books, 1997), chapter 3.

8. Harvey Mansfield, *Manliness* (Yale University Press, 2006), chapter 3. There is also suggestive evidence that specific genes are partly responsible for belligerence in men. At the sixth International Congress of Neuroendocrinology (2006) in Pittsburgh, Dr. Stephen Manuck argued that variations in the genes that regulate serotonin levels are good predictors of male aggression. See "Why Men Are More Aggressive," *Science Daily*, June 21, 2006.

9. Some ancient narratives celebrate the female monster killer, such as Atalanta, who kills the Calydonian Boar, but most monster combatants have been male. With the onset of new popular narratives about female monster killers, such as Buffy Summers in *Buffy the Vampire Slayer* and Ripley in the *Alien* series, one suspects that the traditional gender-based division of labor will change. One wonders, however, whether the biological division of labor (the consequence of androgenic hormones in males) will continue to trump the cultural changes and preserve the age-old masculinity of warriors.

CHAPTER 2

1. Quotes here are from Samuel Butler's translation of the *Odyssey*, book IX.
2. Odysseus and his men escape after blinding Polyphemus with a stake and then strapping themselves to the bottom of the Cyclops's sheep. When Polyphemus lets his sheep out of the cave to graze, he does not feel the undersides of the animals and fails to catch the men as they escape.
3. See Margaret Robinson, "Some Fabulous Beasts," *Folklore* 76, no. 4 (1965).
4. Mandeville himself probably never existed, and his very popular *Travels* were cobbled together from previous (fantastical) travel accounts. In chapter 29 the questionable Mandeville reports, "In that country be many griffins, more plenty than in any other country. Some men say that they have the body upward as an eagle and beneath as a lion; and truly they say sooth, that they be of that shape. But one griffin hath the body more great and is more strong than eight lions, of such lions as be on this half, and more great and stronger than an hundred eagles such as we have amongst us."
5. I am indebted to Adrienne Mayor, who read an early proposal of my work, for leading me to this exciting recent research, and for her general guidance on ancient monsters. My account here draws on her book *The First Fossil Hunters* (Princeton, 2000) and her and Michael Heaney's article "Griffins and Arimaspeans," *Folklore* 104, no. 1/2 (1993): 40–66.
6. The eggs may have belonged to the therapod Oviraptor found nearby, not the Protoceratops.
7. See book IX, "Creatures of the Sea," 9–11, and book V, 128, in Pliny's *Natural History*.
8. Romans seem to have interpreted the "stone" character of the fossilized remains as the result of an encounter with the Gorgon's head, which Perseus used to rescue Andromeda from the sea creature. If you look at a Gorgon, you turn to stone.
9. *The Deified Augustus*, in *Lives of the Caesars*, chapter 72.
10. Most naturalists of the era, particularly Aristotle, were simply preoccupied with current living creatures, whose numbers and varieties seemed quite enough to engage their investigative energies. The idea of "failed varieties," however, was certainly available in the ancient world. Lucretius echoes earlier naturalists when he describes monsters who lived long ago but did not survive to the present day. In chapter 5 of *On the Nature of Things* he says:

> And other prodigies and monsters earth was then begetting of this sort—in vain,
> Since Nature banned with horror their increase, and powerless were they to reach unto
> The coveted flower of fair maturity, or to find aliment, or to intertwine
> In works of Venus. For we see there must concur in life conditions manifold,
> If life is ever by begetting life to forge the generations one by one:
> First, foods must be; and, next, a path whereby the seeds of impregnation in the frame
> May ooze, released from the members all; Last, the possession of those instruments
> Whereby the male with female can unite, the one with other in mutual ravishments.

This passage seems to suggest that prehistoric creatures (not necessarily species, but individuals) could not survive because they lacked the necessary adaptive traits. In particular, they lacked the respective male and female genitalia necessary to have intercourse.

11. Thomas Jefferson originally presented the fossil to his colleagues in 1797 but published the description in 1799. "A Memoir on the Discovery of Certain Bones of a Quadruped of the Clawed Kind in the Western Parts of Virginia," *Transactions of the American Philosophical Society* 4 (1799): 246–60.
12. In all fairness to the Stagirite, Aristotle may not have been so credulous about the Bolinthus. The account appears in a text of dubious origin, called "On Marvelous

Things Heard," in *The Complete Works of Aristotle*, vol. 2, edited by Jonathan Barnes (Princeton University Press, 1995).

13. The quote is from the more fantastic account (the possibly apocryphal pseudo-Aristotle "On Marvelous Things"), but a more sober version, wherein the animal projects its excrement only eight feet, is found in Aristotle's *History of Animals*, 9.45.

14. Robinson, "Some Fabulous Beasts." In "Marvels of the East," Rudolf Wittkower also argues that Pliny had significant influence on medieval lore for well over a thousand years after his death.

15. Augustine, *City of God*, 15.9.

16. See Pliny, *Natural History*, book VII, for the discussion of "bodily parts that possess special powers"; see book IX for the Ganges eel.

17. Pliny, *Natural History*, book VIII.

18. Ibid.

19. For a detailed discussion of monster hoaxes in antiquity, see Mayor, *First Fossil Hunters*, chapter 6.

20. This nightmarish tale appears in Pliny, *Natural History*, book IX.

21. But since this passage is part of Hume's general critique of miracles (or the epistemology of confirming miracles), he goes on to lament, "But if the spirit of religion join itself to the love of wonder, there is an end to common sense." See "Of Miracles" in *An Enquiry Concerning Human Understanding*.

22. These reports from Ctesias, Megasthenes, and Pliny himself are gathered in book VII of Pliny's *Natural History*.

23. Aristotle describes something called a "Barbary ape" (which was really a Macaque monkey), but he probably never saw a real ape.

24. See E. E. Sikes's survey of Greek human origin stories in "Four-footed Man: A Note on Greek Anthropology," *Folklore* 20, no. 4 (1909).

25. In *The Invention of Racism in Classical Antiquity* (Princeton University Press, 2004), Ben Isaac accepts the current wisdom that ancients were not prejudiced about skin color, but he finds them positively prejudiced about people who lived in inhospitable geographic regions (i.e., the unpleasant weather of northern Europe produced inferior human beings).

26. Pliny, *Natural History*, book VI.

27. Jasper Griffin, in "East vs. West: The First Round," *New York Review of Books*, December 6, 2007, points out that Greek negative views of Persians were not groundless; it's just that the accusations against Persians could also be leveled against the Spartans. Griffin says, "The King of Persia referred officially to his most exalted officials and soldiers, the governors of great provinces ('satrapies'), as 'X, my slave....' Greeks commented that, in the Persian system, 'all men were slaves but one.' But we should not forget that Sparta was a slave-owning and highly military society; all over Hellas, Sparta opposed the rise of democracies."

28. The Indian tradition describes ears so big that a person could wrap up in them to sleep. This legend was turned around by Megasthenes and other Westerners and reapplied to Indian races. See Bacil F. Kirtley, "The Ear-Sleepers: Some Permutations of a Traveler's Tale," *Journal of American Folklore* 76, no. 300 (1963).

29. Edward Said's *Orientalism* (Vintage, 1979) has become an important tool for understanding the political agendas of all media representation. While Said refers specifically to the age of European imperialism, many scholars have applied his perspective to other historical eras, with mixed results.

30. Aristotle's famous dictum "All humans by nature desire to know" still stands as a respectable alternative to the view of Foucault and Said that "all knowledge is power." Actually it was Francis Bacon who originated the knowledge = power formula, but

the postmodernists expanded the notion to mean that any pursuit of knowledge about "the other" is primarily imperialist in motivation.

31. Pliny, *Natural History*, book VII.

CHAPTER 3

1. References to Livy are drawn from Naphtali Lewis's collection of ancient primary sources, *The Interpretation of Dreams and Portents in Antiquity* (Balchazy-Carducci Publishers, 1996).

2. Currently the term *hermaphrodite* is a somewhat contested label, and advocacy groups together with the medical community seem to prefer the term *intersexual*. Intersexuality describes a person whose sexual genotype (actually chromosomal makeup) or phenotype (genitalia) is neither exclusively male nor female. It is extremely rare to find both testicular and ovarian tissue in one individual; more commonly, a person will have a male chromosomal pattern, XY, but then have hormonal abnormalities in utero (e.g., adrenal gland problems), causing the growth of external female genitalia. Likewise, XX females will get abnormal doses of virilizing hormones in utero and develop a mock penis. There is some debate about the percentage of intersexuals in a given population. Anne Fausto-Sterling has put the figure very high, almost five million in the United States, while Leonard Sax, with the Montgomery Center for Research in Child and Adolescent Development in Maryland, puts the figure around fifty thousand. Sax argues that Fausto-Sterling has inflated the numbers by including groups who are not truly intersexual. A high number would help validate Fausto Sterling's belief that gender is a "social construction" rather than a biological fact. See Leonard Sax, "How Common Is Intersex? A Response to Anne Fausto-Sterling," *Journal of Sex Research* 39, no. 3 (2002), and Anne Fausto-Sterling, "The Five Sexes: Why Male and Female Are Not Enough," *The Sciences* 33, no. 2 (1993) and *Sexing the Body: Gender Politics and the Construction of Sexuality* (Basic Books, 2000). In *The Ontology of Sex* (Routledge, 2006), Carrie Hull points out that Fausto-Sterling revised her numbers down, from 4 percent of all people to 1.728 percent. When Hull checked the math of the new figure, however, she found significant error; she places the number at a mere 0.373 percent. See chapter 4 of Hull's thoughtful study.

3. Carlin A. Barton, *The Sorrows of the Ancient Romans: The Gladiator and the Monster* (Princeton University Press, 1993), chapter 4, "Envy."

4. Remember Lucretius's description of prehistoric monsters, some of whom were hermaphrodite: "In those days also the telluric world strove to beget the monsters that upsprung with their astounding visages and limbs—the Man-woman—a thing betwixt the twain" (*On the Nature of Things*, chapter 5).

5. Quoted in John Block Friedman, *The Monstrous Races in Medieval Art and Thought* (Harvard University Press, 1981), chapter 9.

6. See Pliny, *Natural History*, book VII.

7. See Luc Brisson, *Sexual Ambivalence: Androgyny and Hermaphroditism in Graeco-Roman Antiquity*, translated by Janet Lloyd (University of California Press, 2002), chapter 1, "Monsters." Also see chapter 2 of Fausto-Sterling's *Sexing the Body*.

8. I have to agree with David D. Leitao, who argues persuasively that the transition from Livy to Pliny was not so simple as a triumph of reason. Interestingly, Leitao seems to suggest that Livy probably exaggerated the drowning of hermaphrodites, but it's equally possible that Pliny was overly sanguine in his report. See Leitao's review of Brisson in *Scholia Reviews*, ns 12 (2003).

9. One wonders if Christianity didn't have a bigger influence than rationality on the growing dignity of hermaphrodites in the millennium that followed.

10. The passages from *Plutarch's Lives: Pericles* are taken from the John Dryden translation.

11. Chapter 5 of *On the Nature of Things*.

12. Plutarch relates the story in his "Dinner of the Seven Wise Men," in book XIII of *Moralia*.

13. See Borges's entry on "The Centaur" in *Book of Imaginary Beings*, translated by Andrew Hurley (Penguin Books, 2006).

14. Aristotle, *Parts of Animals*, 654.

15. Aristotle, *Parts of Animals*, book II, part I. "The ordered and definite works of nature do not possess their character because they developed in a certain way. Rather they develop in a certain way because they are that kind of thing, for development depends on the essence and occurs for its sake. Essence does not depend on development" (Aristotle, *Generation of Animals*, book V).

16. Aristotle is "fixist" in the sense that an essential form preexists the element potentials, and subsequently that form is not a mere accumulation of material (in the atomist sense). Act precedes potency in Aristotle, and therefore, though he recognizes that embryogenesis is epigenetic, form and function are not merely "effects" of that process.

17. Aristotle articulates this "essential form" in the context of his overall causal theory: "There are four causes underlying everything: first, the final cause, that for the sake of which a thing exists; secondly, the formal cause, the definition of its essence (and these two we may regard pretty much as one and the same); thirdly, the material; and fourthly, the moving principle or efficient cause" (*Generation of Animals*, book I).

18. Legend has it that Empedocles threw himself into an active volcano, Mt. Etna in Sicily, to turn himself into an immortal. See Ava Chitwood, "The Death of Empedocles," *American Journal of Philology* 107, no. 2 (summer 1986).

19. In his *Physics* Aristotle contemplates the possibility that nature cobbled itself together without any sense of direction, without purpose:

> Why should not nature work, not for the sake of something, nor because it is better so, but just as the sky rains, not in order to make the corn grow, but of necessity? What is drawn up must cool, and what has been cooled must become water and descend, the result of this being that the corn grows. Similarly if a man's crop is spoiled on the threshing-floor, the rain did not fall for the sake of this—in order that the crop might be spoiled—but that result just followed. Why then should it not be the same with the parts in nature, e.g. that our teeth should come up of necessity—the front teeth sharp, fitted for tearing, the molars broad and useful for grinding down the food—since they did not arise for this end, but it was merely a coincident result; and so with all other parts in which we suppose that there is purpose? Wherever then all the parts came about just what they would have been if they had come to be for an end, such things survived, being organized spontaneously in a fitting way; whereas those which grew otherwise perished and continue to perish, as Empedocles says his "man-faced ox-progeny" did. (*Physics*, book II, part VIII)

20. Aristotle, *Parts of Animals*, book I, part I.

21. Ibid., book II.

22. Lucretius, *On the Nature of Things*, chapter 5.

23. This whole theory has appeared sexist to some scholars, and perhaps Aristotle was and should be chastised accordingly. But in fairness to him on this particular point, he claims that some of the developmental errors in reproduction can be ascribed to semen as well as uterine material. In Aristotle's *Problems* (see volume 2 of Jonathan

Barnes's *The Complete Works of Aristotle*), he says, "Monstrosities come into being when the semen becomes confused and disturbed either in the emission of the seminal fluid or in the mingling which takes place in the uterus of the female." Furthermore, it's not much of an insult to argue that women provide variation unless one is arguing for some strange eugenics position, which Aristotle (unlike Plato) did not, and which seems impossible in principle given his point about the inevitability of variation in the mechanics of reproduction.

24. Aristotle, *Generation of Animals*, book IV.

25. Aristotle, *Problems*, 898a.

26. If malformed creatures are aiming at actualizing their respective essences but missing the mark, so to speak, what about the essences themselves? In other words, individual monsters are "failed" members of actual species, but might there exist monstrous species, monstrous essences? The answer is somewhat nuanced. Technically, there are no monstrous essences or species, because a "monster" for Aristotle is an individual animal that fails to achieve its specific *telos*, or developmental end goal. These end goals are the forms or types, and, unlike individual organisms, they are fixed. But Aristotle does admit the reality of very weird and hard to categorize species, whole taxa that seem to straddle the fence between traditional categories (for example, a "slime mold" that appears *both* animal and plant). These are liminal creatures, on the threshold between categories, but they are not monsters. They are rare and intriguing and form puzzling links in the chain of being (*scala naturae*), but they are not mistakes. Nature poses certain challenges for the taxonomist, but strange and exotic creatures will ultimately find a place in the scheme of nature and on the subtle grid of classification (even if they straddle that grid indefinitely). Monsters and bizarre species do not fall *outside* of nature, but reside inside the complex system.

27. Lucretius, *On the Nature of Things*, chapter 4.

28. See Julius Obsequens's popular *Book of Prodigies*, for example. Nothing is really known about Obsequens, not even his dates. But his book, culled from Livy's history of Rome, appeared sometime between the second and fourth centuries. Napthali Lewis, in *Dreams and Portents in Antiquity*, says, "The simple fact of his making and publishing this collection speaks volumes about the impact of such material on the popular mind."

CHAPTER 4

1. See Plato's love dialogue, *Phaedrus*. It's very rare for Socrates to leave the urban setting of Athens, and he is unapologetic about his distaste for nature, preferring instead the company of people and philosophical dialogue to trees and rivers. Perhaps it is his amorous attraction to Phaedrus, a constant throughout Plato's dialogue, that leads Socrates to depart somewhat from his usual haunts.

2. See *Republic*, book IX.

3. See *Republic*, Stephanus numbers, 573c and 577d.

4. If this harmony argument were not enough to rescue justice from the pessimistic treatment, Socrates points out another profound feature of gangster life. Gangsters can never have true friends: when people are ruled by their appetites, they will sell each other out when times get bad.

5. Ultimately Plato rescues love from the more disparaging characterization and argues famously that eros can be redirected from its selfish nature to a selfless concern for the beloved. But this requires a careful balance, preserving the sexual tension (this intense energy is the engine that brings us to glimpse the Forms) while refraining from the actual sex. See the *Symposium* as well as the *Phaedrus*.

6. In March 1999 Marilyn Lemak of Naperville, Illinois, killed her children, Thomas, three, Emily, six, and Nicholas, seven, by first drugging their peanut butter with antidepressants and then smothering them. The prosecution successfully argued that Lemak killed her children as a means of punishing her husband because he had started to see another woman. In 1994 a South Carolina woman, Susan Smith, intentionally drowned her two children, Michael, three, and Alex, fourteen months, by driving her car into a lake while her children were in their locked car seats. Apparently Smith was attempting to win the affections of a man who had expressed anxiety about getting involved with a woman who had children. These cases of infanticide are quite different, of course, but share the common theme of mothers whose romantic interests seem to have trumped their maternal ones. For a scholarly treatment of the Medea mythology, see Susan Iles Johnson and James J. Clauss, *Medea: Essays on Medea in Myth, Literature, Philosophy, and Art* (Princeton, 1996).

7. When vacationing in Europe in the early 1990s I chanced to flip on the TV in my pensione. The scene haunted me for years afterward and I unsuccessfully quizzed film buffs relentlessly to help me identify the film. Fifteen years later I finally discovered that the scene was from an obscure Danish television version of *Medea* by director Lars von Trier (originally aired in Denmark in 1988). Von Trier reportedly once said, "A film should be like a rock in the shoe." His *Medea* has been like a rock in my shoe for almost twenty years, and counting.

8. One is reminded here of William Congreve's famous passage in *The Mourning Bride* (1697), "Heaven hath no rage like love to hatred turned, nor hell a fury like a woman scorned." The quotations from Euripides' *Medea* are taken from Ian Johnston's translation.

9. In Euripides' tragedy *Hecuba* we see the same sort of descent into inhuman monstrosity, but the injury that provokes Hecuba's vengeance—betrayal by a supposed friend who murders Hecuba's son—makes her more sympathetic in her outrage and her response. Sometimes one must meet monstrosity with something similarly frightening in order to return balance to justice. The metaphor of Hecuba's transformation is that, by sinking to animalistic retaliation, she will become a dog, a hapless hound. In *The Fragility of Goodness*, chapter 13, Martha Nussbaum argues that the whole play is "an assault upon our fondest thoughts about human safety and human beneficence." The play is a rare recognition, in an otherwise much less vulnerable ancient literary culture, of the external uncontrollable factors in human happiness.

10. Scylla was the horrifying sea monster who, together with Charybdis, formed a legendary gauntlet of doom for sailors traveling between Italy and Sicily.

11. See chapter 2 of Dodd's still impressive *The Greeks and the Irrational* (University of California Press, 1951).

12. Sigmund Freud, *Totem and Taboo* (Norton, 1962), chapter 3.

13. *Alastor* is a Greek term that means "avenger" and was personified as a demon that surrounded family feuds in particular. Alastor is the demon that avenges blood crimes, even if he must visit the sins of the father upon the sons.

14. Interestingly, Jason interprets his own sin not as betraying Medea, but as knowing that she was evil (murderer of her own brother, etc.) and still going ahead with their romance. He is being punished because he didn't get out when the going was good.

15. Socrates' famous theory that people never *knowingly* do wrong but only make cognitive mistakes about the good is here undermined by Medea. Socrates' notion that proper understanding clears away immoral action looks rather naïve next to the subtler psychology of Euripides and even Socrates' student Plato.

16. See book II of the *Republic*.

17. Julia Annas, *Ancient Philosophy: A Very Short Introduction* (Oxford University Press, 2000), chapter 1.
18. Aristotle, both in his embryology and his ethics, is perhaps the best exception to this generalization.
19. Christianity came along later and removed this escape plan by making it a sure doorway to more severe and eternal monster harassment.

CHAPTER 5

1. Timothy K. Beal, *Religion and Its Monsters* (Routledge, 2002), introduction.
2. Satan is widely accepted as the engineer of Job's misery, and he unambiguously colludes with Yahweh to begin the torture of Job. But, as many commentators have pointed out, the term translated as Satan is *ha-satan* and means generally "the adversary" or "the accuser"; it is not a proper personal name. In any case, the mainstream exegetical tradition has interpreted the adversary as Satan.
3. *Consurrexit autem Satan contra Israhel et incitavit David ut numeraret Israhel* (Chronicles 21:1). Unless otherwise noted, Bible passages are from the Latin Vulgate Bible.
4. *Intravit autem Satanas in Iudam qui cognominatur Scarioth unum de duodecim.* Of course, the relatively recent discovery and publication of the Gospel of Judas has redefined Judas along Gnostic lines. In that suppressed and then long lost gospel, Judas is more positively rendered. He delivers the body of Jesus to the high priests, but it is with Jesus' full knowledge and blessing. Judas is characterized as a catalyst for ultimate redemption, not an enemy of goodness. See Elaine Pagels and Karen L. King, *Reading Judas: The Gospel of Judas and the Shaping of Christianity* (Viking, 2007).
5. Luther Link, *The Devil: Archfiend in Art from the Sixth to the Sixteenth Century* (Harry Abrams, 1996).
6. Book of Job, chapter 40.
7. See chapter 3 of Beal's *Religion and Its Monsters* for a nice discussion of these various meanings of Leviathan.
8. Ibid., chapter 4.
9. Christian philosophers such as St. Anselm (1033–1109) and St. Aquinas (1126–1198), but also the Muslim scholar Averroes (Ibn Rushd; 1126–1198) all considered some form of the "paradox of omnipotence." Was God bound by logical consistency, or could he violate the laws of rationality? Could God make a square circle or create a stone so heavy that he could not lift it? In general, Western monotheists opted for a rational omnipotent God, one that observed the laws of logic and maintained some level of coherence to our human minds.
10. *Baghavad Gita*, translated by Ramanand Prasad (American Gita Society, 2004), chapter 11, available at http://eawc.evansville.edu/anthology/gita.htm.
11. For an opposing viewpoint, see Partha Mitter, *History of European Reactions to Indian Art* (Clarendon Press, 1977). Mitter argues that Western interpretations of Indian art assume, unsurprisingly, a hierarchy of quality that places a premium on more Western-looking representations (such as the Ghandharan styles). But he also argues that Westerners overemphasize the "metaphysical" and "spiritual values" of Indian art. "I would suggest," Mitter says, "that a more effective and fruitful way of studying the nature and quality of Indian art and the entire relations between art and religion would be in concrete and human terms and not by presenting collective notions or metaphysical generalizations" (286). But while Mitter is certainly correct about the dangers of generalizing, it seems disingenuous to suggest (for the sake of his argument) that metaphysics and spiritual values

are *not* concrete human concerns. The argument that we should divorce Indian depictions of the Buddha or Vishnu or Ganesh from metaphysics seems more like an ordnance volley in the academic battle between cultural materialists and symbolic anthropologists. More trenchant, Mitter never really delivers on his promise for an alternative (nonspiritual) analysis of Indian art. Thanks to my colleague Joan Erdman for referring me to Mitter's interesting discussion of monsters.

12. Myths of Babylonian dragons were well known, and the extended Book of Daniel refers to such a creature in *Bel and the Dragon*. In this version of the Daniel story (originally included in the 1611 King James Bible, but not subsequent versions) Daniel kills a dragon revered by Babylonians by feeding it cakes made from pitch, fat, and hair. The dragon's belly explodes.

13. Historians are divided as to whether Domitian's reign was really marked by Christian persecution. See L. L. Thompson, *The Book of Revelation: Apocalypse and Empire* (Oxford University Press, reprint edition, 1997).

14. Most scholars agree that the infamous number 666 is a coded way of referring to the Roman emperor (a numerological breakdown of his name), though which emperor, Nero or Domitian, is still contentious.

15. The date of the composition of the Book of Daniel is a highly contested business. Most believers, particularly those of a literal bent, date its composition to the sixth century and see its various prophesies validated by the historical events of the second century (namely, the persecution of Jews during the reign of Antiochus IV Epiphanes). In this reading, Daniel's visions come to pass centuries later and help to recommend the Bible as a source of supernatural truth. Others date the work much later, claiming that it was actually written during the second-century persecutions but posing as a much earlier work of prophesy.

16. Most conservative Christian exegetes dubiously interpret the fourth beast as a prophecy about the coming terror of the Roman, rather than Greek, Empire. Among other implications, this move brings Daniel and Revelation into even greater parallel.

17. Among other passages, see chapter 12, part 2 of Maimonides' *Mishneh Torah* and also his *Yemen Epistle* in *Maimonides Reader*, edited by Isadore Twersky (Behrman House, 1976). Martin Luther originally argued that there was "no Christ" in the strange text of John's vision, and he downgraded its importance, considering it a dangerous apocryphal text.

18. The biblical monsters, originally articulated long before the medieval period and properly belonging to the ancient era, are nonetheless highly animated in the literary and pictorial traditions of medieval Europe. Biblical monsters inform medieval thinking about cosmology, geography, anthropology, and theology. For that reason I have chosen to introduce them in this, rather than the previous, chapter.

19. See chapter 3 of Andy Orchard's excellent book *Pride and Prodigies: Studies in the Monsters of the Beowulf-Manuscript* (D. S. Brewer, 1995).

20. Western mainstream Jewish and Christian traditions now consider the Book of Enoch to be an apocryphal work, but it had a significant influence on early and medieval biblical culture. Even canonical scripture, for example Jude 14 and 15, refers unapologetically to the Enoch story. Up until the fourth century Enoch was a respected text, seen as genuine by patristic writers such as Origen and Tertullian. Discovery of Dead Sea Scroll fragments of Enoch at Qumran led scholars to treat the scripture (or parts of it) as originating sometime before the second century BCE. The Book of Giants, also found at Qumran, is another influential apocryphal text (based on Enoch and Genesis); it was recomposed and championed by Mani (216–276 CE) as a Manichaean text that describes, among other things, how God killed the giants in the Flood.

21. Cited in chapter 3 of Orchard's *Pride and Prodigies*.

CHAPTER 6

1. "We cannot deny that Enoch, the seventh from Adam, left some divine writings, for this is asserted by the Apostle Jude in his canonical epistle. But it is not without reason that these writings have no place in that canon of Scripture which was preserved in the temple of Hebrew people by the diligence of successive priests; for their antiquity brought them under suspicion, and it was impossible to ascertain whether these were his genuine writings." Augustine, *The City of God* (*De civitate Dei*), book XV, 23. This and other quotes from Augustine's text are from Marcus Dod's translation (Modern Library, 1993).
2. Augustine, *City of God*, book XV, 9. One suspects that Augustine, like so many other pre-Victorians, actually stumbled on an extinct creature's fossilized part, but he did not have a theoretical paradigm that included dinosaurs.
3. Ibid., book XV, 23.
4. Isidore of Seville, *Etymologiae*, book XI.
5. Isidore's list, and that of every other medieval monsterologist, is heavily influenced by Pliny the Elder's *Natural History*.
6. Isidore of Seville, *Etymologiae*, book XI, chapter 3.
7. This sort of pantheism is hinted at in the doctrines of many ancients, including Heraclitus, Parmenides, and the Stoics, but doesn't get its fullest expression until Spinoza's *Ethics* (1675) and his notion of the *deus sive natura*.
8. Plato's *Timaeus* articulates a well-known version of this cosmology.
9. Augustine, *City of God*, book XV, 23.
10. The Greek word for cubit is *pygme*.
11. All these monstrous races could be read as moral inspirations or warnings: Pygmy races were symbols of humility, giants were symbols of pride, and dog-headed races were symbols of slanderous lying. See Wittkower, "Marvels of the East."
12. Augustine, Sermo 37, "Ad Fratres in Eremo."
13. See chapter 20 of Umberto Eco's entertaining novel *Baudolino* (Harcourt, 2002).
14. Isidore of Seville, *Etymologiae*, book XI, chapter 3, 18.
15. See St. Jerome's *The Life of Paulus the First Hermit*.
16. Augustine, *Confessions*, book XIII, chapter 33. Also see Isidore's *Etymologiae*, book XI, chapter 1, for a similar discussion of *mens* and *anima*.
17. Aquinas, *Summa Theologica*, first part, question 93, article 2.
18. For the captain metaphor, see, for example, Plato's *Republic*, *Phaedrus*, and *Phaedo*. For the ghost metaphor, see Descartes' *Meditations* and *Discourse on Method* and Gilbert Ryle's influential interpretation of Descartes in *Concept of Mind*. For comparison with the East, see the Hindu notion of soul (*atman*) as the captain or rider of a chariot in the *Katha Upanishad* and the Buddha's rejection of soul in the *Potthapada Sutta*.
19. Aquinas, *Contra Gentiles*, book II, chapter 82.
20. "In everything that is apt to arrive at any perfection, there is found a natural craving after that perfection: for good is what all crave after, everything its own good." Aquinas, *Contra Gentiles*, book II, chapter 82.
21. Augustine, *City of God*, book XVI, 8.
22. This and other quotes from the Irish *Passion of St. Christopher* are from a 1913 Fraser translation, which can be found at www.ucc.ie/milmart/chrsirish.html.
23. Most Roman Catholic versions contend that Reprobus, instead of being a dog-headed Berber, was a giant of a man who converted to Christianity and was instructed by a hermit ascetic to help people cross a difficult river. He dutifully carried many people across the turbid waters until one day a small child asked for his assistance. The child was heavier than any other human that Reprobus had previously encountered, and it

was revealed to him that the child was actually the incarnation of Jesus, heavy with the burden of human sin.

24. Cited in chapter 9 of John Block Friedman's masterful study *The Monstrous Races in Medieval Art and Thought*. Guido of Mont Rocher (b. 1333) laid out the relevant considerations for struggling clergy: "And for this reason it may be supposed that if there be two chests and two heads there are two souls. If however, there be one chest and one head, however much the other members be doubled, there is only the one soul."

25. The story of Lazarus and Baptista and this quote from the *Mercury* are nicely discussed in Stephen Pender, "No Monsters at the Resurrection," in *Monster Theory: Reading Culture*, edited by Jeffrey Jerome Cohen (University of Minnesota, 1996).

26. The idea that Ham's descendants were damned to servitude was often employed by anti-abolitionists in nineteenth-century America to justify the slavery of imported Africans, particularly between the years 1830 and 1865. See Stephen Haynes, *Noah's Curse: The Biblical Justification of American Slavery* (Oxford University Press, 2002), chapters 4, 5.

27. For a discussion of the rabbinical and Christian historical exegesis of the Genesis passage, see Haynes, *Noah's Curse*, chapter 2.

28. Augustine, *City of God*, book XVI.

29. This color-coding was based on an interpretation of Ham's name as alternately "burnt" or "hot" or "dark." A more comprehensive listing of the Table of Nations might be as follows: the descendants of Ham would include Egyptians, Ethiopians, Phoenicians, Hittites, and the Mongol tribes; the descendants of Shem would include the Hebrews, Persians, and Assyrians; the descendants of Japheth would include the Greeks, Romans, Spaniards, Celts, Scythians, and Medes.

30. It is interesting to note that the Table of Nations is still the preferred explanation of races among some contemporary fundamentalist Christians. The stories of the relative offspring of Ham, Shem, and Japheth are detailed as "good creation science" in the displays of the Kentucky Creation Museum (opened in spring 2007 in Petersburg). The racist interpretation of the table has been removed in the museum version, and an egalitarian tone is brought to bear on the story of Ham, Shem, and Japheth. For an overview of the museum itself, see Stephen T. Asma, "Dinosaurs on the Ark: The Creation Museum," *Chronicle of Higher Education*, May 18, 2007.

31. Augustine, *City of God*, book XVI.

32. Ibid., chapter 8. It's difficult to penetrate further Augustine's thinking here. The argument as presented begs for further clarification, but none is given. For example, should the deformed baby be considered an actual *member* of a faraway race, or merely an isomorphic token of such a race, a symbol? If the child is in fact a proper member of the monstrous tribe, how are we to understand its gestation in a nonmonstrous woman? Even when we abandon our contemporary notions of heredity, Augustine's theory still seems peculiar. It is as if he were thinking about a biological atavism (a throwback), but along geographical rather than temporal lines. One suspects that the whole argument hinges on treating the parallel between race and individual as symbolic rather than literal. But whatever the case on this issue, Augustine ends the reflections by emphasizing, yet again, that all such oddities are indirect descendants of Adam.

33. It's interesting to note that by the time Columbus set out for the New World, and no doubt long before, the criteria for identifying threatening and irredeemable races had become more explicitly physiognomic. In his famous letter of 1493, Columbus informs his fellow Europeans that the new native races will most likely be receptive to conversion. His optimism is based on his admission that they are not the monsters that he fully expected to encounter. They do not appear to have tails or dog's heads or one eye, or other abnormality.

34. Naomi Reed Kline, "The World of the Strange Races," in *Monsters, Marvels and Miracles: Imaginary Journeys and Landscapes in the Middle Ages*, edited by Leif Sondergaard and Rasmus Thorning Hansen (University Press of Southern Denmark, 2005).

35. For a good discussion of the *mappaemundi* and Alexander's gates, see Evelyn Edson, "Mapping the Middle Ages: The Imaginary and the Real Universe of the Mappaemundi," in *Monsters, Marvels and Miracles*, edited by Sondergaard and Hansen. According to Edson, Alexander's achievements were often included on Christian maps because "he was thought to be a precursor of Christ—as Alexander conquered the physical world, so Christ conquered the spiritual world."

36. My discussion of the Hereford map draws on Kline's fine essay "'The World of the Strange Races."

37. See Friedman, *Monstrous Races in Medieval Art and Thought*, chapter 5.

38. Ibid.

39. Both the *Travels of Sir John Mandeville* and the *Travels of Marco Polo* (1299?) describe Alexander's gates. Both were highly influential travel narratives and helped to codify and transmit ideas about exotic lands and peoples well into the age of exploration. Both are also filled with fantastical and bogus stories (including, quite possibly, the existence of Mandeville himself), and many of these stories resurrect the ancient monsters, but now with travelers' tales that either discredit or more likely corroborate their existence.

40. According to legend, ten Jewish tribes were deported out of Samaria after the Assyrians conquered the region. They disappeared from recorded history, and most modern-day Jews trace their lineage to the remaining tribes of Benjamin, Judah, and Levy.

41. To this extent, Mandeville at least demonstrates a better understanding of Islam than does the twelfth-century French epic *La Chanson de Roland*. In *The Song of Roland* the Moors of Saragossa are erroneously thought to worship a trinity of gods: Mohammed, Termagant, and Apollo. This confusion undoubtedly made it easier for some European Christians to group Muslims in with other forms of polytheistic paganism.

42. For a fuller discussion, see Andrew Fleck, "Here, There, and In Between: Representing Difference in the Travels of Sir John Mandeville," *Studies in Philology* 97, no. 4 (2000).

43. I am obviously tracing the discourse about monsters as it appears in the theological and travel writings of the time, but it bears mentioning that the larger, illiterate European majority was probably not as Christian as is usually supposed. Theological nuances in particular were probably not as relevant in driving prejudices as were things like images and rumors. In *The Black Death* (Harvard University Press, 1997), David Herlihy points out that "early in 1348, the rumor arose that the Jews of Northern Spain and Southern France were poisoning the Christian wells, and thus disseminating the plague" (65). The rumor spread all over Europe, and probably did much more damage than any doctrinal or lettered form of prejudice. Christianity itself, which we usually think of as typifying the medieval mind, probably floated more like a small elite island on a sea of folk religion (animism) and culture. Herlihy argues that the black plague probably helped to Christianize the illiterate populations by driving them to develop cults of saints in order to garner improved protections against the raging disease. He offers compelling evidence for this claim by combing over birth records and finding a huge spike in the saints' names given to newborns during the plague period. I mention these points as a simple reminder that although my study must of necessity track the literate cultures of a given era, much more than literature and education were at work in these eras.

44. Judith Taylor Gold, *Monsters and Madonnas: The Root of Christian Anti-Semitism* (Syracuse University Press, 1999), epilogue.

45. Considerable interpretive differences continue, however, with some scholars arguing that Dhu'l-Qarneyn is Cyrus the Great. Those who suggest that he is Alexander point to the popularity of the early Alexander legends during the Hellenistic era, a popularity that extended throughout Christian and Jewish as well as pagan cultures. The stories of Alexander's gates were probably already in circulation in the Hellenistic era, and it's likely that they would have been known by the people of the Arabian peninsula.

46. *Qur'an, Surat al-Kahf,* verses 92–96, translated by Marmaduke Pickthal.

47. My discussion here draws from Aziz Al-Azmeh, "Barbarians in Arab Eyes," *Past and Present,* no. 134 (1992).

48. See Andrew Runni Anderson, *Alexander's Gate, Gog and Magog, and the Enclosed Nations* (Medieval Academy of America, publication no. 12, Cambridge, Mass., 1932).

CHAPTER 7

1. Quotes from *Beowulf* are from Frederick Rebsamen's translation (Harper Perennial, 1991).

2. In "*Beowulf* as Palimpsest," in *Monster Theory,* edited by Cohen, Ruth Waterhouse points out that the passage attributing Cain's bloodline to Grendel is probably a rewrite by the scribe who replaced the Old English "in chames cynne" (in Ham's kin) with "in caines cynne" (in Cain's kin). We've already seen that both Ham and Cain were historically assigned the status of "monster father," but the *Beowulf* scribe's alteration might indicate a point at which Cain made more sense to European Christians. In medieval folk traditions Cain had become more loathsome, and the tradition of assigning him paternity to the monsters had become more entrenched. But the original use of Ham is telling and reveals the racist genetic connection assumed between the human races of color (African and Asian races, usually assigned to Ham) and the monsters.

3. J. R. R. Tolkien's "Beowulf: The Monsters and the Critics" was read on November 25, 1936, as the Sir Israel Gollancz Memorial Lecture (published by Humphrey Milford, 1937).

4. Tolkien's position, that the poem is a unified Christian critique of paganism, has been taken up more recently by Andy Orchard in *Pride and Prodigies.* Orchard makes a very compelling argument, based on a comparison with the other works bundled together with the Nowell Codex, that an overarching critique of pagan pride can be detected in each. My own discussion of the issue is much informed by both Orchard and Tolkien, but I'm aware that their reading is still a minority report in the sense that they ascribe a purposeful unified voice to the poem.

5. Both Catholics, Chambers and Tolkien were friends and might be said to offer a uniquely Catholic perspective, one that celebrates rather than ignores the issues of evil, on early English literature.

6. Obviously in Christianity there is a parallel narrative that sees the suffering of Jesus as the ultimate monster killer redeeming the world from sin through his suffering. But although this is a familiar version to us now, we must recognize that it made little sense to the pagan cultures of the Mediterranean and northern Europe. The idea that one "wins" (righteousness) by "losing" (undergoing suffering) was paradoxical to the cultures of strength, loyalty, and power.

7. Orchard, *Pride and Prodigies,* chapter 4.

8. "Alexander the Great's Journey to Paradise," in *Legends of Alexander the Great,* edited by Stoneman.

9. Friedrich Nietzsche, *Beyond Good and Evil,* translated by Judith Norman, in *Fifty Readings in Philosophy,* edited by Donald Abel (McGraw-Hill, 2004). Some careless

readers have interpreted Nietzsche's distinction between slave morality and master morality in racial terms. This reading is rendered incoherent when Nietzsche explains that both forms of morality, vying for dominance, can exist within each person: "In fact, you sometimes find them [master and slave morality] sharply juxtaposed—inside the same person even, within a single soul" (aphorism 260).

10. Sam Keen, *Fire in the Belly* (Bantam Books, 1992), chapter 8.

11. Perhaps the more popular "new man" fusion of the pagan and the Christian is the *simpler* fusion. The monster-killing hero is simply baptized and made into a saint. St. George is a monster killer who, like almost every other monster killer, saves innocents from doom. But now he, and other similarly talented saints, do their monster killing in the sanctified context of missionary work. Christianity may have all the merciful and peaceful tendencies in it that believers (like Tolkien) respect and skeptics (like Nietzsche) scorn, but both sides forget that Christianity was a *mythos* before it was an *ethos*. The majority of medieval folk culture would have been less interested in "turn the other cheek" proverbs and more interested in stories of Christian *power*, the supernatural efficacy of Christianity and its God to ameliorate the problems of life.

CHAPTER 8

1. Even while I wrote this chapter a story about a botched exorcism made the daily news. In July 2007 in Phoenix, Arizona, police responded to a report of an exorcism on a young girl. When police arrived they found the girl's grandfather choking her, and they used stun guns on him.

> The 3-year-old girl and her mother, who was also in the room during the struggle between 49-year-old Ronald Marquez and officers, were hospitalized, police said. The relative who called police said an exorcism had also been attempted Thursday. "The purpose was to release demons from this very young child," said Sgt. Joel Tranter. Officers arrived at the house Saturday and entered when they heard screaming coming from a bedroom, Tranter said. A bed had been pushed up against the door; the officers pushed it open a few inches and saw Marquez choking his bloodied granddaughter, who was crying in pain and gasping, Tranter said. A bloody naked 19-year-old woman who police later determined to be Marquez's daughter and the girl's mother was in the room, chanting "something that was religious in nature," Tranter said. (Associated Press, CNN.com, July 29, 2007)

2. Anthony's marvelous episodes have also fueled the pictorial tradition, from the medieval period to the present. Paintings by Hieronymus Bosch, Matthias Grunewald, and Salvador Dalí, for example, have helped to keep Anthony's tribulations in the popular imagination. Anthony's battle with monsters comes to us via his famous biographer, Athanasius of Alexandria (ca. 293–373). Athanasius chronicled Anthony's life in a work titled simply *Vita Antonii*, or *Life of Anthony*.

3. Anthony had a younger sister whom he placed in a nunnery, where she could preserve her virginity.

4. All quotes from the *Life of Anthony* are taken from Rev. H. Ellershaw, *Select Writings of Athanasius*, in *Library of Nicene and Post-Nicene Fathers* (New York, 1957), series II, vol. IV.

5. Anthony offers more evidence of the weakness of evil spirits when he tells the famous gospel story about Christ's exorcism of a man named Legion. This man was

possessed by many demons, and when Christ drew them out of the man, the evil spirits actually *begged* Christ to enter a herd of swine. He granted this transfer, and the swine then ran straight into the lake and drowned themselves. Anthony asks his monks why, if demons are powerful, they have to ask permission and beg for such trivial mischief.

6. Centuries later Aquinas was still refining Christian demonology and giving nuance to the ideas first formed by St. Anthony. In his *Summa Contra Gentiles* Aquinas considers whether demons are inherently evil. He offers some standard theological and scriptural ways of thinking about demons and monsters, but he also gives a more philosophical argument for thinking that demons are not all bad. The wider popular culture believes demons to be inherently evil beings that intentionally seek the pain and suffering of others as their only real goal and purpose. But Aquinas argues that demons are confused and weak-willed and accidentally evil, but not essentially evil. When those demons tortured St. Anthony, for example, they were motivated by their (admittedly selfish and wrongheaded) sense of good. Like other cases of evil and sin, the suffering of St. Anthony is the result of a "false judgment" rather than a "bad will." Properly speaking, for Aquinas, there is no such thing as a bad will really, only a confused will. By definition, a willful choice is always toward a good, so a bad will, one that *always* and *by nature* chooses bad rather than good, makes no sense.

7. It may be objectionable to treat witch monsters in the medieval section of this book. The fact that so many witch trials occurred into the seventeenth century certainly falsifies the idea that witches were confined to the premodern era. Nonetheless, the witch crazes, regardless of their chronological manifestation, seem to have certain metaphysical assumptions and perspectives that can properly be called medieval. An invisible copresent dimension of spirit beings, which both help and harass, is a foundation of medieval theology. Belief in this reality is probably as strong now as it was then, but I include it here because its beginnings, at least in its monotheistic form, were medieval.

8. I don't want to give the impression that *all* this fear was paranoia. Some of it was well founded. In 1453, for example, the Turks captured Constantinople and began their rapid expansion into Europe and North Africa.

9. The pamphlet, and other such treasures, can be found in *Reprints of English Books, 1475–1700*, no. 40, edited by Joseph Arnold Foster, in the regular collections at Chicago's Newberry Library.

10. In the quotes that follow, I've taken the liberty of updating the English spellings.

11. Social psychology seems to confirm that interrogation methods of torture lead many innocents to "name" other innocents, and an unstoppable cycle of paranoia and self-fulfilling prophecy follows. In this regard, the witch trials have something in common with the torture prisons of Cambodia, the Stalin-era gulags, and the excesses of China's Red Guards, among other lamentable purges. In general, the twentieth-century understanding of the hysterical witch period accepts that the accusations and confessions of the time were bogus, containing no kernel of truth. A notable exception is the writing of Margaret Alice Murray, a British anthropologist who published witch trial theories in the 1920s and 1930s. Much maligned in her own day and ours, Murray argued that the strange consistency of witch confessions should be interpreted as confirmation that some underground movement of female-dominated pagan covens did in fact exist. She argued that the rituals, even some of the alleged cannibalism, were real pagan movements operating in the shadows of Christian official culture. Murray treats them as a cult working with a mishmash of local animist and ancient pagan traditions. Her work is largely scorned by academics, but she had some influence on Gerald Gardner's thinking. Gardner (1884–1964) was instrumental in

founding modern Wicca. See Murray's *The Witch Cult in Western Europe* (Clarendon Press, 1921).

12. The seminal work on the ergot hypothesis is Linnda Caporael's "Ergotism: The Satan Loosed in Salem," *Science* 192, April 1976.

13. Historians disagree about the number of witch hunt executions. In *Witchhunt in Early Modern Europe* (Longman, 1995) Brian Levack puts the number at around 60,000, whereas Anne Lewellyn Barstow, *Withccraze* (HarperOne, 1995), puts the number around 100,000.

14. Number 37, "The Divels Delusions," in *Reprints of English Books, 1475–1700*, edited by Foster.

15. Many of the medieval *grimoires* (magic manuals) warn of the dangers of the "diabolical enchantments." Benevolent Jewish and Christian magic was popular among intellectuals, pseudo-intellectuals, and cognoscenti interested in exotica. Good deeds were thought to be possible through magic, but once practitioners had opened the channel to the spirits, they had to be extra vigilant about the dark forces. For example, a fifteenth-century Jewish grimoire, called *The Book of the Sacred Magic of Abramelin, the Mage*, sets forth an esoteric combination of Kabbalah and Greek numerology. The practitioner is warned to "always be on guard, and abstain as from a mortal sin from flattering, regarding, or having respect to the Demon, and to his Viperine Race." Look out, it continues, for a "Man of Majestic Appearance, who with great affability doth promise unto thee marvelous things. Consider all this as pure vanity, for without the permission of God he can give nothing; but he will do it unto the damage and prejudice, ruin and eternal damnation of whomsoever putteth faith in him, and believe in him." *The Book of the Sacred Magic*, translated by S. L. MacGregor Mathers (1900; Dover reprint edition, 1975), chapter 10.

16. Heinrich Institoris, *Malleus Maleficarum*, translated by P. G. Maxwell-Stuart (Manchester University Press, 2007), part I, question 9.

17. Ibid., part II, chapter 7.

18. Ibid., part I, question 9.

19. Here again we find the classic medieval witch logic, so well parodied by Monty Python, in which women under terrible distress and torment are forced to admit to any damn thing in hopes of relief, and then their forced bogus confessions are used against them to justify further ordeals.

20. Pursuant to this cautionary anecdote of the young man, Institoris asks the following astounding question: "So what are we to think about those witches who shut up penises in what are sometimes prolific numbers, twenty or thirty at a single time, in a bird's nest or some kind of box, where they move about in order to eat oats and fodder, as though they were alive—something which many people have seen and is reported by common gossip?" Indeed, what are we to think? In a rare moment of humor, the stern inquisitor completes the story by telling of a man who had been robbed of his penis and then instructed by a witch to fish it out of the swarming collection. When he tried to take a big one, the witch asked him not to take that one because it belonged to the parish priest.

21. Institoris, *Malleus Maleficarum*, part I, question 11.

22. It's hard to imagine a more horrific charge than baby eating, which is precisely why some inquisitors leveled it against the Jews as well. This legend can be added to the others, discussed earlier, that sought to demonize the Jews as monsters. For Institoris, Jews were like witches in another important way. Unlike other heathen, Jews and witches had been exposed to the Christian faith, had understood the teachings of the Gospel, but had then decided to reject it. This was considered worse than being oblivious to the Gospel. It is an old anti-Semitic charge, further nuanced by Institoris's theological attempt to link witches (demons) and Jews directly.

23. Some social historians have suggested that this may be a reflection of general patriarchal anxiety about women such as midwives who were independent, learned in folk wisdom, and autonomous when compared to traditional wives and mothers. Often the entire phenomenon is chalked up to patriarchal misogyny. See, for example, Mary Daly's influential *Gyn/Ecology: The Meta-ethics of Radical Feminism* (Beacon Press, 1978), wherein she inflates the number of executed female witches to astronomic proportions and then blames the whole mess on male aggression.

24. While the *Malleus Maleficarum* offers little clue to the antimidwife campaign, some social scientists in Germany have recently suggested that midwives represented a threat to procreation because they knew the herbal arts of contraception and abortion. In a time when European populations had been decimated by plagues, the Church sought to rebuild its people. Disease, schism, Muslims, and infidels of all stripe seemed to be at the door of Catholicism. Midwives, with their contraceptive "magic," seemed to the Inquisition to exacerbate the problems, and this may be why they became prime suspects in the witch trials. See Gunnar Heinsohn and Otto Steiger, "Witchcraft, Population Catastrophe and Economic Crisis in Renaissance Europe: An Alternative Macroeconomic Explanation," University of Bremen, 2004, IKSF Discussion Paper 31.

25. See Institoris, *Malleus Maleficarum*, part I, question 4; part II, chapter 4 for discussions of incubi and succubi.

26. For all the Inquisition's convictions about the threat of succubi and incubi monsters, they were still plagued with the philosophical problem of an immaterial spiritual substance (having no spatial magnitude) actually moving a material substance (which has spatial magnitude). Because every action occurs from some sort of contact, we are left wondering where the contact point would be between a bodiless spirit and a physical body. The two different metaphysical substances can't find any meeting ground. Asking a spirit to move a human is like asking the abstract number 4 to move a rock. One half-hearted attempt to broach the problem is to make the demon a *carrier* of earthly semen rather than a *producer* of spirit semen. In this way, we don't have the impossibly difficult job of explaining how immaterial spirit seed enters a human womb to produce an actual metaphysical hybrid. Aware of the conundrum, Institoris says that contact between an evil spirit and a human body is not really physical, but only *virtualis*. But then he seems to gloss over the problem by reminding us that spirits are always running around gathering material seeds of every kind in order to cause unpredictable mayhem. In effect, he simply chooses to press ahead and leave the vexed question behind. Apart from this issue of demon-human interaction, the whole issue of how a spirit substance interacts with a material substance is at the core of Catholic dogma itself. The Savior, after all, is himself a metaphysical hybrid. All the same questions can be asked about how Mary immaculately conceived and how the Christ became a carpenter's son. And, just so I don't leave the impression that it's a strictly religious puzzle, one has to add the continuing scientific problem of mind-body interaction.

27. Institoris, *Malleus Maleficarum*, part I, question 1.

28. The werewolf discussion occurs in ibid., part I, question 10.

29. He marshals scriptural precedence for this view: Leviticus 26 and Deuteronomy 32.

30. The *Canon Episcopi* is probably a ninth-century Frankish document (sometimes thought to originate in the fourth century), and its short text on witches had become canon law by the time of the *Malleus*. It characterizes the psychological theory that I've been sketching and that Institoris was reacting against. Roughly speaking, witches are just very confused about their own powers and experiences (delusions), but this still makes them dangerous heretics because they tend to infect other

innocents with their promises of satanic power, and that betrayal is still real even if the magical powers are imaginary. The *Canon Episcopi* famously formulated the scenario of groups of women (hallucinating themselves to be) riding through the air for great distances.

31. Alchemy was a positive practice in Islamic *scientia* for centuries, but when the texts and ideas flowed into Europe after the expulsion of the Moors it came to be seen as a threatening alternative knowledge base with infidel origins. Alchemy became associated with the black arts and heresy, but ironically many of the research programs of alchemy (e.g., the transformation of natural substances) became the foundations of later chemistry. The Dominicans Aquinas and Albertus Magnus and the Franciscan Roger Bacon originally tolerated alchemy, trying to submit its claims to rational criteria. But by the fourteenth century alchemy was outlawed in many places. See Roslynn D. Haynes, *From Faust to Strangelove* (Johns Hopkins University Press, 1994), chapter 1.

32. The idea that nature is filled with invisible seeds of transformation (*rationes seminales*) was very useful to theologians like Augustine, who used the concept whenever he needed to explain natural growth, development, or evolution in a monotheistic paradigm of "fiat creationism" that precluded such transformation. Ecclesiastes 18:1 states that all things were created by God simultaneously (*qui vivit in aeternum creavit omnia simul*), but Genesis gives us a staggered creation over time. Augustine's idea of germs of forms existing within other forms helped to make consistent the *unrolling* of creation and the simultaneous *miracle* of creation. Institoris seems to be drawing on this tradition to help him explain demon creative power.

33. Institoris points out that such demonic alterations of nature can never violate the ways of nature (e.g., bring a dead man to life), but only speed up, slow down, or mix or otherwise mutate changes that could happen anyway (theoretically).

34. For detailed discussion of women's susceptibility to evil, see Institoris, *Malleus Maleficarum*, part I, question 6.

35. See ibid., part II, chapter 6.

CHAPTER 9

1. For a more detailed version of the story of Linnaeus's hydra, see Wilfrid Blunt and William T. Stearn, *Linnaeus: The Compleat Naturalist* (Princeton University Press, 2002).

2. See Harriet Ritvo, *The Platypus and the Mermaid* (Harvard University Press, 1997), chapter 1.

3. See Andy Orchard's fine translation of *Liber Monstrorum* in the appendix to *Pride and Prodigies*.

4. The *Liber Monstrorum* is a strange Latin text that boldly criticizes many specific beliefs in monsters, but then undercuts its own skeptical posturing by relishing the detailed descriptions of these creatures. It officially takes the epistemic high ground of incredulity, but then can't seem to get enough of its own taboo subject. The classicist Andy Orchard offers a more compelling interpretation of this monster critique, suggesting that close attention to the text reveals that the greatest criticism is always leveled against non-Christian legends, not monsters per se. It is "the pagans" with "their rumor-filled talk," according to the author of the *Liber Monstrorum*, that fill our heads with hydras, gorgons, headless men (Epifugi or Blemmyae), and harpies.

5. See Aleks Pluskowski, "Apocalyptic Monsters: Animal Inspirations for the Iconography of Medieval North European Devourers," in *The Monstrous Middle Ages*, edited by Bettina Bildauer and Robert Mills (University of Toronto Press, 2004). For more

discussion of the relationship between the bestiary tradition and the rise of natural history, see Stephen Asma, *Stuffed Animals and Pickled Heads* (Oxford University Press, 2001), chapters 3, 4. Local animals were given symbolic Christian interpretations in these influential texts, creating layers of metaphysical and moral meaning on top of the observable natural world. Edward Topsell's (1572–1625) bestiary, for example, explicitly states the purpose of studying animals: "For the knowledge of man, many and most excellent rules for public and private affairs, both for preserving a good conscience and avoiding the evil danger, are gathered from beasts."

6. L. Jardine and M. Silverthorne, eds., *Francis Bacon: The New Organon* (Cambridge Texts in the History of Philosophy, Cambridge University Press, 2000), book II.

7. Francis Bacon, *The New Atlantis and The Great Instauration* (Harlan Davidson, 1989).

8. For a nuanced treatment of Browne's place in the development of critical natural history, see Kevin Killeen, " 'The Doctor Quarrels with Some Pictures': Exegesis and Animals in Thomas Browne's *Pseudodoxia epidemica*," *Early Science and Medicine* 12, no. 1 (2007).

9. Sir Thomas Browne, *Pseudodoxia Epidemica*, book III, chapter 11. In book II, chapter 20 of Alexander Ross's 1652 *Arcana Microcosmi*, the more credulous Scottish author tries to undo Browne's skepticism and reinstall some integrity to the griffin legend. He argues that many other hard-to-believe hybrid creatures exist, so why not the griffin? "Many other sorts of mixt animals we read of, as flying Cats, and flying fishes; and some kinds of Apes with Dogges heads, therefore called Cynocephali." He makes the classic pro-cryptid move, arguing that there are many unexplored regions in this vast world, and perhaps the griffin lives in these remote lands. But as empiricism grew, Ross became part of the losing side in the battle between credulity and skepticism.

10. Ritvo, *Platypus and the Mermaid*, chapter 4.

11. Madeleine Doran, "On Elizabethan 'Credulity,' " *Journal of the History of Ideas* 1, no. 2 (1940).

12. See Mark Burnett, *Constructing Monsters in Shakespearean Drama and Early Modern Culture* (Palgrave, 2002) for a cultural studies analysis of specific plays and characters. The study is notable for its interesting discussion of the relationship between traditional fairground theater and nearby monster booths.

13. Charles Waterton, *Wanderings in South America* (Century Publishing, 1984), first journey, chapter 1. All quotes from Waterton are from this source.

14. Ibid., third journey, chapter 1.

15. See the Reverend J. G. Wood's biographical essay on Waterton in *Wanderings in South America*.

16. Ibid., fourth journey, chapter 2.

17. Selections from Sidney Smith's review can be found in the explanatory index of Waterton, *Wanderings in South America*.

18. See James W. Cook, "Introduction," *The Colossal P. T. Barnum Reader* (University of Illinois Press, 2005).

19. Quoted in James W. Cook, introduction to gallery 1, "Barnum's Serialized Writings," in *The Colossal P. T. Barnum Reader*.

20. For more detailed information about the Feejee Mermaid, see Jan Bondeson, *The Feejee Mermaid and Other Essays in Natural and Unnatural History* (Cornell University Press, 1999), and A. H. Saxon, *P. T. Barnum: The Legend and the Man* (Columbia University Press, 1989).

21. Gallery 4, *Colossal P. T. Barnum Reader*.

22. The Feejee Mermaid was an old taxidermy hybrid (possibly of Japanese origin) that first made its way to the United States in the possession of a sea captain, Samuel

Barrett Eades, in the 1820s. Captain Eades's son sold the creature to Moses Kimball, who proved to be Barnum's great friend and co-conspirator for many years. Kimball leased the monster to Barnum in 1842, and the rest, as they say, is history.

23. For example, a few days after the effusive *Philadelphia Public Ledger* story, the *Philadelphia Spirit of the Times* decried the Mermaid as a hoax and lambasted the *Ledger* for being suckered. But at the same time, the *New York Tribune* wrote:

> That Mermaid. Has arrived in this city on its way to the British Museum, and we were yesterday gratified with a private view of it. We tried hard to determine where or how some cute Yankee had joined a monkey's head to a fish's body, but had to give it up, though our incredulity still lingers. If such an animal ever *did* exist, it is surely the most extraordinary fact in Natural History. Believe it we can hardly; but how to account otherwise for what our eyes have seen staggers us. We should like to hear the opinion of better judges, after a rigid scrutiny.

See gallery 4, *Colossal P. T. Barnum Reader*.

24. A. H. Saxon, ed., *Selected Letters of P. T. Barnum* (Columbia University Press, 1983), letter 8.

25. Ibid., letter 24.

26. Gallery 2, *Colossal P. T. Barnum Reader*.

27. For an interesting discussion of Barnum's views on slavery and the "What Is It?" display, see Benjamin Reiss, *The Showman and the Slave* (Harvard University Press, 2001).

28. See Marc Hartzman, *American Sideshow* (Tarcher, 2006), part II.

CHAPTER 10

1. This pamphlet was found in the Newberry Library, Chicago, collected under the title *Reprints of English Books, 1475–1700*, edited by Foster. "Relation of a Terrible Monster called a Toad-fish" is found in file number 37 of the collection. I've taken the liberty of modernizing the spellings and grammar for the sake of readability.

2. See Katherine Park and Lorraine J. Daston's important and influential article "Unnatural Conceptions: The Study of Monsters in Sixteenth and Seventeenth Century France and England," *Past and Present*, no. 92 (1981).

3. See Wittkower, "Marvels of the East."

4. *Reprints of English Books, 1475–1700*, edited by Foster, file 34.

5. Sadler's text is included as an excerpt in the appendix of Ambroise Paré, *On Monsters and Marvels*, translated by Janis L. Pallister (University of Chicago Press, 1983). All quotations of Paré are from Pallister's translation.

6. Jean Ceard, *La Nature et les prodigies* (Droz, 1977; 2nd ed., 1996) has been decisive in shaping our understanding of Paré's naturalism.

7. Paré, *On Monsters and Marvels*, chapter 29.

8. See ibid., chapter 33 for Paré's reductionist materialist argument.

9. See ibid., chapter 20.

10. See ibid., preface.

11. He offers an illustrated tour of conjoined twins, parasitic anomalies, and hermaphrodites, all of which are explained by the presence of too much seed at the time of generation. "On the generating of monsters," Paré explains, "Hippocrates says that if there is too great an abundance of matter, multiple births will occur, or else a monstrous child having superfluous and useless parts, such as two heads, four arms, four legs, six digits on the hands and feet, or other things."

12. Paré, *On Monsters and Marvels*, chapter 1.

13. See ibid., chapter 9 for a discussion of the role of the imagination.

14. The Chinese also have a long tradition, still alive in rural areas, of monsters being produced by disturbing maternal perceptions and imaginings. For an interesting discussion of the relevant Qin Dynasty texts, see Frank Dikotter, *Imperfect Conceptions: Medical Knowledge, Birth Defects, and Eugenics in China* (Columbia University Press, 1998), "Torments of Imagination," chapter 2.

15. Galileo's letter to the grand duchess is his most famous articulation of the relationship between science and religion. He ties his humanism to a theological tether: "But I do not feel obliged to believe that the same God who has endowed us with senses, reason and intellect has intended us to forego their use and by some other means to give us knowledge which we can attain by them. He would not require us to deny sense and reason in physical matters which are set before our eyes and minds by direct experience or necessary demonstrations."

16. Descartes followed the important work of his British contemporary William Harvey (1578–1657), who first accurately described the circulatory system, using a mechanical paradigm. In his later studies Harvey became very interested in embryology, arguing for epigenesis over preformationism and even postulating the existence of a mammalian ovum.

17. René Descartes, *Discourse on Method*, translated by Lawrence J. Lafleur (Prentice Hall, 1960), part V.

18. It seems a significant testament to the difference between Descartes' age and our own that he assumes a familiarity on the part of his readers with freshly decapitated heads (and also assumes easy access to large animal hearts).

19. For an interesting interpretation of the change in La Mettrie's thinking from earlier to later writings, see Blair Campbell, "La Mettrie: The Robot and the Automaton," *Journal of the History of Ideas* 31, no. 4 (1970).

20. Julien Offray de La Mettrie, *Man a Machine*, translated by Gertrude Carman Bussey (Open Court, 1999).

21. As if he hadn't dealt enough blows to the egos of his readers, La Mettrie says that even smart people are not uniquely different from imbeciles. Idiots and insane people have brains, he says, but they are mechanically deficient or the tissues are "too soft." Change a tiny fiber in the brain machine, he suggests, and you could change Erasmus or Fontenelle into idiots.

22. Dr. Darwin is mentioned briefly in Percy Bysshe Shelley's introduction to the original 1818 edition of *Frankenstein*.

23. *Frankenstein*, vol. 1, chapter 4.

24. See Marilyn Butler, "*Frankenstein* and Radical Science," in the Modern Criticism section of Norton's Critical Edition of *Frankenstein*, edited by J. Paul Hunter (1996). Butler points out that the earliest versions of Shelley's Dr. Frankenstein show him as a scientific bumbler who knows "too little science rather than too much." The earliest versions of the story are not indictments of science itself.

25. Thomas Pynchon, in his essay "Is It O.K. to Be a Luddite?" *New York Times Book Review*, October 1984, underscores the traditional Romantic interpretation of *Frankenstein* by connecting Shelley, via her husband and Lord Byron, to Luddite anti-technology sympathies of the day.

26. One of the reasons for the now common interpretation that the monster has more humanity than his maker can be found in the fact that Frankenstein reads Paracelsus, Agrippa, and other "dubious" sources, while the monster educates himself on Milton, Goethe, and Plutarch.

27. Isaiah Berlin quotes this in *The Crooked Timber of Humanity*.

28. See Steven Marcus, "Frankenstein: Myths of Scientific and Medical Knowledge and Stories of Human Relations," *Southern Review* 38, no. 1 (2002) for a nice summary of the many ways "Frankenstein" has been employed as a cultural adjective.

29. Although Shelley never met Hunter—he died a few years before she was born—she certainly knew of him. Hunter had trained the physician Anthony Carlisle, who presided over Shelley's mother, Mary Wollstonecraft, while she lay dying (shortly after giving birth to Mary Shelley). John Hunter, who started from quite humble Scottish beginnings, eventually became surgeon to King George III, and after Hunter's death his astounding anatomy and physiology collection became the pride of the Royal College of Surgeons. Hunter and his collection inspired a posthumous yearly lecture series that brought renown and controversy to the Royal College of Surgeons, including the lectures of Shelley's friend William Lawrence.

30. For a description of Hunter's eccentric experiments and specimens, especially as they relate to museology, see Asma, *Stuffed Animals and Pickled Heads*. Also see Wendy Moore's biography *The Knife Man* (Broadway Books, 2005).

31. In his 1837 Hunterian Lectures, Richard Owen described Hunter's contribution:

> With respect to Monstrosities in general, Hunter had drawn out a scheme for their classification, and had produced them by experiment. In the Animal Economy he states that every Species of Animal, and every part of an animal body is subject to malformation, but that this is not a freak of Nature, or a matter of mere chance;—for he observes that every species has a disposition to deviate from Nature in a manner peculiar to itself. It is this principle that forms the basis of the latest and most elaborate Treatise on Monsters, a Work, which Geoffroy St. Hilaire describes as being "the result of having established, by great number of researches, that Monsters are, like the Beings called Normal, subject to Constant rules."

My quotes from Owen's lectures are taken from Philip Reid Sloan's excellent edition of *The Hunterian Lectures in Comparative Anatomy, May and June 1837* (University of Chicago Press, 1992).

32. Ibid., lecture 4, notes section. Karl Ernst Von Baer (1792–1876) seemingly refuted this "law of parallelism" when he demonstrated that "the embryo of a higher animal form never resembles the adult of any other animal form, but only its embryo." Von Baer saw this refutation, erroneously, as a derailment of evolutionism. But in the 1880s Frank Balfour asked a nagging question that resisted Von Baer's generalization: "[Why do animals] undergo in the course of their growth a series of complicated changes, during which they acquire organs which have no function, and which, after remaining visible for a short time, disappear without leaving a trace?" The philosopher Ron Amundson clarifies: "Hypothetical ancestors can be used to explain gill arches and notochords in mammalian embryos. Von Baer's laws cannot." For an excellent discussion of these issues, see Amundson's *The Changing Role of the Embryo in Evolutionary Thought* (Cambridge University Press, 2005). The quotes from Von Baer and Balfour are from Amundson's chapters 3 and 5, respectively.

33. For a provocative earlier theory that combined preformation ideas with evolution, see Gottfried Wilhelm Leibniz's (1646–1716) idiosyncratic "Monadology." In section 74 he writes:

> Philosophers formerly have been very perplexed concerning the origin of forms, entelechies, or souls. Today, however, it has been discovered through precise observations made on plants, insects, and animals that the organized bodies of nature are never produced out of chaos or putrefaction, but always out of seeds, in

which doubtless there has been some *preformation*. Hence it has been concluded, not only that the organized body was already in the seed before conception, but also that there was a soul in this body, and, in short, the animal itself.

34. Owen, *Hunterian Lectures*, lecture 4.
35. Apparently Hunter was the first British scientist to observe and describe the egg-tooth that grows on fetal chicken beaks (the Italian Aldrovandi had actually seen it long before). The "little horny knob at the end of the beak" enables chicks to crack out of their shells. See *Descriptive Catalogue of the Physiological Series in the Hunterian Museum of the Royal College of Surgeons of England* (E. & S. Livingstone, 1971), vol. 2.
36. Owen, *Hunterian Lectures*, lecture 4.
37. The cyclops is better understood as a fusion of two eyes. William Lawrence's entry on "Monsters" in Abraham Reece's *Cyclopedia* anatomized cyclops faces and repeatedly found two optic nerves joined together. "Indeed, in all the instances there have been more or less plain marks of the apparently single organ being composed of the parts of two eyes." This insight probably predates, just barely, Geoffroy's *soi pour soi* explanation of cyclops formation, but the important point is that such mechanical lawful explanations had begun to dominate the discussion of monsters.
38. See Armand Marie LeRoi, *Mutants: On Genetic Variety and the Human Body* (Viking, 2003), chapter 2.
39. William Lawrence, "Monster," in *Cyclopedia*, compiled by Abraham Rees (Longman, Hurst, Rees, Orme and Brown, 1819), vol. 24. All references to the *Cyclopedia* are drawn from an unpaginated original text in the Newberry Library, Chicago.
40. Lawrence begins his encyclopedia entry with a definition: "Monster, in Anatomy and Physiology, a creature in whom the body in general, or some large and conspicuous part of it, deviates remarkably from the accustomed formation. The union of the two eyes into one, with deficiency of the nose, the want of the brain, and of its membranous and bony coverings, the various more or less complete junctions of two bodies, &c. come under this description. A considerable deviation from the ordinary form or structure of a particular part or organ is often called a monstrous formation."
41. Lawrence tells a miserable story:

> In one case, where the bones were wanting, but an imperfect cerebrum seemed to exist, the child lived six days. The child was perfectly formed, excepting the head, and of usual size. It took no food and had no evacuation. Respiration went on naturally: it did not cry, but often made a hideous whining noise. When the soft substance at the top of the head was touched, general and violent convulsions took place. No signs of voluntary motions appeared, and the mother had less feeling of the child in utero, than in her former pregnancy.

42. Here he adds a short addendum to his point, one that must have seemed obvious to his 1819 peers but that would soon prove highly contentious for Darwin's generation. Lawrence says that nature could certainly make many possible extreme variations that would live and flourish rather than perish quickly, "but this would interfere with another principle, which seems to prevail extensively in the operations of nature—preservation of uniformity in the species."
43. "How does it happen," he asks, "that the head should be destroyed in all cases just so far as the orbits?" These and other such arguments refine Lawrence's belief that internal fusions might arise in utero, causing such monsters as conjoined twins or parasite or autosite twins, but sudden external force does not appear to create monsters.

44. Here Lawrence takes the high ground against teleologists like Haller, but his own ground is not quite as high as he thinks, since he's just given a similarly speculative argument about monster variations being held in check by nature's interest in preserving "uniformity in the species." Von Haller supported his idea that violence damaged the acephalic (headless) children by saying that it was contrary to the wisdom of nature to create arteries, veins, and nerves in a skull that was destined to be brainless. "This is a dangerous argument," Lawrence countered. "Is it not equally contradictory that a rectum should be formed without an anus, since life cannot be continued without such an opening? If nature be so wise and careful, why did she not provide against the destruction of the head? And why does she go on working, month after month, to no purpose, in constructing the numerous other monsters, which are incapable of life?"

45. Our current scientific understanding of teratology is still in its infancy. Roughly speaking, we know that 25 percent of anomalous births are attributable to known genetic and chromosomal factors (e.g., fragile X syndrome, Huntington's disease, Down syndrome, cystic fibrosis), and 10 percent are attributable to environmental factors (e.g., chemical teratogens, virus infections, radiation), leaving 65 percent to unknown causes. We now know that most (90 percent) malformed fetuses are spontaneously aborted before birth (compared with only 18 percent of phenotypically normal conceptuses). Those anomalous humans who survive to birth make up between 2 and 7 percent of total human births.

CHAPTER 11

1. See Evelleen Richard's discussion of Robert Knox in "A Political Anatomy of Monsters, Hopeful and Otherwise," *Isis* 85 (1994).

2. This makes more sense when we remember that no one at this time knew what a proper "gene" was. We, on the other side of the neo-Darwinian synthesis, think of the "germ" in purely material chemical terms, but in the 1830s there was more conceptual room to imagine teleological forces at work in the mysterious unit of heredity. Owen argued for a teleo-directed monsterology of preset saltations. The historian Evelleen Richards explains, "By appropriating Hunter's endogenous explanation of teratological change, and the evidence Hunter adduced in its support, Owen was able to oppose Geoffroy's materialistic emphasis on external causation and to validate his own teleomechanism of divinely preprogrammed evolutionary change in the embryo." See Richards's "A Political Anatomy of Monsters."

3. In 1838 Darwin filled his red Notebook D with a summary and gloss of John Hunter's book *Animal Economy*. Darwin's new friend Richard Owen was editing Hunter's work and also lecturing on it at this time, so one finds a mishmash of Hunter's and Owen's ideas about monsters in Notebook D. Darwin focused his musings on the issue of reproduction and whether it had importance for species transmutation.

4. Despite their disagreements, the teratologists still learned much from each other's research. Owen even quotes, approvingly, Isidore Geoffroy Saint-Hilaire's claim that his father had risen above previous theorists: "It was from precisely opposing principles that my father took as his point of departure; and it was also, as it must be, to precisely opposing results that he arrived. Establishing, through a great number of investigations, that monsters are, like those beings said to be normal, subordinated to constant laws, he was led to admit that the method of classification that naturalists employed for the latter, might be applied with success to the former." Thanks to my colleague Kate Hamerton for improving my translation of the French. The

passage is taken from the section of Owen's notes, found in Paul H. Barrett et al.'s edition of Notebook D in *Charles Darwin's Notebooks 1836–1844* (British Museum and Cornell University Press, 1987). All references to Darwin's Notebooks are from Barrett's edition.

5. Apparently Owen sermonized Darwin on the matter regularly, even suggesting to him that such a "production of monsters" presented an "analogy to the production of species." See Notebook B, entry 161. My subsequent discussion of Owen's use of monsters is heavily indebted to Richards, "Political Anatomy of Monsters." For more detailed information on Owen's complex, and sometimes confusing, theories of transmutation, see Nicolas Rupke, *Richard Owen: Victorian Naturalist* (Yale University Press, 1994), and Adrian Desmond, *Archetypes and Ancestors* (University of Chicago Press, 1982), as well as Desmond's *The Politics of Evolution* (University of Chicago Press, 1989).

6. See Darwin, Notebook C, no. 86.

7. This epistemic problem of determining which traits are adaptations and which are simply inherited as neutral continues to trouble some contemporary intellectuals. Jerry Fodor, "Why Pigs Don't Have Wings," *London Review of Books* 18 (October 2007), for example, engages in much hand-wringing over the seeming impossibility of settling such a question. He worries that we have no objective criteria for weighing which traits of an organism are selected for as adaptations versus those that simply piggyback onto the selected traits. We have stats to show that curly tails and tameness are correlated traits in dog populations; we can ask, Fodor points out, if natural selection is targeting tameness, and curly tails are accidental byproduct correlations, or the other way around. It is interesting that Darwin himself was worried as early as the 1830s about the epistemic implications of his budding theory. I tend to think that Fodor's worry is rather exaggerated. Even his own example of tameness (or less aggression) versus curly tail seems to resolve relatively easily. Only the most dogged skepticism (oh, the puns keep coming) would fail to acknowledge the relevance of aggression and tameness to survival, and therefore more likely subjects of selection, whereas curly tails comparatively speaking seem to be the proper candidates for free-rider status. The criticism that we don't have absolute nomological certainty about the relevance of aggression and tameness strikes me as a futile leftover from logical positivism.

8. Darwin's cousin and longtime friend William Darwin Fox had a fascination with hybrid animal breeding, and in Notebook D Charles rehearses a whole series of empirical facts drawn from William's many stories. Hybrids are considered, with special attention to subsequent offspring: dogs bred with wolves, long- and short-necked geese, blue-eyed deaf cats, common and muscovy ducks, and more.

9. Darwin, Notebook D, nos. 12–18.

10. Darwin, Notebook E, no. 3 reveals his first application of Malthus's ideas from *An Essay on the Principle of Population* to the whole range of organic relations.

11. Charles Darwin, *The Origin of Species* (1859 edition), chapter 1, "Variation under Domestication."

12. For example, French bulldogs, artificially selected for flat faces, often give birth to offspring with severe cleft palate. Man, in his history of animal domestication, has created some Frankenstein creatures. Darwin says that man "often begins his selection by some half-monstrous form; or at least by some modification prominent enough to catch his eye, or to be plainly useful to him." In this same passage he plays with the Designer metaphor of natural selection. "Can we wonder," he asks, "that nature's productions should be far 'truer' in character than man's productions; that they should be infinitely better adapted to the most complex conditions of life, and should plainly bear the stamp of far higher workmanship?" Ibid.

13. Darwin's gentle argument with the American naturalist Asa Gray is well known as an example of teleological confusion surrounding natural selection. Gray, who was in most regards very helpful to Darwin's reception in America, nonetheless received a rebuke from Darwin when Gray argued that the Author of nature foreordained the course of evolution. In a letter to Gray, Darwin writes, "If the right variations occurred, and no others, natural selections would be superfluous." Gray was arguing that far from destroying the "argument from design," Darwin in fact buttressed it. Cynthia Russett, in *Darwin in America: The Intellectual Response 1865–1912* (Freeman, 1976), points out that "Asa Gray was...a very distinguished scientist as well as a convinced Christian. But he was not a professional philosopher, and on the question of Darwin's relevance to the argument from design he seems to have been quite wrong."

14. Darwin's eventual theory could explain more than just adaptations. For a discussion of the causal pluralism of Darwin's mature theory, see Stephen T. Asma, "Darwin's Causal Pluralism," *Biology and Philosophy* 11, no. 1 (1996).

15. The homologous body plans of diverse animals were reinterpreted by Darwin as morphological evidence of common ancestry, not evidence of God's divine Ideas. Bats, men, moles, and whales share body plans because they have a distant common ancestor, not because a transcendental archetype is instantiated in them. Darwin believed that homologies give us a glimpse into the flesh-and-blood creatures of our phylogenetic past.

16. For a nice analysis of the various non-Darwinian evolution theories of this time, see Peter Bowler, *The Eclipse of Darwinism* (Johns Hopkins University Press, 1983).

17. Hugo de Vries, *Species and Varieties: Their Origin by Mutation* (Open Court Publishing, 1904), lecture 19, "Experimental Pedigree Cultures."

18. "The struggle for life and natural selection are manifestly inadequate to give even the slightest indication of an explanation of this case. It is simply impossible to imagine the causes that might have produced such a character. The only way out of this difficulty is to assume that it has arisen at once, in its present apparently differentiated and very variable condition, and that, being quite uninjurious and since it does not decrease the fertility of the race, it has never been subjected to natural selection, and so has saved itself from destruction." De Vries continues the argument by extrapolating to other normal plant morphologies: "But if we once grant the probability of the origin of the 'Nepaul-barley' by a sudden mutation, we obviously must assume the same in the case of the Helwingia and other normal instances. In this way we gain a further support for our assertion, that even the strangest specific characters may have arisen suddenly." Lecture 22, "Taxonomic Anomalies."

19. My discussion of Goldschmidt is informed by Michael R. Dietrich, "Richard Goldschmidt: Hopeful Monsters and Other Heresies," *Nature Reviews: Genetics* 4 (January 2003). Also see Stephen Jay Gould's introduction to a reissue of Goldschmidt's *The Material Basis of Evolution* (Yale University Press, 1982).

20. The neo-Darwinians were strenuously reasserting Darwin's gradualist micromutation theory, reformulating it as a part of the new population genetics. The idea of a steady stream of tiny mutations fit nicely with the emerging statistical methods of quantitative genetics, whereas qualitative jumps, such as Goldschmidt's hopeful monsters, did not. The major players of the neo-Darwinian synthesis were Julian Huxley, Theodosius Dobzhansky, Ernst Mayr, George Gaylord Simpson, J. B. S. Haldane, and Sewall Wright. Simpson and Goldschmidt, in particular, argued with each other in their respective writings.

21. Quotes of Pere Alberch are taken from his watershed article, "The Logic of Monsters: Evidence for Internal Constraint in Development and Evolution," *Geobios*, memoire special, no. 12 (1989).

22. Alberch approvingly refers back to the teratological work of his predecessors, such as the Geoffroys, in this case of the three-headed monster.
23. My discussion of Gould's example is drawn from his article "Eight Little Piggies," collected in his book *Eight Little Piggies: Reflections in Natural History* (Norton, 1993).
24. Using his logic of monsters, Alberch showed how the developmental construction of limbs consists of three fundamental processes: branching (the development of two series from one), segmentation (repetition of the same element), and condensation (fusion between elements). A forelimb, for example, builds outward from the shoulder to the fingers and involves a branching construction, pursuant to the humerus, of the ulna and radius. Further branching builds the wrist bones, and then the digits are composed by segmentation. See Neil Shubin and Pere Alberch, "A Morphogenetic Approach to the Origin and Basic Organization of the Tetrapod Limb," in *Evolutionary Biology*, vol. 20, edited by Max Hecht, Bruce Wallace, and Sir Ghillean T. Prance (Plenum Publications, 1986).
25. To be more precise, the penultimate, rather than the ultimate, digit is built first and then forward to the first digit, and back one.
26. Moreover, when animal populations have lost digits, like the horse, they seem to have lost them (morphologically speaking) in the same reverse sequence.
27. Notice that Alberch's logic of development does not give us some absolutely necessary sequence of inevitable body plans; after all, we know that fossil tetrapods can have five, six, seven, or even eight digits. But it does give us a fundamental internal constraint system that can be turned on for longer or shorter periods and thereby provide predictable morphological consequences.
28. A close reading of Gould suggests, however, that this "vindication" is more of a rhetorical device, helping raise awareness for a historically ignored area of study (development). Gould redefines "hopeful monster" in a way that keeps it under the umbrella of Darwinism, and therefore confusingly uses the term differently than Goldschmidt. In his article "The Return of Hopeful Monsters," *Natural History* 86 (June/July 1977), Gould argues that small changes in the embryological "constraint systems" (such as the timing mutation to stop or continue digit building) can produce large morphological transformations in the adult, and possibly macro-evolutionary pathways.
29. See Israel Rosenfield and Edward Ziff, "Evolving Evolution," *New York Review of Books* 53, no. 8 (2006).
30. The same question regarding discrete form and matter was raised at the organismal level of biology. Technically, every cell *can* make the whole organism, in the sense that it contains all the information code. But although each cell has the entire recipe, its job is to specialize and build and maintain something quite particular (muscle, bone, blood, etc.). We might have expected that cells would have only information on a need-to-know basis, like a foot soldier who gets only a part of the overall tactical plan. In fact, they have the entire plan inside them, but chemical gatekeepers are rationing out very limited parts of the total information.
31. My description of Scott Holley's work is drawn from his public lecture "Fish 'n Clocks: How the Vertebral Column Is Segmented in Zebrafish Embryogenesis," delivered on December 6, 2007, as part of the Science and Mathematics Colloquium Series, Columbia College, Chicago. For a more technical articulation of his recent work, see his essay "The Genetics and Embryology of Zebrafish Metamerism," *Developmental Dynamics* 236 (2007).
32. Zebra fish make great models because their process of vertebral construction takes only about twenty-five hours to complete, whereas the same development in humans

takes six weeks. Add to this the fact that zebra fish are transparent and therefore easy to observe in terms of internal development.

33. A simple illustration can be seen in the extremely protracted juvenile traits of humans when compared with other primates, such as chimps. Maximum brain growth for chimps is concluded around one year of age, whereas humans continue until their late teens. The bodily or somatic maturing of an animal can be quite delayed or reduced, especially when compared with phylogenetic relatives, but the sexual maturation of the same animal can seem accelerated by comparison.

34. See Sean B. Carrol, *Endless Forms Most Beautiful: The New Science of Evo-Devo* (Norton, 2005). My quotations are taken from chapter 11.

CHAPTER 12

1. In 1962 S. Shachter and J. Singer demonstrated in their paper "Cognitive, Social, and Physiological Determinants of Emotional State" (*Psychological Review* 69) that an emotion requires both a physiological arousal and a correlate cognition. For example, subjects injected with adrenalin do not automatically have an emotional response to the chemical. However, when the subject is first questioned about a painful event, then the injection will trigger an upsetting emotional response. The cognitive interpretation of, or even just correlation with, physiological arousal is crucial to defining the subsequent felt emotion; the cognitive aspect is not just an epiphenomenon of the chemical. This question of the relationship between cognitive and affective states has an earlier incarnation in the disagreement between William James and Walter Cannon. As Rami Gabriel points out in *Affective Reactions in a Prosopagnosic Patient* (PhD dissertation, University of California at Santa Barbara, 2007), "William James (1890) argued that the internal changes occur because of an arousing event, and we subsequently interpret these internal feelings as an emotion. Cannon (1929) disagreed claiming that the same changes occur in the internal organs in a range of emotional responses, so it is implausible that one emotion is attached to one particular feeling, furthermore artificial changes brought about by for example, adrenalin do not necessarily produce an emotional feeling." I am indebted to Dr. Gabriel for steering me to this important debate.

2. In the 1940s a psychologist named Donald Hebb continued Darwin's experiments on chimp fear of snakes and showed that infant chimpanzees who had no earlier exposure to snakes were nonetheless terrified of them when first presented. Hebb continued to introduce novel objects and animals to the chimps and discovered something more subtle than just snake phobia. He concluded that chimps had alarmed and frightful responses to any extremely varied morphologies they encountered. When something in their perceptual field jumped out as radically different, it could not be processed by the cognitive categories already in place. As Melvin Konner describes it, "Against the background of knowledge already accumulated by the infant chimps, the new objects were different; they aroused many perceptual schemas or patterns stored in the brain but fitted into none, causing arousal and then fear. The brain was somehow designed to generate fear as the result of such a cognitive mismatch." See Melvin Konner's description of Donald Hebb's, Wolfgang Schleidt's, and Mary Ainsworth's experiments in *The Tangled Wing* (Times Books, 2002), chapter 10.

3. Noel Carroll's theorizing about horror can be found in *The Philosophy of Horror* (Routledge, 1990).

4. H. P. Lovecraft, *Supernatural Horror in Literature* (Dover Publications, 1973).

5. The contrast between fear and angst is articulated in Martin Heidegger, *Being and Time* (Blackwell, 1978), part I, chapter 6, "Care as the Being of Dasein."

6. See Immanuel Kant, *Critique of Judgment* (Hackett, 1987), part I, section 27.

7. For Kant, the sublime is an experience of incoherence that results when reason sets a task for the mind for which it does not have enough power to complete. Looking at the night sky, for example, and trying to envision the expanse of space and time stretching before us is a task that cannot be adequately completed. He contrasts this incoherent magnitude with a different kind of incoherent magnitude, which he calls a *monstrous* magnitude. He uses *monstrous* as a technical term to designate an object that contradicts itself, something of a size that renders its own purpose or function impossible. It's hard to know what he means here, except that he may be thinking of absurd objects, such as staircases that are so monumentally big that no one can climb them. Or perhaps he's imagining an animal whose head is so large that it cannot move. In this strict definition, Kant's "sublime" and "monstrous" are both species of incoherence, but with different origins and implications. See *Critique of Judgment*, part I, section 26.

8. Schopenhauer's most formal presentation of this philosophy can be found in his 1819 *Die Welt als Wille und Vorstellung, The World as Will and Representation*, in two volumes (Dover, 1966). See Bryan Magee's interesting discussion of Schopenhauer's influence on subsequent artists in *The Philosophy of Schopenhauer* (Oxford University Press, 1997), part II.

9. The highly emotional and subjective interests of Expressionist art (of which horror might be seen as a subspecies) manifest the philosophical trajectory I've been sketching. The art of human vulnerability and the sense of cosmic fear can be seen in the famous shrieking face of Edvard Munch's *The Scream* (1893). In addition to painting works called *Anxiety* and *Despair*, Munch is reported to have said, "Sickness, insanity, and death were the angels that surrounded my cradle and they have followed me throughout my life." One finds these artistic tendencies toward terror in earlier works as well, in Bosch, El Greco, and Goya.

10. The famous line about nature "red in tooth and claw" is from Tennyson's 1850 poem *In Memoriam A. H. H.*, but it was often applied to Darwinian natural selection. The quote from Thomas Henry Huxley is taken from his 1893 *Romanes Lecture* and can be found in *Darwin: A Norton Critical Reader*, 2nd ed., edited by Philip Appleman (Norton, 1979).

11. As we've already seen in our discussion of Plato, among others, the inner monsters of psychology are not really new at all. But it is fair to make a generalization at the level of paradigms and say that the twentieth century is comparatively subjective in its understanding of monsters.

12. Freud begins his essay by admitting the unorthodox nature of his crossover into aesthetics:

> The subject of the "uncanny" is a province of this kind. It is undoubtedly related to what is frightening—to what arouses dread and horror; equally certainly, too, the word is not always used in a clearly definable sense, so that it tends to coincide with what excites fear in general. Yet we may expect that a special core of feeling is present which justifies the use of a special conceptual term. One is curious to know what this common core is which allows us to distinguish as 'uncanny' certain things which lie within the field of what is frightening. ("The Uncanny," in *Studies in Parapsychology*, edited by Philip Rieff [Collier Books, 1963])

13. Bettina Bildhauer and Robert Mills point out that the German word for monster can be deconstructed in a manner similar to Freud's *uncanny*: "In the same way that Freud divides the word 'un-heimlich' to reveal its literal meaning, 'un-familiar' or 'un-homely,' so, too, the German word for monster, Ungeheuer, can similarly be split into two semantic units—'un-geheuer' likewise means 'un-familiar' or 'un-safe.'

From this it might be argued that monsters are the embodiment of something that is both familiar and foreign, disturbing and reassuring." "Conceptualizing the Monstrous," in *The Monstrous Middle Ages* (University of Wales Press, 2003). Also see Julia Kristeva, *The Powers of Horror: An Essay on Abjection* (Columbia University Press, 1982), and Judith Butler, *Bodies That Matter* (Routledge, 1993), for discussions of "abjection." Abjection is a cultural category, with *unheimlich* overlaps, designating a marginal, liminal being (or beings). Kristeva and Butler appear to be combining the categorical mismatch approach and the psychoanalytical approach to discuss horror and ultimately gender prejudice. I have not found Kristeva's and Butler's work very helpful in understanding monsters, or anything else really, but the work certainly has its own devoted following.

14. Beal, *Religion and Its Monsters*, introduction.

15. One of the first forms of repression that Freud details in the developmental sequence is the now classic case of potty training. "The excreta," Freud says, "arouse no disgust in children. They seem valuable to them as being a part of their own body which has come away from it. Here upbringing insists with special energy on hastening the course of development which lies ahead, and which should make the excreta worthless, disgusting, abhorrent and abominable." Repression transforms values, but, provided the repressions don't become neurotic, those transformations are usually healthy for social life. Freud adds the bold claim, "Anal erotism [infant attachment to excreta] succumbs in the first instance to the 'organic repression' which paved the way to civilization." *Civilization and Its Discontents* (Norton, 1961), chapter 4, note 1.

16. With regard to a theory of "doubles," Freud sees himself enlarging on the good start made by his colleague Otto Rank in his 1914 *Der Doppelganger*.

17. In early civilizations, Freud points out, kings and people of means often created replicas of themselves; artisans were enlisted to fabricate doubles and triples of the royal personage, often burying the additional selves with the original. One wonders if real identical twins feel anything like a lesser sense of finitude or a stronger sense of existential security. Do they feel as though their sibling is a backup copy of their own self (like a hard-drive backup)? The double was originally a positive demonstration or representation of the universal will-to-live (*conatus*). But our narcissistic desire to cheat death is impossible to sustain in the face of maturing experience. Reality reminds us as we are developing that we will not cheat death. To carry on in the fantasy world of the narcissistic pleasure principle is impossible given the brute facts of our animal nature.

18. Zombies, I would argue, are even more disturbing than doppelgangers, and Freud connects them to his psychoanalytic framework. The narcissistic desire for everlasting life is functionally repressed in the healthy adult, but he cannot escape its lure altogether. "Since almost all of us still think as savages do on this topic," Freud explains, "it is no matter for surprise that the primitive fear of the dead is still so strong within us and always ready to come to the surface on any provocation. Most likely our fear still implies the old belief that the dead man becomes the enemy of his survivor and seeks to carry him off to share his new life with him" ("The Uncanny," in *Studies in Parapsychology*, edited by Philip Rieff [Collier Books, 1963]). These uncanny experiences, often rehearsed in the horror genre, trigger complex paradoxical feelings, desires that were once positive but have transformed into negatives in the course of natural maturation. Undead monsters are particularly uncanny, I would argue, because they embody our narcissistic commitment to extended life, but also our mature commitment (via the reality principle) that no such possibility exists.

19. Freud writes, "The sight of Medusa's head makes the spectator stiff with terror, turns him to stone.... Thus in the original situation it offers consolation to the spectator; he is still in possession of a penis, and the stiffening reassures him of

that fact." "Medusa's Head" (1922, published posthumously in 1940), in *The Medusa Reader*, edited by Marjorie Garber and Nancy Vickers (Routledge, 2003). The fear of castration is a root cause, according to Freud, for the general male "horror of women." One is reminded of the *vagina dentata* myths that appear in many cultures: women with teeth in their vagina. We encountered this in an earlier chapter, when we looked at Renaissance travelers' tales (John Mandeville's *Travels*). In 2007 an independent film debuted at Sundance Film Festival called *Teeth*, which attempted to update the old toothed vagina myth. Interestingly, monstrous vaginas don't really fit Freud's theory, in which the vagina is the result of castration, rather than the cause of it.

20. See Lawrence Weschler's discussion of Masahiro Mori's work on the uncanny valley in "Why Is This Man Smiling?" *Wired* magazine, June 2002.

21. See David Hughes, interview with David Lynch, *Empire*, November 2001.

22. David Foster Wallace, "David Lynch Keeps His Head," in *A Supposedly Fun Thing I'll Never Do Again* (Back Bay Books, 1998).

23. Hughes, interview with David Lynch.

24. "Dream Team: Thyrza Nichols Goodeve Talks with the Brothers Quay," *Artforum*, April 1996. Also see Suzanne H. Buchan, "The Quay Brothers: Choreographed Chiaroscuro, Enigmatic and Sublime," *Film Quarterly*, spring 1998, for a more detailed connection between the Quays and sublime aesthetics. Some recent Japanese horror films and their American remakes, such as *Ju-on* (2003) and *The Grudge* (2004), *Ringu* (1998) and *The Ring* (2002), are aesthetically creepy in subtle ways that also explore the uncanniness of mundane objects, motions, and lights.

25. Socrates says, "The moral of the tale is, that anger at times goes to war with desire, as though they were two distinct things." *Republic*, book IV.

26. For a wonderful account of a lesser known serial offender, see Jan Bondeson, *The London Monster: A Sanguinary Tale* (Da Capo, 2002).

27. In *Shots in the Mirror* the criminologist Nicole Rafter draws a distinction between slasher and serial-killer films. She argues that slasher films are closely related to fairy tales and folklore in their celebration of unbelievable supernatural characters (e.g., Freddie from the *Nightmare on Elm Street* series, Michael from the *Halloween* series). The serial-killer genre, however, is more for adults. Rafter sees less humor and less supernaturalism in serial-killer films. The two different genres are made for different audiences, despite occasional overlap. See *Shots in the Mirror*, chapter 3, "Slashers, Serial Killers, and Psycho Movies."

28. Warren Kinsella, "Torture Porn's Dark Waters," *National Post*, June 7, 2007.

29. Mark Olsen, "King of Horror on Horror," *LA Times*, June 22, 2007. This defense seems almost hard to believe and disingenuous because it's unlikely that even the most devoted fans of torture porn would refer to it as "good art."

30. Quotes from E. Michael Jones are taken from the concluding chapter of *Horror: A Biography* (Spence Publishing, 2002).

31. To make his interpretation work, Jones regularly has to suggest that the explicit accounts of some directors cannot be trusted. Jones describes David Cronenberg (*Shivers, Scanners*) as unaware of the real meaning of his own films: "As anyone who has read one of his interviews could attest, David Cronenberg simply does not understand his own films or the forces that drive his own characters. This is precisely why Cronenberg is so good at doing horror. He is himself so completely and successfully secularized, that he can only mirror the incomprehension of the society he was describing in his horror films" ("Conclusion: Misreading Horror," in *Horror: A Biography*). Discounting artists' own explanations of their work seems a little strange at first, but Freudians have always made this same point, and perhaps Jones is no worse on this account. Add to this the earlier quote from David Lynch, who admits that he

doesn't really understand his own subject matter, and we might find it more reasonable to discount the conscious intentions of the filmmakers.

32. For a hilarious analysis of various films from a postmodern psychoanalytic perspective, see Slavoj Žižek's documentary with Sophie Fiennes, *Pervert's Guide to Cinema* (2006).

33. Aristotle's theory of cathartic tragedy is as relevant here as Freud's theory of libidinal release. See chapter 6 of Aristotle's *Poetics*.

34. "Capone and Eli Roth Discuss Horror Movies," interview, at *Ain't It Cool News* Web site, June 3, 2007.

35. The father continues, "You forget what you want to remember and you remember what you want to forget." Cormac McCarthy, *The Road* (Vintage Books, 2006).

36. The unforgettable torture images of cinema are trivial compared to the kinds of inner monsters that veterans have to carry around with them. The debilitating effects of posttraumatic stress disorder are well documented, and we know that long buried or repressed memories can resurface even decades later to wreak havoc on veterans' mental health. For a relatively sensitive discussion of a veteran whose Vietnam memories reawakened decades later, during the invasion of Iraq, see Kathy Dobie, "The Long Shadow of War," *GQ Magazine*, January 2008.

37. Sigmund Freud, *Inhibitions, Symptoms and Anxieties* (Norton, 1977), chapter 7.

38. I hasten to add that all this technology also gives us better access to previously hidden *beauty* in nature. But this is not a book about beauty, and so I'll have to lay emphasis on the more disturbing implications of the new aesthetic of nature.

39. Typical of the association of dinosaur fossils and monsters in the late nineteenth and early twentieth centuries is a book by the paleontology popularizer Rev. H. N. Hutchinson, *Extinct Monsters: A Popular Account of Some of the Larger Forms of Ancient Animal Life* (Chapman and Hall, 1892).

40. The description of the alien as "fanged, phallic and fetal" is from chapter 10 of David J. Skal, *The Monster Show* (Norton, 1993). See Skal's book for more discussion of the links between reproduction anxiety and films like *The Brood* and *Alien*.

CHAPTER 13

1. Quoted in Rummana Hussain, Lisa Donovan, and Mitch Dudek, "Campus Killer," *Chicago Sun-Times*, February 18, 2008.

2. Quotes taken from the Atlanta television companion Web site My Atlanta TV.com. See Denio O'Hayer, " 'Monster' Caught in Murder of Boy, 7," posted December 12, 2007, at www.myatltv.com/news/.

3. The story was reported widely in the British media in 2000 and 2001, when Beart received a life sentence, but these nauseating details are drawn from David Rose, "Crime: 'At the End of the Day, All of Us Sitting Here Are Monsters,' " *The Observer Magazine*, November 20, 2005.

4. Quoted in the English news magazine *The Week*, May 9, 2008.

5. Nathan Leopold, *Life Plus 99 Years* (Doubleday, 1958).

6. See ibid., chapter 1.

7. Robert Louis Stevenson, *The Strange Case of Dr. Jekyll and Mr. Hyde* (Norton, 2002), section titled "Henry Jekyll's Full Statement of the Case."

8. In the Leopold-Loeb case, "alienists" repeatedly interviewed the murderers, and defense attorney Clarence Darrow incorporated their findings into his ultimate argument for some clemency during the sentencing phase of the case. The *Tribune* reported that when the killers were spared the noose, the pro-defense alienist had

to be accompanied home by police guard in case an irate public should try to exact revenge.

9. Nietzsche has a way of speaking to the mania in some young men. Darrow was probably fishing for every defense angle he could find, and one hates to put stock in such a weird argument, especially because it has censorship implications. But every philosophy professor knows, and I speak from experience, that it is always the more wild-eyed kids in class who just can't get enough of the pugnacious German iconoclast. Sad to say that the NIU mass murderer, Steven Kazmierczak, also had a thing for Nietzsche and mailed his girlfriend Jessica Baty a copy of *The Antichrist* around the time he went on his spree. See the interview with Jessica Baty on CNN, February 17, 2008.

10. The Heine quote, and Freud's use of the adage *Homo homini lupus*, are taken from *Civilization and Its Discontents* (Norton, 1989), chapter 5.

11. In this chapter I am focusing on the more influential psychological ideas, but we cannot forget the popularity of post-Darwinian biological determinism. One of the most notable criminology theories was that of the Italian Cesare Lombroso (1836–1909), who, through a quirky interpretation of Darwin, argued for "born criminals." The criminal monsters, said Lombroso, gave themselves away by their "criminaloid" anatomy.

12. See Freud, *Civilization and Its Discontents*, chapter 7, note 10.

13. Of course, aggression is not all bad, and when sufficiently channeled it becomes the driving force in healthy ambition. Peter Gay discusses this aspect of aggression as a "will to mastery" and points out that "solving a tantalizing puzzle, climbing an unclimbable mountain, gaining proficiency in an obscure tongue, inventing a labor-saving device, are all in their way aggressive acts." See *Cultivation of Hatred* (Norton, 1993), appendix. In these more disguised forms, aggression shows up almost everywhere, and this reminds us that aggression itself may be only a heuristic reification of very different behaviors.

14. In praise of rage and other energizing emotional forces, Rollo May reminds us that modern life is filled with boredom, alienation, dullness, and safeness: "Violence puts the risk and challenge back, whatever we may think about its destructiveness; and no longer is life empty." Quoted in Stephen Diamond's fascinating book *Anger, Madness, and the Daimonic* (State University of New York Press, 1996), chapter 1, "The Angry American: An Epidemic of Rage and Violence."

15. Jack Katz, *Seductions of Crime* (Basic Books, 1988), chapter 1, "Righteous Slaughter."

16. The Leopold and Loeb case was often called the "trial of the century," as was Clarence Darrow's earlier "Scopes monkey trial" (1925).

17. I remind readers of the Hobbs case, another case where guilt is arguable, which I discussed in the introduction. Recall that in 2005 Jerry Hobbs was arrested for allegedly killing his eight-year-old daughter, Laura, and her nine-year-old friend, Krystal Tobias. Jerry Hobbs is alleged to have become enraged when his daughter defied his order to come home; he stabbed her twenty times (including once in each eye) and stabbed the Tobias girl eleven times. "This was a slaughter of two little girls," said chief deputy state's attorney Jaffrey Pavletic. "You can see the rage that was exhibited." Quoted in Dan Rozek, "Prosecutor: Girls Punched, Stabbed Many Times," *Chicago Sun-Times*, May 12, 2005. Again, I don't know if Hobbs is really guilty of this crime; a jury will decide. But the state's attorney and the media clearly use the language of the Freudian rage monster thesis. A *New York Daily News* article dated May 11, 2005, and written by Sean Hill and Corky Siemaszko blared a headline referring to an earlier Hobbs conviction, "Dad the Monster: Chain-saw Loving Ex-Con Charged in Brutal Slaying of IL Girls."

18. Stephen Diamond, *Anger, Madness, and the Daimonic* (State University of New York Press, 1996), chapter 6.

19. Plato, *Republic*, book IX.

20. Those who wish to maintain the parallels between *Forbidden Planet* and *The Tempest* might read this monster as an updated Caliban, the mongrel creature servant of Prospero. Caliban is severely treated in Shakespeare's play because he once tried to rape Prospero's daughter, Miranda, so he requires constant surveillance and domination. In Act 5, Scene 3, Prospero says of Caliban, "This thing of darkness I acknowledge mine."

21. Freud is assuming the dualism in his writings as early as the 1924 "The Economic Problem of Masochism," but Eros and Thanatos dominate the posthumous *Outline of Psychoanalysis* (1940).

22. See the highly entertaining note 7 in chapter 4 of *Civilization and Its Discontents*.

23. Like Leopold and Loeb, who were often later characterized as repressed homosexuals, the Columbine High School murderers, Eric Harris and Dylan Klebold, were inseparable mates. Harris and Klebold often suffered "faggot" and "homo" epithets at school. Harris's own suicide note reveals some of the motive for the attack and explicitly indicts his own repressive and abusive society. "By now, it's over. If you are reading this, my mission is complete," Harris writes. "Your children who have ridiculed me, who have chosen not to accept me, who have treated me like I am not worth their time are dead. They are fucking dead." He continues, "I may have taken their lives and my own—but it was your doing. Teachers, parents, let this massacre be on your shoulders until the day you die."

24. See Anthony Chase, "Violent Reaction: What Do Teen Killers Have in Common?" *In These Times*, July 9, 2001.

25. Martin Luther typifies a common Christian "monsterization" of Jews when says, "They are children of the Devil, condemned to the flames of hell…they have a God…he is called the Devil." Quoted in Gold, *Monsters and Madonnas*, chapter 17.

26. Ibid., chapter 15.

27. Ibid., epilogue.

28. Peter Gay, *The Cultivation of Hatred* (Norton, 1993), chapter 1, section 2.

29. Leopold, *Life Plus 99 Years*, chapter 2.

30. Strictly speaking, the unemotional monster is older than the twentieth century. It goes back at least to the accusations by Romantics, some of which we've looked at, against the cold clinical rationalists of the Enlightenment. But the earlier discussion was largely academic, artistic, and ideological, not usually applied to real criminology issues or cases. See Nathaniel Hawthorne's 1846 short story "The Birthmark" for a fictional version of a scientist who has lost his emotional core in the pursuit of abstraction.

31. Erle Stanley Gardner, introduction in Leopold, *Life Plus 99 Years*.

32. Leopold, *Life Plus 99 Years*, chapter 1.

33. One cannot be entirely sure whether Leopold has accurately reported the real meaning of his famous quip. It is possible that he was seeking to revise his own history in a charitable way. Ibid., chapter 2.

34. Personal communication with Michael Harvey. Harvey's novel *The Chicago Way* (Knopf, 2007) is based on his real life experiences with John Wayne Gacy. Harvey was also the creator and executive producer of the television documentary series *Cold Case Files*. He explained to me that Gacy and other such murderers have an intense need to dominate others:

> It's all about power and control. Power and control over the victims. Power and control over the police investigating the crimes. Power and control over the media covering the crimes. All of it feeds the serial killer's massive ego, makes him feel like he is the center of attention, and operates almost as an aphrodisiac for the killer. Many serial killers will go even further, attempting to exert control over their victims even after death. Killers

will keep bodies close by as "trophies," so they can revisit their victims and relive the crimes. Yes, power and control. The stuff of serial killer fantasy.

35. See Hare's now classic book *Without Conscience: The Disturbing World of Psychopaths among Us* (Guilford Press, 1999), but also his more recent book, coauthored with Paul Babiak, *Snakes in Suits: When Psychopaths Go to Work* (Regan Books, 2006) for an interesting discussion of corporate psychopaths. Now Hare only needs to write an additional volume on *academic* psychopaths.

36. Quoted in an interview with Kate Hilpern, "Office Hours, Beware: Danger at Work," *The Guardian*, September 27, 2004.

37. Quoted in Rose, "Crime."

38. Interview with Dick, by John Boonstra, in *Rod Serling's The Twilight Zone Magazine* 2, no. 3 (June 1982): 47–52.

39. Is there some additional property that entities must possess if they are to be considered persons? The philosophical strategy of *Blade Runner* is to slowly build up progressive layers of biological traits on originally inanimate objects (the replicants). And the question is tacitly asked at each stage: Do we have a "person" yet? How about if we add memories? How about if we add learning skills? And so on.

40. One of the crucial traits that *Blade Runner* adds to the replicants is *imagination*, which seems crucial to empathy. When Darwin wrote *The Descent of Man* (1872), he had to argue vehemently that nonhuman animals possess imagination. Prior to Darwin, the idea of animal imagination was both rare (because Descartes had persuaded many that animals had no minds) and heretical (for it seemed to imply some unholy kinship between man and animal). Darwin realized that this trait was a serious hurdle, pronouncing, "The Imagination is one of the highest prerogatives of man. By this faculty he unites former images and ideas, independently of the will, and thus creates brilliant and novel results" (chapter 3). But even so high a faculty as imagination, Darwin argued, could be found in animals, and the place to look for it was the dream. Dreaming is the involuntary art of poetry (chapter 3). If animals can dream, then they are "uniting former images and ideas" and "creating brilliant and novel results": they are imagining. Not unrelated is the original title of *Blade Runner*, Philip Dick's *Do Androids Dream of Electric Sheep?* The question posed here is whether a computer could ever dream at all.

41. The vaguely Christian symbolism is reinforced by Roy's receiving, just prior to the redemption, a nail through his hand.

42. Of course, Descartes would object that you still do not have certainty because the test itself must be read by the senses, and we know how fallible the senses can be.

43. See Matt Crenson, "What Makes a Sexual Predator?" Associated Press, September 6, 2005.

44. In *Anger, Madness and the Daimonic*, Stephen Diamond laments that "the most ascendant and widely accepted explanation for psychotic conditions such as schizophrenia or bipolar disorder (manic depressive illness) is the biochemical model, which presumes that there is an inherited, biochemical abnormality in certain people predisposing them to psychosis" (chapter 5).

45. I will simply state my official embrace of *causal pluralism* and move on to some specific experimental findings. By detailing a couple of brain-based case studies, I am not renouncing or downplaying the spiritual and existential dimensions of mental disorders—dimensions that, I think, can be correlated with rather than reduced to physiochemical events. I tend to agree in principle with George Engel's pluralistic biopsychosocial model of psychiatry, although its critics have pointed out that it lacks implementable details for a strong research program. See Engel's "The Need for a New Medical Model," *Science* 196 (1977).

46. My discussion of Dr. Kiehl's research is based on Crenson, "What Makes a Sexual Predator?"

47. Melvin Konner, *The Tangled Wing* (Times Books, 2002), chapter 10.

48. Information on Dr. Gray's research is taken from Paul Rowland, "Brain Biology of Psychopaths 'Lack Capacity to Interpret Fear,'" *The Western Mail*, December 5, 2006.

49. The lack of empathy that one finds in parts of the autistic spectrum, such as in Asperger's syndrome, has led to some highly speculative questions about neurological similarities with psychopaths. In "Does the Autistic Child Have a 'Theory of Mind'?" *Cognition* 21 (1985), psychologists Simon Baron-Cohen, Alan Leslie, and Uta Frith show empirical evidence that autistics have a much harder time than other mentally challenged subjects in their ability to impute beliefs to other people. Suffice it to say that psychopaths are a species unto themselves, and most autistics are entirely humane, loving, and gentle.

50. Information about Dr. Ralph Adolphs's research is drawn from his article "Damage to the Prefrontal Cortex Increases Utilitarian Moral Judgments," *Nature* 446 (April 2007).

51. Linda Mealey, "The Sociobiology of Sociopathy: An Integrated Evolutionary Model," *Behavioral and Brain Sciences* 18 (1995).

52. Personal communication with Michael Harvey. He went on to say, "There are, of course, many other factors that play into the dynamics here, and those factors will vary greatly from case to case. I just mean to point out that this type of childhood abuse appears to be a common denominator and, perhaps, sets off a chain reaction in certain individuals that leads them to engage in psychopathic behavior as an adult."

53. Quoted in Diamond, *Anger, Madness, and the Daimonic*, chapter 5. My own thinking on this issue is strongly indebted to Dr. Diamond, who continues throughout his book to develop Jung's point further. In our haste to eliminate any egregious emotions, we have pursued a medical model of tranquilization rather than finding other, potentially healthy outlets for madness.

54. Joseph Edward Duncan III described his own struggle with demons on his Internet blog. In April 2005 Duncan wrote, "It is a battle between me and my demons." He continued, "I'm afraid, very afraid. If they win then a lot of people will be badly hurt." Quoted in Crenson, "What Makes a Sexual Predator?" A month later Duncan broke into an Idaho family home and tied up the mother, her boyfriend, and the eldest boy. He hammered the three victims to death, then kidnapped the eight-year-old daughter, Shasta, and the nine-year-old boy, Dylan, repeatedly raping and molesting them for six weeks. Eventually Duncan murdered Dylan. Before he committed these horrific acts, Duncan had already established a pattern of sexual predatory behavior. He did time for raping a young boy at gunpoint and was also arrested in 2004 for groping a six-year-old. He appears to be linked to an earlier unsolved homicide in California as well. He was not just a regular guy who had an isolated bad day. Nor does it appear that he made any normal kind of freewill choice to adopt a new lifestyle of killing people and raping children.

Most would agree that Joseph Edward Duncan III is a monster, in the sense that he has abdicated his own humanity. His deeds are unforgivable. It seems extremely doubtful that *any* causal story could be produced (no matter how accurate) that would *explain* Duncan's actions to most reasonable people. If we could show that Lucifer himself was inside Duncan's heart, or a virus had eaten part of his brain, or a "bludgeoning gene" had been discovered, or he had grown up in a Skinner box...it would hardly matter. And the idea that Duncan himself knows *why* he did it also seems very hard to believe.

55. Social psychologists have long recognized a double standard when judging bad behavior. When I commit some awful deed I am apt to attribute my actions to the stresses of a difficult situation, not my character. But if I observe similar bad behavior in another I am apt to ascribe the deviance to the person's character; I tend to see it as a personality trait rather than a situational response. Most people, Brodsky notwithstanding, have the same inconsistent tendency.

56. Of course, one of the most odious characters of recent political history is Saddam Hussein. Along with other genocidal leaders, such as Pol Pot, Hitler, and Stalin, Saddam has been psychoanalyzed from afar by many scholars. Whichever psychopathological label eventually sticks to his name, it's pretty clear that he had a very difficult childhood. His peasant father died shortly after his birth and his mother left him with relatives for many years, finally returning with a stepfather who abused and humiliated him. By all accounts he had a rather lonely childhood and did not seem to keep up with his peers; he could not read or write until he was ten years old. His deprivations seem to have paved the road to later heartlessness. A malignant heart seems to have developed in the context of political justifications and rationalizations. Saddam seems to fit the diagnosis of malignant narcissist (narcissistic personality disorder) in the sense that he had little empathy for others and a grandiose sense of his own importance. The psychologist Erwin Parson claimed that Saddam had a "Nebuchadnezzar imperial complex"; he even had himself photographed in the style of the ancient Babylonian king. Peter Beaumont, "From Tikrit Boy to Butcher of Bagdad," *The Observer*, December 31, 2006, asks:

> At the end, what can we say about Saddam? That he was a monster? A madman? A malignant narcissist? All of these labels and more have been applied. In the run up to the second Gulf War, the author and columnist Thomas Friedman framed the paradox of Saddam in a different and more subtle way, asking whether Iraq was the way it was because of Saddam? Or was Saddam the way he was because of Iraq? In reality there are no monsters, only men. And it was as a man Saddam went to the gallows, not as a cipher. Those who called him a "madman"—as so many did—were lazy. He was too complex and contradictory a figure for that, as those who tried to profile him discovered. But if there are identifiable hallmarks of narcissistic personality disorder, then Saddam had them times over.

CHAPTER 14

1. Quotations are from Elaine Marshall, "Crane's 'the Monster' Seen in Light of Robert Lewis's Lynching," *Nineteenth Century Literature* 51, no. 2 (1996). Marshall argues convincingly that Crane took some imaginative inspiration for his Henry Johnson character from his brother William's firsthand account of Robert Lewis.

2. Gary Will, "The Dramaturgy of Death," *New York Review of Books* 48, no. 10 (2001).

3. Quotations are taken from Elaine Marshall's article "Crane's 'the Monster' Seen in Light of Robert Lewis's Lynching," *Nineteenth Century Literature* 51, no. 2 (1996).

4. Bureau of Justice, Correctional Populations in the United States, 1996 report, and Bureau of Census, quoted on the Human Rights Watch Web site, www.hrw.org. In the 1990s the Bureau of Justice Statistics estimated that one in every three black men in their twenties was either in prison, in jail, or on parole or probation. See Sasha Abramsky, *American Furies: Crime, Punishment, and Vengeance in the Age of Mass Imprisonment* (Beacon Press, 2007), introduction.

5. Debra Higgs Strickland, "Monsters and Christian Enemies," *History Today*, February 2000.

6. James Aho, *This Thing of Darkness* (University of Washington Press, 1994), chapter 6, "Who Shall Be the Enemy."

7. Mike Prysner, video testimony, Iraq Veterans against the War Web site, http://ivaw .org/.

8. *Faces of the Enemy*, a film by Bill Jersey and Jeffrey Friedman, a Quest Production, 1987, based on the book by Sam Keen.

9. Edward Said, *Orientalism* (Random House, 1978).

10. Noam Chomsky, *Reflections on Language* (Pantheon, 1975).

11. John Locke, *An Essay Concerning Human Understanding* (Dover Publications, 1959), vol. 1, chapter 33.

12. Quoted in Daniel Boorstin, *The Lost World of Thomas Jefferson* (Henry Holt, 1948).

13. Edward Drinker Cope, "The Developmental Significance of Human Physiognomy," *American Naturalist* 17 (1883).

14. Contrary to Chomsky and Said, the philosopher John Searle recognized the potential racism contained within Cartesian rationalism. He points out, "Once you believe that there are innate human mental structures it is only a short step to argue that the innate mental structures differ from one race to another." This "short step" was in fact taken by Nazi racial theorists, and I suspect this step was facilitated by the internalist metaphors (e.g., noumenon, will) that pervade the intellectual tradition from Kant through Nietzsche. John Searle, "The Rules of the Language Game," *Times Literary Supplement*, September 10, 1976.

15. George Mosse, *The Crisis of German Ideology* (Schocken Books, 1981).

16. Adolf Hitler, *Mein Kampf*, translated by Ralph Manheim (Houghton Mifflin, 1971).

17. I'm aware that adaptationist evolutionary explanations of instincts may share some of the same questionable assumptions of the more conscious explanations. One such assumption may be that a trait or behavior exists because it is useful. There is a teleological structure that operates in most adaptationist explanations of trait survival, but I don't think it's circular, nor do I think it falls prey to the charge of Panglossian optimism.

18. Frans de Waal, *Our Inner Ape* (Riverhead Books, 2005), chapter 4.

19. See Samuel P. Huntington, "The Clash of Civilizations," *Foreign Affairs* (Summer 1993), and his more developed argument in *The Clash of Civilizations and the Remaking of the World Order* (Simon and Schuster, 1998). Things have changed so radically in the decade or so after Huntington forwarded his thesis that much of his specific writing about China and the Middle East is rendered out of date. But the general idea of a clash of civilizations has perhaps grown and flourished in the nonacademic popular culture.

20. One of the most famous Muslim creators of the American caricature was the Egyptian scholar and Muslim Brotherhood apologist Sayyid Qutb (1906–1966). Qutb's writings, including "The America I Have Seen," have become especially inspirational for terrorist groups like Al-Qaida. Qutb's anxiety about American debauchery, especially the sexually aggressive American woman, is almost humorous now, because he drew his conclusions from attending a chaste-sounding 1949 Colorado State College dance. "The dance is inflamed by the notes of the gramophone," Qutb laments, "the dancehall becomes a whirl of heels and thighs, arms enfold hips, lips and breasts meet, and the air is full of lust." His anxiety about licentious sexuality was only a piece of a larger-scale cultural disgust, an abhorrence that has intensified in the Islamism of recent years. See Sayyid Qutb, "The America I Have Seen," in *America in an Arab Mirror: Images of America in Arabic Travel Literature*, edited by Kamal Abdel-Malek (Palgrave, 2000).

21. See Brian Whitaker, "Saudi Textbooks 'Demonize West,'" *The Guardian*, July 14, 2004.

22. See Ruth Goldberg, " 'In the Church of the Poison Mind': Adapting the Metaphor of Psychopathology to Look Back at the Mad, Monstrous 80s," in *Monstrous Adaptations: Generic and Thematic Mutations in the Horror Film*, edited by Richard J. Hand and Jay McRoy (Manchester University Press, 2007).

23. Of course, we in the United States also have strongly hierarchic fundamentalist Christian traditions. We, too, have traditions that are accommodating modernism with varying degrees of success. And our tribal and hierarchic sects of the major monotheisms make uneasy company in the egalitarian American democracy. The ostensibly secular playing field of American public life (won by the Disestablishment Clause) thinly veils our private spiritual lives. These private inner lives, whether they are Christian, Jewish, or Muslim, pulse with autocratic deities and submissive devotees, but they are necessarily stunted in the public context of egalitarian tolerance.

24. Dana Steven, "A Movie Only a Spartan Could Love," *Slate.com*, March 8, 2007.

25. Touraj Daryaee, "Go Tell the Spartans," *Iranian.com*, March 14, 2007.

26. The work of Frank M. Snowden Jr., for example *Before Color Prejudice: The Ancient View of Blacks* (Harvard University Press, 1983), offers compelling evidence that ancient Mediterranean cultures were not prejudiced about skin color. Instead, the ancients organized their xenophobia around cultural prejudices against language, art, and religion.

27. Perhaps it's appropriate to acknowledge an even earlier defining moment of this structuralism, namely, Marx's theory that the structures of capitalist political economy "alienate" the worker and transform him into a kind of zombie. See Marx's Paris manuscripts in *The Economic and Philosophic Manuscripts of 1844 and the Communist Manifesto* (Prometheus Books, 1988).

28. Hannah Arendt, *Eichmann in Jerusalem: A Report on the Banality of Evil* (Penguin Classics, 2006), epilogue.

29. See Milgram's *Obedience to Authority*.

30. Philip Zimbardo, *The Lucifer Effect: Understanding How Good People Turn Evil* (Random House, 2007).

31. Unfortunately for Zimbardo's thesis, there is some evidence that some of the U.S. soldiers were in fact bad apples. Specialist Charles Graner, who was sentenced to ten years in prison, has a checkered past, with allegations of domestic abuse and even inmate abuse, when he worked (before Abu Ghraib) as a corrections officer in Greene County, Pennsylvania.

32. Philip Zimbardo, "Revisiting the Stanford Prison Experiment: A Lesson in the Power of Situation," *Chronicle of Higher Education*, March 30, 2007.

33. Gardner, introduction to Leopold, *Life Plus 99 Years*.

34. Quoted in James Dobson, *Fatal Addiction: Pornography and Sexual Violence*, video documentary of the Bundy interview, available from Dobson's conservative nonprofit Focus on the Family.

35. Mark Ames trolls the Web for disgruntled former NIU students complaining about the "shittiest," "ugliest," even the "windiest" campus they've, like, ever seen. From this dubious method of data collection he concludes that DeKalb and NIU represent "a very familiar, flat sort of American Hell," a Middle American place so dreadful that anybody who lives there should be on psychiatric medication: "Indeed, someone who wouldn't turn to antidepressants would, in my opinion, be the sick one." He suggests that the real villain in the massacre was not Kazmierczak, but the oppressively dull and mediocre NIU campus and community. Sadly, this kind of extreme structural theory of monsters can be found everywhere in our contemporary discourse. Ames's argument strikes me as so implausible that I'll offer only the following brief response.

First, disgruntled students can be found decrying the evils of their school in every city and rural town in America. Nothing interesting about mass murderers can be concluded, as far as I can tell, from students grousing about their campus and faculty. The leap in logic here is deplorable. Second, after living amid real poverty in the developing world (as I did in Cambodia), one finds such pretended despair (common among such railers against the system) truly pusillanimous. Ames describes Kazmierczak's home town of Elk Grove, Illinois, which is not far from the odious DeKalb, as a terrifying place of white people, businesses, highways, "and, yes, suburban tract homes." My goodness, one wonders why everybody from such dreadful places isn't killing their neighbors with automatic weaponry. Finally, I myself attended NIU for four years of undergraduate study and two years of graduate work, and, though it was clearly no Paris, I rarely if ever felt the desire to buy some guns and shoot my classmates. As far as I can tell, none of the other hundreds of thousands of NIU graduates who endured the same "bleak" and of course windy campus ever wrestled much with murderous impulses.

36. Eldridge Cleaver, "On Becoming," in *Soul on Ice* (McGraw Hill, 1968).

37. One simple counterargument will sufficiently unmask the hypocrisy and insincerity of Cleaver's explanation for his raping women. He claimed that his goal in raping white women was a form of vengeance because of the historical ill treatment of black women. If this is true, then one wonders why he started out his rape agenda by "practicing on black girls in the ghetto." He admits in *Soul on Ice* that raping black girls would be good "training" to get ready for "The Ogre." Cleaver's incoherent and hypocritical logic makes it clear that some redistributions of criminal culpability, from individual to society, are nothing more than convenient subterfuges.

38. Quoted in Rose, "Crime."

39. Quotes and information from Xavier McElrath-Bey are taken from his presentation in my spring 2008 course "Doing Time in America: The Prison System" at Columbia College, and from his autobiographical sketch in Gordon Mclean's *Too Young to Die* (Tyndale House, 1998). In addition to Xavier, I am also indebted to my coteachers, Professors Garnett Kilberg-Cohen and Sara Livingston.

40. This impersonal aspect of the criminal justice system, among other things, has led Xavier to work with BARJ, the nationwide movement for Balanced and Restorative Justice, which attempts to introduce community justice mechanisms that hold offenders, instead of the abstract "state," directly accountable to their victims. One of the goals of this movement is to humanize criminal justice by contextualizing it in the real lives of those directly effected. BARJ sees the current paradigm as alienating and unhelpful for both victims and offenders.

41. When he was sentenced as an adult and sent to prison for murder, he continued the gang-banger lifestyle inside the even more primitive "jungle atmosphere" of the penitentiary. "At first," Xavier explained, "I blamed the system. I read Marx and I became a communist in prison. I read Nietzsche too, and I came to see myself and my people as 'victims.'" Society was to blame. Gang life was an alternative society, one where he and other disenfranchised men could hold power. Later, after long stretches of what he called "existential isolation" and reflection, Xavier took a more balanced approach and accepted personal responsibility for his actions.

42. According to this view, monsters from the ghetto are brutal and actively aggressive, but the corrupt legal and political systems that overcrowd prisons and build local economies on incarceration are just passive-aggressive, institutional versions of equally dehumanizing tendencies. Michel Foucault's argument in *Discipline and Punish* suggests that modern forms of state-controlled surveillance and psychological manipulation by more "humane" methods (such as the panopticon) only *appear* to be less insidious than the corporeal punishments of pre-Enlightenment Europe.

Suffice it to say that Foucault and his devotees are strong proponents of the structural theory (or social constructivism) of deviance. There are no real monsters except those defined so by the powerful.

43. See Raymond Ibrahim, ed., *Al-Qaida Reader* (Broadway, 2007).

44. See Reza Aslan, "Why Do They Hate Us?" *Slate.com*, August 6, 2007.

45. Alan Krueger, "What Makes a Terrorist?" *The American: A Magazine of Ideas*, December 2007, at American.com. Alberto Abadie, a professor of public policy at the John F. Kennedy School of Government, Harvard University, has argued that the level of political freedom, not poverty, explains terrorism. He told the *Harvard Gazette*, "In the past, we heard people refer to the strong link between terrorism and poverty, but in fact when you look at the data, it's not there. This is true not only for events of international terrorism, as previous studies have shown, but perhaps more surprisingly also for the overall level of terrorism, both of domestic and of foreign origin." Abadie argues that it is areas with intermediate levels of political freedom that experience the most terrorism. Both societies with high levels of political freedom and authoritarian regimes have quite low levels of terrorism. "Tight control and repressive practices keep terrorist activities in check, while nations making the transition to more open, democratic governments may be politically unstable, which makes them more vulnerable." Quoted in Alvin Powell, "Freedom Squelches Terrorist Violence," *Harvard Gazette*, November 4, 2004.

46. Marc Sageman, *Understanding Terror Networks* (University of Pennsylvania Press, 2004), chapter 3.

47. Of course, a higher degree of education in the terrorist population begs the question about what sort of education. If the higher levels of study are just in the Qur'an, Sharia, and Hadith exegesis, then one cannot conclude much about the traditional liberalizing effects of learning. If, however, the higher education is more than indoctrination, then Krueger's findings may be the most compelling evidence that Muslim outrage is not ideological at all, but an informed sense of political injustice. This would not necessarily negate the structural explanation of terrorism, but only reorient it away from religious and economic motivations and toward nationalist ones.

48. Ayaan Hirsi Ali, *Infidel* (Free Press, 2007).

49. From an audiotape, attributed to bin Laden, released in March 2008, quoted in Ian Fisher, "Vatican Dismissed bin Laden Accusation of 'Crusade,'" *New York Times*, March 21, 2008.

   In April 2007 a small publishing house in Malatya, Turkey, was attacked, apparently because it distributed Bibles. Three employees, a German and two Turks, were found with their hands and legs bound and their throats slit. Five suspects were arrested, each of whom carried a letter that said, "We five are brothers. We are going to our deaths." This sort of violence, which admittedly is decentralized, gives credence to the idea that at least some of the terrorism is religiously or ideologically grounded.

50. Sam Harris, *The End of Faith: Religion, Terror, and the Future of Reason* (Norton, 2004), chapter 1.

51. See Martin Amis's three-part essay "The Age of Horrorism," *The Guardian*, September 2006, and Hitchens's *God Is Not Great* (Hachette, 2007) for an extended critique of religion as a species of insanity. Ayaan Hirsi Ali's autobiography *Infidel* includes an extended critique of Islam as backward and dehumanizing.

52. Daniel Dennett, *Breaking the Spell: Religion as a Natural Phenomenon* (Penguin, 2007), chapter 1.

53. Religion, according to these critics, is only one of the monstrosities. Other dehumanizing ideologies include communism, democracy, patriarchy, feminism, and scientism. Joseph Stalin, referring to his own damaging revolutionary policies, is reputed to have shrugged, "If you want to make an omelette, you'll have to break some

eggs." Isaiah Berlin damns all such dehumanizing idealism and reminds us that the twentieth century has been the age of disastrous "final solutions." Utopian thinking, according to Berlin, is divorced from the reality of human lives; it loses the trees for the forest. He characterizes the ideologist as someone whose good intentions (e.g., the future liberation of all mankind) actually blind him to the pain and suffering he is causing in the here and now. "To make such an omelette," Berlin says, "there is surely no limit to the number of eggs that should be broken—that was the faith of Lenin, of Trotsky, of Mao, for all I know of Pol Pot." Isaiah Berlin, "The Pursuit of the Ideal," in *The Crooked Timber of Humanity* (Vintage Books, 1992).

54. Donna Haraway, one of the most influential postmodern monster theorists, attempts to use the metaphor of the cyborg as a liberating and empowering symbol for feminists. In previous decades the cyborg, a hybrid creature, part artificial and part natural, was a disturbing disruption of normality, but now that same disruption is turned into a virtue. Haraway argues that a cyborg, a pastiche creature without essentialist defining parameters, is a kind of model for contemporary women who wish to claim solidarity and political power in a disorderly world that lacks traditional boundaries such as "human nature." For Haraway and other postmoderns, monsters are metaphors of destabilization, and the goal of such subversion is to weaken the patriarchy and strengthen the repressed and excluded. See Donna Haraway, *Simians, Cyborgs, and Women: The Reinvention of Nature* (Routledge, 1991), especially the "Cyborg Manifesto" in chapter 8.

55. The intellectual heirs of Foucault, focused on "othering discourses," are more interested in how some people are made to *appear* to be monsters. Appearance (representation) is of paramount interest, not *reality* (since for them no reality "really" exists outside of these power discourses).

56. I think it is entirely possible to accept the idea that monsters resist classification and inhabit the terra incognita without succumbing to the radical metaphysics of postmodern skepticism. The anomalies and exceptions that comprise the monstrous are not unraveling the center, as postmodernists predicted. The monsters remain, even by definition, outsiders. They do not actually or symbolically overthrow the rational.

My objection to postmodern relativism is that it suffers from a severe case of melodrama. Yes, meanings are partially constructed by society, but that doesn't mean there is no accessible reality. When the semiological linguists noticed that *words* cannot be connected easily to their *referents* (i.e., nothing essential about the word *dog* picks out the four-footed mammal barking outside), they melodramatically inferred that all language (and thought) lacks rational foundation, and *meaning* is just the free play of socially manipulated but ultimately arbitrary signs. This assumption serves as the basis of most postmodern work, but it strikes me as inductively fallacious, empirically false, and strangely provincial (narrowly textual) in its view of human knowledge. The idea that language and thought are sloppy and imprecise is obvious to anyone who has used them and does not indicate a radical relativism of all language, especially in light of the astounding successes of human communication. The assumptions of postmodernism seem slightly ridiculous as soon as we leave the world of literary theory and enter the world of medicine or engineering or even automotive repair. For two quite different but compelling discussions of the relationship between Darwinian theory and postmodernism, see Colin Nazhone Milburn, "Monsters in Eden: Darwin and Derrida," *MLN* 118, no. 3 (2003), and Brian Boyd, "Getting It All Wrong," *American Scholar* (Autumn 2006).

57. The deconstructionist David Gunkel announces, "Monsters signify. And what they signify is precisely the deterioration and demise of philosophical demonstration in general." For Gunkel, rationality, and its servants, have been a controlling force. See

his deconstruction of Hegel's *Philosophy of Nature* in "Scary Monsters: Hegel and the Nature of the Monstrous," *International Studies in Philosophy* 29, no. 2 (1997).

58. The one domain where I think postmodernism has had fruitful effect is *aesthetics*. To keep the analytical thread of my book on monstrous creatures and men, I have had to forgo an interesting discussion about the monster idea in the arts. Without getting in too deeply, it is worth pointing out that most Western narratives have had the structural arc of the Aristotelian curve. That is to say, stories, according to Aristotle's *Poetics*, should have internal cohesion, with beginnings, antecedents and consequential actions, climaxes, resolutions, and endings. Or consider Plato's *Phaedrus*, the second half of which is entirely devoted to showing how a good story should be like a healthy organism, all parts well formed, essential, and functionally connected to each other. Postmodernism, on the other hand, has nicely celebrated the monstrous artwork: deformed stories without teleological justification. Surrealism began the job, it seems, and postmodernism has continued the tradition of mutilated narratives and hybridized stories. Like teratological offspring, novels and films have placed beginnings in the middle and endings at beginnings and generally twisted around character and plot mechanisms until something quite new emerges. Film and literature have celebrated monstrous turns in their storytelling: non sequiturs, inessential episodes, violations of space and time, and so on. One thinks here of the work of writers like Jorge Borges, Italo Calvino, Kurt Vonnegut, and Thomas Pynchon, or the films of David Lynch, Quentin Tarantino, and perhaps Monty Python's Flying Circus.

59. See Noor Khan, "Attackers Behead Afghan Teacher for Education of Girls," *Chicago Sun-Times*, January 5, 2006.

CHAPTER 15

1. Akira Kurosawa gives high praise to Honda Inoshiro, the director of *Godzilla*. The two filmmakers worked together on many films, including Kurosawa's *Kagemusha* (1980) and *Ran* (1985). See "A Long Story: Part I," in *Akira Kurosawa: Something Like an Autobiography* (Vintage Books, 1983).

2. In "Where Wonders Await Us" Tim Flannery gives us a shocking and depressing iteration of waste that we've dumped into the deep hadal zone. During every war hundreds (even thousands) of vessels and their toxic fuel and munitions sink to the bottom, but even during peacetime the pollution is staggering. Between 1971 and 1990 an average of one ship was lost every two days, and up until the 1970s it was common for countries to dump their chemical weapons. "Britain alone," Flannery explains, "has dumped 137,000 tons of unwanted chemical weapons at sea, and some of the chemicals still remain in solid form on the bottom." Moreover, shortly after World War II radioactive waste began to be dumped, and between then and 1993 (when the practice was banned) 142,000 tons had been dumped into the North Atlantic. The mutational results of this kind of pollution are still unclear, but worrisome trends can already be seen. The liver glands of some shrimp species contain a million times the level of polonium-210 than naturally occurs in seawater. Industrial waste causes sex changes in mollusks, and mercury poisoning is so prevalent that most pregnant women already know they should not eat fish. The damaging chemicals that we previously thought would just stay quietly on the bottom of the ocean will in fact come back to haunt us in the food chain.

3. The genre of science fiction is more than just entertainment when it comes to artificial life and artificial intelligence. The hopeful and horrifying imaginary narratives of sci-fi help us to conceptualize the possible outcomes of our current research trajectories. Dan Dinello's *Technophobia: Science Fiction Visions of Posthuman Technology* (University of Texas Press, 2005) does a nice job surveying the pessimistic sci-fi warnings that

Hollywood has been producing for almost a century. The imagined future is furnished with both terrifying and inspiring depictions of human enhancement.

4. See Asimov, *I, Robot* (Spectra Reprint, 2008).

5. See Pete Warren, "Launching a New Kind of Warfare," *The Guardian*, October 26, 2006.

6. Dave Bullock, "Inside the Navy's Armed-Robot Labs," *Wired*, January 2008.

7. Steven Levy, "Real Artificial Life," in *Artificial Life* (Vintage Books, 1992).

8. Cited in Dinello, *Technophobia*, chapter 8.

9. Consult the National Nanotech Initiative Web site, www.nano.gov/html/about/funding.html (October 2006).

10. See Marvin Minsky, "Will Robots Inherit the Earth?" *Scientific American*, October 1999.

11. Bostrom's 2005 lecture for the conference was entitled "Humanity's Biggest Problems Aren't What You Think They Are," available at www.ted.com/index.php/talks/nick_bostrom_on_our_biggest_problems.html.

12. See Kevin Warwick, "Cyborg 1.0," *Wired*, February 2000.

13. What does it all mean? Orlan's own cryptic assessments of her work aren't all that helpful. "My work is not against plastic surgery, but against the dictates of beauty standards which are impressed upon our bodies," she says. "Skin is a mask, a source of strangeness, and by reforming my face, I feel I'm actually taking off a mask. My work is carnal, inasmuch as it deals with flesh; it is blasphemous" (see Stephen Asma's "A Portrait of the Artist as a Work in Progress," *Chronicle of Higher Education*, January 19, 2001).

14. See Stelarc's Web site, www.stelarc.va.com.au/.

15. Quoted in the BBC news story "Making Cindy into Barbie," September 21, 1998.

16. The computational intelligence (CI) movement studies fuzzy-logic systems and computational evolution and may eventually articulate nonbinary theories that answer my objection here. Treating the variable values of a system as somewhere between on/off or true/false seems absolutely necessary in modeling anything like cognition.

17. Perhaps the best evidence for this view is found in Antonio Damasio's research. Damasio worked with a patient who suffered frontal lobe damage and discovered that emotion or affect was absolutely crucial in the correct functioning of decision-making cognition. Emotion assigns value to ideas and heavily influences the ability to reason and calculate. See *Descartes' Error: Emotion, Reason, and the Human Brain* (Picador, 1995).

18. Daniel Dennett, "My Mind Has a Body of Its Own," in *Kinds of Minds* (Basic Books, 1996).

19. The quote and the information about Ashley are found in Nancy Gibb, "Pillow Angel Ethics," *Time*, January 22, 2007.

20. See Russell Goldman and Katie Thompson, " 'Pregnant Man' Gives Birth to Girl," posted July 3, 2008, at http://abcnews.go.com/Health/.

21. An interesting and contentious controversy has surrounded J. Michael Bailey's book *The Man Who Would Be Queen: The Science of Gender Bending and Transsexualism* (Joseph Henry Press, 2003). Bailey, the chair of Northwestern University's psychology department, has argued that transsexual reassignment surgery is not, contrary to dominant views, a fulfillment of long frustrated gender identity. Instead of saying that male-to-female sex changes are done to correct a biological accident, Bailey claims that such transsexualism is about fulfilling specific sexual desires. Some transsexuals, according to Bailey, are extremely homosexual and want to be penetrated by a man; others are men who have autogynophilia, a sexual fascination with having a vagina of one's own. Needless to say, Bailey's views, which seem more conjectural than scientific, have aroused the condemnation of many transsexuals and advocacy groups. For a representative exchange of differing views, see Dennis Rodkin, "Sex and Transsexuals," *Chicago Reader* 32, no. 11 (2003).

22. This popular religious viewpoint really does ignore the true blending of sexual differentiation: confused internal and external genitalia and reproduction equipment and the confusion of chromosomal and somatic gender specifications. Does God privilege the external somatic differentiation, or does he want us to go with the chromosomal differentiation? Anyone who feels that they know God's mind on this issue (and to be frank, any issue) is a subtler thinker than I.

23. In "The He Hormone," *New York Times*, April 2, 2000, Andrew Sullivan describes the "correction" that hormone injections brought to his masculine identity. Sullivan suffers from low testosterone and injects himself with supplemental doses. In a compelling description of his own psychological and physical transformation, he throws serious doubt on the social constructionist theory of gender. In addition to his own phenomenology of chemically based gender, he offers some additional data:

> Testosterone is clearly correlated in both men and women with psychological dominance, confident physicality and high self-esteem. In most combative, competitive environments, especially physical ones, the person with the most Twins. Put any two men in a room together and the one with more testosterone will tend to dominate the interaction. Working women have higher levels of testosterone than women who stay at home, and the daughters of working women have higher levels of testosterone than the daughters of housewives. A 1996 study found that in lesbian couples in which one partner assumes the male, or "butch," role and another assumes the female, or "femme," role, the "butch" woman has higher levels of testosterone than the "femme" woman. In naval medical tests, midshipmen have been shown to have higher average levels of testosterone than plebes. Actors tend to have more testosterone than ministers, according to a 1990 study. Among 700 male prison inmates in a 1995 study, those with the highest T levels tended to be those most likely to be in trouble with the prison authorities and to engage in unprovoked violence. This is true among women as well as among men, according to a 1997 study of 87 female inmates is a maximum security prison.

24. See Freeman Dyson's provocative essay "Our Biotech Future," *New York Review of Books*, July 19, 2007.

25. See Bernard E. Rollin's excellent study *The Frankenstein Syndrome: Ethical and Social Issues in the Genetic Engineering of Animals* (Cambridge University Press, 1995), chapter 2.

26. Quoted in the excerpted text of Francis Fukuyama's *Our Posthuman Future*, published as "Biotechnology and the Threat of a Posthuman Future," *Chronicle of Higher Education*, March 22, 2002.

27. See John Hedley Brooke, "Visions of Perfectibility," *Journal of Evolution and Technology* 14, no. 2 (2005) for a nice tour of some technology- and science-loving religious thinkers. Brooke critiques the simple dichotomy that Fukuyama and others continue to promulgate. Also see Brooke's extensive treatment of the issue in *Science Religion: Some Historical Perspectives* (Cambridge University Press, 1991).

28. Robert Krulwich, interview with Francis Collins for a 2005 *Nova* special on artificial life, www.pbs.org/wgbh/nova/sciencenow/3214/01-collins.html.

EPILOGUE

1. " 'Witches' Burnt to Death in Kenya," BBC News Web site, May 21, 2008.

2. Pilirani Semu-Banda, "Mob Justice in Malawi," WIP (Women's International Perspective) Web site, www.thewip.net, posted May 21, 2008.

3. Andrew L. Wang and Courtney Flynn, "Mom Charged with Stabbing Daughter, 6, Told Waukegan Police the Girl Was Possessed," *Chicago Tribune*, April 8, 2008.

4. Associated Press, "Exorcism Is Protected by Law," available at www.msnbc.com, June 28, 2008.

5. See William Mullen, "Mythical Creatures on Display at Field Museum," *Chicago Tribune*, March 18, 2008.

6. Barry Grant, "Rich and Strange: The Yuppy Horror Film," *Journal of Film and Video* 48 (1996).

7. Wittgenstein's theory of family resemblance is sometimes interpreted as a harbinger of the social constructionist view of knowledge, and he is then claimed as a father of more extreme forms of epistemological relativism. There's some good reason for this interpretation, in the sense that Wittgenstein and others were trying to break the old tradition of typological essentialist thinking. This is not the place to try to settle a question about how to interpret Wittgenstein, but I do want to point out that the metaphor of family resemblance, if considered carefully, actually speaks against a purely relativist reading. Families are populations, and populations are real metaphysical entities, albeit spread over space and time. See Michael Ghiselin's compelling arguments that even species are individuals, in *Metaphysics and the Origin of Species* (State University of New York Press, 1997). What this means for the concept of monster is that, though there is no absolute essence, there can still be an objective population of entities to which such language refers. The death of typological essentialism does not mean the death of objective knowledge about the world.

8. See Eleanor Rosch and Barbara Lloyd, *Cognition and Categorization* (Lawrence Erlbaum, 1978), and George Lakoff, *Women, Fire and Dangerous Things* (University of Chicago Press, 1990).

9. Not all the protagonists in this natural history of monsters have been quick to light torches and cry out for blood. Remember that St. Augustine was not particularly xenophobic about monsters and exotic peoples. And it's worth mentioning that the ancient historian Herodotus was so open-minded about the otherwise demonized Persians that Plutarch later called him *philobarbarus*.

10. Pynchon, "Is It O.K. to Be a Luddite?"

INDEX

Note: Page numbers in *italics* refer to illustrations.

chimeras, 40
chimpanzees, 239–240
China, 5–6, 11, 14
Chinguo, Stanislaus, 278
Cho, Seung-Hui, 205
Chomsky, Noam, 236
Christianity
    and *Beowulf,* 97–98
    and cross symbol, 105
    demons and devils of, 13, 64, 68, 106
    and desire, 117
    and genealogy of monsters, 84–86
    and hell, *71*
    and heresy, 107–108
    and heroics, 99, *102*
    humility-emphasis of, 99–100
    and Jews, 90–91
    and Judgement Day, 100
    and monster killers, 99–100
    and monstrous human races, 37
    and Muslims, 241
    persecution of Christians, 67–68
    and Resurrection, 83
    on souls of monsters, 79–83
    and xenophobia, 86–87
    See also Bible
Christopher, Saint, 81
The City of God (Augustine), 77, 86
civilizations, monstrous, 240–244
Clark, William, 32
clash of civilizations, 240, 248
classicism, 51
Cleaver, Eldridge, 246
Clinton, Hillary, 281
cloning, 189–190
cockroaches, 263
coelacanth, 2
Collins, Francis, 274
Colossus: The Forbin Project, 267
Columbine massacre, 204, 205
Columbus, Christopher, 91
communism, 243
compassion, 224
Confessions (Augustine), 79
conjoined twins, *157, 174*
    Alberch on, 173
    Chang and Eng Bunker, 137
    as expression of God's will, 76
    Lazarus and Baptista, 83, *84*
    souls of, 83
conscience, 188–189, 210, 220
consumerism, 241, 243

contingency, 165
Cope, Edward Drinker, 237
cosmetic procedures, 262, 265–266,
    276–277
cosmic fear, 185, 186, 191, 192, 193, 194
Council of Constance, 107
Crane, Stephen, 231–233
Craven, Wes, 183
creationism, 164, 168, 178–179
credulity, 32–36
    Bacon on, 127
    of Barnum's audience, 136
    in Doran's model, 130–132, 140
    and paleontology, 279
Crimes and Misdemeanors, 281
criminal monsters, 203–228
    aggression and rage, 208–212
    and causes of psychopathology,
        223–226
    and desire, 212–218
    and detachment, 218–223
    judging and managing of, 226–228
    labeling of, 216
    See also serial killers; *specific individuals*
Cronenberg, David, 200, 201
cryptozoology, 32, 279
Ctesias
    on griffins, 28
    on manticores, 33, *34*
    as source for Alexander, 22
    on umbrella-footed humans, 36
    on unicorns, 129
Cthulhu, 184–185, 186
cultural category, monsters as, 13
curiosities, 135, 137–140
Cuvier, Georges, 128, 156–157
cyborg technology, 260–265
cyclops, *158*
    Alberch on, 173
    as creation of God, 86
    and fossil elephant skulls, 31–32
    medieval authorities on, 77
    and Odysseus, 26–27, 98
    popular belief in, 35
    soi pour soi explanation of, 158–159
    teratological explanation of, 156–158
Cynocephali (dog-headed men)
    Augustine on, 77
    and Christianity, 88
    depiction of, *78*
    and embellishment, 36–37

power, human drive for, 187, 217, 244, 265–266
Power, Samantha, 281
Prague, 11–12, *12*
predators, 24, 198–199
preformationism, 45–46
pregnancy, 143, 146–148, 162
"Prester John's Land" (Driesbach), *78*
pride, 101, 102
primates, 239–240
primitivism, 216–217
Prince Randian, 139–140
prison experiment at Stanford University, 244–245
prodigies, 146
Proffitt, Dennis R., 22
projection, 57, 198
Prometheus Bound (Aeschylus), 27, 28
Protestants, 142
Protoceratops, 28–29, *29*
prototype theory, 282–283
Prysner, Mike, 235
Pseudodoxia epidemica (Browne), 127–128
pseudoprophetes (false prophets), 68
psittacosaurus, *29*
psychopaths, 193, 212, 223–226, 228. *See also* criminal monsters
Psychopathy Checklist diagnostic tool, 220
psychosomatic theories, 148
purpose of monsters, 43–44, 48–49, 275–276
Pygmies, 77
Pynchon, Thomas R., 284
Pyrrhus, King of Epirus, 33

Al-Qaida, 249
Al-Qaida Reader, 248
Quay, Stephen, 194
Quay, Timothy, 194
Qur'an, 92

race
    attitudes toward, 235
    and lynchings, 232–233
    monstrous races, 36–38, 233, 235
    and natural selection, 237
    See also xenophobia
racism, 138
rage, 208–212, 227
Raimi, Sam, 183
ram, one-horned, 43, 48

Ramayana, 37
Ramirez, Richard, 280
rape, 210, 246
reality principle, 188–189, 191, 192
reason and rationality
    of the ancients, 42–45, 52–54, 57, 58, 60
    and concept of monsters, 10
    Freudian theory on, 188
    of medieval intellectuals, 80–81
reductionism, 153, 258, 268, 274
Reformation, 142
relativism, 252, 253–254
religion, 188, 192, 216. *See also specific faiths*
repression
    and adulthood, 190
    and conscience development, 210
    and narcissism, 189
    and sexuality, 116–117, 195–196, 215–216
    and torture porn, 197
    and uncanniness, 192
reproduction
    ambivalent reactions to, 184
    and bio-horror, 201
    and demons, 144–145
    and hybridism, 167–168
    and witches, 112–113
Republic (Plato), 52–54, 194–195, 212
repulsion, 5–7
Resident Evil video game, 198
Resnick, Mitchel, 259–260
responding to the marvelous, Doran's model of, 130–132, 140
Rhizocephala ("root-headed" barnacle), 198–199
Ringling Brothers Circus, *139*, 139
Ritvo, Harriet, 129
The Road (McCarthy), 25, 197
Robinson, Margaret, 33
robo-roach technology, 263
robotics, 190–191, 257–260, *263*
Roman Catholic Church
    and Inquisition, 107–108, 112, 113
    and omens, 142
    and papacy, 68, 107, 113
    and witches, 278
Romans, ancient
    and biblical prophecy, 67
    ethnocentrism of, 36
    and hermaphrodites, 39–42
    and infanticide, 40, *41*
    and prophetic arts, 39